John and Anti-Judaism

McMaster Divinity College Press
**McMaster Biblical Studies Series,
Volume 7**

John and Anti-Judaism
Reading the Gospel in Light of Greco-Roman Culture

JONATHAN NUMADA

☙PICKWICK *Publications* · Eugene, Oregon

JOHN AND ANTI-JUDAISM
Reading the Gospel in Light of Greco-Roman Culture

McMaster Biblical Studies Series, Volume 7
McMaster Divinity College Press

Copyright © 2021 Jonathan Numada. All rights reserved. Except for brief quotations in critical publications or reviews, no part of this book may be reproduced in any manner without prior written permission from the publisher. Write: Permissions, Wipf and Stock Publishers, 199 W. 8th Ave., Suite 3, Eugene, OR 97401.

Pickwick Publications
An Imprint of Wipf and Stock Publishers
199 W. 8th Ave., Suite 3
Eugene, OR 97401

McMaster Divinity College Press
1280 Main Street West
Hamilton, Ontario, Canada
L8S 4K1

www.wipfandstock.com

PAPERBACK ISBN: 978-1-7252-9816-3
HARDCOVER ISBN: 978-1-7252-9817-0
EBOOK ISBN: 978-1-7252-9818-7

Cataloguing-in-Publication data:

Names: Numada, Jonathan.

Title: John and anti-judaism : reading the gospel in light of greco-roman culture / Jonathan Numada.

Description: Eugene, OR: Pickwick Publications, 2021 | McMaster Biblical Studies Series | Includes bibliographical references and indexes.

Identifiers: ISBN 978-1-7252-9816-3 (paperback) | ISBN 978-1-7252-9817-0 (hardcover) | ISBN 978-1-7252-9818-7 (ebook)

Subjects: LCSH: Bible. New Testament John—Criticism, interpretation, etc. | Judaism—Relations—Christianity.

Classification: BS2615 N86 2021 (paperback) | BS2615 (ebook)

06/15/21

Contents

Tables / vii

Acknowledgments / ix

Abbreviations / xi

Introduction: The Problem of Anti-Judaism in the Gospel of John / 1

1. Approaches to Creating and Maintaining Social Identities / 25

2. Social Identity among Jews in Greco-Roman Egypt / 47

3. Social Identity among Jews in Greco-Roman Asia Minor / 76

4. Social Identity among Jews in First-Century Rome / 98

5. Diaspora Jewish Social Identity and John's Portrayal of Jesus / 132

6. Interpreting John's Portrayal of Jewish Origins and Collective Destiny / 166

7. Interpreting John's Relationship to Jews and Judaism / 203

Conclusion: Where Do We Go from Here? / 228

Bibliography / 237

Index of Modern Authors / 267

Index of Ancient Sources / 273

Tables

Figure 1: Levels of Abstraction in Social Identity / 35
Figure 2: Relative Difference (Woman Scientist) / 38
Figure 3: Chain of Revelation / 190
Figure 4: Progenitors in John / 198
Figure 5: John, Jews, "the World" / 215
Figure 6: Social Identity of Diaspora Jews and the Johannine Jesus / 215

Acknowledgments

This book is a heavily revised version of a doctoral dissertation submitted to McMaster Divinity College in 2016. Many people have come together to make its writing possible. I owe deep gratitude to my doctoral adviser, Dr. Cynthia Long Westfall, for her mentorship, guidance, and wisdom during my doctoral studies. I would also like to thank Dr. Stanley E. Porter. His Johannine Literature and History of Biblical Interpretation seminars provided a very informative perspective on the history of scholarship. McMaster Divinity College's financial generosity made the graduate work behind this study possible, and I am very grateful for that institution's ongoing support after I completed my studies there.

I would also like to give my thanks to all the faculty and staff of Northwest Seminary and College, and the Associated Canadian Theological Schools at Trinity Western University in Langley, BC. I would like to specifically thank Dr. Howard Andersen for his ongoing encouragement, and Drs. Larry Perkins and Brian Rapske, former teachers who are now colleagues, for their continuing mentorship. They also raised many important questions during my studies at ACTS that played a strong role in motivating the research presented here. I would like to thank Sheffield Phoenix Press for their permission to republish some expanded and reworked material in chapters 2 and 3 that originally appeared as "Aristeas and Social Identity: Creating Similarity from Continued Difference" in the *Journal of Greco-Roman Christianity and Judaism*. Thanks are also owed to my friend Dr. Bradley K. Broadhead, who read this manuscript and offered many helpful suggestions. This book is dedicated to my wife Marie and our son Evan.

Abbreviations

AB	Anchor Bible
AGJU	Arbeiten zur Geschichte des antiken Judentums und des Urchristentums
ANRW	Temporini, Hildegard, and Wolfgang Haase, eds. *Aufstieg und Niedergang der römischen Welt: Geschichte und Kultur Roms im Spiegel der neueren Forschung.* Part 2, *Principat.* Berlin: de Gruyter, 1972–.
BBR	*Bulletin for Biblical Research*
BE	*Bulletin Epigraphique*
BibInt	Biblical Interpretation Series
BJS	Brown Judaic Studies
BSac	*Bibliotheca Sacra*
BTB	*Biblical Theology Bulletin*
BZAW	Beihefte zur Zeitschrift für die alttestamentliche Wissenschaft
CBQ	*Catholic Biblical Quarterly*
CBQMS	Catholic Biblical Quarterly Monograph Series
CEJL	Commentaries on Early Jewish Literature
CPJ	Tcherikover, Victor A., ed. *Corpus Papyrorum Judaicarum.* Vol 2. Cambridge: Harvard University Press, 1960.
CTQ	*Concordia Theological Quarterly*
CurBR	*Currents in Biblical Research*
EJL	Early Judaism and Its Literature

ETL	*Ephemerides Theologicae Lovanienses*
FJTC	Flavius Josephus: Translation and Commentary
GLAJJ	Stern, Manahem. *Greek and Latin Authors on Jews and Judaism*. Vol 2. Jerusalem: Israel Academy of Sciences and Humanities, 1980.
HTR	*Harvard Theological Review*
HUCA	*Hebrew Union College Annual*
IEJ	*Israel Exploration Journal*
JBL	*Journal of Biblical Literature*
JES	*Journal of Ecumenical Studies*
JETS	*Journal of the Evangelical Theological Society*
JGRChJ	*Journal of Greco-Roman Christianity and Judaism*
JIWE	Noy, David. *Jewish Inscriptions of Western Europe*. 2 vols. Cambridge: Cambridge University Press, 1995.
JJS	*Journal of Jewish Studies*
JQR	*Jewish Quarterly Review*
JSJ	*Journal for the Study of Judaism in the Persian, Hellenistic, and Roman Periods*
JSNT	*Journal for the Study of the New Testament*
JSNTSup	Journal for the Study of the New Testament Supplement Series
JSOT	*Journal for the Study of the Old Testament*
JSP	*Journal for the Study of the Pseudepigrapha*
JSS	*Journal of Semitic Studies*
JTS	*Journal of Theological Studies*
LBS	Linguistic Biblical Studies
LNTS	The Library of New Testament Studies
LSJ	Liddell, Henry George, et al. *A Greek-English Lexicon*. 9th ed. Oxford: Oxford University Press, 1996.
LSTS	Library of Second Temple Studies
MAMA	*Monumenta Asiae Minoris Antiqua*. Manchester and London, 1928–1933

Abbreviations

NedTT	*Nederlands theologisch tijdschrift*
Neot	*Neotestamentica*
NovT	*Novum Testamentum*
NovTSup	Supplements to Novum Testamentum
NTL	New Testament Library
NTS	*New Testament Studies*
PACS	Philo of Alexandria Commentary Series
PAST	Pauline Studies
PSPB	*Personality and Social Psychology Bulletin*
RevExp	*Review and Expositor*
SBLDS	Society of Biblical Literature Dissertation Series
SBLMS	Society of Biblical Literature Monograph Series
SBLSP	Society of Biblical Literature Seminar Papers
SCS	Septuagint and Cognate Studies
SSEJC	Studies in Scripture in Early Judaism and Christianity
StPB	Studia Post-biblica
TJ	*Trinity Journal*
TynBul	*Tyndale Bulletin*
TZ	*Theologische Zeitschrift*
VC	*Vigiliae Christianae*
VTSup	Supplements to Vetus Testamentum
WGRWSup	Writings from the Greco-Roman World Supplement Series
WTJ	*Westminster Theological Journal*
WUNT	Wissenschaftliche Untersuchungen zum Neuen Testament
ZAW	*Zeitschrift für die alttestamentliche Wissenschaft*
ZNW	*Zeitschrift für die neutestamentliche Wissenschaft und die Kunde der älteren Kirche*
ZTK	*Zeitschrift für Theologie und Kirche*

Introduction

The Problem of Anti-Judaism in the Gospel of John

INTRODUCTION

PETER W. WARD DOCUMENTS an incident where on May 23, 1914, the *Komagata Maru*, a Japanese passenger liner with 376 immigrants from *British* India, sailed into the *British* Columbia harbour of Vancouver. One would think that under normal circumstances migrating from one part of the British Empire to another would be a simple matter, as all were considered British subjects of one sort or another. However, local Canadian authorities were zealous to maintain a "white" dominion within the Empire, so the passengers of the *Komagata Maru* were labelled "Indians" and barred from entry.[1] As the situation escalated, concerned citizens and police officers frantically manned the ironically-named ex-British cruiser *HMCS Rainbow*, which was hastily deployed to stare down the *Komagata Maru*. This deadly show of force was intended to compel the immigrants, who by this time had taken over the passenger liner, to return to India. The *Komagata Maru* left Vancouver on July 23, 1914 after disembarking only 20 people. The authorities imprisoned or executed many of the passengers upon their

---

1. While the true motive was the fear of a small population being overwhelmed by a much larger number of immigrants whose culture and race those of western backgrounds tended to dislike, it was asserted at the time that Indians and "Asiatics" would be unable to assimilate to Canada's cold climate and Anglo-Saxon culture and allowing them to do so would be "unkindness." Of course, some contested this prohibition on grounds of compassion or Imperial solidarity. See Ward, *White Canada Forever*, 82–93.

return to India. Some British subjects, it seems, were more British than others.

Canadians are not the only historical examples of nationalistic or ethnocentric zeal amidst changing or redefined boundaries. This incident offers something of a historical parallel to the emergence of early Christianity and Judaism, where many different factions vied to define what it meant to be a follower of YHWH. All parties involved claimed the same Scriptures and the same heritage, but to varying degrees denied validity to the interpretations of other parties. The Christian side of this dialogue is commonly referred to as "anti-Judaism."[2] James Dunn poignantly described anti-Judaism as an "embarrassment of history," and Christians have certainly been embarrassed by the treatment of Jews and Judaism by their historical forebears, especially on account of the horrors of the Holocaust.[3] Some scholars see Christian anti-Judaism traditions as the negative interpretation of Christology and Jesus' crucifixion,[4] while others hold anti-Judaism—particularly in the NT—is a matter of internal Jewish debate and therefore is not anti-Jewish at all. Regardless, some NT texts remain problematic; the Gospel of John is a strong example due to verses such as John 8:44,

---

2. "Anti-Judaism" is a conventional term for the literary evidence of the Christian side of conflicts between Christian and non-Christian Jewish groups. Usually these have theological origins but are perceived as motivating the social separation (or maintaining the separation) of Christ-followers from the Jewish parent religion. Here it refers to the author of John's participation in an implied theological or social conflict with (fellow) Jewish opponents and is not to be understood as anti-Jewish prejudice (although see discussion of Culpepper, Tomson, and Reinhartz below).

Investigation of "anti-Judaism" gains its impetus from modern Christians and Jews seeking to come to terms with their conflicted history, and properly understanding that shared history in order to prevent injustices such as the Holocaust from happening again in the future. The fact that "anti-Judaism" is a modern term can potentially be problematic because of the danger of imposing modern preconceptions on ancient situations, since most NT authors would have referred to themselves as Israelites or Jews rather than Christians. We must remember that each conflict is unique, that early Judaism supplied the theological resources for early Christianity, and that conflicts represented in the NT had theological origins.

3. Dunn, "The Embarrassment of History," 41–60.

4. Ruether writes, "But certainly the first Christian theology took the form of Christological *midrashim* on the Jewish Scriptures. The anti-Judaic tradition exists as the negative side of this . . . What we have here are two sides of the same argument" (Ruether, *Faith and Fratricide*, 65; see also 111–12).

Introduction

where it describes "the Jews" as having the Devil as their father.[5] The heightened sensitivity to the Johannine controversy with "the Jews" has, since the Second World War, prompted New Testament studies to produce a burgeoning literature on Johannine treatment of this group. This is a proper response to a serious moral issue perceived to be at the very heart of Christian Scripture:

> John's attitude to and uses of "the Jews" cannot be reduced to an optional topic, easily isolated from other possible areas of interpretative interest, neither is it one that can be abstracted from the very fiber of the text. It directs us to the fundamental theological impulses of the Gospel, which will emerge only through close exegetical dialogue with the text and with the trajectories that run through it from behind as well as into the future.[6]

Judith Lieu's arguments will be discussed below, but here it is sufficient to note that she is correct that anti-Judaism is a serious theological problem for Christians. Most Christians today have little trouble relating to neighbours who are Jewish, Sikh, Buddhist, Muslim, or of no religion in today's pluralistic culture. Yet the exclusive claims of the Christian message demand the conclusion that other belief systems, like Judaism, must somehow be deficient or incorrect. A latent anti-Judaism is arguably a key component of Christian identity, and Christians often face the difficulty of proclaiming their faith against the background of the injustices and embarrassments of their religion's history.

ANTI-JUDAISM IN GENERAL

Scholarship on Johannine anti-Judaism over the last two centuries is too extensive to fully survey here. Instead, I will briefly discuss key scholarship since the Second World War and classify the literature as

---

5. "The Jews" or "Jews" (rather than a specific Jewish party) plot to kill Jesus (John 5:18; 7:1, 19–25; 8:37–40) and sometimes serve as his primary opponents (1:19; 2:18–20; 5:10–18, esp. 7–9). At times they are a more sympathetic group (11:31–36) and many are eventually persuaded by the raising of Lazarus (11:45). Contrast this with the more specific terms used in the Synoptic Gospels. Much of the difficulty lies in determining the goals of John 7–9.

6. Lieu, "Anti-Judaism," 182.

per a taxonomy of scholarly strategies for understanding anti-Judaism. In general, pre-war scholarship reflects the concerns and knowledge then available to scholars. In particular, German History of Religion scholars believed Johannine anti-Judaism resulted from an exchange of a Jewish identity for a Hellenistic-Christian identity.[7] Meanwhile, some conservative theologians who were responding to History of Religion scholarship were anti-Jewish in their views but sought to preserve historical Jewish links to Jesus as part of an attempt to maintain John's theological authority.

The so-called "Parting of the Ways" and anti-Judaism are usually seen as interrelated issues.[8] James Parkes's 1931 dissertation argues that antisemitism in the modern period arises from a Christian theological polemic that gained momentum following the Christianization of the Roman Empire. Parkes argues the Romans were very tolerant of Jews until Constantine, after which the situation deteriorated for Jews.[9] Parkes's thesis that modern antisemitism is the direct descendant of Christian anti-Judaism is convincing, though his assertion that negative relations between Jews on the one hand, and Greeks and Romans on the other, were not a contributing factor is questionable because this creates an unnatural dichotomy between cultural perceptions and the theological and polemical decisions that would follow. That said, Parkes is correctly responding to a supposed "mystical racial reason"[10] found in earlier studies of antisemitism that attempted " . . . to prove that antisemitism was something which inevitably accompanied the Jew wherever he went, and which was due to his own racial and unalterable characteristics."[11]

---

7. Gerdmar, *Roots of Theological Anti-Semitism*, 99–158, 376–407; Kelley, *Racializing Jesus*, 64–88, 135–48.

8. Terence L. Donaldson's work has been useful in writing this overview of the literature. See Donaldson, *Anti-Judaism in the New Testament*, 1–29, and Gager, *Origins of Anti-Semitism*, 14–37.

9. Parkes, *Church and the Synagogue*, 11.

10. Parkes, *Church and the Synagogue*, 372.

11. Parkes, *Church and the Synagogue*, 1–2. For more on the various theological, philosophical, and cultural rationales for antisemitism among European scholars, see Gerdmar, *Theological Roots of Anti-Semitism* for a comprehensive treatment; see also Kelley, *Racializing Jesus*, for a narrower but still very useful discussion. For discussion and limited rehabilitation of Bultmann, see Müller, "das Judentums,"

Introduction

Marcel Simon's monograph *Verus Israel*, first published in French in 1948[12] and released in English in 1964, established the "conflict model" as a paradigm for understanding the history of anti-Judaism and Jewish-Christian relations.[13] Like Parkes, Simon argues that antisemitism as we know it today is a descendant of Christian anti-Judaism.[14] Many no longer consider the constructs that Simon draws on to be credible, such as the idea of a Jewish missionary movement, centralized authority at Jamnia, or even the supposed shallowness of Jewish "legalism." However, many of Simon's insights remain current and, if not entirely revolutionary for their time, helped instill a revised appreciation of Christianity's Jewish heritage and the symbiotic Christian-Jewish theological relationship. Together with Parkes's dissertation, Simon's monograph was instrumental in introducing the "conflict" model that would replace constructs built upon notions of theological or philosophical progressivism.

Having lost a daughter and wife to the Holocaust,[15] Jewish-French historian Jules Isaac wrote *Jesus and Israel* (also published in 1948) while in hiding from the Nazis. Isaac argues 21 theses that re-assert Jesus' Jewish background and the Jewish origins of Christianity. Isaac points out that not all of the Jewish people rejected Jesus, but only certain parties, and that the entire Jewish people cannot be considered reprobate or participants in deicide. While Christian anti-Jewish traditions arose from efforts to consolidate the Church, Isaac maintains that antisemitism will persist so long as the Church refuses to accept responsibility for correcting its historic anti-Jewish traditions. Isaac maintains that anti-Jewish traditions are fundamentally at odds with both Jesus' ethnicity and teachings.[16]

Gregory Baum, a Catholic priest and academic of Jewish family background, attempts to show that the roots of what would become a traditional hatred of Jews do not lie in the New Testament, though

---

439–72; Stegemann, "Das Verhältnis Rudolf Bultmanns zum Judentums," 26–44.

12. Baumgarten, "*Verus Israel* as a Contribution to Jewish History," 465.
13. Taylor, *Anti-Judaism and Early Christian Identity*, 2.
14. Schäfer, *Judeophobia*, 6.
15. Isaac, *Jesus and Israel*, xii.
16. Isaac, *Jesus and Israel*, 399–400.

Baum admits that at times the NT seems on the verge of expressing something similar.[17] Baum presumes a variation of the conflict model but is sensitive to cultural differences in the use of rhetoric and the intent of anti-Jewish writers to more firmly establish Christian identity.[18] Baum concludes that antisemitism, when it is a product of anti-Judaism, is correctly understood as a matter of reception history, a conclusion quite similar to but more forceful than that of Isaac.

In John C. Gager's 1983 monograph, *The Origins of Anti-Semitism*, the cultural tradition of antisemitism results from a convergence of several factors. Again, the conflict model comes to the fore, as Gager maintains that the prime mover among these interrelated issues is internal division sparked by pagan and Christian encounters with Jews and their religion.[19] Gager attempts to establish that the theological anti-Judaism of early Christianity and the racial antisemitism of the modern period are related phenomena. Though gentiles often had positive views of Judaism,[20] and while there was a Roman anti-Semitic tradition motivated by xenophobia and the revolt of 66–73 CE,[21] it was the Christian faith that transmitted anti-Judaism across the generations to become antisemitism in the Enlightenment period.[22]

Dunn's essay "The Question of Antisemitism in the New Testament" denies that Christian Christological claims necessitated a rejection of Judaism as Judaism was, like Christianity, a diverse and developing movement. Dunn emphasizes that Christian-Jewish conflict was a matter of theological, rather than racial disagreement. This theological conflict originated as an in-house debate, rather than an as intergroup conflict between two established parties.[23] From a historical-social perspective, Lieu's 1994 article[24] takes things a step further and

---

17. Baum, *Is the New Testament Anti-Semitic*, 21.
18. Baum, *Is the New Testament Anti-Semitic*, 29.
19. Gager, *Origins of Antisemitism*, 269.
20. Gager, *Origins of Antisemitism*, 41–66.
21. Gager, *Origins of Antisemitism*, 58–62.
22. Gager, *Origins of Antisemitism*, 21.
23. Dunn, "Question of Anti-Semitism in the New Testament," 177–211 (esp. 180).
24. Lieu, "The Parting of the Ways," 101–19.

Introduction

suggests that the "Parting of the Ways" is more of a theological construct and heuristic paradigm than a historical reality. Indeed, from a historical perspective the so-called Parting of the Ways is a problematic concept. Alison Salvesen is correct to point out that testimony from Josephus and Jerome indicate that while an ideological division may have occurred early, the two parties continued to exist side by side and interacted for centuries.[25] This scenario of early theological difference accompanied by the continued association of Jews and Christians, as well as prolonged debates among leaders and laity, would provide more impetus for the development of anti-Judaism traditions in Christianity, not less.[26]

JOHANNINE ANTI-JUDAISM

Until the 1990's there was something of a consensus that the best explanation for Johannine anti-Judaism were synagogue expulsions due to the purported centralization of Jewish religious authority at Yavneh. While the assumptions underlying this version of a conflict hypothesis had long been present in scholarship,[27] it was J. Louis Martyn and Raymond E. Brown who gave this model the coherence needed for it to become almost scholarly orthodoxy. Problems in dating the Birkat Haminim and increasing awareness of first-century Judaism's diversity has led to this model's fall from favor, and some recent studies of Johannine anti-Judaism disregard it.[28] While criticisms of Martyn's dependence upon allegory for providing a history of the community are

---

25. Salvesen, "A Convergence of the Ways," 233–58; also Lieu, "The Parting of the Ways," 101–19.

26. Consider John Chrysostom, some of whose sermons seem to be a response to Jews and Christians getting along too well, seeking each other's help, and celebrating each other's festivals (*Adv. Jud.* 8).

27. In 1933, Benjamin W. Bacon presumes something similar to the community hypothesis of Gospel origins (*Gospel of the Hellenists*, 119) and many works dating from the turn of the nineteenth century presume Christian-Jewish controversies follow a much earlier dating for the parting of the ways (e.g., Scott, *Fourth Gospel*, 70–77; Wrede, *Charaktur und Tendenz des Johannesevangeliums*, 42–58).

28. For instance, Warren Carter and Tom Thatcher interpret the negative portrayal of Jewish authorities as criticism of Jewish imperial collaborators rather than persecutors. Carter, *John and Empire*, 27–39; Thatcher, *Greater than Caesar*, 52–53.

justified,[29] it remains possible there was some sort of "community" in conflict with local Jews or Jewish leaders behind John's Gospel. As far as understanding anti-Judaism is concerned, a positive contribution of the Martyn-Brown hypothesis is it provides a historical and cultural context for polemics perceived in John.[30]

In 1984, Steven Katz questioned the belief that late first-century and early second-century Judaism was a Rabbinic edifice.[31] By pointing to the Bar Kokhba rebellion against Rome and underlining its causes, as opposed to the cautious and conservative mentality of the Yavneh sages, Katz effectively demonstrates that the Birkat Haminim was not universal in effect nor aimed specifically at Christians. Rather, the Birkat Haminim was intended to deal with Jewish heretics of all persuasions, including those who embraced apocalypticism and deviant theologies held by both Christian and non-Christian Jews.[32] That Jewish apocalypticism likely contributed to the Bar Kokhba rebellion shows that the sages in Yavneh were unable to control Judaism, indicating local governance of Jewish communities was largely an *ad hoc* affair.

Katz's poignant criticisms have led many scholars to conclude that John is a response to a theological crisis brought on by the Roman destruction of the temple in 70 CE. As a possible occasion for John[33] this proposal was first raised by James Dunn[34] and further developed by scholars such as Stephen Motyer, Raimo Hakola,[35] and Andreas J. Köstenberger.[36] As supporting evidence they point to the prominence of themes such as the feasts and cult, and the placement of the temple incident in John 2. According to these scholars the Jewish War and its aftermath benefit from greater historical certainty than the hypothetical reconstructions of the Martyn-Brown hypothesis. This proposal

---

29. Motyer, *Your Father the Devil*, 28–30; Hakola, *Identity Matters*, 20–22.

30. Richey, *Roman Imperial Ideology*, 4.

31. Katz, "Issues in the Separation," 48–50.

32. Katz, "Issues in the Separation," 55, 72–74.

33. See also Kirschner, "Apocalyptic and Rabbinic Responses to the Destruction of 70," 27–46.

34. Dunn, "Let John Be John," 293–322.

35. Motyer, *Your Father the Devil*; Hakola, *Identity Matters*.

36. Köstenberger, "Destruction of the Temple," 205–42.

also has the merit of turning an anti-Jewish polemic into a constructive Jewish-Christian theological response to the loss of an important national and religious symbol. However, the validity of this argument depends upon the assumption that John is a faithful Jew, a contention that many scholars doubt.

Building on the foundation of Dunn's "Let John be John!," Motyer argues that John is an attempt made in the aftermath of the temple's destruction to persuade a Jewish audience that Jesus is the Messiah.[37] Motyer draws on various points of salience, such as the temple and Judaism's cultural memory,[38] to show that John was written from a Jewish rather than gentile perspective. While Motyer assumes a variation of the conflict model, he questions the reality of a synagogue expulsion in the Johannine community's history and focuses on the presence of anti-Judaism as evidence of an attempt to persuade.[39] He therefore seeks to set John in a broader setting that downplays the need to understand John as an attempt to cope with psychological trauma from a schism.

Another scholar critical of the Martyn-Brown hypothesis is Raimo Hakola. Hakola holds that the Johannine Christians had an in-depth, although at times distorted, understanding of Judaism.[40] For Hakola, a purpose of John is to confirm the audience in their faith in Jesus while also distancing them from Judaism to provide a self-sufficient theological identity. Hakola sees John reflecting a growing disaffection towards Judaism on the part of Jewish Christians that eventually results in a complete break.[41] Nonetheless, Hakola finds himself operating within something of a conflict paradigm when he asserts that John interprets the temple's destruction as God's punishment for Judaism's rejection of

---

37. Motyer, *Your Father the Devil*, 39, 212–16.

38. Motyer, *Your Father the Devil*, 32–34.

39. Motyer, *Your Father the Devil*, 16.

40. Hakola, *Identity Matters*, 217–20. According to Hakola, an example of caricaturing Judaism is the presence of animals in the temple courts, which he believes was unrealistic but serves to underline Jesus' piety. Hakola also views the portrayal of the Samaritans as Jewish syncretists as unfair, as well as the attempt to stone Jesus for healing on the Sabbath when more lenient penalties were available. For Hakola, these features suggest that the Johannine community was out of contact with Judaism yet used notions such as these in developing their self-understanding in relation to Judaism.

41. Hakola, *Identity Matters*, 85–86.

Jesus to justify separation from Judaism by the Johannine community.[42] Hakola also claims that John 4:22–24 represents criticism of Jewish worship when the focus seems to be more on the positive eschatological fulfillment of worship through re-centering it in Jesus. In *Identity Matters*, some of Hakola's criticisms of this passage appear to derive more from modern values than those of the first or second century,[43] but in later scholarship Hakola avoids the conflict-based community hypothesis and more successfully allows for gradual disaffection and separation using Social Identity Theory.[44] For Hakola, John abandons Judaism by the time of writing[45] but maintains a dualistic worldview with "sub-types" that add a degree of flexibility in providing grounds for social distinction between Jewish and Johannine Christian communities.[46] Caiaphas's counsel in John 11:47–48 reflects cynicism towards Jewish leaders and fosters a symbolic sense of victimhood, again with the purpose of reinforcing Johannine Christian social identity.[47] Hakola understands elements of Johannine anti-Judaism as rationalizing disaffection with Judaism to increase social distance between the two communities, rather than reflecting a response to a real social conflict such as a synagogue expulsion.[48]

While he does not directly address the issue of Johannine anti-Judaism, John A. Dennis proposes that John's Gospel is engaged in

---

42. Hakola, *Identity Matters*, 94.

43. Hakola, *Identity Matters*, 103–4, 108–12. Hakola recognizes that John is in continuity with a long strain of Jewish tradition regarding worship. However, he over-emphasizes the discontinuity with Judaism present in John. The emphasis in the text is upon unity among all who would worship God, and the superiority of worship inaugurated by Christ. There is an implicit rejection of prior Jewish worship, but logically this is unavoidable if one accepts the Johannine claims about Christ. Expressing disaffection with Judaism does not seem to be a thrust of the text (especially given the nature of first-century polemic) but the importance of Jesus.

44. Hakola, *Reconsidering Johannine Christianity*, 43–62. Also the methodology used in this study. See below.

45. Hakola, "Counsel of Caiaphas," 159; reproduced in Hakola, *Reconsidering Johannine Christianity*, 96–117.

46. Hakola, "Burden of Ambiguity" 438–55; reproduced in Hakola, *Reconsidering Johannine Christianity*, 132–46.

47. Hakola, "Counsel of Caiaphas," 146–57.

48. Hakola, "Counsel of Caiaphas," 140.

Introduction

intra-Jewish debate. In his monograph, Dennis maintains that John 11:47–52 reflects an example of restoration theology where Jesus' death facilitates the creation of "True Israel." According to Dennis, " . . . John did not think in a category such as 'supersession' or 'replacement theology'; rather, he believed that his community was the true or *genuine* Israel."[49] Dennis regards John as a largely Judeo-centric document and employs a historical-theological and narrative-critical reading in a manner similar to that advocated by Dunn and Motyer.[50] His conclusions are similar to those of Motyer, where John is attempting to solve issues presented by the destruction of the temple.[51] The Johannine Jews are those who reject Jesus as Messiah, and by implication, the God of Israel. Jews who accept Jesus are "true Israelites."[52]

Terence L. Donaldson argues that we must investigate anti-Judaism by using a three-way grid consisting of *self-definition, degree of separation,* and *rhetorical intent*.[53] Observing that John is very Judeo-centric in its characters and interests, Donaldson concludes the portrayal of the Johannine Jews may be a combination of a synagogue expulsion and an attempt to dissuade other Jews from trusting traditional authorities following the destruction of the temple. However, this position is dependent upon the identity of the intended audience which, if gentile, may reflect negative intentions towards Jews as an ethnic group.[54]

The above discussion, while selective, shows that one's undestanding of anti-Judaism in John is dependent upon how a scholar reconstructs the Gospel's *Sitz im Leben*, which in turn influences a scholar's perceptions of the Gospel author's communicative goals. In short, the paradox of the so-called hermeneutical circle applies very strongly to interpretive issues surrounding the Johannine text, the ethnic, religious, or philosophical background of its author, or any reconstructed Christian community and its social situation lying behind the text of the Fourth Gospel.

---

49. Dennis, *Gathering of True Israel*, 351. Italics original.
50. Dennis, *Gathering of True Israel*, 7–10.
51. Dennis, *Gathering of True Israel*, 341.
52. Dennis, *Gathering of True Israel*, 350–51.
53. Donaldson, *Anti-Judaism in the New Testament*, 29.
54. Donaldson, *Anti-Judaism in the New Testament*, 99–107.

TAXONOMIES OF ANTI-JUDAISM

Different taxonomies for classifying different kinds of anti-Judaism have been proposed to help scholars gain greater insight into the context of Christian documents perceived to be polemical towards Jews. Miriam S. Taylor has proposed a taxonomy consisting of four major types and eleven sub-types of anti-Judaism.[55] She grounds her categories, presented as a response to Simon's conflict model,[56] in psychological motivation rather than argumentative function. This reverses logical priority in the pathology of anti-Judaism, removing the social conflict dynamic as a motivating factor to depict anti-Judaism as a problem created *de novo* by Christian writers to further self-definition. However, in mid-to-late antiquity Judaism remained attractive to many Christians so, *pace* Taylor, it is perhaps best to conclude that conflict and competition prompted the use of anti-Judaism to further the cause of Christian self-definition, rather than the other way around.[57]

Douglas Hare presents a more resilient taxonomy of anti-Judaism, later adopted and modified by John Gager[58] and George Smiga.[59] Hoping to nuance Rosemary Radford Ruether's claim that anti-Judaism has its origins in Christological *midrash*,[60] Hare's taxonomy assumes anti-Judaism originates in theological disagreement between Jewish, and later Jewish and Christian, parties over the significance of Jesus.[61] Hare then organizes his taxonomy according to what an author is attempting to achieve, be it persuasion ("prophetic polemic"),[62] intra-Jewish criticism for rejecting Jesus in favor of another Jewish symbol or theology ("subordinating polemic"), or distancing the Church from Judaism to appropriate its theological identity for gentiles ("abrogating

---

55. Taylor, *Anti-Judaism and Early Christian Identity*, 22–78.

56. Taylor, *Anti-Judaism and Early Christian Identity*, 4–5.

57. In agreement with Baumgarten, "*Verus Israel* as a Contribution to Jewish History," 474–77.

58. Gager, *Origins of Anti-Semitism*, 8–9. Following Hare, "The Rejection of the Jews," 28–32.

59. Smiga, *Pain and Polemic*, 12–23.

60. Ruether, *Faith and Fratricide*, 64.

61. Keith, *Hated without a Cause*, 5.

62. Here I am following Smiga's terminology.

Introduction

anti-Judaism"). Scholarly consensus sees John's Gospel as stemming from a Jewish background with strong elements of prophetic and subordinating polemic; the question is whether abrogating anti-Judaism applies. In large measure this depends on how one interprets John's treatment of "the Jews."

In general, scholarship on John's use of "the Jews" falls into four major approaches to understanding the intended identity of the group who serves as the object of Johannine use of the term. Among the options for interpreting the historical context for Johannine treatment of Jews or Judaism are:

1. *Anti-Judaism is Directed against a Specific Group of Jews*: Understanding Johannine polemic against οἱ Ἰουδαῖοι in this manner limits the polemic to a specific group. In the eyes of some this may exonerate other groups of Jews.

2. *Anti-Judaism is Directed against Jews in General, but in Specific Historical Circumstances*: This approach interprets Johannine polemic as directed against all Jews, but in specific historical contexts. This is emblematic of the two-level reading espoused by J. L. Martyn and Raymond E. Brown,[63] and it limits the rhetorical force of anti-Judaism to a specific situation.

3. *Anti-Judaism is Directed against Literary Constructs who Symbolize the State of Unbelief (the Ontological Approach)*: this approach views οἱ Ἰουδαῖοι as non-historical characters who theologically or ontologically symbolize unbelief. It is usually also assumed that John is primarily a theological document in which "the Jews" serve as foils for the exposition of the meaning of belief and John's Christology.

4. *The Cathartic Approach*: In this approach readers are encouraged to condemn and disassociate the Church from such attitudes exemplified by John's treatment of Jews.[64]

63. Brown, *Community of the Beloved Disciple*; Martyn, *History and Theology*.

64. For more discussion concerning the history and literature behind these categories, please see Numada, "The Repetition of History," 261–84. This is not the first nor only means for categorizing approaches to anti-Judaism in John. For example see Schoon, "Escape Routes as Dead Ends," 144–58; Frey, "'Die Juden' im

The literature examining the Johannine treatment of "the Jews" is extensive[65] but a brief overview shows scholarship follows the patterns outlined above. Reimund Bieringer and others edited an influential volume that devotes five essays to Johannine anti-Judiasm,[66] and Urban C. von Wahlde has written comprehensive review articles.[67] The two historical approaches described above (options 1 and 2) are variable and historically-exegetically unstable.[68] This ambiguity leads some scholars to posit that this reflects stages of redaction behind the text, while other scholars combine the categories above to create explanations to this riddle.

A Specific Group of Jews

As noted, some scholars posit "the Jews" refer to a specific group of Jewish people, usually a leadership group.[69] John Ashton and Daniel Boyarin advance well-developed examples of this position. John Ashton argues in the second edition of *Understanding the Fourth Gospel* that "the Jews" are a coalition of high priests and Pharisees who attempt to exert control over Judaism in Palestine.[70] Ashton in turn draws on an essay by Daniel Boyarin,[71] where he contends that since the time of Ezra

---

Johannesevangelium," 339–77 (esp. 340–53).

65. At the time this was written, a search on the ATLA database produced 64 articles, essays, and books specifically devoted to this topic, not to mention literature where the topic is treated as part of a larger argument but is not the central concern.

66. Bieringer et al., *Anti-Judaism and the Fourth Gospel*.

67. Wahlde, "'Jews' in the Gospel of John," 30–55; Wahlde, "Johannine 'Jews,'" 33–60.

68. Here, in agreement with Stanley E. Porter. I would like to thank Dr. Porter for providing me access to a draft chapter from his *John, His Gospel, and Jesus*, where he performs a linguistic analysis on the use of "the Jews" in John's Gospel. Porter convincingly demonstrates that attempts to confine the referent of οἱ Ἰουδαῖοι to a specific member party of that group are untenable. See also Diefenbach, *Der Konflikt Jesu mit den „Juden"*, 214–16.

69. For example, Lowe, "Who were the Ἰουδαῖοι?," 101–30; Boer, "Depiction of 'the Jews' in John's Gospel," 141–57; Carter, *John and Empire*, 19–42. Elsewhere, Carter understands them as usually but not always representing the Jewish leadership in Jerusalem (Carter, *John: Storyteller, Interpreter, Evangelist*, 70).

70. Ashton, *Understanding the Fourth Gospel*, 78. For more discussion on changes in Ashton's position, see below.

71. Boyarin, "The Ioudaioi in John," 216–39.

Introduction

the title οἱ Ἰουδαῖοι was sometimes used to speak of Jewish religious ingroups over against lesser status "People of the Land" or gentiles. Translating ὁ ὄχλος as "the People" (of the Land), Boyarin argues the resentment against "the Jews" detected in John is that of second-class Israelites objecting to the elite hegemony of a specific Jewish party. This is similar to Martinus de Boer's argument where John directs the polemic against the Jewish leaders, only these leaders would presume to claim for themselves the honorific title "the Jews."[72] A difficulty with this approach is that if the Johannine Jews are a specific group of Jewish people, this group could be almost any one of a number of groups.

Jews in General, but in Specific Historical Circumstances

Another approach is to interpret the negative Johannine portrayal of Jews or Judaism in general as having its origins in a very specific historical context. One scholar who recently argued for such a position is Urban C. von Wahlde.[73] In his recent commentary von Wahlde maintains that while a first edition of John used more nuanced terminology, in its second edition "the Jews" are a group character who are inserted into the text to signify the religious authorities. Von Wahlde concludes "the Jews" are an anachronism who reflect hostility resulting from a synagogue expulsion. He regards the use of the term as hostile in all occurrences where ethnic, political, or geographic senses are absent.[74] Von Wahlde believes earlier editions of John included episodes of disagreement among the religious authorities about Jesus, with some responses even being positive. The second edition, however, obscures this so that polemic is redirected against all Jews. Von Wahlde argues that the profound negativity sometimes detected in John belongs to a later edition, and thus a time different from the original author.[75] He then merges these conclusions with elements of the *ontological approach* by

---

72. Boyarin, "The Ioudaioi in John," 216–39.

73. Others include Motyer, *Your Father the Devil*, 145–50; and Collins, "Speaking of the Jews," 158–75.

74. Wahlde, *Gospel and Letters of John*, 1:144–51.

75. Regarding *Sitz im Leben*, he is following Martyn (Smith, "Postscript," 19–20) and Brown (*Community of the Beloved Disciple*, 22–24, 40–43).

saying the hostile depiction of Jews symbolizes an authoritative Jewish opposition to the Johannine community.⁷⁶

The Cathartic Approach

Some scholars argue that anti-Judaism in John's Gospel is a historical fact and intractable theological problem, whatever its causes or origins may be, and scholars must identify this problem in order to definitively repudiate modern anti-Semitism.⁷⁷ This program makes the *cathartic approach* primarily a corrective response to the dangers of anti-Judaism. While some disagree that John is anti-Jewish or anti-Semitic in the ways sometimes presented, many would agree with its advocacy for confronting modern prejudice.

In summary, the historical approaches to John's treatment of "the Jews" surveyed above reveal a high degree of diversity because different understandings of the historical life setting of John (*Sitz im Leben*) exert a strong interpretive influence. Boyarin's proposal may offer a satisfactory historical explanation because it does not require "the Jews" to function as a metonym for another Jewish party, but the problem is οἱ Ἰουδαῖοι also serves broader ethnic, religious, and geographic senses. Likewise, first-century Jewish writers frequently use the term in a way that is not hostile. An additional factor is that the Johannine penchant for *double-entendre*⁷⁸ leaves open the possibility that John is speaking against a specific party but is exploiting the term to refer to all of Judaism to stress that Jesus is the source of salvation. The carthartic approach to anti-Judaism advances a cause with strong moral foundations that many would agree with, but some may take issue with its

---

76. Wahlde, *Gospel and Letters of John*, 1:149.

77. Scholars who argue this or similar points include Culpepper, "Anti-Judaism in the Fourth Gospel," 61–82, where he deals with this issue very directly. Adele Reinhartz is an important writer who highlights the difficulties of perceived anti-Judaism. See her "'Jews' and Jews in the Fourth Gospel," 213–27; also Reinhartz, "New Testament and Anti-Judaism," 524–37. She maintains that the "ideal reader" of the Gospel of John would understand the Johannine Jews as "villains" (529–32). See also Reinhartz, *Befriending the Beloved Disciple*; and Tomson, "'Jews' in the Gospel of John," 176–212. Hakola promotes a similar course of action (Hakola, *Identity Matters*, 238–42).

78. Cullmann, "Der Johanneische Gebrauch Doppeldeutiger Ausdrücke," 360–71.

Introduction

assumption that anti-Judaism in John is a historical given and prefer to advocate for a more nuanced historical or literary portrayal.

The Ontological Approach

The ontological reading of "the Jews" as symbols for the unbelief of "the world" is quite old. We can trace this interpretive strategy at least as far back as Christoph E. Luthardt in the mid-nineteenth century.[79] It is brought to prominence in the twentieth century by Rudolf Bultmann,[80] and appears in R. Alan Culpepper's *Anatomy of the Fourth Gospel*.[81] The hermeneutical utility of the *ontological approach* lies in broadening and abstracting perceived Johannine polemic against "the Jews" because its symbolic nature implies any anti-Judaism is not really against real historical Jews, but is instead a means for explaining Johannine theology.[82] C. K. Barrett, Judith Lieu, and the early John Ashton are among those who have proposed that the best way forward is by assuming an ontological reading of "the Jews," and then seeking the historical reasons for the author's decision to use "the Jews" as characters who represent unbelief.[83]

In 1985, Ashton engaged in a critical survey of Johannine scholarship concerning the identity of "the Jews" with Lowe and von Wahlde as his primary dialogue partners. Ashton finds historically-oriented proposals deficient on grounds that John is more literary than historical, and at the time viewed "the Jews" as operating as more of a group character than a historical party.[84] Stating that the "choice is between

---

79. Luthardt, *St. John's Gospel Explained*, 185–86. For more discussion of Luthardt see Numada, "The Repetition of History." See also the discussion of the non-historical nature of anti-Judaism in John in Fischer, "Ueber den Ausdruck: οἱ Ἰουδαῖοι im Evangelium Johannis," 96–135.

80. Bultmann, *Gospel of John*, 294–95.

81. Culpepper, *Anatomy of the Fourth Gospel*, 129–30.

82. Cook, "Gospel of John and the Jews," 213.

83. To my knowledge this is most thoroughly discussed by Lieu, "Anti-Judaism in the Fourth Gospel," 101–17 (esp. 112–17). The question is also raised by John Ashton, "The ΙΟΥΔΑΙΟΙ in the Fourth Gospel," 40–75; Barrett, "St. John: Social Historian," 26–39.

84. Ashton, "The ΙΟΥΔΑΙΟΙ in the Fourth Gospel," 57.

the historical, the theological, and the historico-theological,"[85] he sees understanding "the Jews" as representatives of unbelief as the best explanation for Johannine anti-Judaism, although why John chose to use this term remains an open historical question that needs to be answered.[86]

Barrett arrives at conclusions similar to the early Ashton from a more sociological and social-historical approach. Barrett describes Jews in the Roman Empire as being "discontent" but having a degree of privilege as an ethnic group. Barrett draws on the community hypothesis and a two-level reading strategy to make sense of Johannine treatment of "the Jews." He also draws parallels between John 8:44 and statements by Paul in Gal 3:29, Phil 3:2, and Rom 9:1–8; 10:1–3. Noting that Christian Jews and non-Christian Jews likely regarded each other as apostates, Barrett concludes that John 8 is theologizing a "nontheological *social* antagonism." The Johannine Jews are not real people, although as yet unknown conflicts with real people inspired the author to use them as a theological symbol representing unbelief.[87]

Lieu states that John's "Jewishness" has come to the foreground with the discovery of the Dead Sea Scrolls and is almost beyond dispute. She then proceeds to offer brief descriptions of strategies for dealing with Johannine treatment of Jews and Judaism, noting that each has its shortcomings and that attempts to use historical context are conjectural. She concludes that the strongest approach is to understand the Johannine Jews as representatives of unbelief.[88] Yet for Lieu, this is precisely the problem:

> The "problem" of the Johannine Jews is thus generated by the symbiosis of "historical" tradition and [a] dualist thought-world within the Gospel genre. To that extent, it derives from the Gospel's theological substructure, which shares some of

85. Ashton, "The ἸΟΥΔΑΙΟΙ in the Fourth Gospel," 68.

86. Ashton, "The ἸΟΥΔΑΙΟΙ in the Fourth Gospel," 40–70. In the heavily revised second edition of *Understanding the Fourth Gospel*, Ashton changes his mind (70–78). He adopts a diachronic reading and a Palestinian provenance, where "the Jews" are an alliance of priests and Pharisees who attempt to take control of Palestinian Judaism following the destruction of the temple.

87. Barrett, "St. John: Social Historian," 30–33.

88. Lieu, "Anti-Judaism in the Fourth Gospel," 101–12.

Introduction

> the world-denying or world-hostile tendencies of both apocalypticism and Gnosticism.[89]

She does not see the *ontological approach* or historical approaches as mitigating perceived Johannine anti-Judaism because reception history becomes part of the text's received meaning to compound anti-Judaism.[90] She concludes:

> The argument of this essay is that neither of two possible solutions is acceptable, namely, either (1) to see the purportedly accessible, historically contextualized "meaning" as the only meaning, thus remaining tied to the past and delegitimizing any developing or reapplied meaning, or (2) to reaffirm the authority of the text as a part of the canon and as such beyond critical analysis or judgment.[91]

Lieu helpfully argues for the necessity of first engaging in historical-literary investigation of "the Jews" and resolving the legacy of this problem through "responsible interpretation." This would allow the exegete to steer reception history onto a more acceptable course (necessitating the *cathartic approach*).[92]

Tobias Niklas performs a narratological analysis of "the Jews" and the disciples using reader response criticism to guage the effect on a potential reader. He concludes that "the Jews" are a group character that show little character development and primarily function as a foil for Jesus to explan the claims he makes in the Gospel of John.[93] This is in contrast with the disciples, who are used to narrow narrative distance and provide attractive characters for audiences to identify with because the latter are concrete individuals while the former are not. "Entanglement" (enmeshment) of Jews as a deindividuated group character with

---

89. Lieu, "Anti-Judaism in the Fourth Gospel," 113.

90. Lieu, "Anti-Judaism in the Fourth Gospel," 116; also Diefenbach, *Der Konflikt Jesu mit den Juden*, 3.

91. Lieu, "Anti-Judaism in the Fourth Gospel," 117.

92. Lieu, "Anti-Judaism in the Fourth Gospel," 116; Lieu, "Worlds of the Fourth Gospel," 178.

93. Nicklas, *Ablösung und Verstrickung*, 391–409.

real Jews leads to anti-Judaism.⁹⁴ Nicklas's study is convincing because it focuses on the narrative and information that is present in the text.

Likewise, Lars Kierspel undertakes a narratological analysis of ὁ κόσμος and οἱ Ἰουδαῖοι in John that strongly supports the *ontological approach*. Kierspel maintains that "the Jews" are the localized representations of a humanity hostile to the λόγος, and a statistical analysis of οἱ Ἰουδαῖοι and ὁ κόσμος support this contention.⁹⁵ Literary and theological parallelism between these two terms broadens Johannine anti-Judaism so that Johannine polemic is instead directed at a hostile, unbelieving world that is persecuting the Johannine community. Kierspel's study is largely convincing, especially in its exploration of the thematic and theological parallels, but Kierspel's assertion of "a post-Easter context of universal hate and persecution" is questionable and requires further investigation.⁹⁶

Another narratological study that examines anti-Judaism is that of Ruth Sheridan. Sheridan argues that the Gospel's characterization of the Jews "encourages an ideal reader to construct a particular character portrait of 'the Jews' in light of the OT citations in John 1:19–12:50."⁹⁷ Sheridan maintains John purposely portrays Jews as not knowing the Scriptures or being able to recognize Jesus' identity.⁹⁸ For Sheridan anti-Judaism is a negative rhetorical tactic that must bear persuasive value that confirms the Johannine community in its decision to follow Jesus. The crux of her argument is that the Scriptural citations or related subject matter in chs. 1–12 are intended to prompt belief on the part of the Jews in the narrative, but instead prompt an increasing level of hostility as the narrative progresses.⁹⁹

The generalities of Sheridan's argument are convincing, but it is questionable whether we can attribute such weight to the function of the Scripture citations rather than the progression of the narrative as a

---

94. Nicklas, *Ablösung und Verstrickung*, 409.

95. Kierspel, *Jews and the World in the Fourth Gospel*, 165–219. For how John balances his use of the terms "the Jews" and "the world" and their occurrences, see also his third appendix (223).

96. Kierspel, *Jews and the World in the Fourth Gospel*, 213.

97. Sheridan, *Retelling Scripture*, 47.

98. Sheridan, *Retelling Scripture*, 133.

99. Sheridan, *Retelling Scripture*, 235–40.

Introduction

whole. However, for future research Sheridan suggests exploring how the Gospel would engage real Jews of the first century CE, and advocates investigating various contingencies that would prompt the Gospel author to "other" Jews as a group,[100] something that we will attempt below.

Hybrid Approaches

It is common for scholarly investigations to employ one or two of the explanatory strategies above, as there is a diverse range of historical possibilities for explaining the Johannine author's decision to use "the Jews" as symbols for the unbelief of "the world" (the *ontological approach*). Many of these are complimentary, though again this suggests that the life setting of the document is the key variable. We see this in the work of Culpepper, who assumes a synagogue expulsion and merges an *ontological approach* with the *cathartic approach*.[101] H. J. de Jonge at times seems headed in the direction of the *ontological approach*, though for him any conflict involving the Johannine Christians is rooted in an *intra*-Christian dispute, where the Johannine Jews at times represent members of a competing Christian sect. He also maintains that in many cases Jewish characters are ahistorical literary creations that fulfill narrative functions.[102]

Cornelis Bennema accepts that the literary function of "the Jews" is to represent unbelief in a general sense[103] but he also adopts a position similar to von Wahlde where they also represent two specific groups of Jewish leaders, first starting with the Pharisees, and then later transitioning to the chief priests.[104] The *ontological approach* is favored to a degree by von Wahlde, although he sees its uses as originating in problems with *Jews in General, but in Specific Historical Circumstances*. Von Wahlde describes the polemic in John 7–9 as "stereotyped

---

100. Sheridan, *Retelling Scripture*, 244–45. Edward W. Klink makes similar suggestion (Klink, *Sheep of the Fold*, 254–55).

101. Culpepper, "Gospel of John and the Jews," 273–88.

102. Jonge, "'The Jews' in the Gospel of John," 121–40. Footnote 4 on p. 121 has a bibliography of those who hold similar views.

103. Bennema, "Identity and Composition of οἱ Ἰουδαῖοι," 240, 263.

104. Bennema, "Identity and Composition of οἱ Ἰουδαῖοι," 242.

apocalyptic polemic" that is intended to persuade those who failed to believe in Jesus.[105] In his commentary von Wahlde proposes that redactors relabelled Jewish leadership parties as "the Jews," which by implication directs Johannine polemic against all Jews because of a Jewish policy of persecution against Christians.[106] This is very similar to an approach argued by Jörg Frey. Frey argues that, on the basis of traditions concerning John's composition and circumstances deduced from the Gospel itself, the Gospel was composed in Asia Minor. He sees a local Christological conflict in Asia Minor between Christian and non-Christian Jews in the 90's CE, and the subsequent rejection experienced by Christian Jews, as the historical grounds for Jews serving as literary representatives for an unbelieving world.[107]

Stanley E. Porter attempts to merge the various approaches in *John, His Gospel, and Jesus*, where he argues that the debate over the negative Johannine treatment of "the Jews" has been taken to be a more serious issue than is necessary, mitigating the need for the *cathartic approach*.[108] Frequently, he notes, οἱ Ἰουδαῖοι simply functions as an ethno-religious term. He also demonstrates that the catch-all term "the Jews" is very difficult to apply with certainty to distinct parties. Further, Porter argues that the Greek article is not a direct equivalent of the English definite article "the," meaning the article in Greek does not have the same accusatory potential as it does in English. This allows Porter to conclude that οἱ Ἰουδαῖοι simply refers to whichever Jewish people happen to be present. Porter uses this to argue that we need to draw upon contextual evidence to identify the Jewish group in question.

The result of Porter's argument is something of a hybrid of the options presented above so that the identity of which Jewish group appears in a given episode is context-specific. This has the function of merging the *Specific Group of Jews* and the *Jews in General, but in Specific Historical Circumstances* approaches. For this to work, Porter merges this with elements of the *ontological approach* to maintain the requisite distance between Judaism and the author of the Gospel:

105. Wahlde, "'You are of Your Father the Devil' in its Context," 418–44.
106. Wahlde, *Gospel and Letters of John*, 1:194.
107. Frey, "'Die Juden' im Johannesevangelium," 339–77.
108. Porter, *John, His Gospel, and Jesus*, 149–73.

> [Disagreement over Jewish beliefs and symbols in John] . . . reflect tensions present during Jesus' ministry, even to the point of the author not seeing "the Jews" as fellow religious–ethnic followers but as antagonists perhaps even during the life and ministry of Jesus, hence his identification of them, though he shares ethnicity with them, as "the Jews." In that sense, the language regarding "the Jews" reflects internecine debate, with the added dimension that such debate indicates even more fundamental disagreements that led early on to a parting of the ways of Judaism and Christianity.[109]

According to Porter, the antagonism with "the Jews" is grounded in either the ministry of Jesus or the author of the fourth Gospel.[110] His helpful treatment of the Greek article diffuses some the accusatory force of the repeated appearance of οἱ Ἰουδαῖοι. Porter, together with Brook W. R. Pearson, holds the older view of an early dating for the "parting of the ways" between Christianity and Judaism,[111] which would allow for a greater sense of "the other" that would in part justify the use of the term at the time John was written. A difficulty with Porter's position is that the Synoptic Gospels use more diverse and specific terms than οἱ Ἰουδαῖοι,[112] and may suggest a greater level of hostility or social distance behind John than is found in the Synoptic Gospels,

---

109. Porter, *John, His Gospel, and Jesus*, 172.

110. This is reminiscent of some literature from the late nineteenth century until ca. 1930. For a survey see Howard, *Fourth Gospel*.

111. Porter and Pearson, "Why the Split," 82–119. They are no doubt correct from a theological view and trace the parting to the split between Paul and the Jerusalem church (110–15). For Porter and Pearson, the real issue is that the parting occurred on theological, and therefore ethnic grounds (114). The fate of Jewish Christianity as the medial path between Gentile Pauline Christianity and Judaism is the presenting issue of uncertainty (114).

Socially, the picture is less clear, though Porter and Pearson acknowledge continued, extended social interaction (115). The lack of a sufficient parting on a social, and at times a religious level, would remain an issue for church leaders. See the aforementioned discussion of inappropriate Jew-Christian interactions in Chrysostom's *Adv. Jud.* 8.8.4–5; and also canons 34–39 of the Council of Laodicea, which seem aimed at delineating the appropriate limits of Jew-Gentile Christian social and religious interaction.

112. Cook, "Gospel of John and the Jews," 262. By his count, "the Jews" occurs 71 times in John versus 16 times in all the Synoptics combined.

again prompting one to investigate the circumstances motivating more frequent use of this term.

SUMMARY

Recent research has done much to illuminate the nature of Johannine treatment of "the Jews." Interpreters no longer see the Gospel as rejecting Jewish particularism in favor of Hellenistic universalism.[113] Rather, the *ontological approach* for understanding "the Jews" suggests John is rejecting "the world" of which "the Jews" are but a subset. Yet why did John select "the Jews," rather than a specific party, to function in this manner? Further, John seems to be rejecting Judaism, at the very least as a label for the Gospel's audience. This raises the classic problem that while John seems to reject Jews or substantial elements of Judaism, the Gospel consistently uses Judaism's symbols and ideas to explain the Gospel's Christology. This study will investigate the social function of the Gospel's ontological portrayal of "the Jews" and attempt to determine what the author of John is reacting against. It will argue that Johannine anti-Judaism essentializes Jewish symbols through their incorporation into its presentation of Jesus. John also abstracts Diaspora Jewish social identity in order to reduce its salience for the Johannine audience, so that it can be replaced with what is presented as a new identity centered on Jesus.

---

113. For example, Baur, *Das Christenthum*, 1–41, 151–53; Bousset, *Die Religion des Judentum*, 3–76. See also, Gerdmar, *Roots of Theological Anti-Semitism*, 98–158.

1

Approaches to Creating and Maintaining Social Identities

INTRODUCTION

This study will employ methodologies from Collective Memory and Social Identity studies, namely Cultural Memory and Self-Categorization theory, to shed light on why the author of John selected οἱ Ἰουδαῖοι (the Jews) as representatives of unbelief. Treating Hellenistic Jewish texts as material artefacts of cultural memory, this study will reconstruct how Diaspora Jews socially categorized themselves relative to non-Jews. It will also examine evidence concerning their social locations in society, as well as evidence of what Hellenistic Jewish writers thought their social location *should* be. We will use this information interpret John's portrayal of οἱ Ἰουδαῖοι and see that John is reducing the normative fit of aspects of Jewish social identity to reduce its salience for the Johannine audience.

JEWISH NATIONALISM IN THE GRECO-ROMAN PERIOD?

One possible explanation for disaffection with Jewish identity in John that has not been sufficiently examined is Jewish "nationalism." High amounts of enthusiasm for Jewish *cultural identity* (sometimes referred to in scholarship as "zeal") before the Jewish Revolt could easily exacerbate social tensions with both Jewish-Christian and gentile Christian communities and broader Judaism. The disaster of the war with Rome would have offered opportunity for John to advocate for change.[1]

Jewish cultural identity in antiquity is the topic of countless articles, monographs, and essays.[2] A common theme is diversity: some scholars argue that Jews were perfectly at home in Hellenistic culture and enjoyed a peaceful existence outside of Palestine.[3] Others argue Jews were less at ease and envision a more precarious life among hostile gentile neighbours.[4] It is known with certainty that Jews used their religion to maintain social distinctiveness and internal cohesion, but the case of Izates shows how some Jews placed more importance on Judaism's ethnic aspects than others.[5] God-fearers and converts to Judaism may have been regarded as less Jewish than ethnic Jews[6] yet gentiles, some with other religious allegiances, are known to have been benefactors of Jewish synagogues.[7] Further, while Jews as a group were not granted citizenship, some Jewish apologists went so far as to portray Judaism as the origin for the best of human civilization.[8] Whatever the case, and while not all Jewish writers liked it, Jews in the

---

1. See Motyer, *Your Father the Devil*; Köstenberger, "Destruction of the Temple," 205–42. See also Kerr, *Temple of Jesus' Body*, who delineates the temple theme in John; see Hoskins, *Jesus as the Fulfillment* for a more traditional typological and Traditions History study.

2. See the humorous title of the introduction to *Jewish Identity and Politics between the Maccabees and Bar Kochba* by Benedikt Eckhardt entitled "Yet another Book on Jewish Identity in Antiquity" where the author defends the relevance of the volume (1–10). Other recent important works are Barclay, *Jews in the Mediterranean Diaspora*; Boyarin, "Semantic Differences; or, 'Judaism/Christianity,'" 68–85; Cohen, *Beginnings of Jewishness*; Collins, *Between Athens and Jerusalem*; Gruen, *Diaspora*; Williams, *Jews in a Graeco-Roman Environment*. Some of the more significant edited volumes are Bilde, ed., *Ethnicity in Hellenistic Egypt*; Jones and Pearce, eds., *Jewish Local Patriotism*; Levine and Schwartz, eds., *Jewish Identities in Antiquity*.

3. Gruen, *Diaspora*, 53, 69, 105–15; Rutgers, *Hidden Heritage of Diaspora Judaism*, 20–38; Schwartz, "How at Home were the Jews," 349–57.

4. Tcherikover, *Hellenistic Civilization and the Jews*, 309–32.

5. *Ant.* 20.34–48, esp. 20.40–45; Schwartz, "Doing Like Jews," 93–110.

6. Cohen, "Crossing the Boundary and Becoming a Jew," 14–31.

7. Trebilco, *Jewish Communities in Asia Minor*, 58–60; see also Luke 7:5.

8. For the idea that Moses invented literacy, technology, and taught Greek philosophers, see the fragments preserved in Eusebius, *Praep. ev.* 9.26–27. For Moses as being like a Greek philosopher, see *Praep. ev.* 9.6. For Judaism as a "national philosophy," see below.

Approaches to Creating and Maintaining Social Identities

Roman Empire constituted a distinct ethno-religious group and most Jews sought to keep it this way. However, this did not stop Jews from attempting to reinterpret their social identity to advance their position within broader gentile culture.

Self-made changes in Jewish identity are the basis for much of the discussion surrounding the New Perspective on Paul (NPP). Paul attributes himself a history of being "zealous for God and the Law" (Gal 1:14; Phil 3:6; Acts 22:3). Dunn links this to Paul's having formerly been a nationalist[9] and Martin Hengel is probably correct in characterizing these sentiments as a typical expression of Jewish piety in the NT period.[10] There are instances in Acts of encounters with violent zealous Diaspora Jews (13:45; 17:5), indicating that just because certain Jews were "Hellenized" they were not necessarily more "liberal."[11] Although there is disagreement among scholars as to the exact nature of Paul's program, it is generally agreed that Paul is using his theology of justification to make it possible for gentiles to receive the same salvific benefits as faithful Israelites—with potentially radical implications for redefining Jewish identity. A similar scenario of identity-redefinition through theology, as described by Dunn, could supply part of a well-documented and historically secure *Sitz im Leben* for John and explain its treatment of "the Jews." However, this issue is neglected in Johannine studies because most nationalism scholarship focuses on the emergence of nation-states in modern Europe, and so it may be assumed that the phenomenon does not apply to the NT period.[12]

Anthony D. Smith argues that confining the phenomenon of "nationalism" to the modern period is "Eurocentric" because it (1) assumes the political history of eighteenth- to twentieth-century Europe is normative,[13] and (2) it neglects the fact that nations and states existed

---

9. Dunn, *New Perspective on Paul*, chapter 15.

10. Hengel, *Zealots*, 177.

11. These examples would refute the most important presuppositions of writers such as F. C. Baur and Wilhelm Bousset, which construe Diaspora Jews as somehow less Jewish than their Palestinian brethren. See Gerdmar, *Theological Roots of Anti-Semitism*.

12. Smith, *Ethno-Symbolism and Nationalism*, 4–8.

13. Smith, *Antiquity of Nations*, 102.

in antiquity and outside of Europe.[14] Smith prefers to define a nation on the basis of the Greek word ἐθνή (which in his writing is substituted for by the French word *ethnie*), where states are constructed by a dominant ethnic group but also include other ethnic groups.

First proposed by John Armstrong but more fully developed by Smith, the ethnosymbolic approach focuses on the subjective elements of nationalism.[15] Building on Fredrik Barth's transactional model[16] Smith classifies two major types of nationalism: (1) political nationalism that seeks to establish a sovereign state, and (2) cultural nationalism that seeks "moral regeneration" of an ethnic community and its traditions.[17] According to Smith the characteristics of an *ideal type* nation are: " . . . a named and self-defining human community whose members cultivate shared memories, symbols, myths, traditions and values, inhabit and are attached to historic territories or 'homelands,' create and disseminate a distinctive public culture, and observe shared customs and standardized laws."[18]

Nations are built around an *ethnie* which may or may not have a political expression in a political state. According to Smith an *ethnie* " . . . possess[es] a myth of common ancestry, shared memories, one or more elements of common culture, including a link with a territory, and a measure of solidarity, at least among the upper strata."[19] Smith notes that a nation never has a single conception of itself due to regional, class, or subcultural differences. What is necessary for a nation to be a nation is for people to think of themselves as one; a nation is an

---

14. Smith is responding to what he calls "modernist" scholars such as Ernest Gellner, who maintain that efficient centralized power and widespread literacy were vital precursors to the emergence of national identities on account of their function in mobilizing collective action on behalf of the state. According to such thought, pre-modern absolute monarchies are not "nations" because they relied on coercive power for internal cohesion and collaborative action instead of a collective identity (Gellner, *Nations and Nationalism*, 88–89).

15. Armstrong, *Nations before Nationalism*; Smith, *Ethno-Symbolism*.

16. Barth, "Introduction," 9–28; Jenkins, *Social Identity*, 60–69.

17. Smith, *Ethnosymbolism and Nationalism*, 24. This builds on Hutchinson's concept of cultural nationalism (Hutchinson and Smith, *Nationalism*, 124–29).

18. Smith, *Ethnosymbolism and Nationalism*, 29.

19. Smith, *Ethnosymbolism and Nationalism*, 27.

empirical reality grounded in subjective experience, even if it is fractured by internal conflicts.[20]

Smith argues that nationalism has eight major themes: (1) autonomy of the nation, (2) the perceived unity of the nation, (3) a common national identity, (4) authenticity,[21] (5) a homeland, (6) dignity (the belief that members of the group should enjoy a certain level of prestige or status),[22] (7) continuity with a common progenitor, (8) and a collective destiny (usually glorious and unique).[23] These themes can be divided into two categories: the objective or material (1, 2, 3, 5) that focus on the political, and the subjective (4, 6, 7, 8) that focus primarily upon the cultural.[24]

In *Dynamics of Cultural Nationalism* John Hutchinson seeks to demonstrate that cultural nationalism can be expressed in ethnic renewal movements that attempt to inspire realization of national destiny. In this paradigm cultural-nationalist leaders typically see nations as going through historic cycles of decay, renewal, and restoration.[25] Leaders of cultural-nationalist movements therefore develop new myths or revise old ones to reinvigorate the nation's sense of purpose,

---

20. Smith, *Ethnosymbolism and Nationalism*, 33.

21. *Authenticity* (4) is what is perceived to be prototypical of that particular culture, and is closely associated with what Smith calls its "dignity." Smith notes that a nation's idea of its authentic self is often perceived to be embodied in the cultural memory of its so-called "Golden Age," where a group realizes and expresses what is perceived to be its authentic identity (Smith, *Chosen Peoples*, 215).

22. *Dignity* (6) is the prototypical social status that the culture thinks it should be attributed relative to other groups (Smith, *Chosen Peoples*, 213–14). An oft-cited example of this being worked out is the Maccabean revolt—at least as portrayed by 1 Maccabees—which was remembered as divinely-assisted resistance to assimilation into Hellenistic paganism (Bickerman, *God of the Maccabees*, 90; Mendels, "Memories and Memory," 45), and this seems to have been immortalized even among the Greek-speaking Jews of the Diaspora (Rappaport, "Connection," 90–100).

23 Smith notes that conceptions of a group's collective destiny often uses past "Golden Ages" as a template (Smith, *Chosen Peoples*, 215–17). Also Smith, *Ethnosymbolism and Nationalism*, 62–63.

24. Collins makes a similar distinction in the organization of his study of Jewish identity. See Collins, *Between Athens and Jerusalem*, 25–26.

25. Hutchinson, *Dynamics of Cultural Nationalism*, 9–10.

identity, and destiny.²⁶ Key players are often religious groups who may be internally divided but united against outsiders.²⁷

When speaking about Judaism in the Hellenistic and Roman periods, ideas of Jewish political-national aspiration are easily supported as Hellenistic Judaism saw itself as a nation that should have political autonomy. Further, Judaism saw itself as united in its obedience to Torah and YHWH (although parties vehemently disagreed on precisely how to do this) and had a traditional homeland. It is the subjective elements that are qualitatively difficult to define, and it seems how Hellenistic Jews related to gentile cultures varied from case to case. Yet for an individual to remain a Jew, they would need to value their identity as a Jew, claim continuity with Abraham as progenitor, and either anticipate a future collective destiny or seek to realize the proper collective place of Jews in broader society.

The ethnosymbolic approach to "nations" and "nationalism" allows for the application of these concepts prior to the modern period without risk of anachronism. According to this paradigm Judaism was an ethnic group, religion, and nation. Tendencies we would describe as nationalistic were expressed in Jewish rebellions against Rome in Palestine and the Diaspora,²⁸ though it remains possible for Jews to have been culturally but not politically nationalistic.

There are plenty of signs John is responding to matters of Jewish theology and identity that mirror political and cultural nationalism,²⁹

26. Hutchinson, *Dynamics of Cultural Nationalism*, 14, 22–30.

27. Hutchinson, *Dynamics of Cultural Nationalism*, 39.

28. Between 66 CE and the early 130's CE, Jews engaged in three major violent revolts against Rome, one of them being in North Africa (Cohen, *From the Maccabees to the Mishnah*, 30–34). See Farmer, *Maccabees, Zealots, and Josephus*, 122–200 for a survey of primary sources.

29. The NT does not speak directly of Jewish nationalism (or political and *cultural identity*) in detail, but there are several indicators that they formed a significant element of Jewish cultural memory. Hengel has shown that the Zealot movement that led to the Jewish War of 66–70 CE was inspired by the Maccabean revolt (Hengel, *Zealots*). In the NT there is mention of one of Jesus' disciples being known as Simon the Zealot in Luke 6:15 and Acts 1:13. Mention is made of the ironically-named Barabbas (Son of the Father), who was accused of being a rebel against Roman rule (Mark 15:7; Luke 23:18–19; also mentioned in Matt 27; John 18:40). In John 10:22 Jesus goes to Jerusalem to celebrate Hanukkah, while in John 6:15 Jesus has to dismiss a crowd that sought to force him to become king. Perhaps to debunk

but in order to examine this phenomenon one needs to be able to avoid conflating sentiments held by members of a group with their political expression. While the ethnosymbolic approach to nationalism helpfully opens up new avenues for NT research, it faces certain methodological and terminological difficulties in placing separate areas of sociology and psychology under the political term "nationalism." The ethnosymbolic approach also depends upon the symbolic interactionist paradigm to social psychology; while useful for mapping out the symbolic universe of a closed group, it can become unwieldy when examining human interactions in poly-ethnic contexts. The discursive nature of texts suggests that in this context Self-Categorization Theory (SCT) is more appropriate due to reliance on observed behavior as exhibited in texts. This study will therefore redefine what Smith calls "political nationalism" as *national identity*, and "cultural nationalism" as *cultural identity*. The symbolic resources for constructing group identity are sometimes referred to under the umbrella term of *collective* (or *cultural*) *memory*, which are amenable to social-psychological methodologies that explore social identity.

COLLECTIVE AND CULTURAL MEMORY

Collective memory is less about the recall of information and more about present experience of the past. Collective memory scholarship usually posits a constructed and reinterpreted past that serves as a paradigm for interpreting the present circumstances of communities.[30] *Collective Memory* also serves as a metaphor for the media that transmit culture and group identity across generations by means of narratives that are reformulated, simplified, and meet some sort of psychological or social need.[31]

---

such implied militant claims Jesus makes a point of entering Jerusalem on a donkey, demonstrating (acknowledging?) his kingship but conveying peaceful intentions (Matt 21:5; Mark 11:4–10; Luke 19:30–44; John 12:14–16).

30. Misztal, *Theories of Social Remembering*, 9–13; Assmann, "Collective Memory and Cultural Identity," 130.

31. Misztal, *Theories of Social Remembering*, 11–15; Erll, *Memory in Culture*, 100–101. While Maurice Halbwachs proposed the idea of collective memory, he has drawn criticism for not clearly establishing how it operates. Still, past history continues to influence group memories (Misztal, *Theories of Social Remembering*, 52–55). An extreme "presentist" stance may view memories as created by those in power to

Cultural memory[32] involves groups creatively using their shared history to reinterpret the narratives leading to the present situation through selectively remembering and forgetting elements of it (*distortion*; *innovation*).[33] We can traces these developments in traditions over time.

Collected memory is the means by which socially-shaped individual memories can be propagated in a population through media.[34] *Collective memory*, on the other hand, is the social employment of symbols, media, institutions, and practices that are communicated in collected memory and used to build a culturally-specific reality. However, it is phenomenological and only exists to the degree that individuals express or understand these in a common manner. These phenomena are involved in three major dimensions or domains—the sociological, material, and mental:

1. *Material dimension*: mnemonic artefacts, media, and technologies of memory; symbols, landscapes, architecture, books, film, photography.

---

foster social cohesion (58–61), though many prefer to see collective memory as continuously formulated in dialogue with the past with an eye to present social needs, constantly mutating as culturally-conditioned frameworks change but not entirely unfaithful to the past (69–82).

This study treats the formation of memory as a process of negotiation, traceable through a process similar to biblical *Traditions history*. An instrumental view of memory as a tool that meets present needs presumes that memories are elaborations on earlier versions of the same tradition. This approach acknowledges that collective memories change over time but it allows one to presume a degree of continuity with actual events or individuals from the past while recognizing the tendency to mythologize history to foster identity formation (99–100).

32. Misztal, *Theories of Social Remembering*, 12.

33. Misztal, *Theories of Social Remembering*, 17; Schudson, "Distortion in Collective Memory," 346–61. *Distortion* involves intentionally reinterpreting the past, though *distortion*'s pejorative connotations suggest *innovation* may be a more appropriate term to use. *Remembering* and *forgetting* refer to inclusion or exclusion of material in cultural/collective memory. *Forgetting* often occurs due to embarrassment. Sara Pearce observes that in *Antiquities* Josephus "forgets" and omits the Golden Calf episode in his Exodus narrative, probably from embarrassment. Philo, on the other hand, blames the episode on Egyptian influence (*Moses* 2.161–62). See Pearce, "Belonging and Not Belonging," 91.

34. Erll, *Memory in Culture*, 128.

Approaches to Creating and Maintaining Social Identities

2. *Social dimension*: mnemonic practices such as commemorative rituals, forms of production, storage, persons (leaders; specialists), social institutions.

3. *Mental dimension*: shared values, concepts, codes that allow collective remembering by means of symbolic mediation.[35]

In the case of historically-situated collective memories, we have direct access to its material aspects (texts, archaeological data) but only indirect access to sociological or mental elements (usually via texts).[36] This study will survey the subjective elements of Jewish *cultural identity* resulting from individual psychological processes that operate among groups holding similar values.[37] The remnants of cultural memory available to us are primarily texts, though can also to a limited degree be inscriptions or testimony from non-Jewish texts.

We can trace patterns of memory distortion and innovation by means of (1) how something is remembered, and (2) the content that is remembered.[38] As a textual study, this examination will focus on the material artefacts of Jewish cultural memory's preservation, transmission, and development.[39] Biblical studies typically examines this process by means of the *biblical traditions* in *reception history* of ideas or lines of thinking that appear in canonical and non-canonical literature. Analogous is what Siegfried Schulz terms *Themageschichte*, or thematic traditions history study in biblical scholarship, which traces a biblical tradition over a period of its reception history, paying attention to motivations for innovations added to the tradition.[40] Closely related are *interpretive traditions* pertaining to a biblical tradition.[41]

35. Erll, *Memory in Culture*, 102–3.

36. Erll, *Memory in Culture*, 104.

37. Turner, *Rediscovering the Social Group*, viii–ix.

38. Rodriguez and Fortier, *Cultural Memory*, 9.

39. This is what Rodriguez and Fortier term a memory's *traditio* (*Cultural Memory*, 9).

40. Schulz, *Untersuchungen zur Menschensohn-Christologie*, 43–89 (esp. 88–89).

41. Rodriguez and Fortier's division of Cultural Memory's mechanisms into *Traditio* and *Traditus* are helpful, but still remain broad categories that in the context of this study would benefit from further definition. For greater specificity, the terms biblical tradition, interpretive tradition, and reception history are used in place of the general term traditio proposed by Rodriguez and Fortier.

As for (2) the content of cultural memory, this study interacts with several ideas that facilitate cultural memory's use in identity formation. The first consists of specific events or circumstances, a *cultural memory* (singular noun), within the broader stream of a culture's social memory (uncountable noun). The second consists of the individuals who played significant roles in Jewish history and were of importance for the construction of Jewish identity, or what Smith terms the "common progenitors." Thirdly, this study attempts to examine the more subjective elements of cultural memory, such as Jewish ideas of authenticity or prototypicality (discussed below). The means for remembering and the contents of remembrance discussed above played a vital role in the construction of how Jews understood themselves and related to other groups of people. The subjective elements, in particular, are perhaps best understood in terms of how people form their social identities.

SOCIAL IDENTITY THEORY AND SELF-CATEGORIZATION THEORY

Social Identity Theory (SIT) and Self-Categorization Theory are two closely related social-psychological theories. Here we will attempt to apply SIT and SCT as methodologies for reading the Johannine text, which along with Cultural Memory can help interpret John's treatment of "the Jews."

SCT and SIT understand groups as individuals operating according to consensual criteria of similarity,[42] though individuals may bear multiple social identities from different contexts.[43] Social identity is therefore not a fixed property but is contingent and situational in nature. Based on a number of experiments conducted in the early 1970's,[44] SCT and SIT presume that individuals are predisposed to evaluate themselves, their groups, and in-group members positively. Individuals negatively appraise disloyal group members because this benefits faithful members.[45] The basis of in-group favoritism, known as in-group bias, is not the

42. Turner, *Rediscovering the Social Group*, 10.

43. Nkomo and Cox, "Diverse Identities in Organizations," 348.

44. See Hornsey, "A Historical Review," 205.

45. Turner, *Rediscovering the Social Group*, 29–30; Haslam, *Psychology in Organizations*, 28–30.

group *per se* but the agreed-upon criteria of similarity (categories) used to establish a person's identity.[46] However, the categories that people use to alternately place themselves and others into in-groups and out-groups are established on a situational basis and do not exist independent of social contexts.[47] These categories are known as *self-categorizations*, also referred to as *social categorizations* in this study.

Central to SCT and SIT is that individual and group categorizations exist as part of a cline of classification systems. The chart below illustrates how social identities begin with more generalized classifications with a higher level of abstraction that can become more specific or concrete:

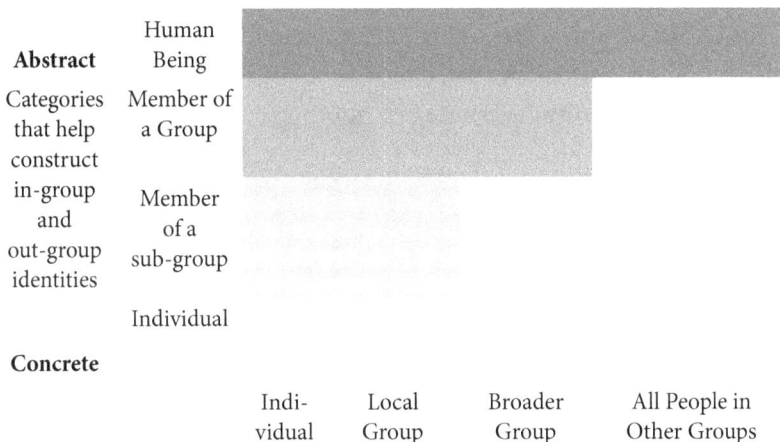

Figure 1: Levels of Abstraction in Social Identity[48]

Marilynn B. Brewer argues that people favor intermediate group identities because they more readily balance between being too individualistic and too inclusive. A more abstract and broadly applied categorization is no longer helpful for asserting an identity because it now has anonymizing qualities, essentially depriving them of a social

---

46. Rabbie and Horwitz, "Categories versus Groups," 117.

47. Rabbie and Horwitz, "Categories versus Groups," 119–20.

48. Adapted from Haslam, *Psychology in Organizations*, 47. The terms "group" and "sub-group" are themselves relative and contingent, serving to illustrate the cline of relationships between social levels. A group may consist of nations, tribes, clans, families, or even sports teams, while a sub-group may be a constituent part of a larger group. Used with permission.

identity with any degree of uniqueness.[49] We will see below that the partially-defined medial identity categories can give rise to social conflict at the inter- and intra-group levels because people bear multiple categorizations for establishing a social identity.[50] To a certain point the likelihood of ambiguity can increase as categorizations become less abstract because individuals may disagree over what should govern the criteria for determining similarity, and whether someone fits the category.

Prototypes, Meta-Contrast, and Comparative Fit

SCT and SIT argue individuals try to advance their group's status as a means of advancing their own prestige.[51] Whether or not a given categorization for social identity is salient enough to act upon is dependent upon several factors related to self-interest.[52] Social categorization of individuals involves evaluating an in-group member's *prototypicality*

---

49. Individual categorizations render a person too distinct and isolated if they are the sole categorization that is salient. Likewise, categorizations that are too abstract or inclusive again render the individual isolated because they lack distinction. See Brewer, "On Being the Same and Different at the Same Time," 475–82 (esp. 475).

50. Turner, *Rediscovering the Social Group*, 45–49.

51. Haslam, *Psychology in Organizations*, 32–40. Earlier expressions of SIT and SCT maintained that this was motivated by the need to maintain self-esteem, although it was contested as to why advancement of the group would improve individual self-esteem. Later developments broadened the motivational basis to include a spectrum of analogous factors, such as the need to find a sense of belonging in their social sphere in order to promote ontological security and reduce ontological anxiety. Another explanation is that individuals seek to reduce subjective uncertainty by providing order to their social existence. Together, these replaced self-esteem as the explanation for why people attempted to advance the group and evaluated in-groups positively (Hornsey, "A Historical Review," 214–15), or to attempt to situate one's group advantageously relative to others (Hogg and Williams, "From *I* to *We*," 87). See also Giddens, *Modernity and Self-Identity*, 35–47.

52. Hogg states that these are: "(a) individual motives for self-enhancement (self-esteem) or self-evaluation (uncertainty reduction), (b) the contextual accessibility of specific social categorizations, (c) the accessibility of specific social categorizations in memory, (d) how well a specific categorization accounts for relevant similarities and differences among people (structural or comparative fit), and (e) how well a specific categorization accounts for others' actual behavior (normative fit)." See Hogg, "From *I* to *We*," 89.

but an out-group member's *stereotypicality*.[53] Prototypes are similar to David Weber's "ideal type"—they are individuals or constructs who are representative examples of group members. Different bases of comparison can determine the level of difference or similarity: a high degree of perceived interclass difference is more likely to result in someone being attributed *prototypicality* (they are very different from out-group members), but only if there is also a high degree of similarity with in-group members.[54] As criteria for determining comparative fit (similarity) changes with the social context, individuals adjust what they think is salient (relevant) for establishing who is similar and different.[55] This principle of comparison is known as "meta-contrast." which people generally use in such a way that ensures their in-groups maintain a positive self-image.[56] S. Alexander Haslam provides an example:

> ... if a woman's social self-category "scientist" becomes salient, other scientists will be perceived to be more similar to each other (and her) and more different from other non-scientists (whose similarity to each other will also be accentuated) on dimensions that are seen to define membership of those categories (e.g. commitment to the scientific method).[57]

Some scientists may choose, for example, to view gender as a salient category. If the majority of scientists are men, the woman scientist becomes dissimilar. Similarity or difference is established upon which category is considered salient at the time[58] and the degree to which people are willing to evaluate others as individuals and not as depersonalized

---

53. Haslam, *Psychology in Organizations*, 161–64.
54. Haslam et al., "Contextual Changes," 524.
55. Haslam et al., "Contextual Changes," 525.
56. Haslam, *Psychology in Organizations*, 165.
57. Haslam, *Psychology in Organizations*, 49.
58. Turner, *Rediscovering the Social Group*, 46, 80; Haslam, *Psychology in Organizations*, 71. For empirical studies see Haslam et al., "Contextual Changes," 509–12. On the formation and acceptance of stereotypes and prototypes, see Haslam et al., "When do Stereotypes Really Become Consensual," 757–72, where formation of group identities and categories are not solely based upon definition vis-à-vis an outgroup but also in-group consensus.

members of an out-group.⁵⁹ We can see below an illustration for how relative difference is perceived when different factors are salient.

Figure 2: Relative Difference (Woman Scientist)

Different (stereo-type)					Similar (prototype)
Salient Category: SCIENCE (not gender)					
Taxi Drivers	Retail Employees	Baristas		Male + Female Scientists	Albert Einstein
Salient Category: GENDER (not academic specialization)					
Daughters	Mothers	Female Scientist		Taxi Drivers	Male Scientists

The creation of religious and ethnic categories involve similar social identity processes.⁶⁰ Again, these social categories are phenomenological, meaning these categories lack salience if there is no exposure to people from another group that are understood as different.⁶¹

Levels of Identification and Convergence

SCT and SIT are relevant for historical literary study because written forms of communication provide evidence of SCT schemata that give information on how writers viewed themselves and others. Sociolinguistic methodologies that rely on SCT argue that when people share similar identities, they are more likely to communicate with one another. Where people do not think they share an identity of some kind, they are less likely to communicate or form community.

Perceived common identity is vital for exerting non-coercive influence over others. Language, vocabulary, and communication styles

---

59. Haslam, *Psychology in Organizations*, 70–72; Hogg and Williams, "From *I* to *We*," 88.

60. For example, see Eriksen, *Ethnicity and Nationalism*, 14–69.

61. According to Eriksen, some African ethnic groups were unaware that they possessed different ethnicities until the arrival of colonialism. When colonial authorities made it known to these groups that the parties were different from one another, sometimes simply on account of geography, only then did the relevant factors become salient and distinct ethnic identities emerged. Eriksen, *Ethnicity and Nationalism*, 98–107.

may also serve as identity markers to demonstrate that the communicator is part of the same categories as their audience, if the category the communicator aspires to is accessible to them.[62] When people want to minimize intergroup differences, communication styles become more similar to the recipient in a process known as social convergence. When communicators want to maintain inter-category difference, divergence in communication style occurs to maintain that difference in a form of linguistic self-stereotyping.[63] SIT and SCT maintain that, in general, individuals from groups of lower social status have a tendency to claim or emulate the qualities of groups with a higher social status when barriers maintaining distinction between groups are permeable.[64] In such a context someone may over-communicate (emphasize) or under-communicate (play down) their perceived differences or similarities.[65] This may also involve the "forgetting" of undesirable qualities that are attributed to their group. This is more likely when an individual is a high identifier because their group identity is important to them. However, people who are low identifiers may similarly act like out-group members because group identity is not important to that individual.[66] When in-group members view attempted social convergence unfavorably, they consider those attempting such convergence as violators of the in-group.

In summary, for SIT and SCT, identities and social categories are situational. As a general rule, categorizations move from abstract and

62. Haslam, *Psychology in Organizations*, 126–29.

63. Haslam, *Psychology in Organizations*, 136. For example, Hakola has applied SIT to non-Johannine contexts, such as the Qumran community ("Social Identities," 259–76) where he maintains that polemic may arise as a result of similarities between parties and the need to establish difference.

64. Haslam, *Psychology in Organizations*, 137.

65. Eriksen, *Ethnicity and Nationalism*, 27–28.

66. Sahdra and Ross, "Group Identification and Historical Memory," 384–395. Arguing from Schema Theory, Sahdra and Ross maintain that since people are inclined to view the in-group positively, people forget negative aspects of their group's history because it is not consistent with preconceptions of that group, though this is difficult to prove definitively. Additionally, it is more plausible to suggest that when someone who is well-informed omits mention of something, there is likely a motivation behind its omission. Manstead and Spears argue that high-identifiers tend to feel less guilt over their group's misdeeds, while low-identifiers tend towards more guilt over their group's misdeeds (Manstead et al., "Guilty by Association," 872–86).

generalized to more specific and well-defined. Meta-contrast determines the degree of comparative fit, or whether an individual fits the expected in-group prototypes or out-group stereotypes; the determining criteria are chosen on the basis of whether people think a category is salient for that situation. In a process known as convergence, individuals may attempt to move themselves or their group closer to another group, usually to increase their prestige or security. Evidence of SCT may be observed in acts of communication, such as texts.

INSIGHTS FROM PRIOR APPLICATIONS OF SIT, SCT, AND SOCIAL MEMORY THEORY

In biblical studies, Philip Esler pioneered the use of SIT in social scientific criticism and has produced the most comprehensive treatment and application of SIT as a methodology for biblical studies, particularly in his *Conflict and Identity in Romans*. This work is notable because of the breadth of its bibliography and its synthetic applications of multiple paradigms.[67] Elsewhere, Esler is clear in stating that he regards the social sciences as a source for heuristic tools in reading texts.[68] Esler's work on Romans demonstrates a keen ability to situate Paul's theology in relation to ethnic issues in mixed Jewish-gentile churches and the social goals behind Paul's argumentative techniques.[69] However, while very insightful, Esler's monograph tends to be model-driven. It is Esler's mastery of Social-Scientific criticism demonstrated by the sheer number of social models and paradigms that he employs that prevents his work from being deterministic in its application of models.

Philip Esler and Ronald Piper later apply SIT, SCT, and social memory theory to the Johannine community. They attempt to contextualize the Johannine Jews as religious leaders in opposition to Jesus.[70] Meanwhile, Esler and Piper interpret Lazarus, Mary, and Martha (but not the disciples) as exemplifying prototypes for the Johannine community. In the social memory paradigm, they also provide prototypical "ancestors" for the community to promote greater unity by fostering a

---

67. See the survey in Esler, *Conflict and Identity in Romans*, 1–76.
68. Esler, "Social-Scientific Approaches," 339.
69. Esler, *Conflict and Identity in Romans*, esp. 109–270.
70. Esler and Piper, *Lazarus, Mary, and Martha*, 159–64.

sense of fictive kinship.[71] Esler and Piper do not address the issue of relative difference between the Johannine Christians and Judaism, or between non-believing Jews, Jewish and gentile Christian parties, and non-believing gentiles. While their attempt to frame Johannine Christian identity positively is laudable, they understand the Johannine Jews in a purely official, authoritative oppositional role. It addresses Johannine anti-Judaism's broader social function, but not its origins.

As mentioned earlier, Raimo Hakola also applies SIT and SCT to the Gospel of John. In a number of articles later reproduced in monograph form, Hakola employs SIT to understand the identity of the Johannine community relative to Nicodemus and Caiaphas.[72] Like his previous work, and Esler and Piper above, he concludes the Johannine community interpreted reality in dualistic terms as part of a social-constructivist agenda,[73] though it had also adopted a non-Jewish way of life on account of perceived cynicism detected in the text.[74] Hakola's application of SIT models is more descriptive than the work of Esler and Piper but it risks resulting in preconceived conclusions.[75] Positively, Hakola's scholarship more directly addresses the purpose and social function of Johannine polemic and is not dependent upon a reconstructed *Sitz im Leben*. Additionally, Hakola's work attempts to address the issue, very important in SIT and SCT, of relative difference and meta-contrast, and suggests that differences between the Johannine community and Judaism may not have been as significant as John desired.[76]

---

71. Esler and Piper, *Lazarus, Mary, and Martha*, 90–100.

72. Hakola, "Burden of Ambiguity," 438–55; Hakola, "Counsel of Caiaphas," 140–63.

73. Hakola, "Burden of Ambiguity," 455.

74. Hakola, "Counsel of Caiaphas," 159.

75. For instance, note the widely divergent views of Raimo Hakola and John A. Dennis on Caiaphas' prophecy. Hakola, "Counsel of Caiaphas," 159; Dennis, *Gathering of True Israel*, 341–53. More useful is Hakola's application of meta-contrast in "Social Identities," 259–76. According to his argument in this article, Johannine anti-Judaism is just as likely the result of similarity to other Jews as it is a sign of disaffection with Jewish identity, which would be more in keeping with the conclusions of Dennis.

76. Hakola, *Reconsidering Johannine Christianity*, 58–62; a similar point made by Rodney Whitacre, though he frames it in terms of the Martyn-Brown hypothesis

Hakola's work largely confines itself to matters of election and Jewish orthopraxy. Hakola's contention is that the Johannine writer had become disaffected with Judaism's practices and cynical towards members of a Jewish community, but leaves the reasons for this unexplained. Hakola addresses the issue of relative difference between Johannine Christians and Jews, but he does not situate this in the broader context of relative difference between Jew and gentile and he regards the positive Johannine references to Jewish figures or symbols as superficial. His treatment of Johannine dualism is beneficial, and in heuristic terms he applies SIT and SCT models well, though in socially-descriptive terms there remains much room for further investigation as to the nature of the new social identity created by John for Johannine Christians and how it is different from Diaspora Jewish social identity.

The above discussion shows that biblical scholars have previously made use of SIT and SCT as paradigms for interpreting biblical texts. At times the application of SIT and SCT border on being model-driven,[77] or, more positively, simply serve heuristic rather than descriptive

---

and holds a more self-isolationist understanding of Diaspora Judaism than is supported in this study (Whitacre, *Johannine Polemic*, 11).

77. A widely acknowledged limitation of social-scientific approaches. For example, following E. A. Judge, Porter notes that (1) "all socio-historical models seem to take the same external or extrinsic approach to data." That is, the theoretical frameworks applied to interpret texts are often only loosely linked to the texts. Furthermore, Porter observes that there is (2) a tendency to cursorily group different isolated texts together and ignore their individual significance. This results in literary evidence being organized into one data set, when in fact it may consist of many. A further difficulty, Porter notes, lies in (3) applying modern sociological frameworks to ancient social settings when there may be insufficient historical information to properly apply the model. This is also observed by J. Sanders, who surveys aspects of various models and approaches. For Sanders, models remain useful, so long as they can be properly applied. See Porter, "Pauline Social Relations," 14; Judge, *Social Distinctives*, 127–30; Sanders, *Schismatics*, 82–151, esp. 113.

Porter also takes issue with social descriptivist approaches but notes that they rely far less on theoretical frameworks, which Porter sees as being the most variable element in socio-historical approaches. Yet for Porter, social descriptivist approaches have the merit of being textually based, with a more confined scope restricted to social phenomena specifically described in texts under study. The disadvantage is that while it offers a more complete picture of individuals, it can miss the broader picture. Further, social descriptivist approaches also tend to lack strong theoretical frameworks. Porter, "Pauline Social Relations," 19–20; Kee, *Knowing the Truth*, 36; Judge, *Social Distinctives*, 127–42.

functions. The result is that SIT and SCT as social-psychological paradigms still, at least in their application in biblical studies, suffer from the pitfalls of structuralist sociological methods. While previous studies are helpful and constructive, and Hakola especially understands social relations as being on a cline or continuum rather than as parts of a dichotomy, scholars tend to present Jewish and Christian identities as two opposing forces rather than situational constructs resulting from social situations. Jews and adherents of Judaism, on the one hand, and Greek gentiles on the other, likewise continue to be seen as polarities, even though scholarship has long since shown this was not the case. A more situational, descriptive reading of Johannine anti-Judaism is therefore required.

PROCEDURE

This study will aim to be both socially descriptive and analytical to avoid some of the shortcomings of sociological methods in biblical studies. Aspects of Collective/Cultural Memory examined in this study are primarily drawn from documentary phenomena to explain social behavior, making it more a hermeneutic for understanding texts than a model to be imposed on them.

The meta-contrast inherent to SCT necessitates a heavy reliance on information regarding social categories and how people compare themselves to each other, which in our case we can only derive from literary or inscriptional evidence. Since the bases for comparison and relevance of social categorizations are determined on a situational basis, the procedure used here functions descriptively and analytically.

The procedure for this study will involve examination of Hellenistic Diaspora Jewish literature by writers such as Josephus, Philo, and Aristeas, proceeding on a regional basis (Rome, Egypt, Asia Minor).[78]

---

78. Readers may notice this study has several affinities with the work of Barclay and Collins (Barclay, *Jews of the Mediterranean Diaspora*; Collins, *Between Athens and Jerusalem*). Like Barclay, the first part of this study proceeds geographically, though my interpretations are usually more in line with those of Collins. The use of cultural memory and SCT disposes me to reading texts as historical documents only secondarily. Texts reflect what historical people think or say, though one must conclude that for a document to be a convincing fiction, it must contain much accurate social information. As Rutgers correctly observes, a document may reflect

For the sake of practicality this will be done thematically, analyzing Jewish self-categorizations in primary documents to determine Jewish authenticity (prototypes versus stereotypes), Jewish origins in a common progenitor, and desired social status. Next, I will interpret the social processes at work in the primary sources by making use of secondary literature, papyri, and inscriptions.

Relatively frequent embellishment or misrepresentation of historical "facts" in first-century Jewish literature makes it necessary to determine patterns of *distortion* in Jewish cultural memory. Particular attention will be paid to mechanisms of increasing and decreasing relative difference through over-communication and under-communication, as well as collective *remembering* and *forgetting*. Again, these will be evaluated descriptively because each writer is unique in their thoughts and circumstances; distortion is assumed to be advantageous to the interests of the writer under examination, effectively functioning as part of their social categorization systems. In other words, inferences regarding the importance of memory for identity can be drawn from a cultural tradition's reception history. From a cultural tradition's reception history, we can detect trends in how that cultural tradition is changed and infer an author's social goals.

We will follow this with an examination of how John treats the subjective elements of Jewish *cultural identity* exemplified in the reception history of cultural traditions important to contemporary Jewish cultural memory. This examination will focus on the same themes as the preceding section and interpret the use of these themes to

---

the author's aspirations rather than historical reality (Rutgers, *Hidden Heritage of Diaspora Judaism*, 20–22).

Barclay's *Jews of the Mediterranean Diaspora* has been criticized for its conclusions being too generalized, but not for being explicitly wrong (Schwartz, "How at Home were the Jews," 351–53; Rutgers, *Hidden Heritage of Diaspora Judaism*, 34–38). For his part, Barclay views his own conclusions as tentative (*Jews of the Mediterranean Diaspora*, 99). I would suggest a contributing factor for this negative assessment is that Barclay's criteria for measuring assimilation (social integration), acculturation (language and education), and accommodation (use of acculturation), are determined by acculturation. According to Barclay's criteria, the use of Greek language and evidence of education determines one's level of acculturation (Barclay, *Jews of the Mediterranean Diaspora*, 93–98). However, education does not necessarily imply acculturation because people can pursue it for economic reasons, and therefore it does not necessarily imply assimilation.

establish the Johannine picture of the prototypical Christ-follower and stereotypical non-believer. It will also attempt to discern patterns of *distortion* (or innovation) in its treatment of Jewish cultural memory. Intepreting innovations upon cultural memory assumes that there is an "actual past" for an author to reinterpret to meet present needs. More historically-oriented approaches to memory seek this history; a presentist approach seeks the current circumstances of an author and their final product in order to try to understand their situation and perhaps their motivations, though it will not identify all of the factors that led up to the time of writing, be they experiences of the author, any community they belong to, or Jesus himself. In particular, we will attempt to pay adequate attention to mechanisms of over-communicating and under-communicating identity, as well as remembering and forgetting elements of cultural/collective memory to facilitate or mitigate social convergence.

The examination of John will involve a systematic comparison of the data observed in the study of Jewish self-categorizations found in Hellenistic Diaspora Jewish literature with that found in John's Gospel. This will be followed by an interpretation of the results of the preceding comparison and will bring the various elements together to support the thesis of this project. The presumed conclusions of this study are falsifiable based on how one interprets Jewish Hellenistic literature. The diversity of Jewish literature in the Hellenistic period offers some assurance that we can draw observations of social categorizations from a broad spectrum, which allows for greater comprehensiveness and accuracy.

This study seeks to combine the *ontological approach* to understanding Johannine treatment of "the Jews" with the understanding that this is motivated by controversy with *Jews in general, but in specific historical circumstances*. It will contribute to Johannine studies by demonstrating that these specific historical circumstances are attraction to, and zeal for, Jewish cultural identity. Another contribution is that it will show that well-documented ideas and behaviors from the broader cultural context are sufficient for explaining Johannine anti-Judaism perceived in its treatment of "the Jews." This will help mitigate the need for reliance upon tentative hypothetical reconstructions of *Sitze im*

Leben and allegorical mirror-readings of the text to account for Johannine anti-Judaism. Fully knowable historical factors will be shown to be adequate for explaining the Gospel of John's treatment of Jews and Judaism in that it increases the level of abstraction for Jewish social identity in order to reduce its salience for the Johannine audience. This allows for it to be replaced by a Christologically centered social identity.

2

Social Identity among Jews in Greco-Roman Egypt

INTRODUCTION

Prior to the discovery of the Dead Sea Scrolls it was common to postulate the Gospel of John had an intellectual and cultural background similar to that found in the Alexandrian-Jewish writings that were then available. While scholarship has known for some time that John draws on a broader range of Jewish cultural backgrounds, I will argue that John is addressing many Diaspora Jewish self-categorizations, of which the Alexandrian evidence is the exemplar. In much scholarship the Alexandrian and Egyptian evidence effectively functions as a frame of reference for understanding data from elsewhere because it is extensive, so it will serve as a starting point for interpreting the Johannine categorizations of Jews within a Greco-Roman cultural context. Jewish social situations in Egypt varied widely due to political and social changes resulting from the Roman conquest of Ptolemaic Egypt, growing anti-Jewish sentiment, and the consequences of the Jewish revolt of 66–73 CE.

There are differences in what writers thought it meant to be Jewish, but SCT applied to reading literature, papyri, and epigraphy reveals that there are discernable patterns in terms of how Jews situated themselves in the broader context of gentile cultures. We will examine

Ptolemaic-period documents first in order to establish a basis for comparison. This will be followed by a comparison with later documents to determine what features of Jewish social identity changed and remained consistent.

In this chapter I will argue that, in what Sylvie Honigman and Karl Galinsky term "cultural competition,"[1] Jews categorized themselves as exemplars in matters of piety and ethics. Diaspora Jewish authors did not view themselves as racially, ethnically, or culturally superior to non-Jews, except when it came to Egyptians, but this exception is not consistent. Generally, Jews attempted to reduce relative difference in order to categorize themselves as similar as possible to the ruling classes (Greeks and Romans) by appealing to salient categories. Jewish writers recognized differences in class and status: they said they were *like* Ptolemaic Greeks, and *never maintained they were* Greeks, but for the sake of positive social relations and integration may present themselves as the best of that which is Greek.[2] Evidence ranging from literature to epigraphy and papyri suggest Jews wanted to integrate and participate in the culture but not necessarily assimilate to the culture,[3] practicing social convergence but holding to their distinctive ethno-religious identity.

The primary source material from Hellenistic and Roman Egypt is abundant and requires selective treatment. Since John was probably written in the first century CE,[4] this chapter will speak to inscriptional

---

1. Honigman, "Jews as the Best of all Greeks," 213–15; Galinsky, "A Cooperative Agenda," 222. Honigman and Galinsky propose that cultural competition was not necessarily always negative stereotyping, but often amounted to claiming to be the best representation of common values.

2. Honigman, "Jews as the Best of all Greeks," 207–32.

3. I am using the term *integration* (as opposed to *assimilation, marginalization,* and *separation*) in the sense found in Berry et al., "Psychological Acculturation of Immigrants," 62–67. Those seeking integration wish to remain members of their own culture but have relations with those of other cultures. Assimilationists completely give up their culture for that of another.

4. Many of the readings in this study remain valid regardless of how one dates the Gospel of John. While John is generally dated to the 90's CE, some traditions might date to earlier (e.g., the 40's–60's CE; Brown, *Gospel according to John*, 1:lxxx–lxxxvi), and possible allusions to Peter's martyrdom (John 21:18–19) and the temple's destruction suggest a post late-60's date for composition, while P52 suggests the Gospel cannot post-date the first half of the second century (Keener, *Gospel of John*,

or literary evidence to Jewish self-categorizations that either reflects circumstances available in first-century Egypt, or literary evidence that would have been available. One key witness is Philo, whose *Against Flaccus* and *On the Embassy to Gaius* discuss important matters of Jewish social identity in the face of hostile ethnic sentiment against Jews. Since controversial documents could provide false impressions about daily Jewish life, I will examine evidence from the Ptolemaic period (Letter of Aristeas, 2 and 3 Maccabees) in order to provide a basis for comparison. The evidence contemporary to Philo reveals a controversy stemming from wounded Ptolemaic Greco-Egyptian pride, political miscalculations by the leadership of minorities such as Jews, and Roman mismanagement.[5]

Literary evidence tends to originate with writers who were better-off and closer to the dominant groups of the time. This is the case with Philo and likely also Aristeas.[6] 3 Maccabees' provenance is unknown but it appears to have been intended for popular consumption.[7] 2 Maccabees was likely composed for a second-century BCE Greek-speaking Jewish audience,[8] while its appended epistles reflect the priorities of a Palestinian Jewish audience.[9] 2 Maccabees likewise probably sought to influence ideas about what an Egyptian Jewish identity should look like.

1:140–42; Robinson, *Redating the New Testament*, 256).

5. See especially Tcherikover, "Decline of the Jewish Diaspora in Egypt," 1–33; also Barclay, *Jews in the Mediterranean Diaspora*, 19–81; Collins, *Between Athens and Jerusalem*; Horst, *Philo's Flaccus*, 18–34.

6. Wright dates Aristeas to the mid-second century BCE (Wright, *Praise Israel for Wisdom and Instruction*, 280), as does Hadas (between 150 and 130 BCE) (Hadas, *Aristeas to Philocrates*, 54). Wasserstein and Wasserstein date it to between ca. 200 BCE and the Maccabean revolt (Wasserstein and Wasserstein, *The Legend of the Septuagint*, 25). Translations of Aristeas in this study are Hadas' unless otherwise stated. All translations of biblical literature are from the NRSV, unless otherwise stated, while I will use the NETS translation for LXX quotations.

7. Most scholars tentatively date 3 Maccabees to sometime in the first century BCE, probably during the Roman period (Collins, *Between Athens and Jerusalem*, 126; Croy, *3 Maccabees*, xiii; Hadas, *Aristeas*, 37–38; Johnson, *Historical Fictions*, 130–41).

8. See Schwartz, *2 Maccabees*, 11–14; Goldstein, *1 Maccabees*, 4; according to Robert Doran, 2 Maccabees' apparent mastery of Greek is not sufficient grounds for eliminating a Jerusalem provenance (Doran, *Temple Propaganda*, 112–13).

9. 2 Macc 1:1, 10; Schwartz, *2 Maccabees*, 134.

These documents show how Diaspora Jews pursued social strategies of convergence while maintaining ethnic and religious distinctions. The Gospel of John may have sought to undermine these sorts of social identities in order to create a Johannine Christian identity.

COMMON PROGENITORS

The evidence from Egypt shows that Jewish identity and religious social categorizations were understood in ethnic terms. However, the evidence also shows that Diaspora Jews sought to reduce their relative difference with their non-Jewish neighbors, usually through reinterpretation, rather than reduction, of different social categorizations.[10] This involved reinterpretation of the social significance of Judaism's common progenitors Abraham and Moses, as well as the Mosaic Law. Abraham's origins in Ur bolstered Jewish claims to antiquity, something that was respected in Greek and Roman culture. Meanwhile, Moses is presented as an enlightened human legislator who creates a distinct Jewish identity.

The Letter of Aristeas presents Moses, mentioned directly only once (Let. Aris. 144), as the Jewish people's legislative founder and therefore its common progenitor.[11] Otherwise, it traces their lineage to the war captives and slaves brought to Egypt (23) and whose descendants Ptolemy Philadelphus emancipates. The status of Moses is exalted by means of the Law. Its divine origins are paramount,[12] and

---

10. For identifying the social categorizations used, I am elaborating upon Paul Spilsbury's research on Josephus. While he does not write from an SIT/SCT perspective, his work has been very helpful in discerning the patterns of argument in the materials surveyed in chapters 2 through 4. Key points in Josephus' argument as Spilsbury lists them are: (1) "the Jews are an ethnic entity that must be understood in the light of its particular history," (2) "the Jews are a virtuous people," (3) "the Jews have a profound knowledge of the true God and stand in intimate relationship to this God," (4) "the Jews are a people under authority," (5) "the Jews are a conservative people," (6) "the Jews are a harmonious and peaceable people," (7) "the Jews are a loyal and co-operative people," (8) "the Jews are a populous and international people," (9) "the Jews are a people apart, yet should not be regarded as anti-social," (10) "the Jews are a persecuted and a hated people" (Spilsbury, *Image of the Jew*, 217–27).

11. For example, Let. Aris. 131–32, 139, 148, 240 speak of a human being as ὁ νομοθέτης. God is acknowledged as the ultimate origin of the Law in 312–13.

12. Wright regards *Aristeas* as providing information more on the LXX's reception

Social Identity among Jews in Greco-Roman Egypt

the discussions at the *symposia* (182–300) act as an apology for the Law by presenting the Jewish people as philosophically enlightened.

3 Maccabees places a more explicit emphasis on common ancestry than does the Letter of Aristeas. Moses is never mentioned, and it describes Jews as the "seed of Abraham" and "consecrated of Jacob" and as foreigners in Egypt (6:3) with their own ancestral songs (6:23) and customs (1:3). In the narrative Jews are referred to as Israel seven times,[13] and characters plea for the redemption of "the nation of Jacob" and fear on the part of gentiles (6:13). Likewise, 3 Macc 2:12 positions the narrative as part of Israelite salvation history.

Ancestry and Israel's relationship with God are closely collocated in 3 Maccabees,[14] probably in an attempt to prevent what it sees as unacceptable levels of cultural assimilation in terms of participation in the civic cults that was necessary for citizenship (3 Macc 2:30; 3:21, 23). This conviction was likely shared with Aristeas because Aristeas did not consider a Jewish lack of Alexandrian citizenship to be a problem given their citizenship in Judea (Let. Aris. 36, 44).[15]

2 Maccabees displays a similar regard for Judaism's progenitors, where receiving God's blessing is described as God remembering his covenants with the patriarchs (1:2). In the narrative the Jewish characters clearly understand themselves as members of a single group—Jews, Hebrews, or Israel—with a history centered on important symbols such as the Mosaic law (7:30), Solomon, Jeremiah, and cult items (2:5–10). Greco-Roman Jewish writers, however acculturated to Greek culture they are perceived as being, reveal a strong consciousness of a distinct ethnic identity centered in symbols such as Moses, the Law, and the patriarchs.

---

than its origins (Wright, *Praise Israel for Wisdom and Instruction*, 277–95). Wasserstein and Wasserstein add that *Aristeas* is useful for acting as an indirect source for testimony about the background of *Aristeas'* authors and their social circles (*Legend of the Septuagint*, 26).

13. 3 Macc 2:6, 10, 16; 6:4, 9; 7:16, 23.

14. It refers to the Law in ancestral or divine terms (1:23; 3:4; 7:10, 12). God is described as "God of their ancestors" (7:16) with a kindship-like relationship with Israel (5:7; 6:3, 8; 7:6).

15. For instance Barclay, *Jews of the Mediterranean Diaspora*, 192–203. See Collins' position in *Between Athens and Jerusalem*, 68, 127–29.

SOCIAL CATEGORIZATIONS

Citizens (of Judea)

In the Greco-Roman world, it was the well-off who usually held citizenship, which made it a sign of dignity and social status. For this reason, Aristeas ascribes Judean citizenship to Alexandrian Jews to compensate for their lack of Alexandrian citizenship (Let. Aris. 36, 44). Aristeas also idealizes Jerusalem and its environs to evoke Judean ethnic pride by creating similarities with Alexandria. Hadas states, "Every reader would have recognized that he was dealing with an imaginative work and not a history claiming literal truth" while Tcherikover suggests Aristeas's Judea symbolizes a theocratic utopia.[16] Even the Jordan River meets the ideal of the Nile by following similar seasonal patterns (Let. Aris. 89–116).

Aristeas implies Jews as a whole enjoy the dignity of citizenship because it portrays the LXX translation project as a joint venture by two allied states. Ptolemy Philadelphus sends an embassy (πρεσβεία) to Judea in Let. Aris. 3, 15 and the translators come from what amounts to Judea's diplomatic corps (Let. Aris. 122). The names of the translators reflect Hellenistic acculturation and bear a cosmopolitan mix of Hebrew, Persian, and Hellenistic names. Each of the historic twelve tribes is represented by six translators each, with Plato's ideal city-states also having twelve civic tribes.[17] Philadelphus's largesse towards his guests,[18] reverence for the Jewish Law, and placing the Law in Alexandria's famed library also reflect this dignity (Let. Aris. 9; 310–12; 317). The result is that Aristeas effectively portrays Jews and Greeks as members of the same extended in-group.

3 Maccabees outlines different perspectives on Jewish social circumstances in Hellenistic Egypt, including negative gentile perceptions of Jews. These reflect some traditional accusations such as Jewish

---

16. Hadas, *Aristeas to Philocrates*, 50; Tcherikover, "Ideology of the Letter of Aristeas," 77–78.

17. Cohen, "Names of the Translators," 33, 62; also Honigman, *Septuagint and Homeric Scholarship*, 57.

18. Seen in Philadelphus' largesse (e.g., Let. Aris. 27; 33, 40–42; 52–82; 294; 319), which Honigman notes is probably intended to contrast with the Pharaoh in Exodus (Honigman, *Septuagint and Homeric Scholarship*, 56).

religion obstructing patron-client relationships (3 Macc 3:18–19),[19] or that ethnic practices and beliefs should be interpreted as misanthropy (3 Macc 3:6–7). 3 Maccabees also outlines Jewish stereotypes of gentiles in 5:13, 6:9 and 6:11, with gentile persecution of Jews being labelled an example of "insolence" (μίσυβρι) that require the protagonists to in some way be vindicated (6:9, 13, 15). The refusal of citizenship because of the requisite participation in civic cults provokes further accusations of gentile-directed animosity (3:21–24).[20]

The narrative of 3 Maccabees also describes varying Jewish strategies of cultural accommodation, ranging from (1) assimilation (1:3), (2) partial cultural integration, or (3) outward polarization.[21] Yet others, apparent low-identifiers with Judaism, (4) embrace Alexandrian citizenship (2:31). In each case, it depicts Judaism as a Judean civic religion that performs a function similar to that of Alexandrian civic religion, suggesting a Jewish ethnic self-consciousness centered on religious practices that otherwise allows for the embrace of non-religious aspects of Hellenistic culture. 3 Maccabees portrays the narrative's conflict as an exception to the rule of good relationships between Jews and Greek.[22] Nevertheless, the narrative relies on stereotyped use of in-group and out-group language to tell its story.

2 Maccabees uses Hellenistic political and cultural frames of reference to portray Jews and Greeks as members of a common culture.[23] Yet it also shows that the homeland and religious issues were important to Egyptian Jewish identity, all the while embracing Greek ways of thinking about foreigners.[24] Schwartz suggests the author of 2 Maccabees

---

19. Croy, *3 Maccabees*, xv, 68.

20. Croy, *3 Maccabees*, 70.

21. One possible implication of ὁμοεθνεῖς in 3 Macc 4:12 could be that some Alexandrian Jews were visibly indistinguishable from other Alexandrians, while some Jews dressed in a distinctive manner. The passage could also be taken as mean some Alexandrian Jews were in hiding. According to Croy, 4:12 reflects an editorial mistake that combines sources (Croy, *3 Maccabees*, 79).

22. Suggested by 3 Macc 3:4–10, 27–29.

23. Doran, *2 Maccabees*, 1, 3–6.

24. See the use of "Barbarians" (τὰ βάρβαρα) in 2:21.

"is attempting to present himself as a good Greek (of the Jewish type), hoping thereby to gain the sympathies of Greek readers."[25]

In Ptolemaic Egpyt, a mutual status as foreigners appears to have been a salient category shared by both Jews and the ruling Greek classes, as the Greek aristocracy considered Jews to be fellow "Hellenes."[26] The literature shows that Jews sometimes reciprocated this sentiment. The notion of "Judean citizenship" enabled participation in the Ptolemaic regime and helped mitigate social and cultural differences between Greeks and Jews, but not the religious differences. As we will see below, this has relevance for how we understand the portrayal of Johannine Jewish participation in the Roman regime.

Pious and Faithful to Ancestral Customs

Jewish piety and faithfulness to ancestral customs were key social categorizations for Jews in Aristeas and 2 and 3 Maccabees. Interestingly, Aristeas assumes that these are prototypical social categorizations for Jews that make them distinct in appearance and practice from gentiles (Let. Aris. 158). Yet Aristeas extends this category to include some gentile characters who are appreciative of Jewish ancestral customs, allowing for some social convergence (Let. Aris. 15-16).

While there are some exceptions, 3 Maccabees likewise categorizes the prototypical Jew as pious and faithful to the Law (2:31-33). This categorization is served in the narrative's vindication of Jewish protagonists and retribution against unfaithful Jews (7:1-15),[27] which advances 3 Maccabees' agenda of promoting orthopraxy and faithfulness.[28]

In 2 Maccabees the prototypical Jew is categorized as pious, faithful to the Torah and ancestral customs, and courageous. Narrative devices that indicate this are God's punishment for a coup led by impious Jews that is resolved by the martyrdoms in 2 Macc 6:18-31 and

---

25. Schwartz, *2 Maccabees*, 174.

26. Modrzejewski, "How to be a Jew in Hellenistic Egypt," 65-92, esp. 75-77.

27. Contrast this with the myriads of faithful Jews who cause authorities to run out of paper while conducting the census in 3 Macc 4:20 (Johnson, *Historical Fictions*, 153).

28. Cousland, "Reversal, Recidivism, and Reward," 40, 51; Croy, *3 Maccabees*, xix. See also Berthelot, "Hasmonean Wars," 50-51.

7:1–42,[29] and the subsequent enablement of Judas Maccabeus' victories against the Selucids (2 Macc 8:5).[30] While often using Greek frames of reference for cultural values, these examples demonstrate that the author(s) of 2 Maccabees believes piety should be prototypical of Jews.[31]

The ethnic and religious functions of the Law are equivocated through parallelism in 2 Macc 6:1.[32] 2 Maccabees frequent use of the term "ancestral laws" (πατρίων νόμων) may suggest a connection to Hellenistic cultural values, since the writings of Plato consider violating ethnic customs reprehensible. 2 Maccabees therefore uses a Greek cultural referent to demonstrate the validity of a Jewish one. Obedience to the Law is depicted as a hereditary ancestral custom (7:2, 24, 37), and when the martyrs die for the Law it is equated with dying for their "people" (τὸ ἐθνός) (2 Macc 7:9, 37) and remaining faithful to God (7:2). The Law is sometimes equivocated with other national symbols such as the land or temple (2 Macc 13:10, 14). Faithfulness to these results in the positive appraisal of a Jew in 2 Maccabees, but does not serve as the basis for the positive appraisal of gentiles.

Prayer, as an expression of piety, is prototypical of Jews in both 2 and 3 Maccabees. In 3 Maccabees, the representative prayers of the High Priest Simon, the Egyptian-Jewish priest Eleazar, and ordinary Jews exemplify this trait.[33] 2 Maccabees, in contrast to 1 Maccabees, also downplays bravado and presents prayer as precipitating the divine intervention[34] that made the revolt successful.[35] Prayer also takes a prominent role in the appended introductory blessing and epistle from Jerusalem Jews to Egyptian Jews (2 Macc 1:2–8, 23–36; 2:10).

It is unsurprising that Jewish literature categorizes Jews according to their piety and faithfulness; the interesting thing is how these categorizes are used in relation to social context. In Aristeas they function as

---

29. Schwartz, *2 Maccabees*, 299.
30. Goldstein, *2 Maccabees*, 325.
31. Doran, *2 Maccabees*, 292; Schwartz, *2 Maccabees*, 239.
32. Schwartz, *2 Maccabees*, 275.
33. 3 Macc 1:16; 1:24; 2:1–20; 5:7–9; 5:50–51; 6:1–17.
34. Angels, portents, or visions appear in 2 Macc 3:24–29; 3:33; 5:2–3; 10:29; 11:8; prayer that is followed by divine assistance appears in 2 Macc 1:8; 3:15–20, 31; 10:16, 25; 11:6; 12:6–7; 14:15; 15:21–27.
35. Schwartz, *2 Maccabees*, 48, 417.

points of salience that reduce relative difference; in 2 and 3 Maccabees the Greek monarchs validate Jewish religious claims after witnessing God's vindication of their enemies. 2 Maccabees gives prayer an important role in its narrative. Despite the fact that it narrates a revolt, the appearance of Jeremiah to Judas in 2 Macc 15:13–16 suggests the author does not normally condone anti-gentile violence, an idea perhaps also implicit in Onias's submission to Seleucid authorities after the temple's profanation (2 Macc 3). In conclusion, we can see that Jewish piety is presented as a defining *difference* between Jew and gentile but sometimes it is also a major point of *potential salience* that allows Jew and gentile to relate to one another.

Philosophical

Aristeas, with its emphasis upon the compatibility of Hellenistic and Jewish culture and values, suggests that the author has the goal of integrationist-identity formation in a Greek-speaking context. Its social categorization of Jews as "philosophical"[36] reflects this goal because, as in the case of the categorization of both Jews and Greeks as *pious* in Aristeas, it reduces the comparative difference between the two and redefines them both as part of an extended in-group.[37] The Mosaic Law is categorized as philosophical and preserves ethnic identity while also fostering virtue and worship simultaneously (e.g., Let. Aris. 131, 139, 144). Moses—and therefore Jews—are theologically philosophical on account of this medium of instruction (240).

Philadelphus's response to the Law's philosophical sophistication reinforces this point (Let. Aris. 177–78; 312, 317), as does his role as patron for symbols of Alexandria's cultural sophistication: the Great Library and the Great Lighthouse. Aristeas makes use of these symbols by associating the LXX translation with Pharos, site of the Great Lighthouse, and having the translation placed in the Great Library.

---

36. Evidence for this social categorization possibly dates to Artapanus (third century BCE); also seen in Aristobulus. Collins, *Between Athens and Jerusalem*, 46–50, 186–93; Wasserstein and Wasserstein, *Legend of the Septuagint*, 27–32.

37. Zuntz, "Aristeas Studies I," 32–34.

Participants

The general social categorization "participants" serves as an umbrella term for other potential in-group categorizations such as "peaceful," "cooperative," or "civilized," and provides warrant for Jewish integration into imperial social systems. Aristeas portrays Jews as key participants in building the Ptolemaic state (e.g., Let. Aris. 13), and it deflects responsibility for the Ptolemaic oppression of Jews from the king (Let. Aris. 14, 23–24, 26). Aristeas portrays Jews as essential to the kingdom's prosperity. They serve in court positions and military roles in the service of the Ptolemaic kingdom but Aristeas still labels them as foreign citizens (σοῖς πολίταις) in Let. Aris. 15, 36–37. Aristeas even claims that Jews and gentiles share monotheism (Let. Aris. 15–16),[38] though theological commonality falls short of the religious integration upon which citizenship was predicated.[39] Nonetheless, Aristeas envisions full participation at almost all levels of Ptolemaic society.

3 Maccabees also envisions a role for Jews within Greco-Egyptian society similar to that of Aristeas. Sara Raup Johnson states:

> Third Maccabees, a late Hellenistic text often seen as confrontational, was not designed to encourage the Jews of Alexandria to separate themselves from their fundamentally hostile surroundings, for all its awareness that confrontation could occur. On the contrary, through the fictional story of a persecution happily averted, it sought to construct a model of identity allowing the preservation of Jewish piety while at the same time making possible Jewish involvement in the wider Greek world.[40]

---

38. M. A. L. Beavis notes there is some tension on this point within the Letter of Aristeas. See his "Anti-Egyptian Polemic," 146–147. In Let. Aris. 134, the high priest Eleazar states that monotheism is unique to Jews, but in lines 15–18 some Greek characters say Jews and Greeks worship the same God. Beavis maintains that Aristeas is reducing differences so that the only issue dividing Jews and Greeks is the Jewish purity regulations.

39. Honigman contrasts this to the slave-status of the Hebrews in Exodus, making them collectively more akin to a later form of the patriarch Joseph (Honigman, *Septuagint and Homeric Scholarship*, 56).

40. Johnson, *Historical Fictions*, 217.

3 Maccabees portrays Jews as loyal members participating in all levels of the Ptolemaic state.[41] Even though 2 Maccabees narrates a Jewish rebellion against the Seleucid Empire, it seems to envision relationships similar with those of Aristeas and 3 Maccabees.[42]

God's Elect Chosen People

Egyptian Jewish literature testifies to a strategy of social convergence with Egyptian Greeks, but monotheism and a unique relationship with God are still used to maintain relative difference, as Jewish social memory reinterprets historical events and creates distinctly Jewish narratives. This is also seen in how these documents treat continued religious observances and how, on select occasions, they categorize gentiles. In so far as monotheism and the status of their election were concerned, Jewish writers did not seek to reduce relative difference but instead used it to augment distinction, though being "elect" is not synonymous with being "pious." This is because non-Jews were considered capable of discerning what is ethically and theologically proper.

The categorization of Jews as God's people is seen in Aristeas's idealized description of Jerusalem and the alleged grandeur of the temple cult (Let. Aris. 92–99). It is also seen in the purportedly unique wisdom of Eleazar and the translators (129–71; 182–300). In Aristeas, Jewish election does not mean that gentiles are categorized as idolaters while only Jews are pious, but rather that Jews are the exemplar of what is best about humanity on account of the Law.

3 Maccabees emphasizes God's special relationship with Israel, especially in the prayers of Simon and Eleazar recounting Jewish history and reiterating Jewish in-group status (2:1–20; 6:1–15). It portrays

---

41. Faithfulness to the Law is closely associated with being a faithful subject (3 Macc 7:11). Jews remain loyal to their rulers, including in military service (3:3; 5:31; 6:25–26) and government administration (3:21). They are also loyal clients of their patron (1:5–8) who use non-violence in religious conflicts (1:23).

42. For example, Onias remains a submissive client despite the Heliodorus episode and the deteriorating situation under Simon (2 Macc 3:16–17; 4:5–6). Both Jew and Gentile mourn Onias' death because of his virtue—even Antiochus IV—who later "converts" to Judaism (2 Macc 4:35–37). See also Goldstein, *2 Maccabees*, 222, 241; Doran, *Temple Propaganda*, 110; Doran, *2 Maccabees*, 118; Doran, "Independence or Co-existence," 65–102.

Jews as one-part ethnic group, one-part political-legal entity, and one-part theological community. The privileged relationship with God is the most important factor in Jewish self-categorization, and this allows for participation in Ptolemaic society so long as the religious aspects of citizenship do not violate this God-centered and law-centered identity.

The special theological status of Jews is also a significant categorization for 2 Maccabees. 2 Maccabees 1:2–6 contains an epistle likely composed by Jerusalem Jews that urges Alexandrian Jews to greater faithfulness to the Law, covenant, and their own views of worship.[43] The epistle denigrates gentile conquerors, but a few verses later a gentile ruler acknowledges and vindicates certain Jewish claims (1:27–28; 33–36). Not only was it important for Jews to see themselves as God's elect—it was important for non-Jews to see it too.

PATTERNS OF MEMORY INNOVATION

The compiler of 2 Maccabees accepts that God has restored Israel under the Hasmoneans, and the use of portents and angelic assistance suggests the author(s) sees the war as one of restoration to the proper state of affairs. However, the initial significance of Hasmonean independence is exaggerated by ignoring that the struggle first resulted in local autonomy and was perhaps more of a intra-Jewish civil war.[44] Daniel R. Schwartz notes that 2 Maccabees has a strong awareness of contemporary international politics,[45] including awareness that the Seleucids are subject to Roman tribute, and in turn uses the Romans to ascribe legitimacy to the Jewish cause.

2 Maccabees also attempts to maintain that the prototypical Jew is submissive to the imperial government, seemingly in contradiction with the revolt. 1 Maccabees, on the other hand, uses Phinehas's action in Num 25:7–13 as warrant for violence in defiance of Jeremianic political theology that God had appointed foreign rulers over the Jewish

---

43. D. S. Williams holds 3 Maccabees may be a response to a sense of superiority on the part of Palestinian Jews over Alexandrian or Diaspora Jews, and the content of 2 Maccabee's epistles suggests there may be some credence to this view (Williams, "Defense of Diaspora Judaism," 23–24).

44. See Bickerman, *God of the Maccabees*, 77–90; Mendels, "Memory and Memories," 41–54; Eddy, *The King is Dead*, 213–17.

45. Schwartz, *2 Maccabees*, 42.

people.⁴⁶ 2 Maccabees is hesitant to follow 1 Maccabees, so it preserves the biblical mandate for peaceful coexistence by depicting the *postmortem* Onias and the prophet Jeremiah as granting the rebellion exceptional legitimatization (2 Macc 15:12, 13–16). Likewise, the actions of Antiochus and other antagonists are used to suggest that the revolt was avoidable, a sentiment that would be valued in the Diaspora,⁴⁷ and which preserves a generally positive view of Jew-gentile relations.

JEWISH INSCRIPTIONS

Contemporary Jewish inscriptions provide useful corroborating evidence for the Jewish social categorizations discussed above, though these are fragmentary and cannot support conclusions on their own. For example, one common Hebrew name used by Egyptian Jews in inscriptions is "Eleazar" (or "Lazarus").⁴⁸ The various characters named Eleazar in Jewish literature from the Ptolemaic and early Roman periods were likely fictitious, but it is probable this name was chosen because of its popularity.⁴⁹ However, its priestly connotations do not stop a person named Lazarus from visiting the Egyptian temple of Pan three times.⁵⁰ It is possible to speculate that this represents something akin to Artapanus's view that Egyptian religion was acceptable for Egyptians,⁵¹ but Karen B. Stern argues convincingly that graffiti at the temple of Pan was a part of local travel culture that did not signify religious acceptance or devotion. It is more probable that these Jews were travellers participating in a local custom than it is that they were apostate Jews making a pilgrimage,⁵² which would suggest these Jews saw themselves as participants in the local culture.

---

46. Cohen, *Maccabees to the Mishnah*, 28–30.

47. Schwartz, *2 Maccabees*, 48–49, 54.

48. Horbury and Noy, *Jewish Inscriptions of Graeco-Roman Egypt*, 108–9, 260–61.

49. Perhaps on account of Exod 6:25; Josh 14:1; 1 Sam 7:1.

50. Horbury and Noy, *Jewish Inscriptions of Graeco-Roman Egypt*, 211–12, nos. 123, 124.

51. Eusebius, *Praep. ev.* 9.27.4 (quoting Artapanus). Barclay suggests this possibility on the basis of "Pan" meaning everything in Greek. Barclay, *Jews in the Mediterranean Diaspora*, 100.

52. Stern, "Pan Temple of Egyptian El-Kanais," 177–88.

Social Identity among Jews in Greco-Roman Egypt

Loyalty formulae inscriptions have been found on the remains of Jewish synagogues in Egypt. In one instance Ptolemaic monarchs appear to declare a *proseuche* (synagogue) inviolate, which given the dating of the inscription and the fact that a Latin translation is appended suggest a desire to reiterate rights conferred on the building in the face of Roman occupation.[53] During the Ptolemaic period, the loyalty formulae on Jewish *proseuche* appear to have been regularly dedicated to the monarchy,[54] which is significant because some inscriptions even acknowledge incestuous marriages that violate the Mosaic law while there is no evidence of similar formulae in Egypt dedicated to the rule of the Romans.[55] There is a risk of arguing from silence, but it may suggest that Jews more strongly identified with Ptolemaic Egyptian society and, like others, felt unease with Roman rule.

Papyrological and inscriptional data supports literary evidence that Jews served in a number of roles in Ptolemaic Egypt,[56] and people with Jewish names appear to have sponsored shrines to non-Jewish deities—both Egyptian and Greek.[57] An "Abraham son of Alosmathous" donated to the construction of a shrine built on behalf of the "patron gods" (Θεῶν Εὐεργετῶν) Ptolemy and Cleopatra for Egyptian deities,[58] and some soldiers who appear to have been Jewish and whose level of consent cannot be determined,[59] were included in a dedication on behalf Greek gods.[60] In the case of Abraham son of Alosmathous, either non-identification with Judaism or simple generosity to non-Jews may

---

53. Horbury and Noy, *Jewish Inscriptions of Graeco-Roman Egypt*, 212–13; no. 125.

54. Horbury and Noy, *Jewish Inscriptions of Graeco-Roman Egypt*, nos. 13, 22, 24, 25, 27, 28, 117, 125.

55. Horbury and Noy, *Jewish Inscriptions of Graeco-Roman Egypt*, nos. 22, 25, 117. On incest as a symbol of power, see Ager, "Power of Excess," 165–86.

56. *Ant.* 14.99; Kasher, "First Military Units in Ptolemaic Egypt," 57–67; Collins, *Between Athens and Jerusalem*, 66; Gruen, *Diaspora*, 68.

57. Horbury and Noy, *Jewish Inscriptions of Graeco-Roman Egypt*, 246–50.

58. Horbury and Noy, *Jewish Inscriptions of Graeco-Roman Egypt*, 246, no. 154.

59. A point made by Horbury and Noy, *Jewish Inscriptions of Graeco-Roman Egypt*, 247–48, no. 155 (similarly no. 156).

60. Nos. 155, 156.

be involved. Contribution of funds does not automatically equal religious assent, though it could reflect tolerance.

The Hebrew name "Joseph" was one of the most common used by Egyptian Jews.[61] Again one cannot make definitive inferences from common use of a name, but it possibly reflects sentiments from the biblical Joseph story of prosperity amid faithfulness in a foreign environment. Otherwise, there is no pattern in how Jewish parents named their children, which may itself mark the trend by suggesting Jews practiced a degree of social convergence with Egyptians, Greeks, and Romans. Roman-period ostraca at Edfu documented in the second volume of *CPJ* further supports this contention,[62] as some families tended towards Hebrew names and others Egyptian names, other families followed no particular pattern,[63] and one family had a leader who bore a Roman name while other members took Greek and Egyptian ones.[64] The apparent piecemeal identifications with Romans, Egyptians, and Greeks fits well with the situational nature of SIT and SCT.

THE ANTI-JEWISH RIOTS IN ALEXANDRIA

The anti-Jewish violence in Alexandria in 38 CE is often labelled by scholars as a "pogrom," or violent anti-Semitic riot consisting of disorganized ethnically-driven expressions of hatred against Jews. Philo, the most important historical source for these events, describes it as mob violence, though this may be tendentious. Likewise, in P. London 1912 (*CPJ* 153) the emperor Claudius urges ethnic reconciliation following what he compares to a war, and Josephus mentions periodic violence against Jews throughout the Eastern Empire. It is also known that ethnic violence prompted by a Jewish rebellion in North Africa in the early

---

61. It appears in *Corpus Papyrorum Judaicarum* under various spellings 22 times, and in Horbury and Noy's edition of Egyptian and Cyrenaician inscriptions 4 times. Also Horbury and Noy, *Jewish Inscriptions*, 1.

62. *CPJ* 116. All translations pertaining to *CPJ* documents appearing in this study are taken from this volume (volume 2).

63. For further examples, see also the inscriptions in Horbury and Noy, *Jewish Inscriptions of Graeco-Roman Egypt*, 264, xviii.

64. *CPJ* 117–18. Also, Honigman, "Different Responses to Different Environments," 117–35.

second century resulted in the annihilation of the Jewish people in that region.[65]

The papyri published in the second volume of *CPJ* show that as a rule most Jews were of lower status than someone like Philo.[66] The papyri do not provide much direct evidence of Jewish self-categorizations but give good evidence of Alexandrian self-categorizations and negative Jewish stereotypes that can be useful for understanding meta-contrast dynamics. The available social categorizations give the impression that first-century Alexandrian society was economically and ethnically stratified with the Greek minority viewing itself as having a Greek identity that was under threat from direct Roman rule and the majority Egyptian population, and perhaps also other groups such as Jews.

The *Boule Papyrus* (*CPJ* 150) is one such document that underlines these dynamics. Dating to the early Roman period (reigns of Augustus or Claudius)[67] it represents a petition to the emperor for restoration of the city council, in exchange for which it promises full cooperation with the Roman prefect (lines 8–9) and stable tax revenues by reducing loses due to social problems and corruption (lines 7–11) and tax evasion (lines 1–4). It claims a city council would ensure that full citizens, who are exempt from the poll tax, be limited to those who are pure (ἀκέραιος; Line 5). While the edited text indicates this reading is uncertain, it is consistent with the vocabulary of lines 6 and 14. In general the petition appears preoccupied with ethnic and cultural identity, and whoever wrote it is willing to promise the Romans money if it allowed them to protect their identity. The emperor appears to demur the request (lines 21–23).

The petition to a prefect in *CPJ* 151 further underlines social stratification and instability in Greek Alexandrian identity, where a Jew named Helenos claims he was wrongly removed from the *ephebate* by Horos, a clerk who was probably of Egyptian background. The papyrus

---

65. Gruen, *Diaspora*, 63; Horst, *First Pogrom*, 22–23; Kasher, *Jews in Hellenistic and Roman Egypt*, 356; Smallwood, *Jews under Roman Rule*, 225–26; Lüderitz, "What is the Politeuma," 214–22.

66. *CPJ* 3.

67. *CPJ* 26.

has been interpreted several different ways.[68] Despite the uncertainty, this document illustrates the importance of citizenship and that the elite had little interest in enfranchising lower classes. The complicated regulations suggest that the Greek population wanted to preserve social homogeneity while the Romans were focused on protecting their tax base.[69]

In summary, some Alexandrians grouped Jews together with Egyptians and labelled them out-group members.[70] Greek Alexandrians also resented the loss of political sovereignty to Rome,[71] a further violation. The most likely reason for the anti-Jewish violence at Alexandria was that the social categorization "Alexandrian" was perceived to be under threat, perhaps compounded by many factors such as cultural prejudice against Jews or perceived Jewish political opportunism in alleged support for the Romans. In the countryside at places such as Edfu the social boundaries among people of Jewish, Greek, and Egyptian backgrounds appear to have been more permeable.

PHILO'S ACCOUNT AND SOCIAL CATEGORIZATIONS

Philo discusses the persecution of Alexandrian Jews in two documents: *Against Flaccus* describes the anti-Jewish violence and its origins, while *On the Embassy to Gaius* covers the Jewish delegation's attempt to persuade the Roman emperor Gaius[72] to stop the persecution of Jews and prevent the installation of a statue of the emperor in the Jerusalem

---

68. Kasher, *Jews in Hellenistic and Roman Egypt*, 202–3; *CPJ* 30; Smallwood, *Legatio ad Gaium*, 10–11.

69. This is the likely goal of the complicated regulations found in the *Gnomon Idios Logos*. Further distinctions were drawn between ξένοι (foreigners) and κατοίκοι (foreigners with rights of residence). See discussion in Smallwood, *Legatio ad Gaium*, 10; Barclay, *Jews in the Mediterranean Diaspora*, 49, 64–65; Kasher, *Jews in Hellenistic and Roman Egypt*, 19, 76; but esp. Niehoff, *Philo on Jewish Identity*, 19–22, esp. 22n21.

70. *CPJ* 156c, lines 25–27. Horst, *First Pogrom*, 22. Jews, Egyptians, and Chaldeans were at times stereotyped as magicians and untrustworthy. See Lacerenza, "Jewish Magicians and Christian Clients in Late Antiquity," 396–99; Gruen, *Diaspora*, 16–18.

71. Kasher, *Jews in Hellenistic and Roman Egypt*, 26.

72. Also known as "Caligula"; reigned c. 37–41 CE.

temple.⁷³ These documents are useful for exploring Alexandrian Jewish self-categorizations in the 30's and 40's CE because they give detailed description of Jewish attempts to navigate the conflict from a Jewish perspective.

Historians regard Philo as a generally credible witness to events but as less reliable in regards to their causes,⁷⁴ perhaps because he could not afford to offend those in power or lose local political support, reserving his vitriol for the now-deceased Flaccus and Gaius.⁷⁵ There are indicators that Philo suppresses mention of violent retaliation by Jews known from other sources and seeks to portray the divine vindication of Jews.⁷⁶

Philo depicts the catalyst for the anti-Jewish violence as the ascension of Gaius as an emperor who seeks to erect his own statue in the Jerusalem temple.⁷⁷ The other catalysts were a visit by a newly-appointed king Herod Agrippa and a politically compromised prefect with anti-Jewish advisors.⁷⁸ However, *On the Embassy to Gaius* and other sources describe anti-Jewish violence as occurring in Rome and elsewhere.⁷⁹ Perhaps Sandra Gambetti is correct that there was a Roman policy that prompted the violence at Alexandria,⁸⁰ or it may be that Philo is misrepresenting its true causes. Regardless of the true nature of events described, Philo's social categorizations parallel those found in other Jewish literature and are consistent with his Jewish self-identification. Like other documents, Philo seeks to contextualize (but

---

73. Niehoff, *Philo on Jewish Identity*, 79–94. For the Roman perspective on Gaius' fascination with self-divinization, see Suetonius, *Cal.* 22.2–4.

74. Schürer, et al., *History of the Jewish People*, 3.II:859.

75. Zeev, "New Perspectives on the Jewish-Greek Hostilities in Alexandria during the Reign of Emperor Caligula," 230.

76. E.g., *Ant.* 19.278–279; *CPJ* 153, lines 88–90.

77. *Embassy* 188.

78. *Flaccus* 9–29.

79. Philo notes violence in *Embassy* 159–60; 200–203; *Flaccus* 1; also Josephus in *Ant.* 16.27–28; 16.169–70; later at Caesarea under Felix in *Ant.* 20.173–77. Mason notes instances in the revolt of 66–73 CE of anti-Jewish violence erupting in other cities as recorded in Josephus, *War* 7.51, 57, 367–68 (Mason, "An Invitation to Judean Philosophy," 146).

80. Gambetti, *Alexandrian Riots of 38 C.E.*, 3–5, 249.

not eliminate) the relative difference between Jews on the one side, and Romans and Greek Alexandrians on the other.

Common Progenitor

Philo exalts Abraham and Moses to ascribe greater dignity to Judaism because of the cultural belief that progenitors exemplify that which characterizes their descendants.[81] Philo produced two major accounts of Abraham's life: one allegorical (*On the Migration of Abraham*) and one "literal" (*On the Life of Abraham*).[82] There is insufficient space for full discussion of both here, so we will briefly examine the "literal" *Abraham* because it gives a useful example of Philo's treatment of Jewish self-categorizations and cultural memory. Philo often glosses over Abraham or Moses' flaws to render them examplars of philosophical virtue and piety who conform to his ideas of a prototypical, but not typical, Diaspora Jew.

Philo portrays Abraham as a paragon of virtue and as an ideal "philosopher king" (*Abraham* 261) who founded a nation of philosophers.[83] This is seen in examples such as his recounting of the incident where Sarah is made a part of Pharaoh's harem: Philo blames Pharaoh's lust; Genesis attributes it to Abraham's fearful dishonesty (*Abraham* 94; Gen 12:11–20).[84] A similar example is the account of the aborted sacrifice of Isaac is made to more powerfully portray Abaraham's faith (*Abraham* 174–178; Gen 22:8), with Abraham verbalizing his faith in God and the improbability of intervention before trying to slay him, which is far more dramatic than the biblical account.

Philo's Abraham is described as rich, popular (*Abraham* 209), and a great military leader (*Abraham* 226–232). Philo depicts Abraham as coming to knowledge of God through philosophical reasoning, who then leaves Ur in order to create more opportunity for theological

---

81. Yoshiko Reed, "Construction and Subversion," 189–95; Feldman, "Origen's *Contra Celsum*," 120.

82. For full discussion, see Sandmel, "Philo's Place in Judaism," 151–332.

83. Niehoff, *Philo on Jewish Identity*, 139–46.

84. Sandmel, "Philo's Place in Judaism," 239. Philo also suppresses a similar story involving Isaac and Rebekah (Gen 26:7–11//*Planting* 169).

contemplation (*Abraham* 69–74).[85] Though Judaism remains the most perfect expression of monotheistic values, Philo also describes ethics and piety as though they were universal virtues. This allows for him to portray Abraham as a pious and ethical individual, even though at this point in the narrative he does not keep the Law of Moses (Gen 26:5// *Abraham* 275–276).

In a similar manner, Philo suppresses Moses' flaws and exaggerates his positive qualities. Philo uses Moses to attribute glory to Judaism's customs by lauding Moses' lineage, character of his parents, self-control, and physical appearance. (*Moses* 1.4–9, 19).[86] Moses' flight from Egypt is portrayed as due to false accusations (*Moses* 1.45–46), nor does Moses smash the tablets of the Law at the sight of Israel's idolatry (Exod 32:19), nor does he hit the water-giving rock twice in disobedience to God's instruction for Moses to command the rock to yield water (Num 20:11–12). Likewise, Philo portrays the flight of Israel from Egypt as a Greek colonial expedition to Palestine (*Moses* 1.163, 220), and Philo goes to great lengths to portray Moses as an ideal philosopher and legislator (*Moses* 2.8; 2.12; 2.36). He is also careful to attribute great antiquity to the Law by claiming it was written in the Chaldean language. His version of the Aristeas legend also attempts to show that the LXX, the Greek version of the Scriptures that many Diaspora Jews at that time relied upon in place of the Hebrew Bible, is equal in authority to the Hebrew text itself (*Moses* 2.26, 27–44).

Philo is not simply an apologist; he recasts the progenitors of the Jewish people in order to reduce the relative difference between Jews and the Greco-Romans of his day. According to Philo, Jews possess a dignified lineage and are the collective embodiment of the ideal citizen, and their ascribed philosophical and cultured nature depicts an intellectual sophistication that exemplifies the virtues of Greek culture. This facilitates social convergence so that Jews will be able to claim their rightful social identity as participants in the life of Alexandria, a social strategy that provides an interesting point of comparison with John's portrayal of "the Jews" discussed below.

---

85. Sandmel, "Knowledge of the Existence of God," 138; Sandmel, "Philo's Place in Judaism," 234 [26].

86. Feldman, "Philo's View of Moses," 270–72.

SOCIAL CATEGORIZATIONS

Philosophical, Virtuous, and Peaceful

Philo categorizes Jews as a people trained for contemplating "the prime Good," or God (*Embassy* 4–6). Philo argues that the Law's social manifestations exemplify respect, orderly behavior, self-control, and noble character, and depicts Judaism as an "ancestral philosophy" (τὴν πάτριον . . . φιλοσοφίαν) in which Jews are well-educated to foster virtue (*Embassy* 156). Philo uses these virtue categories to make Jewish morality analogous to that of broader society, especially by using terms such as "ancestral customs," restraint,[87] love for peace,[88] philosophy, and the four virtues.[89] Similarly, Philo reduces relative difference with Romans and Greeks by categorizing them as sharing the Jewish categorizations of dignity, virtue, loyalty, and peacefulness (*Embassy* 161). Philo therefore evidences a pattern of social convergence similar to the Letter of Aristeas above, where Jews are the ideal participants in society.

Faithful to Ancestral Customs

Against Flaccus and *On the Embassy to Gaius* frame the conflict at Alexandria as over whether or not Jews should be considered in-group members on account of their differing customs.[90] In order to create similarity, Philo reinterprets the faithfulness of Jews to their ancestral customs as satisfying the Greek in-group criterion of loyalty to a person's culture.[91] Philo presents Jewish culture as inclusive of the theological elements of monotheism, unwritten customs, and the sacred

---

87. See the discussion of Philo's use of ἐγκράτεια (self-control) in Niehoff, *Philo on Jewish Identity*, 94–107. Niehoff does not discuss its parallel, σωφροσύνη (prudence, discretion), which was considered one of the four virtues.

88. *Flaccus* 48; *Embassy* 306.

89. Φρόνησις (wisdom), δικαιοσύνη (righteousness, justice), ἀνδρεία (bravery), σωφροσύνη (prudence, discretion).

90. Πατρία (ancestral customs) and ἔθος (customs; usually ἐθῶν). Philo portrays Jewish perseverance in their customs as a display of the universal value of patriotism. E.g., *Flaccus* 48.

91. Horst, *Philo's Flaccus*, 145–46.

Social Identity among Jews in Greco-Roman Egypt

laws.[92] Philo argues that this loyalty to their heritage is what places Jews in open opposition to self-deifying emperors, though others dislike Gaius's goals as well.[93]

Philo portrays Jews as ideal citizens when he argues that Jewish faithfulness to ancestral customs is more important than life (*Flaccus* 48–50), with traits such as Jewish zeal for the Law and temple described positively (*Embassy* 192, 212). However, Philo also portrays loyalty to one's own culture as a universal positive quality (*Embassy* 210, 277; *Flaccus* 48).[94] Philo attempts to use Jewish zeal for ancestral customs and religion, elements which would normally set Jews apart, to reduce relative difference with the broader culture. He employs generalized ethnic language to achieve a level of social abstraction that makes loyalty to Jewish identity compatible with a loyalty to one's broader cultural background.

Loyal Clients

Given the persecution at Alexandria was probably at least partially state-sponsored, Philo attempts to categorize Jews as loyal subjects of the empire. Philo avoids mention of irreconcilable theological issues that some Greeks had with Jewish "atheism" or lack of participation in civic cults,[95] but takes issue with Gaius's attempts at self-deification (*Embassy* 118) while maintaining loyalty to deserving human benefactors such as good emperors is not an issue.[96] The goal is to portray the conflict at Alexandria as an exception to the rule of normally good relations between Roman rulers and Jewish subjects (*Embassy* 153–154, 157). Fault for the conflict therefore, lays not with loyal Jews, but an unstable emperor.

---

92. Philo is likely referring to *Halakah* here, but this cannot be proven (Smallwood, *Legatio ad Gaium*, 208–9).

93. *Embassy* 116–117; compare with P. London 1912 = *CPJ* 153.48–51 (pp. 2:40, 42).

94. See also Pearce, "Jerusalem as 'Mother City' in the Writings of Philo," 20.

95. For example, see Gaius' complaint in *Embassy* 357.

96. Horst, *Philo's Flaccus*, 146. Horst observes that the loyalty language in *Flaccus* 48–49 is very strong. See also *Embassy* 8, 147, 159.

Philo sometimes seems to exhibit genuine admiration for Rome and protects Roman protagonists from blame,[97] but his rhetorical strategies also accord well with SIT and SCT, where dominated groups, such as Jews, often attempt to situate themselves closer to what are perceived as legitimate power structures.[98] We see this when Philo contrasts Augustus and Tiberius with Gaius as a failed benefactor (*Embassy* 22; 8–13; 141–49; *Flaccus* 74). Philo likens the current situation to that of a faithful slave on the wrong side of an irrational master (*Embassy* 119), attacking Gaius's legitimacy while aligning Jews with the general legitimacy of the imperial system.

A Great Nation

Philo also attempts to show that Judea is a major world power. He makes veiled threats against persecutors of Jews by claiming Jews are so numerous they inhabit the whole world.[99] Philo uses the Greek colonization pattern, where the mother-city's cult serves as the basis for the cult of its colony, as an analogy for the ethnic and religious unity of Jews.[100] For Philo, the Diaspora is not Judea's empire, but are ἀποικία (colonies) similar to those of Greek city states.[101] He claims that Jews have a positive view of martyrdom for the sake of the Jewish nation, its beliefs, customs, and institutions such as the temple (*Embassy* 191–192). Philo warns that Flaccus's mishandling of the situation in Alexandria could result in a world-wide conflict, such is the extent of the Diaspora (*Flaccus* 44–45).[102]

---

97. As seen in the examples of Tiberius and Augustus; Niehoff, *Philo on Jewish Identity*, 124–25.

98. For similar discussion, see Connolly, "Being Greek/Being Roman," 24–30.

99. *Embassy* 214, 245, 281–282; *Flaccus* 43, 45. See Pearce, "Jerusalem as 'Mother City,'" 32.

100. Pearce, "Jerusalem as 'Mother City,'" 21; Horst, *First Pogrom*, 142.

101. See *Flaccus* 46; *Embassy* 281–282.

102. Also, *Embassy* 330. The extent of the Roman-Jewish war of 115–17 demonstrates Philo's fears were not unfounded.

Participants

Despite these threats, Philo seeks to show that Alexandrian Jews are participants in broader society. One way Philo does this is through labelling Jews as "citizens" (πολίτης). He uses πολίτης loosely; at times it sounds as if Jews should be treated as collectively possessing citizenship, though the term may also mean "resident."[103] Since Philo is seeking to elevate the status of the Alexandrian Jewish community in the context of ethnic strife, it is likely that Philo's ambiguous use of the term is deliberate. While Philo is aware that not all Jews are citizens, he still ascribes them a dignity similar to those of citizens from Roman or Greek cities.[104] For example, in *Flaccus* 47 Philo labels the desecration of synagogues with images as an affront to "Jewish citizens." Philo also maintained that Jewish identity was determined through both patrilineal and matrilinear descent, likely influenced by the Roman regulations found in documents such as the *Gnomon Idios Logos*, where one's ethno-social status generally defaulted to whichever parent's was lower.[105] So in order to be fully Jewish, Philo maintained both parents must be Jewish—consistent with criteria for remaining part of the Alexandrian upper class of "citizens."[106]

In *Flaccus* 48–50, Philo portrays Jewish synagogue worship as a form of demonstrating loyalty to benefactors such as the emperor, and therefore imperial loyalty.[107] In the Letter of Aristeas and 3 Maccabees the categorization of Jews as participants is optimistically made using Jewish categories, but Philo abstracts his own Jewish identity by appealing to broader civic categories to achieve similar ends. Like the Letter of Aristeas and 3 Maccabees, Philo still portrays Jews as uniquely valuable to their rulers, but he achieves this through increasing similarity,

---

103. For where πολίτης appears to mean "citizen" see *Embassy* 157 on Roman Jews as citizens; *Flaccus* 80 with langauge suggestive of Alexandrian citizenship; *Embassy* 265 on Jews in general as πολίτης. In keeping with Lüderitz's article and Horst's comments (Horst, *First Pogrom*, 145, 174–75), πολίτης does also seem to refer to "residents" in Philo.

104. Niehoff, *Philo on Jewish Identity*, 34–38.

105. Kasher, *Jews in Hellenistic and Roman Egypt*, 313; Niehoff, *Philo on Jewish Identity*, 21–22.

106. Niehoff, *Philo on Jewish Identity*, 17–20.

107. Horst, *First Pogrom*, 146.

showing Jews are one of many participant groups who benefit from the Empire.

Brave (and Zealous)

Many Greek and Roman authors considered Jews and Egyptians to be similar to one another, in part due to a number of denigrating versions of the Exodus story[108] and the shared practices, in some Egyptian circles, of circumcision and abstention from pork.[109] Jews and Egyptians, however, did not consider themselves similar, and Philo attempts to make Jews as distinct from Egyptians as possible. He divides the "inhabitants" (οἰκήτορες) of the city and Egypt into two classes: "us and them" (ἡμᾶς τε καὶ τούτους), to increase relative difference. The specific ancestral custom Philo sees as being violated in the conflict is Exod 20:4's prohibition against idols, in this case violated when people, allegedly Egyptians, place Gaius's image in Jewish places of worship. Philo categorizes the Jewish resistance as brave and zealous (*Embassy* 215). Philo also points to other occurrences of persecution to portray Jews as brave and zealous, such as a recent persecution in Rome under Sejanus (*Embassy* 160).

Philo presents Gaius as an antithesis of Jews and dutifully catalogues his shortcomings, intrigues, and self-deification as expressions of his weak and effeminate character (*Embassy* 111). Further, if Philo's accusations against Helicon are to be trusted, it appears it was relatively easy for Alexandrians to buy assistance in the Roman court, further undercutting perceptions of Gaius's integrity (*Embassy* 172, 178, 205). Philo uses Gaius's faults to present authentic Jews as brave monotheists in *Embassy* 115–117 so that while most residents in the empire thought Gaius's ambitions were improper, only Jews were brave enough to protest the emperor's violation of monotheism. Jews are therefore unique in their faithfulness due to their bravery and zeal.

---

108. See the discussions of *Against Apion* and Roman writers below.
109. Horst, *First Pogrom*, 30.

SOCIAL PROCESSES IN PHILO

The above survey of Philo provides a general picture of his categorizations of Jews. Philo saw social barriers as permeable, and he believed Jews could elevate their social position and take a more prominent role in Greco-Roman society. This is especially evident in his attribution of citizen status to Alexandrian and Roman Jews. As leader of the Jewish-Alexandrian delegation to Gaius, and as a member of the extended family responsible for governing the Jewish client states in Palestine, he was probably fully aware of the political and social issues affecting his people. Yet his background meant he was still hopeful of potential roles they could assume if given the opportunity, as reflected by the invective in some of his writings.

Philo's selective use of history allows him to claim antiquity and philosophical sophistication for his religious beliefs and ethnicity. For example, he portrays Moses as a worthy founder on account of his good looks, erudite mind, and virtue. Moses' ascribed educational background allocates to Judaism a mystique, sophistication, and intellectual respectability. Abraham's unique embrace of monotheism resulting from use of his reason and obedience to natural Law further underscores this portrayal, while the appeal to natural Law supplies common ground for interaction with gentiles, much like philosophical monotheism does in the Letter of Aristeas. It appears that Philo's innovations upon Jewish cultural memory have the goal of fostering greater respect for his people.

Philo claims prototypical Jews are not a threat to the social order—a consideration especially important to the Roman elite (see below). In a culture where worship was seen to please the gods and invoke assistance in providence, agriculture, and political stability, Philo maintains that Jews benefit the empire by their mere residence within it. Philo's avoidance of explicit mention of Sabbath, circumcision, and food laws in *On the Embassy to Gaius* and *Against Flaccus*, and their substitution with the general terms τῶν ἐθῶν and τὸ πατριά, indicates Philo is attempting to abstract both Greco-Roman and Jewish identities. This would reduce relative difference by increasing the salience of a broader human, or imperial, identity as the basis for comparison. Of course, Judaism remains a very salient category for Philo; he is not appealing to relativism, nor does he argue for the assimilation of Jews. Rather, Philo seeks the integration of Jews into the social structures of the empire in such a way that Jewish identity is maintained. With similar self-conceptions as found in 2 and 3 Maccabees and the Letter of Aristeas, Philo blames persecution of Jews on individual lapses in judgment and misunderstanding of Jewish intentions on the part of gentile rulers. Philo may have been aware of government policies that prompted events in Alexandria to escalate but he contents himself with indirect criticism. In any case, they run against Jewish Alexandrian self-categorizations originating in the Ptolemaic period where Jews are categorized as foreign, but valued, participants.

CONCLUSION

During the Ptolemaic period, at least according to the evidence available, Jews appear to work at social integration while maintaining religious separation. Jews were an important part of the Ptolemaic regime, and this role became part of their social identity as Jews in Egypt. The Roman period evidences efforts to exclude Jews as likely a product of wounded Alexandrian pride and ethno-social reorganization made due to the excesses of the Roman tax system. The major self-categorizations observed in Alexandrian Jewish literature are Jews as *pious*, *philosophical*, *loyal*, and *dignified participants* in the imperial projects of Ptolemaic and Roman Egypt. Categorizations of Jews as brave or zealous for their heritage are also operative but less prominent. Portrayals of Moses and Abraham reflect these self-categorizations, indicating they were deemed central to Jewish Diaspora social identity in this region.

One may hesitate to take Philo as representative of Alexandrian Jews, but the continuity and longevity of these categorizations suggests a Jewish socially-integrationist strategy among social strata where these values were considered important. This strategy of integration is supported by epigraphic and papyrological evidence, with Jews participating in local travel customs and pledging allegiance to local monarchs. Yet Jews remained distinct enough to be considered "the other" by more nationalistic Alexandrians. The question remains: how representative are the self-categorizations and social strategies found in the literature just surveyed? Establishing their representative character will be the purpose of the next two chapters that explore Jewish social identity in Asia Minor and Rome.

3

Social Identity among Jews in Greco-Roman Asia Minor

INTRODUCTION

Jews in Egypt and Alexandria during the first century faced a period of ethnic and political instability that lasted until the destruction of the war under Trajan in 115–17 CE. Chapter 2 showed that in the Ptolemaic period Jews pursued strategies of integration with the general population. During the early imperial period, elite Jews sought upward mobility until this was curtailed by Claudius's edict (41–42 CE),[1] demonstrating the partial success of anti-Jewish campaigns in Alexandria. Tax records dating to after the Jewish War of 66–73 CE indicate that Jews still sought to integrate with the population at all levels, even if government policies worked against these aspirations. These conclusions are based on the evidence that Jewish writers contextualized their relative difference to facilitate social convergence. The self-categorizations of Jews as "pious" and "philosophical" maintained a degree of positive Jewish distinctiveness, while self-categorizations of Jews as "loyal" and "participants" demonstrate that Jews saw themselves as a unique sub-group within an extended in-group. Graffiti, inscriptions, and other evidence suggest that Jews employed this social strategy in relation to the native Egyptians as well. These social categorizations

1. Fitzpatrick-McKinley, "Synagogue Communities," 56.

will reveal their relevance to understanding John's anti-Judaism below, but the task at hand in this chapter and the next is to show their representative nature for the Western Jewish Diaspora.

Jewish social identity in Asia Minor is particularly important for understanding Johannine anti-Judaism because Church tradition commonly places the composition of John's Gospel in Ephesus.[2] Paul R. Trebilco's study of Judaism in Asia Minor is extremely useful for our investigation but risks anachronism. He relies on later evidence and continuity of circumstances to read retroactively what a picture of Jewish life in the first century would have been like.[3] His conclusions are for the most part broad and tentative, but generally they correspond with the conclusions regarding first-century Egypt. Jews sought integration rather than the alternatives of assimilation or total separation, and categorized themselves as similar to their neighbors when possible. The gradual rise in the political and economic prominence of the Jews of Asia Minor over the centuries suggests Jew-gentile relations took a more positive course than they did in Egypt. It is possible that this may have been due to initially more positive circumstances created (or reflected?) by the rise of Christianity, which, as the council of Laodicea would later indicate, may have attributed to Judaism an antiquity, respect—even a mystique—that it appears to have lacked elsewhere.[4]

Evidence from Asia Minor is sparse compared to that found in Egypt. Very few Jewish inscriptions can be dated to the first century, and there is virtually no Jewish literature originating from this region.[5]

---

2. The tradition is based upon the second-hand testimony of Polycrates preserved in Eusebius in *Hist. eccl.* 3.31.3; 5.24.2. For its influence on modern scholarship see Tilborg, *Reading John in Ephesus*; Carter, *John and Empire*, among many others, though most would maintain provenance from any Hellenistic urban setting as a possibility.

3. This is Trebilco's own description (Trebilco, *Jewish Communities in Asia Minor*, 165–66). Some of the criticisms directed against Trebilco focus on individual historical instances, rather than his thesis as a whole. For example, Strubbe, "Jewish Epitaphs from Asia Minor," 100–104; Horst, "Jews and Christians in Aphrodisias," 106–21.

4. This is implied in canons 34–39 of the Council of Laodicea (360 CE).

5. Even though they would provide potentially useful data, I have chosen not to discuss Jewish manumission inscriptions from the Bosporan Kingdom in modern Crimea due to its geographic separation from Asia Minor. That said, I believe the evidence there supports the argument here.

The possible exception is Josephus who, though a Judean Jew writing from Rome, preserves decrees pertaining to Jews in Asia Minor. Most of these are of a legal nature, but they do suggest points of potential friction with the local gentile population. Recently scholars have evaluated the decrees as authentic, though they obviously betray Josephus's agenda, which he openly declares in *Ant.* 16.175–178.[6]

Josephus's presentations of Claudius's edicts are different in language from *CPJ* 153, with the most significant differences being a high number of laudatory adjectives pertaining to Jews, but these are most noticeable because of the mundane language that appears to be faithfully preserved by Josephus in other edicts. While probable, it cannot be proved conclusively that these elements of laudatory language really are insertions, and if so, if they were made by Josephus himself or one of his presumably pro-Jewish sources. Cicero's *Pro Flacco* provides important corroborating evidence for issues raised in Josephus, and we will see below that the book of Acts preserves similar evidence as well. While Acts is written largely from a pro-Christian point of view, it should be noted that Acts probably comes closest to directly describing how Jews related to gentiles during the period in question. The fragmentary nature of the evidence for Jewish social identity in Asia Minor means this chapter will be brief, but it is sufficient to indicate that Jewish cultural identity in this region did not result in marginalization.

INSCRIPTIONS AND SYNAGOGUES

Trebilco's study examines inscriptions and other archaeological data from Asia Minor to argue that Jews integrated with and prospered in Greco-Roman society—most clearly seen in his discussion of the data from Akmonia and Sardis.[7] However, like John M. G. Barclay's and John J. Collins' studies,[8] his investigation incorporates data gathered from sources spread over a lengthy period. This increases the danger of anachronism—the social, political, and economic circumstances of the late twentieth and early twenty-first centuries are not the same as

---

6. Zeev, *Jewish Rights in the Roman World*, 291.

7. Trebilco, *Jewish Communities in Asia Minor*, chapters 2 and 3.

8. Barclay, *Jews of the Mediterranean Diaspora*; Collins, *Between Athens and Jerusalem*.

those of the seventeenth century—and continuity of circumstances is difficult to prove definitively. It is therefore necessary to confine the survey here to data from the first century CE, occasionally drawing on earlier data, but not information dating from much later than the period during which John was composed. Like literary evidence, inscriptional evidence generally speaks on behalf of those with some money to the neglect of the poor. As will be seen below, this does not necessarily mean it cannot provide useful insight into the social strategies of Jews in general in Asia Minor.

One of the most interesting pieces of evidence is the famous Julia Severa inscription, dating to the middle or latter first century CE.[9] Scholars note that elsewhere she is described as an influential individual, served as a priestess of the imperial cult,[10] and was probably not a Jew,[11] though "[i]t is significant that the Jewish community was able to attract her support. The fact that she was a high priestess of the Imperial cult did not deter them from accepting her gift or from recalling it a number of years later."[12] Given that literary evidence from Philo and Josephus, as well as inscriptions in Rome and Egypt, testify to Jewish assertions of loyalty to the government, it is not entirely out of the question that Jews would entertain the patronage of a priestess for a civic cult. Julia Severa is simply named with nothing being said of her other occupations. Jews at Akmonia seemed willing to accept Julia Severa's financial assistance in the construction of their synagogue. No issue was made of her identity as a priestess for a non-Jewish organization, just as nothing is made of incestuous marriages or claims to divinity among Ptolemaic monarchs.

---

9. Ameling no.168; See Ameling, *Inscriptiones Judaicae Orientis*, 2:349; Trebilco dates it to the 50's or 60's CE (*Jewish Communities in Asia Minor*, 59); see also discussion in Ramsay, *Cities and Bishoprics of Phrygia*, 637–40, for other information relevant to dating.

10. Trebilco, *Jewish Communities in Asia Minor*, 59; Ameling, *Inscriptiones Judaicae Orientis*, 2:351.

11. Trebilco, *Jewish Communities in Asia Minor*, 59; Barclay, *Jews of the Mediterranean Diaspora*, 168; also Lifshitz, *Donateurs et Fondateurs*, 673.

12. Trebilco, *Jewish Communities in Asia Minor*, 60.

The inscription describes Julia Severa as "archisynagogos for life" (ὁ διὰ βίου ἀρχισυνάγωγος),[13] probably an honorary title,[14] and it implies further honor and importance by the prominent placement of her name in the inscription. Some suggest she was a gentile sympathizer, though because of the high status of her family it is possible she served as a patroness for many groups as a matter of course. Trebilco notes that Luke 7:5 mentions in passing that a Herodian centurion sponsored construction of a synagogue, so a person connected to the government sponsoring a Jewish synagogue would not be unprecedented.[15] It lists Severa as first among others who donated funds, suggesting she either made the largest contribution or had the highest social status among members involved. Either way, the Jewish community wanted it clear she was one of their supporters and counts her among those who are "virtuous" (ἐνάρετον) and have "zeal" (σπουδήν).

The synagogue was probably decorated with two pillars depicting a Menorah and a Torah scroll that were found elsewhere.[16] The image of the Torah scroll represents the theological elements of Judaism that shape Jewish identity through the teachings of Moses. The Menorah is a multivalent symbol that could represent the temple, the Jewish people as a whole (as symbolized in the temple), or the festival of Hanukah and the rededication of the temple under the Maccabees. Whatever its connotations, Akmonian Jews should not be understood as necessarily compromising their Jewish identity or their cultural memory.[17]

This imagery suggests a community that was proud of its heritage and cultural identity. In chapter 2 we noted that 2 Maccabees is not strictly anti-gentile, but promotes religious fidelity in a way that corresponds to sentiments present in broader Hellenistic culture. 2 Maccabees' supernatural episodes exhibit God's assistance and vindication of Jews in the eyes of other peoples. Perhaps in the eyes of Akmonian

---

13. Williams' translation (Williams, *Jews among Greeks and Romans*, 168).

14. Ameling, *Inscriptiones Judaicae Orientis*, 353.

15. Trebilco, *Jewish Communities in Asia Minor*, 59.

16. Trebilco, *Jewish Communities in Asia Minor*, 60. However, the date of the pillars remains unknown and could come from a later period (none is given by Catto in his *Reconstructing the First-Century Synagogue*, 69; *MAMA* VI:347; or Robert and Robert, *BE*:512).

17. *Pace* Parker, "Works of the Law," 68–74, esp. 69, 72.

Jews, Julia Severa's patronage reflects an integrationist Jewish social identity and its social relationships with the broader community. It is probable that Akmonian Jews categorized themselves as both loyal to the local authorities, as well as participants in the local community. The decorative pillars also suggest that this same Jewish community categorized itself as pious and faithful to its ancestral customs, yet was probably willing to share its self-categorizations of "virtuous" and "zealous" with the likes of Julia Severa. We can tentatively conclude that the social identity of Jews in Akmonia was, in these regards, similar to that of Alexandrian Jews.

OTHER INSCRIPTIONS

Another inscription that coheres with the interpretation above is Ameling 21, a second-century BCE inscription which comes from Iasos.[18] In an action that would violate the sensitivities of the author of 3 Maccabees, a "Niketas Jason the Jerusalemite" (Νικήτας Ἰάσονος Ἱεροσολυμίτης) donates one hundred drachmae[19] to a festival for Dionysius.[20] In an inscription from Smyrna, dating to 123–124 CE, a group of "former Jews" makes a donation of ten thousand drachmae for some unknown cause.[21] Both inscriptions suggest some Jews were (1) were willing to set aside their beliefs in certain situations, or (2) did not feel these actions betrayed their convictions. Likewise, an *ephebe* list from Iasos dating from 80 to 174 CE features names commonly used by Jews who studied in the gymnasium, a practice with which 1 Maccabees may take issue but not necessarily many Alexandrian Jews.[22]

---

18. Ameling notes the dating of this description is debated. One study attempts to date it to 196–194 BCE, while another study prefers the mid-180's BCE. Ameling prefers a date after 150 BCE. All that is really known is that it probably dates to the second century BCE (Ameling, *Inscriptiones Judaicae Orientis*, 2:128).

19. Ameling edits it as "drachma" (δ[ραχμὰς]), and Frey as "denarii" (δ[ηνάρια]).

20. Williams, *Jews among Greeks and Romans*, 112. Some doubt that he was Jewish (129). Ameling notes that before the Maccabean revolt Jews were known to have supported pagan festivals (Ameling, *Inscriptiones Judaicae Orientis*, 2:128–29). An argument possibly in favor that Niketas was Jewish is that he is listed as a "foreign migrant" (μετοικία) rather than as a "permanent foreign resident/colonist" (κάτοικος), "foreign sojourner" (πάροικος), or "citizen" (πολίτης).

21. Ameling 40; Ameling, *Inscriptiones Judaicae Orientis*, 2:177–79.

22. Ameling 22; Ameling, *Inscriptiones Judaicae Orientis*, 2:129–31.

According to a first-century inscription in the town of Tlos in Lycia, Asia Minor, a Jew named Ptolemy Leukios sponsored construction of a tomb for use by the Jewish community. Shaye Cohen uses this inscription in the introduction to his book[23] because the dual identity of the subject is apparent:

> Although he does not call himself a Jew, his social horizons are defined by his Jewishness. The phrase "among us Jews" reveals a strong public identification with the Jewish community, which defined itself as an "us." And wherever there is an "us," there is also a "them."[24]

Cohen is correct that the "us and them" language is interesting, but even in the midst of this dichotomy there is also a sense of Jew and gentile as together constituting an "us." The entire inscription is below. I have italicized the parties with which Ptolemy Leukios appears to have socially identified himself:

> Ptolemy, son of Leukios *of Tlos* (Τλωεὺς),
> built the tomb from its foundations out of
> his own resources (for) himself and on behalf of his son Ptolemy, son
> of Ptolemy, son of Leukios, on account of the archonship
> which he has held *amongst us Jews* (παρ' ἡμεῖν Ἰουδαίων).
> It is to be the property of all the Jews and
> no one else is to bury anyone else
> in it. If anyone is discovered burying someone else,
> *he will owe the people of Tlos* (ὀφειλέσει Τλοέων τῇ δήμῳ)
> (amount lost—rest of text missing).[25]

Ptolemy forbids the tomb's use by non-Jews, but fines for violations are paid to the town's δῆμος (people), which appears to have been at least partially responsible for its protection and maintenance. Walter Ameling conjectures that there may be a missing line involving fines paid to the local synagogue,[26] but whether or not this is the case, it is

---

23. Cohen, *Beginnings of Jewishness*, 1.
24. Cohen, *Beginnings of Jewishness*, 2.
25. The translation is adapted from Williams, *Jews among Greeks and Romans*, 119.
26. Ameling, *Inscriptiones Judaicae Orientis*, 2:480.

interesting that the δῆμος of the town had a role in caring for the Jewish grave even though only Jews were supposed to be buried there.

It is also interesting that Ptolemy is described as Πτολεμαῖος Λευκίου Τλωεὺς (Ptolemy Leukios of Tlos), a phrase one would use if they had a higher social status,[27] though the case of Helenos in *CPJ* 151 shows that this may not necessarily be the case. Ptolemy appears to have been both a Jew and at least a resident of Tlos who used the Jewish tomb as a symbol to commemorate his influence. A secondary goal may also be to help ensure the welfare of the Jewish community by providing a link between the Jewish and gentile residents. This could indicate either good relations between the populations or serve as evidence of Jews building bridges between the two groups. Overall, this tomb inscription suggests positive Jews–gentile relations in Tlos in the first century CE. This suggests that in terms of social identity Jews and gentiles placed themselves in distinct categories when theological factors were salient. It also indicates that, at least in Tlos, Jews and gentiles saw relatively little difference between their two groups when civic or social categories were salient, indicating social convergence. The inscriptions above also provide tentative support for the Jewish self-categorization of "participant" and perhaps also "loyal" to the broader local community as well.

ASIA MINOR JEWISH IDENTITY IN JOSEPHUS

In *Ant.* 14.267 Josephus attempts to use various *senatus consulta*, civic, and imperial decrees to exploit traditional Jewish alignment with the Romans as a salient factor held in common with gentiles. Josephus claims that the Romans preserved evidence of Jewish rights and privileges in engraved tablets stored at Rome or on display in public places,[28] though in truth it was the beneficiaries of decrees who had them engraved, not the authorities in question.[29] Josephus writes as though the "fact" that Jews were traditionally friends and allies of Rome was

---

27. Williams, *Jews among Greeks and Romans*, 119.

28. Josephus claims the various decrees were engraved by the Romans on "tables" or "tablets" (δέλτος) and stored in public places (*Ant.* 12.416; 14.191, 219-21, 319; 16.48). Zeev, *Jewish Rights in the Roman World*, 27-28.

29. Zeev, *Jewish Rights in the Roman World*, 304.

obvious, but many others within the empire would no doubt declare this as well.

The decrees contained in Josephus's *Antiquities* provide much evidence for Jewish social identity and self-categorizations in the Diaspora, but its historical value is of a mixed character.[30] Zeev and others are likely correct that *Antiquities* contains many legitimate decrees,[31] but given Josephus's apologetic program there is the probability that Horst R. Moehring is correct in his contention that the decrees are poorly preserved and textually corrupt.[32] Again, as per Moehring, the Roman archives had burned down in 69 CE,[33] so Josephus's documentary sources are either summaries or copies produced by someone such as Vespasian,[34] or Josephus was able to obtain these from Diaspora Jewish communities.[35] It is uncertain if the laudatory language concerning Jews is simply a part of patron–client language included in the originals, or if they are embellishments made by Josephus or his sources to serve their own purposes. Considering Josephus's tendentiousness, not all the observations listed below will be of equal value. As part of the cumulative evidence presented in this chapter, however, it would suggest there is some truth to what Josephus tells us. The difficulty is less a matter of establishing truth or falsehood and more a matter of determining what is exaggeration or embellishment.

---

30. In summary, Josephus is less than reliable when he discusses his own career, abilities, or roles in events, but he seems to be somewhat reliable when he is not speaking about himself. His appraisals of events and Jewish beliefs can simply be taken as his own. See Rappaport, "Josephus' Personality," 70–80; Nodet, "Josephus' Attempt," 111; Bilde, *Flavius Josephus between Jerusalem and Rome*, 41–45, 51–52, 234.

31. Zeev, *Jewish Rights in the Ancient World*, 6–21; Gruen, *Diaspora*, 85; Barclay, *Jews in the Mediterranean Diaspora*, 262–63; Levinskaya, *Acts in its Diaspora Setting*, 140; Rajak, "Was there a Roman Charter," 109.

32. Moehring, "*Acta pro Judaeis*," 149.

33. Moehring, "*Acta pro Judaeis*," 132.

34. Levinskaya, *Acts in its Diaspora Setting*, 140.

35. Gruen, *Diaspora*, 85; *CPJ* 143; Rajak notes that synagogues did store copies of documents recording legal provisions made by authorities to accommodate Jewish populations. See Rajak, "Synagogue and Community," 36.

Social Identity among Jews in Greco-Roman Asia Minor

Social Categorizations in Josephus

Participants (Allies)

An example of exaggeration is Josephus's portrayal of Jews as allies and friends of Rome. In the cultural context such statements are somewhat conventional and formulaic,[36] but in Josephus's broader argument he attempts to portray prototypical Jews as good residents and supporters of the Roman government. In a letter outlining a decree to the Sidonians dating to 47 BCE[37] (*Ant.* 14.190–195), Julius Caesar describes Hyrcanus as demonstrating fidelity and diligence in promoting Roman interests because he provided military assistance for the invasion of Egypt (*Ant.* 14.192). Hyrcanus showed valour for the Romans (ἀνδρείᾳ ... ὑπερέβαλεν) which earns the status for himself and his descendants as friends (φίλοις) and allies (συμμάχους), in turn earning Roman respect for Jewish customs (*Ant.* 14.192–195; 212).

In a letter containing a decree to the Greek town of Paros dating to 42–41 BCE, Josephus describes a Roman intervention due to complaints made by Delosian Jews on the basis of Jewish friendship and alliance with the Romans (*Ant.* 14.213–216).[38] This pattern is followed several times.[39] It expresses Josephus's aspiration that Jews be seen as cooperative members of society in spite of the recent Jewish revolt. Whether or not Josephus is trustworthy on this point, Levinskaya believes that for Josephus to falsely make this statement would not have been worth the risk, suggesting that he is being truthful.[40] The decrees portray the prototypical Asia Minor Jew as "pious" and "law-abiding,"

---

36. Gruen, *Diaspora*, 88.

37. The dates for the documents presented here are those of Zeev, *Jewish Rights in the Ancient World*. See the appropriate section.

38. Zeev, *Jewish Rights in the Ancient World*, 107.

39. This appears in Gaius Caesar's decree dating to 47 BCE that Roman respect for Jewish customs be engraved in brass tablets and displayed in Sidon, Tyre, and Ashkelon (*Ant.* 14.196–198). There is also the letter sent by the Laodicean magistrates to the Roman proconsul (46 or 47 BCE; *Ant.* 14.241–243). Alliance between the Jewish people, the Romans, and the city of Halicarnassus serves as the rationale for respect of Jewish customs dating to 47 CE in *Ant.* 14.256–258, "because of fidelity and friendship for the Romans" (διὰ τὴν πρὸς Ῥωμαίους πίστιν καὶ φιλίαν). This underlines Claudius' support, dating to 41 BCE, for Jewish customs in *Ant.* 19.287–291.

40. For example, Levinskaya, *Acts in its Diaspora Setting*, 140.

though it is Jewish laws and observances that are being obeyed and protected, meaning these kinds of statements really describe Jews as faithful to their ancestral customs. Repeated claims to the right to observe the Law of Moses imply that since the prototypical Jew in these locations kept the Mosaic Law, they would therefore be inclined to obey local laws as well.[41]

Since Josephus is keen to categorize Jews as "friends" of Rome and the emperor,[42] he catalogues numerous Roman legal provisions allowing Jews to maintain their identity in the face of local ethnic tensions.[43] These identity markers often show both the Romans and Josephus understood Jewish distinctives as ethnic practices, using terms such as "ancestral customs" (τὰ πατρία), "laws of [their] forefathers," or ἔθος/ἔθη (custom[s]).[44] In Josephus this concern for ethnic heritage reflects Plato's ideal citizen or resident in a city-state, and therefore functions as a salient categorization held in common with the local gentile culture.[45] Further, Josephus expressly uses the Jewish concern for their ethnic heritage to demonstrate that Jews are not ethnocentric. In his presentation of the numerous Roman measures to protect Asia Minor Jews, Josephus states in *Ant.* 16.176–78:

> For there is no nation which always follows the same customs, and it also happens that there are great differences among cities. And it is most profitable for all men, Greeks and barbarians alike, to practice justice, about which our laws are most

---

41. The materials concerning the region of interest in this chapter speak to Paria, an island in the Aegean (*Ant.* 14.213–216); Delos, another Aegean island (*Ant.* 14.231–232); Ephesus (*Ant.* 14.225–227, 228–230, 262–264; 16.167–168, 172–173); Sardis (*Ant.* 14.235, 259–261; 16.171); Laodicea (*Ant.* 14.241–243); Milesia (*Ant.* 14.244–246); and Halicarnassus (*Ant.* 14.256–258). Other materials pertain to Rome (*Ant.* 14.211–212), Alexandria (*Ant.* 19.280–285), Sidon (*Ant.* 14.190–195), the Palestinian coast (*Ant.* 14.196–198), and the empire in general (*Ant.* 19.287–291).

42. *Ant.* 14.267; Zeev, *Jewish Rights in the Roman World*, 3.

43. Zeev, *Jewish Rights in the Roman World*, 5.

44. For example, τοῖς πατρίοις τῶν Ἰουδαίων νόμοις (or, the ancestral Jewish laws) in *Ant.* 14.116; more commonly τοὺς πατρίους νόμους (ancestral laws). E.g., *Ant.* 14.194, 214, 216, 245, 260, 263; 16.173; 19.290.

45. For example see Plato, *Leg.* 12.949e–950a on the destructive effect of cultural innovation versus faithful preservation of ancestral customs; *Leg.* 7.793b–d on "ancestral customs" as buttresses for protecting core laws.

concerned and, if we sincerely abide by them, they make us well-disposed and friendly to all men. We therefore have a right to expect this same attitude from them, *for one should not consider foreignness a matter of differences in practice* (δέον οὐκ ἐν τῇ διαφορᾷ τῶν ἐπιτηδευμάτων οἴεσθαι τὸ ἀλλότριον) but of whether there is a proper attitude to goodness. For this is common to all men and alone enables society to endure.[46]

Josephus uses Jew's unique ethnic identity as a salient category held in common with other ethnic groups and draws an analogy with the Greek *polis* to claim that ethnic distinctives are really markers of similarity given that so many groups live together within the empire. By doing so, Josephus tries to use Jewish differences to align them more closely with their host culture. Likewise, peculiar Jewish customs are presented as fostering open attitudes on the part of Jews if they are sincerely followed.[47] This is because Jewish laws, like laws in general, promote the shared virtue of justice, making generalized morality a salient category held in common with gentiles. If civic or regional differences are a salient factor in Greek identity, and if the virtue "justice" is another, then difference and concern for justice represent aligned social identities despite ethnic and religious differences.

Pious

Josephus also categorizes the prototypical Jew as pious. In *Ant.* 14.213–214, Josephus's Julius Gaius proclaims that by keeping their ancestral customs Jews are performing "sacred rites" (ἱεροῖς χρῆσθαι; τὰ ἱερά). The ἱερὰ Ἰουδαϊκὰ (Jewish rites) and somewhat derogatory δεισιδαιμονία (superstition) are enough to get Jews out of military service (*Ant.* 14.228, 232). Piety is a quality shared with gentiles, as the people of Halicarnassus permit Jewish observances on this basis (and alliance with the Romans).[48] The Sardinians also imply that they share this value since they simply refer to the Jewish god as "God" rather

---

46. This is Marcus' LCL translation. Italics mine. All translations of Josephus used here are from their Loeb editions unless otherwise stated. See also Zeev, *Jewish Rights in the Roman World*, 291.

47. *Ant.* 16.177.

48. *Ant.* 14.256–258.

than their god, and state they value the Jewish presence in their city enough to make provision for marketplace goods that meet Jewish dietary requirements (*Ant.* 14.259–261).[49] In *Ant.* 16.162–173, Josephus's Agrippa decrees that synagogues[50] be treated along the lines of temples where robbers are deemed ἱερόσυλος (temple robbers), though Caesar Augustus also notes his own piety when he orders synagogues be protected, as is also the temple collection as an expression of Jewish piety (*Ant.* 16.163–172). Josephus makes the point of giving evidence that rights of assembly and Sabbath observance are protected,[51] indicating that these are expressions of piety practiced by prototypical Jews in Asia Minor.

Faithful to Ancestral Customs

The Jewish self-categorization of being faithful to the ancestral customs is closely related to the categorization of "pious," the former being distinct from the latter in that gentiles could at times be categorized as pious but not observe Jewish customs. This is notably framed in Josephus's presentation of Nicolaus's speech in Ionia before the Roman governor and local rulers (*Ant.* 16.31–57). The speech is clearly presented as part of Josephus's broader apologetic agenda, but if the provisions preserving Jewish rights to maintain their identity are authentic, then Nicolaus's speech reflects the self-categorizations of Asia Minor Jews, albeit indirectly and selectively via Josephus.

Nicolaus asserts that fidelity to one's ethnic ancestry is a prime virtue not unique to Jews and is considered something more important than the preservation of one's life. Nicolaus, conveniently for Josephus's purposes, also asserts that preventing groups from demonstrating fidelity to τὰ πάτρια ἔθη (ancestral practices) are a common cause of wars (*Ant.* 16.35–36). Nicolaus urges his listeners to follow common Roman practice and allow Jews to preserve their ancestral customs, here labelled as "ancestral piety" (τὴν πάτριον εὐσέβειαν), to acquire

---

49. See Trebilco, *Jewish Communities in Asia Minor*, chapter 2, for information on the future history of the Sardian Jewish community.

50. The probable meaning of σαββατείου (Sabbath-place) and perhaps also ἀνδρῶνος (usually, banqueting hall).

51. *Ant.* 14. 215, 226–227, 235, 242–246, 258–264; 16.163, 171.

the favor of the Deity (*Ant.* 16.41–42). As in *Against Apion*, Jewish observances such as the Sabbath are a sign of wisdom and education because the study of ancestral customs and laws fosters justice and virtue, supposedly aligning the Jews in question with a variation on Plato's ideal that the citizens and residents of a city know its laws thoroughly.[52] Authentic Jews do not hate gentiles or restrict themselves to secretive rites, but are open to people from other groups (*Ant.* 16.42–44).

Josephus's framing of Jewish identity in ethnic terms enables him to present via Nicolaus's speech religious self-categorizations that label authentic Jews with items that traditionally lack ethnic connotations among modern western readers. In Josephus's presentation, Jews as an ethnic group identify themselves as pious, wise, ethical, and law-abiding—ideals that closely parallel the four virtues held in common with their gentile neighbors. Again, Josephus attempts to exploit morality as a common salient category to demonstrate that, like gentiles, Jews are in fact loyal participants in local society.

Loyal Clients

Preserved in the works of Josephus and Eusebius, the first-century BCE Rhodesian scholar Apollonius Molon was among the first to write against Jews and popularize many anti-Jewish stereotypes later used by writers such as Apion,[53] including atheism, arrogance, xenophobia, and being insular (*Ag. Ap.* 2.148, 258). Apollonius Molon also seems to have originated the claim that the Holy of Holies contained an image of a donkey (*Ag. Ap.* 2.80).[54] The Roman aristocrat Cicero likewise denigrates Asia Minor Jews for practices deemed superstitious. The payment of the temple tax supposedly implied ingratitude to Rome because Pompey had spared the temple (*Flac.* 67),[55] as also would later Jewish rebellions against the Roman rule (*Flac.* 69). Attitudes in

---

52. *Leg.* 4.718c; *Leg.* 4.723a; 10.888d. For more, see the discussion of *Against Apion* below in chapter 4.

53. Barclay, *Jews in the Mediterranean Diaspora*, 272. Josephus describes Apollonius Molon as the original slanderer of Jews (*Ag. Ap.* 2.79)

54. See discussion of Josephus' refutation of this and other allegations below in chapter 4.

55. For fuller discussion of Cicero, see chapter 4.

Apollonius Molon and Cicero provide literary evidence that some regarded Jews as suspicious outsiders alien to Greco-Roman culture.

An example of Josephus's counterargument against these accusations is his citation of Claudius's decree on behalf of Alexandrian Jews. Though scholarly suspicion has been raised over its veracity,[56] SIT and SCT deal with mental conceptions of where a person belongs, or *thinks they should belong*, in their social context. If the document is unreliable from a historical point of view[57] it remains useful for our purposes because it communicates *what its author thinks should be true* of the place of Jews in the host culture, and therefore remains useful as evidence to Jewish social identity. In *Ant.* 19.281, Josephus claims that Claudius stated that Jews were equal partners in the establishment of Alexandria, and therefore co-citizens with traditional ethnic rights that continue under Roman rule. The substance of the decree regarding Jews outside Alexandria in *Ant.* 19.287–291 is similar to *CPJ* 153, though Josephus's version emphasizes the friendships of Herod and Agrippa with the Emperor and equates Jewish privileges with those of citizens in Greek cities. In *Ant.* 19.288–89 Jews deserve the preservation of their rights because Jews and their national rulers exhibit "fidelity and friendship (πίστιν καὶ φιλίαν) to the Romans." Josephus ascribes Jews a civic dignity similar to those held by other groups while also portraying them as part of broader composite Hellenic society.

PATTERNS OF MEMORY INNOVATION

Most of the material in Josephus's *Antiquities* dates to the Roman civil war (49–48 BCE)[58] and are the result of Roman pragmatism rather

---

56. Tcherikover regards *Ant.* 19.280–285 as a partial forgery because of its laudatory portrayal of Jews (Tcherikover, *Hellenistic Civilization and the Jews*, 409–15), though Zeev's conclusion is more reserved (Zeev, *Jewish Rights in the Roman World*, 326). The narrative nature of the decree in *Ant.* 19.281–284 is suspect, but its substance in *Ant.* 19.285 matches that of *CPJ* 153. Further, *Ant.* 19.281 contradicts the premise of 3 Macc 2:30; 3:21–23, which states that Jews rejected Alexandrian citizenship out of fidelity to Judaism.

57. Josephus states: τοῦτον ἦν τὸν τρόπον γεγραμμένον (*Ant.* 19.286), which Zeev translates as "such was the tenor of the edict" (Zeev, *Jewish Rights in the Roman World*, 327). This mitigates the need to understand it as a direct quotation.

58. Gruen, *Diaspora*, 86; Barclay, *Jews in the Mediterranean Diaspora*, 267.

than altruism,[59] *ad hoc* interventions rather than permanent legislative policy.[60] Another way Josephus misrepresents these materials is they pre-date his time of writing by almost 150 years, yet he applies them to his contemporary situation anyway. This marks a degree of misrepresentation that allows Josephus to vindicate Jews in light of social pressures they were probably facing as a result of the war against Rome. He capitalizes on past military assistance and historical alliances with the Romans[61] to portray the rebellion against Rome as an abnormal occurrence. Josephus attempts to describe a peaceful and cooperative state between Jew, Roman, and gentile, but in the the sixty years following the revolt this would not hold true in Palestine and North Africa.[62] Further, once the Romans started directly ruling the Jewish homeland, North Africa, and Alexandria the situation for Jews steadily deteriorated, in many cases due to Roman mismanagement. In the context of the decrees Josephus does not mention actions taken by Lucius Flaccus against the temple tax, but he does provide evidence protecting it, even though many in Roman leadership would agree with Lucius Flaccus's attempted intervention over the opinions of Josephus or Rome's Jewish allies.[63]

Yet Josephus may be acting in accordance to Jewish cultural memory and beliefs regarding Jew-gentile interaction in allowing positive references of gentile piety into his account of Jew-gentile relations. This is because LXX Exod 22:28 translates a commandment to respect "God" (אלהים) and the national leadership as "You will not revile the gods (Θεοὺς) or speak evil of your ruler." The concern for mutual respect is also present in Josephus's version of Claudius's decree affirming Jewish rights in the empire (*Ant.* 19.290).[64] Roman rule and

---

59. Gruen, *Diaspora*, 90, 100.

60. Trebilco, *Jewish Communities in Asia Minor*, 16; Gruen, *Diaspora*, 104.

61. For instance, 1 Macc 8; 12; 2 Macc 11:34–38.

62. In the case of Asia Minor, Josephus may have been correct as it appears that Jews there, as a whole at least, abstained from participation in the various conflicts with Rome. See Goodman, "Diaspora Reactions," 36.

63. Cicero, *Flac.* 67.

64. According to W. Weren, Luke makes a similar argument for toleration with the town clerk serving as Luke's voice (Acts 19:35–40). It was probably not an uncommon sentiment. See Weren, "Riot of the Ephesian Silversmiths," 456.

relations with Jews in Asia Minor were not perfect, and Josephus's ideas concerning SIT and SCT can only be accepted to the degree that they are supported by other evidence such as inscriptions or other literary sources.[65]

JEWS IN GREEK CITIES IN ACTS

Josephus's apologetic agenda is vulnerable to suspicions that his depiction of Jewish diaspora attitudes may be tendentious in portraying Jews as well-acculturated and seeking integration with the larger population. Is this picture accurate? The Letter of Aristeas, Philo, and to a degree in 2 and 3 Maccabees echo this portrayal. Fearghus O. Fearghail would argue that there is agreement with the book of Acts as well:

> Luke paints a picture then of Jews in various cities of the diaspora who show a tolerance towards Christian missionaries that is surprising given the lack of tolerance on the part of the Jewish leaders in Jerusalem. These missionaries are allowed to preach in their synagogues repeatedly and often over an extended period . . . Luke's narrative also portrays an openness on the part of the Jews to the Gentiles in the cities of Asia Minor, Macedonia and Greece.[66]

Tannehill argues at some length that Luke-Acts has tragic undertones in Israel's consistent rejection of the Christian message.[67] Jack T. Sanders argues that Luke-Acts borders on anti-Jewish slander,[68] though he bases this contention on the rhetorical context of the protagonists's speeches and not the course of the narratives. Fearghail is nonetheless correct to argue that Luke describes some Jews from Asia Minor and Greece as showing a high degree of tolerance for gentiles and Christian missionaries. Paul preaches in Ephesus for two years,[69] and he preaches in its synagogue for three months (Acts 19:8), so Fearghail's point that

---

65. On the whole, however, Josephus seems to accurately reflect some assumed Jewish social categorizations reflected in John. These will be discussed below.
66. Fearghail, "Jews in the Hellenistic Cities of Acts," 47–48.
67. Tannehill, "Israel in Luke-Acts," 74–85.
68. Sanders, "The Jewish People in Luke-Acts," 110–29, esp. 122.
69. Fearghail, "Jews in the Hellenistic Cities of Acts," 47, citing Acts 19:10.

Ephesian Jews had the patience to allow Paul to make his case over an extended period remains valid. Even when Paul leaves the synagogue the local Jews do not attempt to have his party expelled from the city, and during the Artemis riots it is a Jew attempting to intervene who is shouted down by the gentile crowd (Acts 19:33–34).

An indicator of nuanced situational Jewish self-categorizations in Acts appears at Pisidian Antioch (Acts 13:13–52). Paul preaches a sermon in a synagogue where he appeals to Jewish cultural memories of deliverance (Acts 13:16–41) and refers to national symbols such as the Davidic monarchy (13:21–22), Davidic typology (Acts 13:33–37), and Abrahamic descent (13:26, 32) before asserting that salvation is through trust in Jesus and not the Law (Acts 13:38–39). He ends his sermon by appealing to the Jewish cultural memory that Israel was perpetually unfaithful to YHWH and had rejected all the prophets (13:40–41).[70] It is important to note that in Luke's portrayal the audience, consisting of Jews and proselytes, responds to Paul's sermon positively (13:42–44).

For our purposes it is the negative resolution of the episode that is most interesting. Things turn in Acts 13:45, "but when the Jews saw the crowds, they were filled with [zeal] (ἐπλήσθησαν ζήλου); and blaspheming, they contradicted what was spoken by Paul" (NRSV). Here, ζῆλος seems to indicate "jealousy" because Luke presents it as a response to the crowds Paul and Barnabas were gathering, but it is more likely that "zeal" is the correct translation since the conflict may reflect concern over apostasy and the importance of obedience to the Law.[71] Intervention against Paul comes through high-standing devout women and civic leaders,[72] who were probably connected to the proselytes mentioned in 13:43.

In terms of SCT, what this means is that certain Jews saw themselves as a distinct group whose identity centered on the Law of Moses, though this did not preclude social relations with gentiles. This Law-centered Jewish identity was undermined by Paul's teachings, but

---

70. Neh 9:26; 4 Esdras 1:32; also 2:1; 7:130. See Knight, *Rediscovering the Traditions of Israel*, 144–46, citing Steck, *Israel und das gewaltsame Geschick*, esp. 60–195.

71. See Schnabel, "Jewish Opposition," 233–70; Ortlund, "Zeal without Knowledge," 23–37; Ortlund, "Phinehan Zeal," 299–315.

72. Acts 13:50; Trebilco, *Jewish Communities in Asia Minor*, 22; Fearghail, "Jews in the Hellenistic Cities of Acts," 43.

apparently to the relative lack of concern of most at the synagogue (at least in Luke's telling). At the same time, it appears many in the audience had a strong sense of Jewish theological identity and probably a strong sense of ethnic and cultural identity as well. This is more likely given Paul's heavy use of Jewish cultural memory in his sermon, which with a few exceptions Luke portrays him as successfully using to open his audience up to the message of Jesus. The synagogue audience probably held a spectrum of views that led to a conflict when Paul's sermon brought these differences to the surface.

At the same time, Paul's opponents did not see themselves as so separated from gentiles as to avoid all contact with them, meaning they were not social isolationists. The issue is therefore what constitutes Jewish identity, rather than the more socially-abstract level of how to relate to gentiles in the context of a shared cultural environment. The antagonists in the narrative maintained enough social currency with the upper classes and civic leadership to use their help to evict Paul and his party from the region, something which could hardly be possible had Jews not integrated themselves into the local culture and its power structures. It is implicit in the narrative, therefore, that Jews in Pisidian Antioch categorized themselves as members of that city. While maintaining a distinct identity centered on the Law and other Jewish symbols, Jews did not present this identity as being so distinct as to remove all common ground with their gentile neighbors, suggesting adherence to a limited degree of relative difference. This suggests that the Jews in question had little difficulty remaining faithful to the ancestral customs while also maintaining social relations with non-Jews, even though they responded negatively to Paul's message.

Events in Iconium in Acts 14 follow a similar pattern, and again for the Acts narrative to be historically credible similar social dynamics must have been salient. Paul and Barnabas enjoy some success with Jews and gentiles at the synagogue and "remained a long time" (ἱκανὸν μὲν οὖν χρόνον διέτριψαν) in Iconium (14:3) before non-believing Jewish and civic rulers become involved in Iconium ridding itself of Paul and Barnabas (Acts 14:5). A similar dynamic appears to be at work as at Pisidian Antioch where Jews carry some influence with the local population, something made much more likely if they identified themselves to a degree as Iconians, though while also observing the ancestral customs that preserved their ethnic and religious identity.

In Ephesus some Jews again reject Paul's message, most likely for similar reasons as in Pisidian Antioch (the role of the Law). However, Ephesian Jews still allow him to speak in their synagogue for *three months* before things degenerate below civility, and thereafter the conversation continues for another *two years* "so that all the residents of [the province of] Asia, both Jews and Greeks, heard the word of the Lord" (Acts 19:8–10). In Luke's presentation, Paul later decides it is prudent leave after civil unrest results from his conversion of too many gentiles (Acts 19:21–20:1). In the spectrum of relative difference here, where the salient category is Artemis as a symbol of Ephesian identity, the silversmiths and mob categorize Christians and Jews as similar to each other but different from "Ephesians." Alexander's Jewishness appears to be the salient category, along with Ephesian pride in the Artemis cult, which prompts rejection of his attempt to end the conflict in Acts 19:34.

Alexander's role as a representative of the Jewish community implies that within the Ephesian Jewish communities there were differences of opinion on what it meant to be Jewish and that it was a topic of discussion for Ephesian Jews, and perhaps the Christian controversy may have benefited the numbers of the Jewish community by raising interest in proselytism. We can infer that the Jewish population did not closely categorize themselves alongside those who revered Artemis,[73] but they did apparently share salient categories with many of their gentile neighbors and felt free to discuss their way of life with them.

PATTERNS OF MEMORY INNOVATION IN ACTS

An apparent intention behind the Jewish cultural memory of Israel rejecting, killing, or ignoring all the prophets was to motivate greater obedience to the Law and ancestral customs as these were considered coterminous with faithfulness to God. Obduracy on the part of the spiritual in-group (Israel) is a consistent theme in this tradition, as is the view that being a good Israelite entailed obedience to both the Law

---

73. Trebilco, *Jewish Communities in Asia Minor*, 25.

and divinely appointed prophets as expressions of belief. Paul uses this cultural memory as part of his missionary strategy by using it to elevate Jesus as the rejected prophetic figure, but he does so at the cost of the subordination of the Law, which effectively reverses this cultural memory's social function. It also creates the perception of Jewish opponents of Paul as obdurate, though in truth they were probably attempting to remain true to Jewish customs and the aims of the tradition concerning the prophets. Likewise, the Jewish opponents were probably not particularly anti-gentile, given that they drew on support from their gentile allies to confront Paul.

The result is that for those not familiar with historical Jew-gentile social dynamics, Luke could be accused of portraying Jews as opposed to non-Jewish or non-Torah observant people worshipping the one God. In reality there was probably a spectrum of views, with some Jews willing to make allowances for gentile proselytes. We can conclude that Acts provides accurate information to Jewish social circumstances in broader gentile culture in Asia Minor, and probably an accurate picture of Jewish responses to Paul's preaching. While Acts may appear to present a one-sided portrayal of Paul's opponents, this is not nearly as negative a depiction of all Jews as some maintain.

CONCLUSION

The cumulative evidence indicates that Acts' portrayal of Jewish-gentile-Christian relations is plausible and therefore reliable enough to supply supplementary evidence for the study of social relations between Jews and their neighbors in first-century Asia Minor. Plausibility does not equal historicity, but even if one holds Acts is a theological fiction it would appear to be a historically convincing one. The testimony from Acts indicates Jews maintained their existence as separate social groups but saw their place of residence as a salient category held in common with their gentile neighbors, meaning they categorized themselves as participants, and probably also as loyal. A cursory reading of the brief Acts narratives can lead to the false impression of constant and immediate rejection of Paul's message by Jews. However, Fearghail correctly points out that the lengths of time involved in various episodes indicate that Paul's Jewish audiences gave his proposals serious thought, and the intervention of gentile members of Jewish communities suggest high levels of social Jew-gentile integration that correspond with later evidence presented in Trebilco's study.

Most of the literary and epigraphic evidence available from the first century or before indicates Jews in Asia Minor used socially convergent integrationist strategies. We can assume not all Jews adopted this strategy and sought to separate themselves from gentiles, but even "zealous" Jews in Asia Minor still had sufficient social capital with the gentile leadership of Iconium and Pisidian Antioch to cause problems for Paul and Barnabas. Josephus's portrayal of Asia Minor Jewish identity indicates that its practices—Sabbath observance, practice of ancestral customs, and food laws—were important to Asia Minor Jews. Though of questionable reliability, Asia Minor Jews in evidence from Josephus likely adopted similar social strategies, seeking common ground, when possible, with gentiles on theological-philosophical and ethical issues. Like the Letter of Aristeas, the various documents and accounts preserved in Josephus categorize Jews as pious, and gentiles claim to share this categorization with their Jewish neighbors. Jews are also categorized as loyal participants in the local society and imperial enterprise. This suggests that if the Johannine literature had been composed in Ephesus or another Asia Minor center, Jewish social categorizations and strategies of social convergence in Egypt, at least broadly, would have import for reconstructing the Gospel of John's *Sitz im Leben* and may be able to aid in understanding Johannine treatmant of Judaism and "the Jews."

4

Social Identity among Jews in First-Century Rome

INTRODUCTION

IN CHAPTERS 2 AND 3 we saw that Jews appear to have situationally negotiated and balanced ethno-religious distinctiveness with social convergence. More abstract social categorizations such as "loyal" or "participants" enabled them to reduce their relative difference so that they could identify themselves with their gentile neighbors and the local society and culture. More specific categorizations such as "faithful to ancestral customs" and "pious" were used to maintain ethnic social distinctiveness, though these could also be viewed positively in Hellenistic culture. At times Jews were willing to share social-categorizations pertaining to piety and virtue with gentiles. In these cases, ancestral customs maintained ethnic distinctiveness and served as the exemplar of these shared categorizations. In first-century Asia Minor and Ptolemaic Egypt Jewish attempts at social convergence appear to have been accepted by gentile culture, though the Alexandrian anti-Roman movement opposed use of this social strategy. As for Rome, I will argue that many Romans opposed Jewish use of integrationist social strategies due to a sense of socio-economic and cultural superiority, suspicion resulting from Roman-Jewish conflicts, and Roman financial problems.

Social Identity among Jews in First-Century Rome

Examining Jewish identity and social categorizations in first-century Rome is fraught with difficulty due to a dearth of contemporary Jewish literary evidence. Some first-century inscriptional evidence exists elsewhere in Italy but less than is found in Asia Minor. The Jewish synagogue in Ostia appears to date to the first century, but its inscriptions probably date to the second century. There are ample epitaphs available from Roman Jewish catacombs but their dates are contested.[1] If carbon dating proves correct, then analyses by scholars such as Harry J. Leon that make use of this evidence may provide insight into the social locations of Rome's first-century Jewish population.

As for the literary testimony, most of the helpful first-century evidence derives from Roman writers who are generally opposed to Judaism. These writers vary from presenting a relatively accurate picture of Judaism to holding willfully distorted and prejudicial views.[2] The only Jewish writer known from first-century Rome is Josephus, with *Against Apion* written to an elite Roman audience as an apology,[3] but demonstrating that *Against Apion* represents the views of the Roman Jewish community requires supporting evidence. Philo notes that Roman Jews lived mostly in poorer areas, which suggests the dominant demographic was lower-class.[4] This is confirmed by Harry Leon, who documents interest in Judaism among the Roman upper classes. He also notes Jewish naming conventions in the catacombs predominantly used single-name formulae, suggesting humble socio-economic status.[5] While

---

1. David Noy argues they date to the third or fourth centuries (Noy, *Jewish Inscriptions of Western Europe*, 421–88). Others believe they date much earlier. See Rutgers et al., "Radiocarbon Dates," 541–47; Rutgers et al., "Radiocarbon Dating," 339; Williams, *Jews in a Graeco-Roman Environment*, 13–14.

2. Perhaps due to the descent of a significant number of Jews from war captives, and discomfort at the growing influence of the Jewish population on Roman culture and religious beliefs. This is the thesis of Schäfer, *Judeophobia*; combining the "functionalist school" with the "substantialist school" (represented by Sevenster in *The Roots of Pagan Anti-Semitism in the Ancient World*) of arguments for the origins of pagan antisemitism. Schäfer holds that pagan antisemitism was the result of a combination of political-military conflict and intercultural conflict over Jewish ethnic observances.

3. Barclay, *Against Apion*, L.

4. Catto, *Reconstructing the First-Century Synagogue*, 49.

5. Leon, *Jews of Ancient Rome*, 13–19; 106–12.

he considers Roman Jews to have been predominantly from the lower classes in the first century, Peter Lampe suggests members of different social strata, including higher socioeconomic levels, were interested in Judaism. Lampe argues different classes adopted different strategies in joining local Jewish communities, and that by the second century the Judeo-Christian tradition would increase in its socio-economic status.[6]

Fortunately for our purposes, the subjective and situational nature of SCT means the partial evidence available can still grant some insight into how meta-contrast influenced Roman–Jewish social dynamics, which can provide context for evaluating statements made by Josephus in *Against Apion*, gentile writers, and information for understanding the few Jewish inscriptions available. No piece of evidence is singularly representative, though self-categorizations seen in Josephus and the inscriptions indicate that Roman Jews sought to integrate into Roman society as they had done in Ptolemaic Egypt. That said, circumstances ensured that most Jews continued to occupy lower social levels in first-century Rome.

We will see that Roman anti-Jewish stereotypes and attempts at marginalization of Jews have little in common with Johannine rhetoric and treatment of Judaism. Nonetheless, a clearer understanding of Jewish social location in Rome provides historical perspective for the social categorizations and strategies used in Asia Minor and in Ptolemaic and Roman Egypt. When combined with data from John below, the cumulative evidence from Egypt, Asia Minor, and Rome will show that John's portrayal of both Jews and Jewish issues is highly abstracted and stylized.

---

6. Lampe, *From Paul to Valentinus: Christians at Rome in the First Two Centuries*, 51–79; 409–10.

Social Identity among Jews in First-Century Rome

DISCUSSIONS OF JEWS BY ROMAN WRITERS

Common Progenitor

In his accounts of Jewish origins, Alexander Polyhistor[7] initially follows the biblical narrative of Jewish origins[8] but later elaborates with legends. Polyhistor reports that some thought Moses was a woman,[9] perhaps reflecting the recurrent categorization of Jews as weak-willed and impressionable adherents of a *superstitio*. Elsewhere Polyhistor suggests Jews are an ancient and philosophical people, with Polyhistor following the Jewish historian Eupolemus in claiming Moses gave Jews the Law and invented literacy, later passed on to the Phoenicians and Greeks.[10] The multiple accounts presented in a single author demonstrate the lack of a coherent Roman narrative regarding the historical origins of their Jewish subjects.

Diodorus of Sicily[11] follows a similar pattern in initially presenting a mundane picture of Jewish origins before offering more fanciful ones. Roman views of Egypt and the East generally mean that none of Diodorus's accounts are particularly flattering. At first, he merely states that circumcision, also practiced by other cultures with alleged Egyptian origins such as the Colchi in Pontus, proves that Jews originated as an Egyptian colony.[12] In Roman eyes this would be sufficient denigration, but Diodorus also offers another account where the Jewish

---

7. Alexander Polyhistor was active in Rome in the first century BCE. Menahem Stern's *Greek and Latin Authors on Jews and Judaism*, hereafter *GLAJJ*, proved an invaluable resource in developing this section. All translations of primary sources come from their Loeb editions unless otherwise stated.

8. In Eusebius, *Praep. ev.* 9.19.

9. This passage is preserved in *De Roma* (see Jacoby, *Die Fragmente der griechischen Historiker*, III.A273, F70).

10. Alexander Polyhistor referencing Eupolemus, preserved in Eusebius, *Praep. ev.* 9.26. Eupolemus was active in the second century BCE and served as a Hasmonean ambassador to Rome (1 Macc 8:17; 2 Macc 4:11). See Collins, *Between Athens and Jerusalem*, 46–47. Polyhistor also makes use of the Jewish tradition that a Chaldean Abraham taught astrology to the Phoenicians and Egyptians, though he also cites alternate theories where astrology is traced to Atlas, identified as Enoch (Eusebius, *Praep. ev.* 9.17).

11. Diodorus was active in the first century, BCE.

12. Diodorus, *Bib. hist.* 1.28.1–3; 1.55.5. The other circumcision-practicing culture mentioned is the Colchi of Pontus.

people originated as refugees who were expelled from Egypt due to skin diseases and an irreligious nature, with the bitterness of this rejection prompting Moses to develop racist and misanthropic laws.[13] Diodorus also states that when Antiochus IV profaned the temple as part of a crusade against Jewish racism, he saw in the Holy of Holies an idol of Moses seated on a donkey with a book in his hand,[14] which in Egyptian lore drew a negative association between Moses and the evil god Typhon. Other gentiles simply associated donkeys with stupidity. Jewish food laws prompted others to claim the Jewish God was really a pig.[15]

Likewise, the Roman historian Tacitus[16] offers some innocuous, even venerable accounts, of Jewish origins, though he tends to emphasize that Jews originated as displaced refugees.[17] On the whole, however, he seems to give the most credence to accounts propagated by Apion and Apollonius Molon[18] in what Bilhah Wardy characterizes as "old wives tales."[19] Like Diodorus, Tacitus portrays Moses as a diseased, impious, and megalomanianic leader who, with the guidance of wild donkeys, leads his people out of Egypt. Moses then creates the Jewish lifestyle and religion to establish his authority over the Jewish people and institutionalize the bitterness of their experiences at a cultural level.[20]

In general, Roman writers considered Jews an "Eastern" people and associated them with many of the same mystical or superstitious attributes ascribed to Chaldeans and Egyptians that prompted Romans

---

13. See Diodorus, *Bib. hist.* 35.1.1–5; See also 40.3.8, where he credits Hecataeus.

14. Diodorus, *Bib. hist.* 35.1.3.

15. The myth of a donkey in the Jerusalem temple likely arose in Egypt. Donkeys were associated with Seth/Typhon, who was the enemy of Horus. Horus' father, the god Osiris, was killed by Seth-Typhon. According to Jan Assmann, Egyptians associated Jews with the Hyksos, and the Hyksos were in turn conflated with the monotheists led by Akhenaten. For discussion, see Assmann, "Egyptian Anti-Judaism," 365–78; Bar-Kochva, "Origins and Development of the Slander," 310–26; Feldman, *Jew and Gentile in the Ancient World*, 195; Henten and Abusch, "Jews as Typhonians," 275–95; Horst, *Philo's Flaccus*, 31; Schäfer, *Judeophobia*, 168.

16. Tacitus, c. 56–c. 120 CE.

17. Tacitus, *Hist.* 5.2.

18. Tacitus, *Hist.* 5.3.

19. Wardy, "Jewish Religion in Pagan Literature," 614.

20. Tacitus, *Hist.* 5.3–4.

to regard people from this region with suspicion. Jews were subject to many of the preconceptions held of their region generally, and negative misinterpretations of the Exodus specifically. Along with a perceived Jewish militarism and xenophobia that were read back into Jewish origins, Roman writers were predisposed to assign Jews correspondingly negative social categorizations.

Social Categorizations

Law-Abiding and Moral

Roman writers sometimes grudgingly categorized Jews as moral and law-abiding, though the laws and morals in question were considered suspect. In Diodorus, obedience to the Law of Moses and reverence for Scripture are signs of a prototypical Jew,[21] though he suspects the veracity of the Law's claims to divine origins.[22] Pliny the Elder[23] implies that sexual self-restraint, which he considers a melancholic and superstitious practice, is prototypical of some Jews.[24] While his intent is to denigrate Jews, the Roman satirist Juvenal stereotypes synagogues as places where beggars congregated, perhaps betraying a Jewish reputation for being charitable to the poor.[25] However, Cicero's comments concerning Jewish solidarity suggest some would construe this as Jews being charitable to Jews who were beggars.[26]

In a similar vein, Tacitus attempts to counter possible positive Roman social categorizations of Jews. We will see below that his portrayal of Jewish religion and charity as expressions of misanthropy may be aimed at undermining a possible Jewish reputation for justice. Likewise, his attempts to reinterpret Jewish respect for human life, charity,

---

21. Diodorus, *Bib. hist.* 35.1.3.

22. Diodorus, *Bib. hist.* 1.94.1–2. Diodorus maintains the practice of keeping written laws originated in Egypt, and attributes the divine mandate for obedience to other legal codes as well.

23. Active from c. 23 to c. 79 CE.

24. For more on the significance of the categorization "superstitious," see below. On sex abstinence, see Pliny the Elder, *Nat.* 5.15.73; in 31.44.95. Sex abstinence is labelled a superstitious practice.

25. Juvenal, *Sat.* 3.290–96.

26. See below.

and acceptance of converts through the lens of militarism may be an attempt to mitigate a respect held by others for Jewish bravery, morality, and temperance.

Pious

A social categorization of Jews as pious can be detected in some Roman writers, though most would prefer the antonyms "impious" or "superstitious."[27] According to Augustine, the Roman scholar Varro[28] saw Jews as exemplars of piety, something originally shared with Romans as both groups originally worshipped the gods without images, though Varro also juxtaposes Jewish piety to a relative decline in a Roman piety that demonstrates the emergence of idol worship is detrimental to this virtue.[29] Varro reconciles Jewish religious devotion with Roman beliefs by claiming the Jewish god was really Jupiter.[30] Horace[31] considered enthusiasm for religion a sign of weakness but a trait emblematic of Jews;[32] Seneca[33] admits Jews were theologically well-educated.[34]

Monotheists

Jewish monotheism was well-known by Roman writers but seldom discussed at length, with perhaps the exception being Tacitus, who attempts interpret monotheism as another form of Jewish misanthropy because it is antithetical to the polytheistic beliefs of the majority culture. Tacitus's presentation of Jewish beliefs is not coherent, since in *Hist.* 5.4 he seeks to undermine Jewish theological credibility by making use of the rumor that Jews worshipped a donkey in the temple, yet in *Hist.* 2.78 Tacitus claims Vespasian visited a shrine at Mount Carmel where people (presumably Jews or Samaritans) worshipped God without an

27. See under the categorization "superstitious."
28. Varro was active in the first century BCE.
29. In Augustine, *Civ.* 4.31; Stern cites the parallel in Plutarch, *Num.* 8.7–9.
30. Augustine, *Cons.* 1.22.30; 23.31; 27.42.
31. Horace, c. 65 BCE to 8 BCE.
32. Horace, *Sat.* 1.9.71–72.
33. Seneca was active near the end of the first century BCE.
34. In Augustine, *Civ.* 6.11.

image. Likewise he also reports that Pompey found the Holy of Holies to be empty (*Hist.* 5.9) and describes Jewish theology as unique in its avoidance of idols, though this does not stop him form denigrating Jewish culture (*Hist.* 5.5). In describing the persecution of Christians under Nero, Tacitus labels Christianity as a distasteful Jewish sect from Judea, though he complains it is in Rome where everything "horrible and shameful" becomes fashionable.[35] Despite Tacitus's opinions, it appears that Jewish, and later Christian, monotheism enjoyed some respect in Rome.

Petty

Jewish piety, monotheism, and morality were expressed by means of distinct practices and behaviors. These enjoyed some resonance with elements of the population, but ethnically specific practices such as the Sabbath did not always enjoy this respect. There are indications that Roman writers considered the Sabbath an expression of laziness, making the exercise appear petty in light of the strictures applied to it, and an evaluation which extended to other specifically Jewish observances as well. For example, Suetonius recounts an episode where Tiberius attempts to attend a lecture by the Jewish Rhodesian grammarian Diogenes, but a servant intercepts him to tell him to attend the following Sabbath. Later, Diogenes tries to pay his respects to Tiberius after he became emperor but he is told to return seven years later.[36] It is uncertain if this tale was in general circulation among the population, or if there was even a theological motive behind Diogenes's affront as opposed to some practical concern. The tale as told, however, indicates that people such as Suetonius were under the impression that among Jews the Sabbath trumped other important matters, even demonstrations of respect by future emperors.

---

35. Tacitus, *Ann.* 15.44.

36. Suetonius, *Divus Tiberius* 32.2. That Diogenes was Jewish can be seen in the reference to the Sabbath (*sabbata*). Further, Williams maintains that the Sabbath would have been the principal day for study and teaching among Jews (Williams, *Jews in a Graeco-Roman Environment*, 627–29).

John and Anti-Judaism

Faithful to Ancestral Customs

In Rome Jews were well-known for their observance of "ancestral customs" and were categorized accordingly, often with the practice in question serving as a synonym for the *demonyms* "Jew" or "Judean." Horace takes circumcision and Sabbath observance as prototypical of Jews,[37] and "circumcised" functions as a metonym for Jews in Petronius.[38] Ovid understands Sabbath observance as a Jewish identity marker that is an obstacle to the pursuit of love.[39] Augustine states some Romans regarded Sabbath observance as a sign of Jewish laziness,[40] while Seneca held the lighting of lamps on the Sabbath to be a wasteful practice since the gods apparently did not need lamps.[41] In Persius, the "day of Herod" functions as a synonym for the Sabbath,[42] and there was even a legend that a stream in Judea "rested" on the Sabbath day by drying up as part of an evil omen.[43] The hyperbole found in these examples show Jews were known for adhering to their customs.

Suetonius categorizes Jews as being faithful to their ancestral customs, namely mourning practices. Suetonius claims that Jews were deeply grieved at the murder of Julius Caesar and spent several nights mourning at the site of his cremation, labelling it an ethnic trait.[44] Since this part of the narrative is preceded by military and government honors and tributes paid by other ethnic groups that commemorate Caesar's rule, this suggests Jews are presented as the climax in the succession of mourners for Julius Caesar, since the narrative then moves on to describe forms of retribution and commemoration that underscore the Caesar's repute. Regardless, Suetonius portrays Jewish prototypicality

---

37. Horace, *Sat.* 1.9.65–73.

38. Literally "skinned" (*recutitaque*), which is probably intended to be more derogatory than the use of *circumcido* (circumcise). Persius, *Sat.* 5.179–180. Petronius sees circumcision's significance lying in the fact that it is permanent (*Poems* 97). In Baehrens, *Poetae Latini Minores*, 4:98.

39. Ovid, *Ars* 1.75–80; 413–416; *Am.* 217–220.

40. Augustine, *Civ.* 6.11.

41. Seneca, *Ep.* 95.47.1–3. See also Persius, *Sat.* 5.180–181.

42. Persius, *Sat.* 5.179–180.

43. Pliny the Elder, *Nat.* 31.18.24.

44. Suetonius, *Jul.* 84.

as centered on faithfulness to both ancestral customs and patrons.[45] Another well-known example from Suetonius concerning the Sabbath reinforces this point (*Aug.* 76). Here, Suetonius discusses the Emperor Augustus's habit of eating frequent snacks, at times refusing to share meals with guests because of his lack of appetite:

> 'Not even a Jew, my dear Tiberius, fasts so scrupulously on his Sabbaths as I have today; for it was not until after the first hour of the night that I ate two mouthfuls of bread in the bath before I began to be anointed.' Because of this irregularity he sometimes ate alone either before a dinner party began or after it was over, touching nothing while it was in progress (*Aug.* 76.2).

This account presents Jews as setting the standard for fasting that Augustus claims to exceed, belying a Jewish reputation for being faithful to ancestral customs.[46]

Superstitious

Roman writers usually regarded Judaism as a *superstitio* (superstition), with its connotations of magic, divination, and religious illegitimacy and futility, rather than as a legitimate *religio* (religion).[47] Given the low socio-economic status of many Jews and a general suspicion of foreigners, the categorization of Judaism as a supersition was probably used to stereotype Jews as weak-minded, impressionable, and unstable compared to supposedly well-disciplined Romans.[48] Beyond the more obvious cases of observing the Sabbath and practicing circumcision, Jews were thought to have valued certain mystical practices abhorred

---

45. Suetonius, *Jul.* 85.

46. Williams proposes that for historical reasons Roman Jews treated the Sabbath as a fast day, while other scholars suggest fasting on the Sabbath is a misrepresentation on the part of Gentiles. Williams, *Jews in a Graeco-Roman Environment*, 33–48 (esp. 36).

47. See Grodzynski, "Superstitio," 36–60.

48. Cicero regarded being superstitious as an effeminate trait and uses the adjective *anilis* (like an old woman). See *De Nat. d.* 2.70; 3.90–92; *Div.* 1.7; 2.19; Grodzynski, "Superstitio," 39.

by the Romans such as astrology and dream interpretation.[49] In *Flac.* 67, Cicero states that the yearly Jewish temple tax is a "barbarous superstition" (*barbarae superstitioni*). Some writers use this categorization for the dramatic effect of elevating suspense and ascribing some Roman leaders a divine mandate for their military exploits through prophecy or fortune-telling, while others use it to explain the causes of the revolt in 66–73 CE.

Horace provides a strong example of social prejudices and discomfort with non-Roman cultures. Being a very independent and self-reliant Roman, Horace considered Jews to be part of the unruly mob[50] because he thought all religious beliefs, let alone Jewish ones, made people impressionable and credulous.[51] Horace stereotypes Jews as being particularly offended when their religious sensibilities are affronted.[52] Quintilian[53] describes Moses as the founder of a problematic, superstitious nation,[54] while Suetonius claims Jews persistently created "civil disorder" (*assidue tumultuantis*) due to controversy over a *Chrestus* that prompted Claudius to expel Jews from Rome.[55] In Petronius, Jews symbolize Roman discomfort at the eroding of cultural homogeneity when a Jewish slave is portrayed as subject to random incoherent outbursts in unthinking mimicry of what he hears around him.[56] In these examples, Jews embody the perceived weaknesses of the general population that prompt crowded cities to degenerate into chaos, civil disorder, and a loss of individuality.

---

49. For example, observe Cicero's low views of dream interpretation and astrology (*Div.* 1.36, 124–26; *Nat. d.* 1.55).

50. Horace, *Sat.*1.4.139–143. Stern thinks this passage is an indicator of Jewish proselytizing (Stern, *GLAJJ*, 2:429), but the use of *turba* suggests getting caught up in mob action. Perhaps this serves as a metaphor for conversion to Judaism, but one must consider Cicero's comments on Jewish activism (see below) and Horace's regard for personal independence.

51. Horace, *Sat.* 1.5.100–101: *Credat Iudaeus Apella, non ego* (Apella, the Jew may believe it, not I).

52. Horace, *Sat.* 1.9.69–71.

53. Active in the second half of the first century CE.

54. Quintilian, *Inst.* 3.7.21.

55. Suetonius, *Claud.* 25.4.

56. Petronius, *Satyricon* 68.4–8.

The temple and idol culture of the ancient Mediterranean also prompted credulity at the relative intangibility of Jewish beliefs. Petronius categorizes Jews as unstable and superstitious by stereotyping Jewish worship as clamoring at the sky and trembling at Sabbath observances and that the Jewish God was a pig.[57] He also satirically claims circumcision was imposed to prevent apostasy and assimilation to more rational gentile culture. Pliny the Elder portrays sexual abstinence as a superstitious Jewish rite.[58] Sometimes theological justification is even used to justify anti-Jewish views. For example, Seneca maintains that religious observance and knowing God can be different things, and that rituals are a sign of "depravity" because God was accessible to all.[59] For his part, Persius uses Jews as proof to argue that superstition enslaves humanity,[60] while Juvenal questions the value of worshipping an invisible God.[61] These stereotypes of Jews as superstitious may reflect attempts to prevent serious consideration of Jewish theological claims while reaffirming Roman identities.[62]

Jews were categorized alongside Egyptians and astrologers as spiritual mystics with access to hidden spiritual knowledge.[63] Though a *superstitio*, Suetonius still attributes to Judaism (or Eastern knowledge generally) a mysterious power. Though probably part of his use of the *encomium* genre to set the stage for exaltating the protagonist, Suetonius states that "the Orient" believed that Judea would somehow determine who became emperor,[64] citing an oracle at Mount Carmel and Josephus's prophecy, both of which predict Vespasian's ascension.[65] Suetonius also claims astrologers gave Nero conflicting predictions of his ultimate fate: some prophesied that Nero would lose the throne,

57. Petronius, *Poems* 97.
58. Pliny the Elder, *Nat.* 31.44.95.
59. Seneca, *Ep.* 95.47.
60. Persius, *Sat.* 5.176–184. See also Stern's comment (Stern, *GLAJJ*, 2:436).
61. Juvenal, *Sat.* 14.96–106.
62. Schäfer, *Judeaophobia*, 192–94.
63. Suetonius, *Tib.* 36.
64. Suetonius, *Vesp.* 4.5.
65. Suetonius, *Vesp.* 5.6.

others that he would be king in Jerusalem.[66] Suetonius categorizes Jews as similar to astrologers on account of their prophecies, though Jews are granted greater credibility but not a corresponding amount of trust. Part of the basis for categorizing Jews negatively probably comes from Egyptian Jewish integrationist literature claiming Jewish contributions to practices Romans later regarded as illegitimate. Overall, this reflects a sentiment that the East, including Judea, was a land of exoticism and supernatural events, or at least this reputation granted him poetic license.

Indolent

Romans also expressed suspicion of Judaism by categorizing Jews as an indolent or unwanted presence, contrary to claimed Roman self-categorizations of being hard-working or tough,[67] and in part probably derived from the low socio-economic status of the group as a whole.[68] They reinforced these ideas categorizing Jews as practitioners of dubious occupations, association with Egyptians, and distortion of biblical claims or statements by Jewish writers such as Eupolemus. For instance, Pliny the Elder describes Moses, being the supposed progenitor of an eastern people, as the founder of a magical order.[69] Similarly, Juvenal stereotypes Jews as seeing special meaning in dreams,[70] which categorizes Jews as participants in the lower-class occupation of magic.[71] Pliny depicts the Essenes as a destitute and isolated sect consisting entirely of men who are "tired of life" and "regretful of life,"[72] while Cicero accuses Gabinus of favoring mere slaves (Jews and Syrians) over tax collectors.[73] Much in the same way Philo characterizes Egyptians, Horace characterizes Jews (or Jewish sympathizers) as members of the

---

66. Suetonius, *Nero* 40.2. There were also rumors that Nero did not die but would return with Parthian armies to take power. Collins, *Combat Myth*, 174–75.
67. Barclay, *Against Apion*, 366–67.
68. Sevenster, *Roots of Pagan Anti-Semitism*, 81–82.
69. Pliny the Elder, *Nat.* 30.2.11.
70. Juvenal, *Sat.* 6.542–47.
71. Aune, "Magic in Early Christianity," 1521.
72. Pliny the Elder, *Nat.* 5.15.73.
73. Cicero, *De Provinciis Consularibus* 5.10.

unruly mobs of Rome.[74] Cicero also portrays Jews in similar light[75] and describes them as an influential political force in his speech defending Lucius Valerius Flaccus.[76] Cicero also labels his enemy, Julius Caesar, a "Jerusalemite plebeian-monger" (*Hierosolymarius traductor ad plebem*) on account of his Jewish support,[77] and Jews themselves an unruly mob "hot with passion" (*multitudinem Iudaeorum flagrantem*).[78]

Tacitus also regarded Jews as indolent. Tacitus acknowledges Jews posses the respected attribute of antiquity, but again he interprets this as a sign of depravity.[79] While in *Hist.* 5.4 Tacitus attributes Sabbath observance to the god Saturn, it being the seventh and loftiest planet, Tacitus also depicts the Sabbath as fostering laziness, with Jewish food practices reflecting indolence because Jewish refugees were forced to go without food for long periods. Further, since pigs were considered prone to leprosy, Jews, stereotyped as still traumatized by their expulsion from Egypt due to skin diseases, are construed as abstaining from pork for this reason (*Hist.* 5.4). The Sabbath therefore reflects Jewish origins as refugees. Meanwhile, Tacitus categorized Jews as violators of the in-group because in his perception they were "superstitious" and because large numbers were members of the lower social classes. In the latter case the lower classes were not suspect because they were Jewish, but because they were lower-class.

Militaristic

Jews were categorized as militaristic due to conflicts with Rome, continued perceptions of Jewish misanthropy, practices such as endogamy, and dietary laws. Following the revolt of 66–73 CE, Palestinian Jews are sometimes described as fierce militarists and irrationally violent in

---

74. Horace, *Sat.* 1.9.70–73.

75. In Cicero, *Flac.* 66–67.

76. Flaccus was a former governor in Asia Minor whom Cicero defended against charges of embezzlement and misgovernment, which Wardy suggests may have been politically motivated (Cicero, *Flac.* 66–69; Wardy, "Jewish Religion in Pagan Literature," 598–99).

77. Cicero, *Att.* 2.9.1.

78. Cicero, *Flac.* 67.

79. Tacitus, *Hist.* 5.5.

battle.[80] Diodorus claimed Jews were racist and ethnocentric, which according to him were the rationale for Antiochus IV's program of forced assimilation to Hellenistic culture.[81] Juvenal implies a similar thing when he accuses Jewish converts of being willing to participate in cannibalism.[82]

The most outspoken allegations of Jewish militarism and misanthropy are found in Tacitus. He claims circumcision marks inclusion in the Jewish people to the exclusion of other ethnicities as part of socializing people in an ethic of hatred for other groups.[83] He also claims sacrificial animals are so chosen by Moses in order to be an affront to the Egyptian cults of Hammon and Apis (*Hist.* 5.4), indicating an aggressive posture at the very foundation of Jewish religion and lifestyle. Positive religious practices such as the temple collection or Jews practicing charity are misconstrued as part of a conspiracy theory to increase their wealth and numbers.[84] Meanwhile, Tacitus claims that Jews forbid infanticide to increase their troop numbers, that an afterlife is posited to encourage bravery in battle, the Sabbath is presented as a celebration of military victory in the conquest of Palestine, and that eating unleavened bread at Passover commemorates grain-theft during the Exodus.[85] Overall, Tacitus attempts to categorize Jews as militaristic and disorderly refugees, and attributes them a status consonant with the origins of some in Rome as war captives or slaves. The above categorizations are in response to strong Jewish nationalism at the time and the fact that, by 70 CE, Rome had conquered Judea three times under Pompey, Sosius, and Titus. While to moderns this suggests thrice-manifested Roman aggression, to Romans this implied resistance, insubordination, and a disregard for the *Pax Romana*. The irony should not be lost that elite members of the most militarily powerful and imperialistic society at that time categorized Jews as militarists.

80. Pliny the Elder, *Nat.* 12.54.112–13; Silius Italicus, *Punica* 3.605–606.
81. Diodorus, *Bib. hist.* 35.1.5.
82. Juvenal, *Sat.* 14.96–106.
83. Tacitus, *Hist.* 5.5. But compare Philo, *Virtues* 102, also 103, 181–182 (Borgen, *Early Christianity*, 57).
84. Tacitus, *Hist.* 5.5.
85. Tacitus, *Hist.* 5.3–5.

Social Identity among Jews in First-Century Rome

Foreigners

Roman literature consistently categorizes Jews as foreign. Positively, this could ascribe to Jews and Judaism a sense of exoticism, and possibly a mystique; negatively, this was accompanied by latent assertions of Roman cultural superiority and suspicion of Jewish beliefs and influence. Both probably enabled Judaism, on the one hand, to become influential among Romans while, on the other hand, also preventing many in the Roman Jewish community from integrating with the population. In SIT and SCT terms, Roman writers from the period in question typically categorized Jews as out-group members who surreptitiously violated the in-group, conceived of as a "pure" Rome, and undermined its norms and social cohesion.[86]

Diodorus underscores the categorization of Jews as a foreign and eastern people when he labels people from Nabatea "barbarians" (βάρβαροι), something which would apply to Jews from neighboring Judea.[87] Petronius perhaps reinforces this description in his account of a Jewish slave with a strange accent.[88] In terms of the Roman perspective on their relative differences from these groups, Jewish dietary restrictions saw Jews categorized alongside Egyptians, Libyans, Syrians, and Thracians,[89] and none of these groups were considered to hold values congenial to Roman culture. For example, while Varro was sympathetic to Jewish theological views about God, he nonetheless held Jews to be out-group members, in this case "Chaldaeans," and considered YHWH to be part of the Chaldaean pantheon.[90] The tradition that Jews originated as refugees from Egypt further associated them with others from their region, separating them from Romans as violators of the in-group.

Some categorizations of Jews as out-group members and foreigners are positive. In Suetonius Jews are listed as the exemplars of "foreigners" who mourn Julius Caesar as loyal clients.[91] In the *Chrestus* passage (*Claud.* 25.4) no further explanation is provided when Jews are expelled

---

86. Haslam, *Psychology in Organizations*, 225.
87. Diodorus, *Bib. hist.* 2.48.7; also 19.99.3.
88. Petronius, *Satyricon* 68.5.
89. Sextus Empiricus, *Pyr.* 3.222–23.
90. Lydus, *De Mensibus* 4.53.
91. Suetonius, *Jul.* 84.5.

for creating disturbances. If Jews were commonly characterized as part of the "mob," and foreign at that, perhaps Suetonius felt no further explanation was necessary if Jews were also known to be violators of the in-group. Tiberius's legal reforms aimed at improving the moral fabric of Rome involved expelling Jews along with other "foreign cults" (*externas caerimonias*), probably because they were considered troublesome foreigners similar to Egyptians.[92] Josephus attempts to place the emphasis on the Egyptian factor in his account (*Ant.* 18.79), but Suetonius only makes passing mention of the Egyptians.[93] Suetonius and Josephus disagree on who was treated better, though in Suetonius it is enough for astrologers to simply renounce their profession to remain in Rome while the punishment for the Jewish men involves military conscription.[94] The important point is Suetonius thinks Jews threatened Roman cohesion and identity.

Meanwhile, it appears Jews socially integrated into various professions and may have been able to blend into the population, though the available evidence indicates a distinctly Jewish identity often persisted. The Jewish Rhodesian grammarian Diogenes was apparently of sufficient stature to allegedly brush off Tiberius (*Tib.* 32.2). Whether or not this account is true, Diogenes's identity as both grammarian and Jew were sufficiently well-known to make the story convincing enough for it to be included in Suetonius's writings. After the war, there were incidents of public inspection of males to see if they were circumcised (*Dom.* 12.2), suggesting appearances, observable lifestyles, and personal names were not always enough to determine Jewish identity. Jews were able to simultaneously integrate into the society while also remaining distinct, but these continued distinctions were enough to have Jews categorized as violating the in-group at Rome.

A Subjugated Nation

The most important categorization of Jews, as far as many Roman writers were concerned, was that they were a subjugated people. Romans

---

92. Williams, *Jews in a Graeco-Roman Environment*, 63–80 (esp. 77–79); Rochette, "Juifs et Romains," 27–30.

93. Suetonius, *Tib.* 36.

94. Williams, *Jews in a Graeco-Roman Environment*, 67.

did not ascribe a high degree of esteem to ethnic groups that were included in their empire, and much is made of Jewish resistance and defeat being coterminous with the weakness of their god.[95] It therefore seemed preposterous to some Roman writers that Jews would persist in their religion and ethnic identity.[96] Diodorus labels Judea, having local autonomy in the Hasmonean period, a subjugated Roman vassal state.[97] Augustine reports Seneca's chagrin that Jews positively influenced elements of Roman society with their religion but deemed this unacceptable because of their status as a conquered people.[98] Likewise Pliny labels Jews as vicious fighters to underline Roman superiority in light of their victory and imposition of the *fiscus Iudaicus*.[99] Cicero argues defeat by the Romans humiliates Jews and their religion, and asserts it was the will of the gods that Jews be conquered, enslaved, and taxed.[100] Tacitus also stereotypes Jews as worthy of being conquered and subjugated in describing Antiochus IV's attempt at forced Hellenization, but credits the success of the Maccabean revolt to distractions caused by the Parthians.[101] In Tacitus's eyes, Jews were opportunistic militarists whose destiny it was to be dominated and kept under control.

Social Processes

The writings of Cicero evidence strong negative social categorizations of Jews.[102] The patterns of memory distortion and innovation are obvi-

---

95. Wardy, "Jewish Religion in Pagan Literature," 604.
96. Wardy, "Jewish Religion in Pagan Literature," 625.
97. Diodorus, *Bib. hist.* 40.2.
98. Augustine, *Civ.* 6.11.
99. Pliny the Elder, *Nat.* 12.54.112–113.
100. Cicero, *Flac.* 69.
101. Tacitus, *Hist.* 5.8.

102. Cicero disparages many different groups and ethnicities that were subject to his client's governance in Asia Minor in an attempt to claim that political motives lay behind his client being falsely accused of corruption. Wardy maintains accusations of Cicero being anti-Jewish may be unfair (Wardy, "Jewish Religion in Pagan Literature," 597–99; 609) and Stern notes that, despite his association with Apollonius Molon, Cicero did not make use of typical Hellenistic anti-Jewish traditions (Stern, *GLAJJ*, 193). However, it is apparent that charges of anti-Jewishness are in fact accurate, though this should not be considered remarkable given Cicero's views of mysticism (in agreement with Schäfer, *Judeophobia*, 280n15).

ous: he is a politically active member of the ruling class whose political adversary was Julius Caesar. In his turn, Julius Caesar was favored by Jews due to his opposition to Pompey, who had conquered Jerusalem and profaned the temple during the Roman Civil war. Cicero's letter to Atticus betrays personal views of Jews as low-status rabble, and Cicero then uses this as grounds to denigrate Julius Caesar (rather than using Caesar to denigrate Jews). In his defence of Flaccus, Cicero is at times simply doing his duty, but to achieve his goals he must assert the superiority of the Roman in-group by using points that would be salient and shared with his audience, which would involve negative portrayal of conquered peoples.

There is some distortion in the presentation of Jews found in Suetonius. Though he does not say Jews are astrologers, their religion is a *superstitio* like those of Egyptians or astrologers. It is assumed, rather than made explicit, that Jewish beliefs and practices were a threat to Rome. Jewish foreignness and supposed indolence position them as in-group violators, yet this did not stop Rome from conscripting Jews into the Roman military. In Suetonius, Jews attempted to evade the *fiscus Judaicus* but also demonstrate in-group behavior by acting as loyal clients of Julius Caesar in their mourning his death. Jews rebel against the empire (out-group behavior), but Josephus, a Jew, predicts Vespasian's ascent to emperor (again demonstrating in-group behavior). In Suetonius's presentation Jews are an ancient, exotic, but at times troublesome people who were preoccupied with their own customs but were not necessarily always anti-Roman in their collective disposition.

Peter Schäfer correctly describes Tacitus as harboring a dislike of Jews (and non-Romans in general)[103] and as probably Judaism's most outspoken Roman critic.[104] Writing in the aftermath of the revolt of 66–73 CE, he interprets Judaism through the lens of being "on the wrong side" of the war. Yet Menahem Stern observes Tacitus does not hold Jews morally responsible for the war, and Tacitus sometimes hints that Roman mismanagement was partially to blame.[105] This suggests Tacitus was proud of the traditions and values that characterized his

---

103. Stern, *GLAJJ*, 2:5.
104. Schäfer, *Judeophobia*, 193.
105. Tacitus, *Ann.* 12.54; cited in Stern, *GLAJJ*, 2:3.

in-group, but he did not necessarily have high regard for Roman imperial governance. Ethnocentrism, cynicism, and general in-group bias are reflected in Tacitus's descriptions of the social location of Roman Jews. His regard for Judaism as a *superstitio* rather than a *religio* frames Judaism as antithetical to Roman values, and Tacitus engages in depersonalization of the other and maximizes relative difference between Jews and Romans to secure Roman identity.[106] In elite Roman conceptions, Greeks were most like Romans while Jews, Egyptians, Chaldeans, and Phoenicians were most dissimilar to Romans but similar to one another. The conclusion to draw from Tacitus's persistent polemic is that, ironically, many Romans were probably either ambivalent or favorably disposed to Jews.[107] For this to be possible, people other than Tacitus probably saw the relative differences between Jews and Romans as minimal or simply not salient. Likewise, relatively strong attempts at social integration must have existed for them to build common ground with the Roman in-group.[108]

CATEGORIZATIONS OF JEWS IN JOSEPHUS'S *AGAINST APION*

Given the self-contradictory information in Tacitus or the shallow stereotypes of Juvenal, it is easy to discern the motives behind Josephus's *Against Apion*. Composed after 94 CE for a Roman readership,[109] *Against Apion* may reflect the concerns underlying Josephus's apologetic program. In *Ag. Ap.* 1.2 Josephus complains his 20 volume *Antiquities* project was unsuccessful and necessitated more direct rebuttals, though *Against Apion* employs similar materials, arguments, apologetic strategies,[110] and social categorizations.[111] Josephus is also the sole source that preserves the polemics of Egyptian writers such

---

106. Hogg and Williams, "From *I* to *We*," 88.

107. Schäfer, *Judeophobia*, 192–94; Feldman, *Jew and Gentile*, 177–231.

108. Note, for instance, Aristius Fuscus' comments in Horace, *Sat.* 1.9.60–78.

109. Barclay, *Against Apion*, XXVI, 369; Feldman, "Pro-Jewish Intimations in Anti-Jewish Remarks," 195–96.

110. Spilsbury, "*Contra Apionem* and *Antiquitates Judaicae*," 348–68; also Barclay, *Against Apion*, XXIII.

111. Spilsbury, *Image of the Jew*, esp. 92–93; 217–27.

as Manetho (1.227–287) and Apion (2.1–144). Apion was a well-known Greco-Egyptian scholar who was very critical of Alexandrian Jews,[112] and served as leader of the Alexandrian delegation to Rome that opposed the Jewish one led by Philo. The survey of categorizations suggests a brief analysis of *Against Apion* and its presentation of Jewish social categorizations is appropriate here,[113] as it was written to confront a broader anti-Jewish tradition merely represented by Apion.[114] Its composition also suggests that the ethnic-social conflicts in Alexandria were a very significant problem for many Jews in other parts of the western diaspora, perhaps more serious on a day-to-day level in its consequences than even the revolt of 66–73 CE. Though the subject matter Josephus deals with has Greco-Egyptian origins, Josephus tailors his responses to socially align Jews with the Roman in-group as represented by the elite. Making no claims to provide a definitive list, Barclay notes six major Roman values reflected in *Against Apion* that Josephus argues are shared by Jews and Romans.[115] These are:

(1) admiration for endurance[116]

(2) contempt for death

(3) frugality

(4) agricultural background

---

112. In *Ag. Ap.* 2.28. Barclay, "Josephus v. Apion: Analysis of an Argument," 201. Apion is profiled elsewhere as being a verbose but respectable scholar and grammarian, though somewhat vain and opinionated (Barclay, "Josephus v. Apion: Analysis of an Argument," 200. See also Aulus Gellius, *Noct. att.* 5.14.1–4; Pliny, *Nat.* preface 25).

113. Bilde, *Flavius Josephus between Jerusalem and Rome*, 121.

114. The third and fourth-century so-called *Acts of the Alexandrian Martyrs* indicates that the pogrom against the Jews would be remembered as a heroic struggle by some Alexandrians. They lionize Isidoros, one of Flaccus' anti-Jewish associates against whom Philo directs his invective (e.g., *Flaccus* 135; *CPJ* 154–59). They also seem to portray Isodoros as consistently outwitting emperors and Herod Agrippa in a comedic manner (*CPJ* 156b, 156d; also *Flaccus* 36–38), suggesting that many Alexandrians did not approve of Claudius' resolution of the issue in *CPJ* 153.

115. Barclay, *Against Apion*, 369. Niehoff notes a similar apologetic strategy in Philo (Niehoff, *Philo on Jewish Identity and Culture*). See above.

116. What Barclay terms "admiration of Spartan toughness" (Barclay, *Against Apion*, 366).

(5) family morality

(6) strict (but just) punishment.[117]

If a reader were successfully persuaded that these claims were salient, these values could be used to reduce the relative difference between Jew and Roman to allow for social convergence. However, Josephus also provides direct rebuttals to many of the ideas surveyed above, using many arguments and social categorizations similar to those found in Philo or in *Antiquities*.

Social Categorizations

Antiquity/Common Progenitor

The first two-thirds of book 1 of *Against Apion* are devoted to proving Judaism's antiquity,[118] because ancient traditions were respected while innovative new systems were thought to lack legitimacy. Further, Manetho and Apion's claims that Jews originated as a group of diseased Egyptian refugees separated Jewish origins from the Patriarchal period that preceded settlement in Egypt (*Ag. Ap.* 1.227–2.144). Josephus therefore finds it necessary to prove the distinctive and ancient origins of Jews.[119]

When age is the salient factor Josephus categorizes Jews as similar to Egyptians, Phoenicians, and Chaldeans due to their originating in the same geographic region. He also preserves the ancient authority of Jewish Scriptures by comparing it to other ancient records while asserting the superiority of their accuracy over Greek histories (*Ag. Ap.* 1.7–10, 28–29, 42).[120] According to Josephus, Greek society was predisposed to instability and turmoil, and Greeks lagged behind Jews and Phoenicians in the employment of writing, with their early history being unreliable because it relied upon oral traditions that pre-dated their written records.

---

117. For fuller discussion see Barclay, *Against Apion*, 362–69.

118. Barclay, *Against Apion*, 4.

119. *Ag. Ap.* 1.1.

120. Although Barclay states this was more an unverified cultural assumption that Josephus exploited (Barclay, *Against Apion*, 23).

Though Jewish origins in Ur are defended by Josephus (*Ag. Ap.* 1.71), Abraham is not discussed in *Against Apion*.[121] Instead, Moses stands in as the founder of the Jewish people so Josephus can defend him from the deprecatory descriptions found in anti-Jewish writings.[122] The reasons for Abraham's omission are not stated, but the residence of the patriarchs in Egypt as refugees from famine was likely considered embarrassing because Josephus glosses it over in *Ag. Ap.* 1.92. Instead, Josephus emphasizes Moses' identity as a wise ruler, law-maker, and philosopher so that he can portray Jews as socialized in these characteristics through Moses' wisely-crafted laws, piety, and prescribed lifestyle. Josephus lauds Moses as the most ancient, thorough, and divinely-led legislator who lived a life of virtue and crafted a highly philosophical lifestyle imparted via a religious system that doubled as an education system (*Ag. Ap.* 2.156–60, 173, 181).[123] Of course, the depiction of Moses as the Jewish "legislator" (νομοθέτης) functions to promote Jewish dignity through defense of its laws and lifestyle.

Philosophical

Josephus categorizes Jews as intellectually sophisticated to demonstrate they are not unstable, superstitious, irrational, or immoral. Josephus presents Jewish prototypicality as distinctively concerned for piety, ethics, education, and philosophical reflection. Exploiting the positive connotations of εὐσέβεια (piety), he presents Judaism as the superlative expression of this attribute, under which all other virtues are catalogued. For Josephus, Moses created a unique theocratic "constitution"

---

121. Josephus' description of Abraham in *Antiquities* has affinities with that of Philo (*Ant.* 1.154–55), though unlike in Philo, Josephus' Abraham arrived at monotheism through noting inconsistencies in astronomy and astrology and left Ur due to persecution for his beliefs (*Ant.* 1.156–57).

122. *Ag. Ap.* 1.250–253; 265; 279; 290; 309.

123. Rajak notes that Josephus provides two lists of virtues. In *Ag. Ap.* 2.146 it is "piety" (εὐσέβεια), "fellowship" (κοινωνία), "universal goodwill" (τὴν καθόλουφιλανθρωπίαν), as well as justice, supreme perseverance, and contempt for death. Elsewhere, εὐσέβεια (piety) is equivalent to ἀρετής (virtue), and additionally includes "temperance" (σωφροσύνη), perseverance (in place of courage), "harmony" (συμφωνία), and "wisdom" (φρόνησις). Rajak, "Against Apion," 231–32.

and lifestyle that embodies worship, which expresses itself through virtue and a philosophical lifestyle.

The greatest of Greek philosophers are portrayed as in agreement with, or unwitting adherents, of Judaism (*Ag. Ap.* 2.255; 281). Labelling Judaism and its books a philosophy (*Ag. Ap.* 1.54), none other than Aristotle explains Jewish relative obscurity by connecting Jewish origins to Indian mystics.[124] Likeiwse, borrowing from the Aristeas legend, Josephus depicts Ptolemy Philadelphus as curious about Judaism as a philosophy (*Ag. Ap.* 2.47). Philosophical sophistication is further emphasized in Moses teaching that God is judge, which stresses the need for personal ethics (*Ag. Ap.* 2.160).

Likewise, Josephus also uses Plato to defend Jewish monotheism (*Ag. Ap.* 2.168). While he criticizes Plato's political philosophy as amateurish compared to the Torah (2.223–224), Josephus finds agreement between Plato and Moses on the need maintain ethnic homogeneity for a society to know its laws well.[125] He uses citizenship language to create a point of salience that defends his categorization of his people as participants,[126] but also creates grounds for depicting Jews as philosophical. Josephus claims Jews collectively show that "the Law is the most virtuous and most indispensable instruction" (κάλλιστον καὶ ἀναγκαιότατον . . . παίδευμα τὸν νόμον).[127] He claims the education of all Jews in the Law is the paragon of piety and virtue (2.176–178, 291, 293, 204). Josephus argues this focus on religious education demonstrates Jews are not superstitious, and better situates them in the categorizations of well-educated, law-abiding, and moral participants.

Meanwhile, this argument from education is validated by his assertion that Greek philosophers had similar but less-developed ideas

---

124. *Ag. Ap.* 1.176–181. Barclay is suspicious of Josephus' veracity in recounting this episode (*Apion*, 103).

125. *Ag. Ap.* 2.257: μεμίμηται τὸν ἡμέτερον νομοθέτην (he imitated our legislator). See Barclay, *Against Apion*, 315, citing *Prot.* 326c; *Leg.* 10.810e–811e; 12.949e–953e. Barclay suggests that Josephus assumes Plato's use of Moses on account of the latter pre-dating the former.

126. *Ant.* 14.188; *Ag. Ap.* 2.38–42, 61–67; Barclay, *Jews in the Mediterranean Diaspora*, 70. Barclay is unsure if this is willful or due to ignorance, but I would suggest it is intentional given Josephus' broader program.

127. *Ag. Ap.* 2.175. Translation mine.

about God (2.168–169). For example, Josephus claims Pythagoras was pious to the God of the Jews and zealous for Jewish laws and customs (*Ag. Ap.* 1.162–165). He even claims obedience to Greek customs by Greek philosophers was really adherence to the Mosaic Law (2.281). Similarly, he claims Hermippus reports that Pythagoras says that unnamed Greek cities adopted Jewish customs (1.164–166). He also asserts it is Greeks who are superstitious when, according to his account from the Greek historian Hecataeus, a Jewish soldier serving under Alexander the Great who violates these Greek superstitions by killing an omen-granting bird to establish warrant for monotheism, therefore presenting all Jews as philosophically astute (1.200–204).[128]

Faithful to Ancestral Customs and Zealous

Religious beliefs and practices were understood as markers of Jewish ethnicity, so to defend the part was to defend the whole. Concurrent with categorizations of piety and philosophical sophistication is defense of authoritative scriptural laws and ancestral customs. Josephus therefore defends the Law from charges of being a *superstitio* or δεισιδαιμονία (superstition).[129] Likely drawing on zeal cultural traditions, Josephus states Jews are so educated in their laws and customs they would rather die than disobey them to demonstrate their strength of conviction, endurance, and bravery as prototypical of Jews.[130]

In a paraphrase of pseudo-Hecataeus, Josephus states that Jewish bravery reinforces the education in ancestral customs that make them philosophical. A positive attribute of Jews is that they are a highly conservative people who only assimilate innovations if they cohere with their pre-existing traditions from antiquity (*Ag. Ap.* 2.182–183). Since Josephus does not deal with the issue of circumcision and only refutes Apion's etymology of the Sabbath (2.27), it seems Josephus is focusing on broader intellectual and cultural matters that would have salience for gentile members of his audience. Josephus employs a degree of relativism in his defense of the Jewish lifestyle, culture, and beliefs,[131]

---

128. Barclay, *Against Apion*, 115–17.
129. Schäfer, *Judeophobia*, 188.
130. *Ag. Ap.* 1.42–43; 1.191–192; 2.218–219.
131. Consisting of "laws" or "legislation" (usually νομοθεσία and cognates),

Social Identity among Jews in First-Century Rome

pointing to similar misconceptions about Gauls and Spaniards (*Ag. Ap.* 1.67), and since each culture is unique, Judaism is simply the best of many unique belief systems (2.164; 278).

Participants

In chapter 3, we examined a series of Roman documents pertaining to Jewish rights that Josephus portrayed as evidence of Jewish-Roman friendship. In *Against Apion* Josephus attempts to achieve similar aims through positive description of the Romans.[132] A second strategy employed is his describing Jews as historically reliable allies of Rome against Egypt which, as in Philo, functions to reduce relative difference and facilitate social convergence. Josephus categorizes Jews as loyal participants under their imperial rulers on account of anti-Egyptian actions taken, as in when they provided military assistance to Cleopatra against Physco and the Egyptian mob (2.49–52) and when Jews helped to conquer and garrison Egypt under the Ptolemies (2.44, 49). Further, during the Roman civil war Jewish troops assisted Caesar when he was trapped in Alexandria (2.56–61).[133] Josephus therefore portrays Rome and Judea as aligned against Egypt.

Jews also demonstrate their loyal participant categorization through rendering honors to the Roman emperor. While Jews do not worship the emperor, Josephus claims Jewish loyalty is sincerely demonstrated (2.63; 75–76). He claims it is not extraordinary or distressing that Judea was dominated by Rome—he notes most nations are eventually conquered by the Romans, though Judea remained independent longer because of their alliance with Rome (2.134). In sum, Josephus asserts that Jews remain willing and loyal participants in the Roman Empire.

Pious (and Virtuous)

Josephus attempts to counter the belief that Jews were indolent members of the impressionable, superstitious masses, by stating that Jewish

---

customs (usually, ἐθῶν) and ancestral customs (τὰ πάτρια, with various descriptors).

132. Barclay, *Against Apion*, 363.
133. Barclay, *Against Apion*, 203.

conservativism in their unique belief system is an expression of "prudence and virtue" (φρόνησιν καὶ ἀρετὴν) that is "abounding wisdom" (μάλιστα σοφίας), which grants the Mosaic Law credibility.[134] Using his related arguments about Jewish education above, Josephus categorizes Jews as highly disciplined individuals rather than ill-disciplined members of the masses. In Josephus, Jewish piety and virtue are the natural results of monotheism—something that can be arrived at apart from the Law of Moses as with Pythagoras or Plato. As Josephus would have it, anyone who embraced monotheism and virtue was on the path to becoming like a Jew, because his conception of a prototypical Jew is ultimately a pious and ethical human being, which can also be found among other peoples such as Romans and Greeks, but of which Jews were the exemplars.

Social Processes

Josephus seeks to defend Jewish dignity grounded in its antiquity while reducing relative difference to enable social convergence with Roman readers. When antiquity and record-keeping are salient, Josephus portrays Jews as similar to Egyptians, Chaldeans, and Phoenicians, but when cultural sophistication is salient Josephus contrasts these groups with Jews. Likewise, Josephus appeals to Greek philosophy when the intellectual respectability of Jewish monotheism and ethics are salient, but openly criticizes Greek historians as neophites when antiquity is salient. Josephus usually avoids directly criticizing Romans, although some of his criticisms of Greek culture would apply to them as well.[135] Josephus maximizes relative difference between Jews and groups disliked by Romans and Greeks, such as Egyptians and Chaldeans, to create salient shared categories with Romans. While writers such as Apion culturally identified as Greeks, slandering Apion as racially Egyptian is a useful rhetorical tool for Josephus to advance his goals of social convergence with Romans.[136] While Jewish-Israelite culture was heav-

---

134. *Ag. Ap.* 2.184–186.

135. Barclay, *Against Apion*, 363.

136. For fuller treatment, see Barclay, "Judeans and Egyptians," 109–27. For similar discussion of treatment of Egyptians by Jewish authors see Beavis, "Anti-Egyptian Polemic," 130–65; Niehoff, *Philo on Jewish Identity*, 45–74.

ily influenced by Mesopotamian and Egyptian politics and culture, Josephus increases relative difference by underlining regional rivalries while preserving antiquity as a salient category.

In terms of memory innovation, Josephus plays Greeks and Romans against Egyptians while aligning Jews with those in power. In *Against Apion* Josephus does not focus on external markers of Jewish identity such as circumcision, Sabbath, or purity practices, but does make open reference when necessary. Instead, he prefers to focus on more abstract salient points that cater to his audience's preferences. Another area of innovation in Jewish cultural memory and biblical tradition is evident in Josephus's claims that groups resent the Jewish people out of envy for their greatness. While the intent of a Eupolemus or an Artapanus was probably to help integrate Jews into the ethnic and political structures of Ptolemaic Egypt, Josephus's writings make these kinds of statements in the hopes of prompting Roman acceptance of Jews at the expense of Egyptians. In Ptolemaic Egypt Jews served on the side of the conquerors, while in the time of Josephus his people were among the conquered and subjugated, making it necessary to mitigate Roman prejudice and perceived cultural superiority.

Distortion and innovation are also evident in Josephus's reliance upon pre-war evidence to underscore Jewish-Roman allegiance and similarity as it ignores recent conflicts. While his goal is to mitigate the negative social consequences, Josephus prefers to emphasize prior history to establish a history of Jewish loyalty to Rome. In so doing he ignores obvious motivators, such as self-interest in the Hasmonean allegiance to Rome as a counterbalance to the Seleucids, or Jewish assistance of Julius Caesar as a form of retribution against Pompey.[137] Josephus repackages these as expressions of altruistic affinity between Romans and Jews.

CATEGORIZATIONS OF JEWS DERIVED FROM OTHER EVIDENCE

A significant minority of the Roman Jewish community were probably the descendants of slaves brought to Rome by Pompey and Sosius.[138]

137. Leon, *Jews of Ancient Rome*, 9.
138. Williams, *Jews in a Graeco-Roman Environment*, 49; Rutgers, "Roman

Others probably migrated to Rome of their own accord.[139] In 19 CE the Jewish community was expelled from the city for uncertain reasons. Josephus unconvincingly claims it was in response to the actions of four Jewish con men.[140] Dio Cassius maintains the expulsion was in response to Jews winning too many proselytes,[141] while Tacitus claims too many Jews were migrating to Rome. Given the diversity of opinion, and Tacitus's anti-Jewish bias, these explanations may simply reflect their writers's opinions.[142] Josephus and Suetonius agree that Egyptian religions were somehow involved, and that a large number of Jewish men were conscripted for garrison duty in Sardinia.[143] Gruen and Williams suggest there may not have been a tangible reason for the expulsion: Jews were scapegoats punished for political expediency,[144] while Bruno Rochette argues that for ethnocentric Romans it was a gesture towards cultural preservation.[145] Given the categorizations of Jews as indolent in Latin authors above, an expulsion of astrologers and "Chaldaeans" in 139 BCE,[146] and persecutions under Domitian, this is not likely. However, the Domitian episode confirms that Judaism fascinated some from among the Roman elite, and Agrippa and the Herods were well-acquainted with ruling Roman families.[147]

Jewish naming conventions of Roman synagogues may shed additional light on social aspirations of the Roman Jewish community. By means of their names some synagogues identify with distinctly Jewish elements of their cultural memory. There were probably two synagogues named after Jewish monarchs: a "synagogue of the Herodians" and a "synagogue of the Agrippians,"[148] both of whom were probably

Policy towards the Jews," 96.

139. Rutgers, "Roman Policy towards the Jews," 97.

140. Leon, *Jews of Ancient Rome*, 17; *Ant.* 18.65–84.

141. Dio Cassius, *Rom. hist.* 57.18.5a; Rutgers, "Roman Policy towards the Jews," 100; Levinskaya, *Acts in its Diaspora Setting*, 30.

142. Rutgers, "Roman Policy towards the Jews," 99.

143. Suetonius, *Tib.* 36.

144. Williams, *Jews in a Graeco-Roman Environment*, 9; Gruen, *Diaspora*, 52–53.

145. Rochette, "Juifs et Romains," 29–30.

146. Leon, *Jews of Ancient Rome*, 3.

147. Leon, *Jews of Ancient Rome*, 13–22.

148. Richardson, "Augustan-Era Synagogues in Rome," 21–24.

pro-Roman and indicate that vestiges of national independence were important to these communities. There were also synagogues named after Roman figures such as "the synagogue of the Augustesians," Augustus being remembered as a generous Jewish patron. There was also a "synagogue of the Volumnians," possibly named after a Roman general who furthered Jewish interests in a war fought for other purposes.[149] The "synagogue of the Hebrews" was likely the original synagogue and not a group of Jewish isolationists in Rome; other synagogues were named after the Romans neighborhoods or cities where members may have originated.[150] These synagogue names may indicate confidence in Jewish heritage, a desire to remember important Roman figures, as well as identification with local neighborhoods where the synagogue was located. Synagogues named after other cities probably indicate identification with those locales as well. Roman Jews appear to have accommodated themselves to the Roman context, and naming conventions do not indicate discomfort at being among Romans.

In his study of the Ostian synagogue, L. Michael White maintains that Jews held their identity and assimilation in "creative tension," as seen in the Greek dedication inscription that announces loyalty to the emperor.[151] For Ostia, White maintains that "[w]hat the Ostian evidence does reveal is the high degree of acculturation of Jews within the social life of these Italian cities, even as they worked to retain their Jewish cultural identity and religious traditions."[152] White suggests that there was probably a range of acculturation to Rome among Jews.[153]

The Ostia synagogue possibly indicates a degree of wealth, at least on the part of the main citizen-patron behind the construction of a tomb for the Jewish community,[154] and a patron responsible

---

149. Richardson, "Augustan-Era Synagogues in Rome," 22. Leon (*Jews of Ancient Rome*, 158) notes Volumnius is a very common name and may not refer to the general from *Ant.* 16.277–283; 332; 344; 354.

150. Richardson, "Augustan-Era Synagogues in Rome," 20.

151. White, "Synagogue and Society in Imperial Ostia," 35. Citing *JIWE* 1, #13. I am not aware of any Egyptian synagogue inscriptions pledging allegiance to the Roman emperors.

152. White, "Synagogue and Society in Imperial Ostia," 67.

153. White, "Synagogue and Society in Imperial Ostia," 68.

154. *JIWE* 1, #18. The main patron mentioned in a second-century CE inscription

for the renovation of the synagogue proper appears to have been a freed-person.[155] Its location on the edge of town was not unusual and could be interpreted in various ways.[156] The Ostian and Roman Jewish communities's main language appears to have been Greek rather than Latin,[157] in Ostia possibly simply reflecting the economic importance of Greek as a trade language. In the catacombs of Rome, Latin names and titles dominate, but Greek names and titles also feature prominently in first- and second-century burial inscriptions. Since Greek served as a literary language at Rome its use or non-use is not in itself an accurate indicator of social position,[158] but the dominant use of single names again suggests Jews were of lower socio-economic status since freed-persons held two names and citizens possessed three.[159]

The significance of Latin (or Greek) language usage and Latin names is difficult to estimate. Graydon F. Snyder's study of Jewish symbols used in the catacombs indicates Roman Jews did not adopt many symbols from Roman culture, instead preferring to use Jewish ones.[160] Margaret Williams argues that until the revolt, Roman Jewish identity was conceived of ethnically and nationally, at least as evidenced by use of symbols such as the temple and monarchy. As elsewhere, the demise of the temple and the Jewish state gave rise to emphasis on the Law and synagogue.[161] Williams also postulates that the reason Latin writers understood the Sabbath as a fast day is because Pompey and Sosius both

---

is Gaius Julius Justus, who appears to have been a citizen.

155. *JIWE* 1, #13, a Mindius Faustus; Noy dates the inscription to the latter second century CE.

156. Fitzpatrick-McKinley, "Synagogue Communities," 62.

157. Richardson, "Augustan-Era Synagogues in Rome," 19; Leon, *Jews of Ancient Rome*, 75–92.

158. Due to cultural competition it was common for Romans elites to outwardly revile the Greek culture and language, all the while valuing education in Greek language, literature, and philosophy (Guite, "Cicero's Attitude to the Greeks," 142–59). This was less of an issue among other social classes, for whom the matter was not of much importance (Wedeck, "Roman Attitude toward Foreign Influence," 98).

159. Leon, *Jews of Ancient Rome*, 67; 93–121.

160. Snyder, "Interaction of Jews with non-Jews in Rome," 69–90.

161. Williams, *Jews in a Graeco-Roman Environment*, 33–48, citing the incident of a Hasmonean pretender who was enthusiastically received by Roman Jews in *Ant.* 17.324–38.

exploited the Sabbath to press their successful attacks on Jerusalem that resulted in the enslavement of many Jews brought to Rome and was commemorated accordingly.[162] Yet Williams also sees the use of titles in some funerary inscriptions as reflecting an aristocratic Roman mindset.[163]

The result is that many Roman Jews were probably well-acculturated to Rome but took care to mark themselves off as non-Roman. Many Roman Jews also seem to have continued to use Greek, again possibly reflecting a lack of integration in a Roman society that was traditional and at times xenophobic. Judaism had an allure for some Romans, but this was likely due to exoticism, difference, and the attraction of Jewish monotheism. Unlike the Letter of Aristeas or 3 Maccabees, there are no indications that Jews were visibly distinct in terms of clothing; Sabbath lamps were deemed a defining feature of Jewish residences. Sejanus engaged in discriminatory activities against Roman Jews, yet despite Philo's vitriol Gaius had little trouble politically justifying his actions. Violence did not break out in Rome as in Alexandria, but similar social tensions probably existed.

SUMMARY OF CHAPTERS 2 TO 4

We must try to ground our understanding of the identity of the Johannine Jews on the social identity of Jews in the ancient Mediterranean. Evidence applicable to social history is relatively sparse, but what literary and archaeological evidence does exist shows that when Jews lived outside of Palestine they were able to purse socially-integrationist strategies while maintaining a Jewish identity. To a certain degree this conclusion is largely common sense; economically and socially Diaspora Jews were not a world unto themselves. Jews would have required the services, employment, and protection of gentiles. Integration was an absolute necessity for an ethnic minority in ancient poly-ethnic environments, just as it is for immigrants today.

The situational nature of SIT and SCT present an interesting picture of Jewish identity at the turn of the era. Philo and Josephus pursue similar strategies to reduce the relative difference between Jew and

---

162. Williams, *Jews in a Graeco-Roman Environment*, 49–61.
163. Williams, *Jews in a Graeco-Roman Environment*, 46.

gentile. Josephus depicts Jews as loyal Roman allies; the Letter of Aristeas, Josephus and Philo appeal to the salience of universal values and philosophy to make Jews appear less alien. 3 Maccabees reminds its readers that not all Greeks are anti-Jewish and narrates the vindication of Egyptian Jews and reconciles them to king Philopator. 2 Maccabees interprets the success of the Maccabean revolt in such a way as to portray a picture of Jewish prototypicality that can survive in non-violent, non-confrontational conditions under foreign rulers in the Diaspora. The Letter of Aristeas, Philo, and 3 Maccabees present Egypt as home for their Jewish readers. These documents all use Greek and Roman values, not Jewish, as the standard of judgment, though Judaism was certainly the lens used by Jews to interpret their broader cultural contexts. Philo and Josephus cannot hide Jewish distinctiveness, but they facilitate social convergence by reducing relative difference, again suggesting desire for social, political, and economic acceptance.

Archaeological evidence largely corroborates this picture. Inscriptions from Ptolemaic Egypt indicate Jews identified with their local social environment, even in participating in travel customs at the temple of Pan. One Latin Jewish synagogue inscription in Egypt may indicate a discomfort shared with other local Greeks and Egpytians with the Roman presence. No published Jewish synagogue inscription in Egypt pledges allegiance to the Roman emperors, though one does so in the Roman port of Ostia in Italy, something corroborated by the naming choices of certain Roman synagogues. Roman Jews identified with Roman figures, while Egyptian Jews largely appear to have not. Despite what the archival materials in Josephus seem to suggest—long outdated by the time Josephus uses them—inscriptions and testimony from Acts seem to describe Jewish integration and identification with local gentile populations; Trebilco demonstrates this would become even more apparent in coming centuries.

Evidence from Alexandria indicates high levels of hostility to local Jews in the first century. *Acts of the Alexandrian Martyrs* suggests that it also occurred at the popular level, and not just among elite teachers like Apion, possibly a legacy of Ptolemaic employment of Jews as garrison troops and civil servants to control the local Egyptian population. Jews appear to have been influential in Mithridates' attack on Egypt (*Ant.*

14.127–136, esp. 131), but this Jewish support may have been more about anti-Pompey sentiment than anything pro-Roman, as other indicators suggest Jews took pride in Ptolemaic Egyptian identity. However, resentments would simmer until the pogroms under Flaccus and Gaius and the eventual genocides of the Kitos war.

In Rome, the Jewish community having developed from a nucleus of former prisoners and slaves from conquests of Judea, the literary evidence presently available suggests Jews were largely regarded as a foreign underclass. The actual socio-economic status of most Roman Jews appears to have reflected these origins, and the elite treated their customs and values accordingly. Meanwhile, wealthy Roman Jews appear to have adopted Roman names, the Latin language, and Roman ways of thinking. The Roman Jewish community, as a whole, appears to have been defined more strongly on the basis of ethnicity and religion—no doubt reinforced in part by the prejudices of the Roman ruling classes and the sheer size of the city. A similar dynamic was likely operative in Alexandria, but this was countered to a degree by traditions of Jewish participation established during the Ptolemaic period.

Asia Minor appears to have been the exception, where eventually Jews successfully integrated. This may be due to Asia Minor consisting of numerous smaller states with smaller cities that had less significant local identities than the grand cultural and imperial centers of Alexandria or Rome. Contrary to modern popular urban-versus-rural prejudgments concerning a lack of cultural sophistication in the Western world, what appears to have been the case is that locals in these less significant communities in Asia Minor were apparently more willing to accept Jews as members of their communities. Jews successfully became a part of these less urbanized societies in Asia Minor and Egypt, though this was later undermined in Alexandria. Roman evidence suggests attempts at integration and participation, but many Jews were kept at arm's length by Roman authorities or the upper classes. However, when we can hear Jewish voices we see they attempted to socially integrate and appealed to common values to present social identities that could be well-received by many non-Jews.

5

Diaspora Jewish Social Identity and John's Portrayal of Jesus

INTRODUCTION

IN THE PRECEDING CHAPTERS we explored Jewish cultural identity and social categories that were used in the Jewish Hellenistic diaspora. Jewish writers who composed accounts of Jew-gentile interaction were frequently open towards non-Jews in creating a social niche for Jews and Judaism in the broader culture. Jews categorized themselves to allow participation and integration, using social categories that reduced relative difference and fostered social convergence within the context of an extended in-group. The primary literature suggests Jews attempted to position themselves as the epitome of shared values on account of the Law's wisdom.[1] Jews were faithful to their "ancestral customs," as were the ideal citizens of other cultures. Jews were philosophical and ethical, as also were like-minded gentiles. Jews were but one participant ethnic group in the Roman Empire, as were many others. The Law was used to maintain ethnic difference while the salience of its shared values fostered social convergence.

Stanley E. Porter and Brook W. R. Pearson argue the "Parting of the Ways" originated in the ethnic issues undergirding the Galatian controversy, and suggest this dynamic has not sufficiently been

---

1. Honigman, "Jews as the Best of All Greeks," 207–32.

understanding John's reinterpretation of Jewish prototypicality because social categorizations of Jewish prototypically are also grounded on a lifestyle derived from knowledge that comes from divine revelation in the Law of Moses, something which is somewhat re-ordered in the Prologue.

Pious and Philosophical

As discussed earlier, Jewish writers often socially categorized themselves as philosophical or pious, relative to gentiles, on account of obedience to the Law of Moses. The Johannine critique of this social categorization is the negative result of the Johannine stress on belief and its use of the misunderstanding motif. Being pious and theologically philosophical are arguably the most important Jewish social categorizations, and so they receive the most treatment in John. The theme of belief intersects with authority, signified by Moses, the Law of Moses, or credible Jewish authority figures such as the Pharisees. It follows from John's argument that if belief in Jesus is the sole criterion for life, other issues must take secondary importance and therefore become less relevant for maintaining a social identity that considers Jesus the salient factor. This holds true for ethnic social identity, since being "pious" or "philosophical" in knowledge of God reflects personal dedication to divine revelation relative to those who are not. The self-categorization "pious" is critiqued though presenting Jews as imperceptive or resistant in their opposition to Jesus as the ultimate revealing agent, while categorizations of being theologically "philosophical" are undermined through persistent misunderstanding. The analysis below follows the chronology of the narrative in the first part of the Gospel (the Book of Signs), because this is where most overt discussions between Jesus and Jewish characters, or discussion of ideas derived from Judaism, take place.

John 3 and 4

John usually addresses the matter of Jewish ethnicity indirectly. Terms reflecting ethnic identity such as πάτριος/πατρίων (ancestral customs), commonly found in Josephus or Philo, are absent from John. More generalized terms such as ἔθος (custom) or συνήθεια (custom, habit) do appear once each, but only in passing.[8] Indirect discussion is common in John[9] and the same holds true for examining ethnicity.

This indirect approach is reflected in the discussions of Jewish purification practices in John 3:25, building on information found in John 3:22–36 and the Prologue.[10] John 3:25 mentions a dispute between John's disciples and an unnamed Jew over purification practices. The passage connects water, Spirit and life by means of Baptism to reiterate that Jesus is the source of both the Spirit and life.[11] While keeping the ceremonial Law was necessary for demonstrating faithfulness, in John 3:27 the Baptist himself states no one can receive anything "except what has been given them from heaven" (ἐὰν μὴ ᾖ δεδομένον αὐτῷ ἐκ τοῦ οὐρανοῦ), rendering the act of purification dependent on God and subordinating its importance to belief.

The Baptist's testimony is followed by the claim in John 3:31–36 that Jesus is the source of revelation (3:31–32) who dispenses the Spirit without measure and speaks the words of God (3:34). In John 4 God is said to be Spirit, and Jesus tells the Samaritan woman that those who worship God must do so in the Spirit and Truth (John 4:23–24). This partially merges the two symbols because God is Truth as much as he is Spirit,[12] and it is the Son who gives the Spirit and speaks the truth.[13] The emphasis on the Spirit and Truth, over and against Mosaic stipulations on where to worship, indicates belief in Jesus is the most important element in worshipping God:[14]

> Judgment comes upon every person when confronted with the word of Jesus; to believe in him is to pass beyond judgment into life but to refuse to believe is to bring judgment upon oneself (iii.18ff) . . . In each of these confrontations a

---

8. See the use of ἔθος in John 19:40 regarding Jesus' burial according to Jewish customs; also see συνήθεια in John 18:39 where Pilate comments that release of a Jewish prisoner at Passover was a Jewish custom or habit.

9. O'Day, *Revelation in the Fourth Gospel*, 25–32; and Duke, *Irony*, 144.

10. Neyrey, "Debate," 125.

11. Dodd, *Interpretation*, 309–12.

12. Porter, *John, His Gospel, and Jesus*, 176–180; 190.

13. Thompson, *God of the Gospel of John*, 160–79. See John 1:33; 6:63; 7:38–39; esp. 20:22.

14. Porter, *John, His Gospel, and Jesus*, 177–78; Neyrey, "Debate," 122.

curious pattern emerges in that the judged one becomes the Judge and those judging are judged.[15]

Belief in Jesus is the "judgment" (κρίσις) of the world;[16] as is the rejection and crucifixion.[17] While again the text does not make this explicit, the dispute over baptism and purification is used to lessen the significance of ethnic identity for determining one's spiritual status since Jesus himself is now the mediator of eternal life, making him the salient factor for identifying someone as one who has eternal life, and therefore a spiritual in-group member.[18]

John 4 adds an interesting nuance to this social process, where Jesus and the Samaritan woman engage in a discussion of ethnicity, shared origins, and worship. In discussing the Judean-Samaritan feud over the proper place of worship, Jesus categorizes himself as a Jew vis-à-vis Samaritans when the salient category is knowledge of God (4:22). He states ἡμεῖς προσκυνοῦμεν ὃ οἴδαμεν (we worship what we know), indicating that in John's eyes the Jews in the narrative do worship the one God and are cognizant of their object of worship when they do so.[19] Jesus' statement ὑμεῖς προσκυνεῖτε ὃ οὐκ οἴδατε (you worship what you do not know) establishes Samaritan worship as sincere but inferior—Jews are knowledgeable of God while Samaritans possess a lesser degree of insight. These two statements shift the basis for meta-contrast that at first maintains the relative difference between Jew and Samaritan, but Jesus presents new grounds for comparison in 4:23–24 by introducing the new salient category of "true worshipper"

---

15. Neyrey, "Debate," 117.

16. John 3:19; 5:24; 12:48.

17. John 12:31–32.

18. Dodd notes a Christian audience would consider baptism the sacrament for inferring the Spirit (Dodd, *Interpretation*, 309). It is therefore appropriate to include more discussion of the Baptist here.

19. Thompson, *God of the Gospel of John*, 189–225; Keener, *John*, 1:610–11; Schnackenburg, *Gospel according to St. John*, 1:435–36; Brown, *John*, 1:172. Francis J. Moloney writes: "[Jesus] speaks confidently of the superiority of Jewish traditions . . . and he criticizes the vague Samaritan traditions for not having such authority" (Moloney, *Belief in the Word*, 150). Following Bauer and Bultmann against "conservative interpreters," Ernst Haenchen maintains this statement in 4:22 to be a later insertion (Haenchen, *John*, 1:222).

(ὁ ἀληθινός προσκυνητής).[20] The statement in 4:24 that πνεῦμα ὁ θεός (God is Spirit) with the salient category of "true worshipper," taken with the statement καὶ τοὺς προσκυνοῦντας αὐτὸν ἐν πνεύματι καὶ ἀληθείᾳ δεῖ προσκυνεῖν (and [for] those worshipping him it is necessary to worship in spirit and truth), together with the "I Am" statement in 4:26, establishes Jesus as the basis for worship and spiritual in-group membership.[21]

However, in this exchange John deems Jewish social identity a better fit to claims to knowledge and worship of God than Samaritan identity. Yet when the salient category is the worship introduced by Jesus, the new criteria alters the basis for comparison and renders "Jew" as an inadequate category, more similar to Samaritan than dissimilar. Further, Jesus crosses gender, socio-ethnic, and social deviance barriers to be positively received by a Samaritan woman who cohabitated with a man after being divorced multiple times.[22] Older social identities are no longer salient in establishing one's status as a worshipper, but there is a greater degree of similarity between Jew and Jesus-believer than Samaritan when knowledge of God is the salient factor.

In the Gospel of John the word εὐσεβής (pious, godly), one of the Jewish additions to the cardinal virtues, does not appear at all.[23] However, in the literature surveyed in this study εὐσεβής, along with its verbal forms, is the primary term used to speak of Jewish ancestral customs that relate to worship and is a key element of Jewish social identity. Greek Jewish writers claimed their ancestral practices taught

20. This passage underlines that true worship can only occur through faith in Jesus and being empowered by the Spirit. It is not a contrast of "internal" worship versus "external" (Schnackenburg, *Gospel according to St. John*, 1:436–39). Brown adds that the association between Jesus on the one hand, and "spirit" and "truth" on the other, are so close that "Spirit" does not make a unique contribution to worship in itself, but by means of enabling belief in Jesus (Brown, *John*, 1:180–81). Haenchen agrees with Schnackenburg and Brown, though he maintains a Johannine polemic against temporal-external forms of worship that denies "true worship" to Jews and Samaritans alike (as opposed to making it available to both). See Haenchen, *John*, 1:222–23.

21. Moloney, *Belief in the Word*, 152.

22. Keener, *John*, 1:584–85.

23. With the exception of the related term θεοσεβής (devout) in John 9:31, an attribute which Jesus is accused of lacking. For discussion of piety, see the discussion in chapters 2 to 4.

this virtue and instilled it into their individual and national character, though to a certain degree it was conceded that this category could apply to non-Jews as well. Meanwhile, προσκυνέω and προσκύνησις (worship, reverence) appear much less frequently.[24] Εὐσέβεια and προσκύνησις are related, however—the latter is a narrower term. Piety or godliness can be fostered by means other than worship and may speak to an individual's character as one who reveres the deity.[25] Προσκυνέω is the preferred term in John 4:20–24 and John generally, indicating a perspective where worship is deservedly received by God but lacks its connotations of human virtue.

The category of "true worshipper," who worships in a state of "spirit and truth," is made possible by the sending of the Paraclete, who is named τὸ πνεῦμα τῆς ἀληθείας (the Spirit of Truth) in John 14:16–17. The Paraclete comes to those who believe in Jesus, so it is therefore not possible for those who do not believe to categorize themselves as a "true worshipper." Since "true worshipper" is itself dependent upon an individual's reception of Jesus, the social categorization of εὐσεβής (pious, godly) is no longer salient because in the Johannine schema it cannot establish who is a true worshipper. John ignores this social categorization in favor of a more narrowly defined ontological state derivative of belief in Jesus as the precondition for worship. Since the category "true worshipper" is dependent upon reception of Jesus, the category of εὐσέβεια (piety) would be viewed as irrelevant for self-definition because the grounds for comparison have changed. This theme will become consistent in the Gospel, as seen in our discussion of John 5, 6, and 9 below.

---

24. The term εὐσέβεια (and its adjective εὐσεβής) appear in Let. Aris. 2, 24, 37, 42, 131, 210, 215, 229, 233, 255, 261; 2 Macc 1:19; 3:1; 12:45; 3 Macc 2:31–32; Philo, *Abraham* 1.24, 60–61, 98, 129, 171, 177, 179, 190, 198–199, 208, 268; Philo, *Moses* 1.146, 183, 187, 189, 198, 254, 303, 307, 317; 2.66, 108, 136, 142, 159, 165, 170, 192, 216, 260, 270, 284; Philo, *Flaccus* 48, 98, 103; Philo, *Embassy* 213, 216, 242, 245, 279–280, 297, 316, 319, 335, 347; Josephus, *Ag. Ap.* 1.60, 162, 212, 224; 2:125, 130–31, 144, 146, 159, 170–71, 181, 184, 188, 282, 291, 293. Versus the frequency of the terms προσκυνέω and προσκύνησις, which appear in Let. Aris. 135, 137–38, 177, 317; 3 Macc 3:7; *Abraham* 65; *Moses* 2.23, 40, 165; *Embassy* 116; *Ag. Ap.* 1.239, 261 (although not infrequently in *Antiquities*).

25. For example, its function in its sentences in Let. Aris. 2, 24, 37, and 131.

John 5

One of the clearest ways to understand John's treatment of social categorizations is in how the Jewish characters are contrasted with Jesus in the trial-like scenes.[26] A key example is the Sabbath controversy in John 5, where Jesus declares his relationship to the Father and his identity as the true judge and life-giver.[27] The Sabbath controversy in John 5:9–30 has profound implications for Jewish social identity in the implicit critiques and comments on the origins of Jewish ancestral customs. Its unstable irony presents the topic of discussion as Jesus' claim to God's sovereign agency, something which the Johannine lawsuit motif is concerned with validating.

The *pericope* begins when Jesus heals the lame man at the pool (5:1–9a), but John does not note it is a Sabbath until 5:9b. Jesus tells the man, ἆρον τὸν κράβαττόν σου καὶ περιπάτει (take your matt and walk) in 5:8. The presenting problem is the man follows Jesus' instructions (5:10); John leaves Jesus' intentions vague, but it may have been intended as a celebratory act rather than a defiant instruction to do work on the Sabbath.[28] The Jews in the Gospel do not give the man further trouble after he is questioned, but later the man feels the need to report that he was healed by Jesus when he learns his healer's identity (5:15). The lack of initial consequences for the man in 5:13 suggests the reasons for the conflict are not yet made known.

The nature of the conflict is seen in 5:16 when Jews persecute Jesus for multiple, but unreported, Sabbath violations.[29] There is no opposi-

---

26. For the trial motif in John, see Ashton, *Understanding the Fourth Gospel*, 373–76, 411–14; Neyrey, "Trials (Forensic)," 107–24; Lincoln, *Truth on Trial*, 73–81; also 20–33; Huie-Jolly, "Constructing Ideology in John 5:17–23," 567–95 (esp. 578–86).

27. Lutz Doering notes "the Sabbath motif is christologically focused" (Doering, "Sabbath Laws," 248); "The purpose is not to undermine the Sabbath but to support the high Christology" (Keener, *John*, 1:636).

28. As an act of celebration and demonstration of Jesus' power, see Keener, *John*, 1:641; Beasley-Murray, *John*, 74. For interpretation of the command as a deliberate provocation to instigate a confrontation, see Haenchen, *John*, 1:246; Schnackenburg, *Gospel according to St. John*, 2:97.

29. Brown suggests ταῦτα means "these sorts of things," implying John 5:16 reflects a recurrent pattern. Brown, *Gospel according to John*, 213. The καὶ διὰ relates v.16 back to the Sabbath healing beforehand; the following ὅτι clause makes this explicit.

tion to the previous healing in 4:46–54, but no Sabbath is mentioned. This suggests escalation: at first the Jewish opponents are not upset by the man's healing and they do not persecute him for carrying his matt. While it was significant enough for them to question him, it apparently required no further action. The situation changes when they learn it was Jesus who had healed him on the Sabbath—something about the Sabbath prompts them to take issue with the healing. It is implied in John 5:18 that they want to kill Jesus over his Sabbath violations, given the phrasing μᾶλλον ἐζήτουν αὐτὸν οἱ Ἰουδαῖοι ἀποκτεῖναι (the Jews were seeking all the more to kill him), but any prior decision to kill Jesus is not made explicit in the narrative. The desire to seek his death originates with his self-identification with the Father.[30]

A further indicator of this is that, in an example of unstable irony, the narrative withholds the most important information from the audience until John 5:17–18,[31] which is portrayed as a response to his persecution. John presents the issue so that on the surface it appears Jesus' opponents are upset over minor Sabbath violations,[32] but the debate shifts to the issue of Jesus' equality with God. John 5:18 states that by claiming God as Father, Jesus makes himself equal to God. However, for Jesus this is derivative authority, rather than independent agency, because it is contingent on his relationship to the Father.[33] Likewise, unstable irony presents the conflict as a Sabbath violation, but it is associated with Jesus' claim to be sent by the Father.

In the following dialogue, Jesus applies to himself a synthesis of Wisdom and *Shaliach* Christologies.[34] Jesus claims the right to exer-

---

30. Schnackenburg suggests this response demonstrates a lack of theological perceptiveness on the part of Jesus' opponents (*Gospel according to St. John*, 2:100); Keener draws attention to the recurrent Christological debates, noting that Jesus' attitude towards the Sabbath was relatively mild (*John*, 1:644–45).

31. Thatcher, "Unstable Irony in the Fourth Gospel," 53–77.

32. Keener notes that some held that breaking one part of the Law was tantamount to dismissing its entirety. Yet, John withholds this information. Keener, *John*, 1:641.

33. A connection made by many commentators, among them Keener, *John*, 1:641–42; Beasley-Murray, *John*, 75; Haenchen, *John*, 1:249–50; Brown, *John*, 1:218; Moloney, *Signs and Shadows*, 8–10.

34. Scott, *Sophia and the Johannine Jesus*, 94–169. The personification of Wisdom in a human is unusual but not without precedent. Fletcher-Louis suggests that John

cise judgment on God's behalf, as well as the right to grant life (John 5:22–27), both of which are God's prerogatives.[35] Further, life and judgment are metonyms that connect Jesus to the functions Judaism normally assigns to the Law.[36] In reception history Israel's openness to Wisdom and the Law ascribes Israel/Judea the social categorizations of "pious" for their obedience and devotion, and "philosophical" for the theological knowledge acquired from the Law, but the Johannine incident closes when Moses, who is often presented as the creator of the written form of God's Law, acts as the accuser of Jesus' opponents who cling to the Law at the cost of rejecting Jesus (5:45–47). Ironically, the narrative implies that Moses would recognize Jesus as God's Wisdom and understand him as the Lawgiver (5:46), while the Jewish opponents in the Gospel fail to do so.

Jesus' origins and identity revealed in the Prologue validate his actions and self-claims in the narrative. The imagery connecting Jesus to Wisdom traditions in John 5:19–30 appropriates for Jesus key Jewish self-categorizations. He is the most theologically philosophical and pious because he is taught directly by God, and it is Jesus who sees what the Father does in 5:19–20 and 5:30 (also, 6:45–46). This subordinates Jesus to the Father,[37] but also mirrors Wisdom's claim in Prov 8:25–31 that she was present with God at creation.[38] Jesus' right to exercise judg-

---

would not have been the first to interpret a human as the embodiment of Wisdom, as Sirach personifies wisdom in the *office* of the high priest. John breaks with precedent in personifying it in an individual (Fletcher-Louis, "Wisdom Christology," 52–68).

35. Keener notes that in this context, it justifies worship of Jesus, though warrant for this is dependent upon information presented in the following exposition interpreted in light of information presented in the Prologue (Keener, *John*, 1:650–54); Schnackenburg emphasizes that Jesus is not claiming these prerogatives for himself, but that God exercises them through Jesus as God's agent (Schnackenburg, *Gospel according to St. John*, 2:107).

36. Life is a benefit of keeping the Law in Deut 30:15–20 and the Wisdom traditions (Prov 8:35–36). In Sir 24, Israel is deemed especially wise and appreciative of Wisdom, which chooses to dwell in Israel (Sir 24:8–17). In Sir 24:23, Wisdom is equated with the Law.

37. Keener, *John*, 1:647.

38. Moloney points out that "Jesus does not claim to replace God in any way. For 'the Jews' Jesus' claim to equality was a claim to independence from the Father's authority, to equality of status, 'as if Jesus were setting himself up as a rival to God.'" Moloney, *Signs and Shadows*, 13 (quoting Severino Pancaro in *The Law in the Fourth*

ment in 5:22–24 reflects Wisdom's claim in Prov 8:15 to be the one who enables rulers to govern justly, further underlining this theologically "philosophical" categorization in John. This contradicts ideas in Jewish biblical and interpretive tradition where it is Israel who is "taught by God" in Isa 54:13 (also 48:17),[39] or Philo's etymology of "Israel" as those who see God.[40] Further, תורה (Torah), normally translated as "the Law," bears connotations of "instruction" missing from English or Greek translations, meaning Jews are taught by God through the Law. John effectively juxtaposes instruction received by Jesus against that of his opponents for comparison. This emphasizes the relative difference between the Jews in the Gospel and Jesus, and presents Jesus as this categorization's prototype at the expense of his opponents who do not meet the Gospel's criteria for similarity.

Jesus' *logion* in John 5:17 and the hostile response in 5:18 are examples of Johannine innovation upon Jewish biblical and interpretive tradition. Metaphorical Israelite and Jewish claims to God as Father in a parent-like relationship with Israel are not uncommon in Greek Jewish literature. Jesus' claim to God as his personal father reflects categorizations that Jews generally claimed for themselves, though collectively as a nation. Jesus' innovation is that he claims God as *his* father, rather than *their* (collective) father. The hostile response of the Jewish opponents is justified by the implications of this statement, but not necessarily the surface meaning of the claim.[41] The offense is Jesus' claim to co-equality with God, misunderstood as independence, when the following dialogue demonstrates Jesus' derivative agency to act in union with God on his behalf as the son.[42]

Gospel, 55).

39. Borgen, *Bread from Heaven*, 150.

40. Ὁρῶν θεόν (*Embassy* 4).

41. Schnackenburg maintains that the scandal lies not in claiming God as Father, but in the claim to a unique filial relationship that maintains continuous activity independent of God (Schnackenburg, *Gospel of St. John*, 2:102). Keener makes a similar point (*John*, 1:646–47).

42. Schnackenburg, *Gospel of St. John*, 2:102; Odeberg, *Fourth Gospel*, 203–4, who notes a potential rabbinic parallel where independence from a father would be asserted by means of rebellion on the part of the father's agent. For Odeberg, John presents Jesus as asserting his dependence upon the Father in 5:19.

Jewish attitudes toward the Sabbath were not as monolithic as a cursory reading of John 5 would suggest. The decision to engage in warfare on the Sabbath in 1 Macc 2:34-38 is implemented in order to preserve life, which was considered acceptable grounds for temporary suspension of the Sabbath. Borgen also notes that Philo observes that LXX Gen 2:2 has κατέπαυσεν (he caused to rest) rather than ἐπαύσατο (he rested), implying God does not cease from labor: οὐ παύεται δὲ ποιῶν αὐτός (but he himself does not cease creating). Causing Creation to rest instills the Sabbath practice into the created order, which for Philo is why keeping the Sabbath is beneficial for created beings.[43] Yet Philo complains that some Jews violate the Sabbath on grounds that it is merely a demonstration of God's power, that God continues to create on the Sabbath, and that the Sabbath is for the benefit of humans.[44] Philo therefore informs his readers, presumably Jews, of the need to continue literal Sabbath observance. Since Philo's discussion probably reflects Sabbath issues in the Alexandrian Jewish community[45] and many Jews were probably less stringent in their observance,[46] Jesus is not the first Jew to use God's presumed Sabbath work as warrant for human Sabbath activity.

In a similar manner, Jesus is far from the first Jew to claim God as his father, since this metaphor appears numerous times in the Hebrew Bible[47] and is claimed by the Jews in the Gospel at John 8:41. Jesus' claim to being the son of the Father reflects the royal connotations of Ps 89:26-27 and, in light of the Prologue, his divinity and authority. Most biblical applications of the fatherhood metaphor occur in contexts of restoration and forgiveness where God instructs Israel as would a father his child. The father metaphor (and mother metaphor in Isa 66:13) applies to Israel collectively, and sometimes to all of humanity. 3 Maccabees also claims God as father of Israel, who takes its side against persecuting gentiles and shows compassion to Jews at the exclusion of

---

43. *Alleg. Interp.* 1.18.
44. *Migration* 89-91.
45. See the discussion in Borgen, *Gospel of John*, 180-91.
46. Keener, *John*, 1:642.
47. Pss 68:5-6; 103:13; Prov 3:12; Isa 63:16; 64:8; Jer 31:7-9.

gentiles.[48] The metaphor of God as father reflects the privileged categorization of Jews as philosophical and pious, in the sense of being theologically well-informed and in intimate relationship with God, in comparison to other groups of people. Jesus' use of the metaphor would exclude Jews who do not believe in him from this group.

John 6

John 6 provides a second discussion of Wisdom Christology that elucidates Jesus' identity and authority while negatively categorizing his discussion partners. While the *pericope* would seem to be a narrative continuation of John 4 in geographic terms because it is set in Galilee, it is a thematic development of John 5 in terms of the discussion of Jesus' identity. John 6:4 places the incident near Passover which, together with Jesus' depiction in a role as a provider, shows him to be like Moses.[49] Porter argues John 6 is the third of seven instances of the Passover theme.[50] While the fulfillment motif is important,[51] our focus here is the treatment of symbols pertaining to ethnicity and social identity, of which the Exodus, Moses, and the Law are prime examples. In the following we will focus on how John presents the fulfillment motif in social identity terms, and less on its theological substance.

The Bread of Life discourse has three "I Am" statements where Jesus presents himself as the Bread of Life (John 6:35, 48, 51) and that follow a general pattern of explanation, contrast, and further explanation. The predicative (metaphorical) "I Am" statements allude to Jewish ideas and images and present Jesus as their fulfillment.[52] David Mark Ball sees the predicative "I Am" sayings as functioning primarily as typological fulfillments of Old Testament imagery,[53] though the images

---

48. 3 Macc 2:21; 5:7; 6:3, 8.

49. Hylen, *Allusion and Meaning*, 120–30; Porter, *John, His Gospel, and Jesus*, 214.

50. Porter lists the more explicit appearances of the Passover theme as: (1) John 1:29–36, (2) John 2:13–25, (3) John 6:1–14, 22–71, (4) John 8:31–47, (5) John 11:47–12:8, (6) John 13:1–17:26, and climaxing in (7) John 19:13–42; Porter, *John, His Gospel, and Jesus*, 206.

51. See discussion of the fulfillment motif in chapter 7 below. Also Porter, *John, His Gospel, and Jesus*, 200–204.

52. Ball, *"I Am" in John's Gospel*, 204.

53. Porter takes issue with Ball's exclusive focus on the Hebrew Bible and prefers

operate in a manner very similar to metaphor through the addition of connotations that exemplify his identity, rather than simple replacement.[54] Their function is to point to Jesus as the source of life and demonstrate the necessity of accepting his claims and the need to believe in him. Most of the predicative "I Am" sayings or their associated imagery have connections to key symbols used in the construction of Jewish biblical and interpretive tradition, cultural memory, and social identity—in this case allusions to the Law in the use of the Bread metaphor.

In John 6:22–59, Jesus recounts how Moses served as a leader and produced the Law, associating himself with these ideas and using them to elucidate his identity. John 6 draws many allusions between Jesus and the career of Moses, and the use of Moses imagery illuminates Jesus' identity as the Messiah and as a religious authority.[55] Further, the use of the Bread image denotes Jesus' life-giving function (John 6:48–51). Bread is commonly considered a source of life;[56] Jesus' metaphorical self-comparison with the manna frames him as its eschatological realization. The symbolic use of bread also bears connotations of the Law, metaphorically considered the source of life. Ball notes that "[w]hile this certainly implies that the role of the law within Judaism is now obsolete, John does not focus on this negative aspect but on the positive nourishment that Jesus affords to humanity."[57] Concluding the Law is obsolete may be a hasty conclusion at this point, but it is the logical consequence of the supremacy of Jesus' self-claims because what the Law was said to accomplish through cultural practices is now associated with belief in Jesus.

---

to view them in the broader cultural context, such as the Isis cult (Porter, *John, His Gospel, and Jesus*, 123–25). For further discussion of the embeddedness of early Christianity and Judaism in Greco-Roman culture, see Galinsky, "A Cooperative Agenda," 215–25, esp. 222. Also note his discussion of the imitation of concepts and vocabulary as evidencing the plurality and hybridity of ideas and identities in the Roman world (Galinsky, "Cult of the Roman Emperor," 1–21); Honigman, "Jews as the Best of All Greeks," 213–15.

54. Ball, *"I Am" in John's Gospel*, 223–24, 240.

55. Porter, *John, His Gospel, and Jesus*, 134–35; Harstine, *Moses as a Character*, 72; Boismard, *Moses or Jesus*, 69; Schapdick, "Religious Authority Re-Evaluated," 181–209.

56. Morris, *Jesus is the Christ*, 110–11.

57. Ball, *"I Am" in John's Gospel*, 213–15.

After the feeding miracle in John 6:1–13, the people conclude in 6:14 that: οὗτός ἐστιν ἀληθῶς ὁ προφήτης ὁ ἐρχόμενος εἰς τὸν κόσμον (This is indeed the prophet who is to come *into the world*), and the crowd attempts to force Jesus to become king (6:15). The reason for this, if the following discussion is any indicator, is the crowd sees Jesus as a prophet-king like Moses.[58] In another act similar to the one under Moses' leadership, Jesus leads his disciples across "the sea" (of Galilee) to their destination (6:16–21), as Moses had the Israelites.[59] This is followed by the Bread of Life Discourse (John 6:22–71).

The above creates intertextual allusions[60] to two cultural memories and traditions: (1) the story of the Exodus, and (2) the promise in Deut 18:15–18 of another prophet similar to Moses.[61] These are connected to (3) the Wisdom Christology discussed in the Prologue and John 5. Deuteronomy 18:19, which marks the need to obey subsequent prophets,[62] connects Deut 18:15–18 to the post-exilic cultural memory begun in Neh 9:26 where Israel persistently rejected the prophets. This is seen in John 6 as the pattern of recognition of Jesus as sent by God, the desire to obey him (6:14), and subsequent resistance to Jesus' claims (6:41–42).

---

58. Harstine, *Moses as a Character*; Maronde, "Moses in the Gospel of John," 23–44. The reference to the king motif likely stems from cultural memories that interpret Moses as acting as a founding legislator and king. While it appears in the Synoptics, Jesus' Davidic descent never appears in John (see the inclusive discussion surrounding John 7:42), though, thematically-speaking, Davidic-type kingship is alluded to in John (Daly-Denton, *David in the Fourth Gospel*, 102–12). John also connects incidents from the Psalms to Jesus' career in the narrative. This is significant because reception history of the Psalms, particularly as shown in the LXX superscriptions, similar events were also connected to the life of David.

59. The crossing of the Sea of Galilee being an allusion to the crossing of the Red Sea by the Israelites is attractive due to contextual thematic consistency with the rest of John 6, though establishing a firm basis for this is difficult. For discussion of the sea crossing as a possible allusion to the crossing of the Red Sea, see especially Hylen, *Allusion and Meaning*, 131–34; more generally, Yee, *Jewish Feasts*, 64–65.

60. I am using Porter's definition of "allusion" from Porter, "Further Comments," 108–10.

61. Boismard, *Moses or Jesus*, 70; Schnackenburg, *Gospel according to St. John*, 2:42–43.

62. Glasson, *Moses in the Fourth Gospel*, 27–32.

What prompts rejection of Jesus is the expectation that, as one perceived to be a prophet like Moses, he offers a revelation similar to that of Moses in John 6:28. Jesus' audience in the Gospel was expecting a medium of revelation similar to the Law—God's instructive legislation—that would delineate the action necessary for pleasing God. Meanwhile, Jesus reinterprets the work of obedience in terms of belief in 6:29. The subjunctive ἵνα clause marks Johannine *double-entendre*: belief in Jesus is both the "work" that God demands in 6:28 and "proof" that he is speaking through Jesus.⁶³ Meanwhile, his audience apparently understands ἵνα in John 6:29 as introducing a purpose clause instead of a content clause. In response, they request a legitimating sign and further instructions (6:30). Jesus' audience expects a sign similar to the manna as proof of Jesus' prophetic legitimacy (6:30–31), which would be followed by belief and obedience. This prompts Jesus' discussion of his identity in 6:32–40 when the crowd's expectations go unsatisfied.

In John 6:31 the crowd alludes to the manna tradition but leaves the subject indefinite so that the bread from heaven can be portrayed by the crowd as a legitimating prophetic miracle for Moses.⁶⁴ In the Wisdom tradition "bread" functions as a metonym for the Law, and "eating" as a metaphor for studying or keeping it.⁶⁵ In Jewish cultural

---

63. See also John 20:31. Schnackenburg reads this stereotypically, with a bifurcation between "works" and "belief" (*Gospel of St. John*, 2:39); My reading agrees with Keener, who follows the more nuanced reading used in this study where Jesus says "belief" is the "work" required that also acts as Jesus' legitimating sign (*John*, 1:678).

64. Hylen, *Allusion and Meaning*, 129; Menken, "Provenance and Meaning of John 6:31," 40. At its worst, it indicates the crowd simply wants more food (Keener, *John*, 1:676). Menken, however, suggests this misidentification of the giver of the manna by the crowd intimates views of Moses held by Jews in John's social context. Ideas that Moses was transformed into a deified intermediary had some currency at the time (46–56). The miracles and signs that Jesus performs in John serve a legitimating function. For example, John 2:18 versus 2:23; 3:2; 4:48; 6:14; 10:38; 14:11. Deuteronomy 13:1–5 says a prophet's legitimacy is determined by the fulfillment of their predictions. However, "signs" (σημεῖα) seen during the Exodus events legitimate trust in YHWH in Deuteronomy (4:32–35) and are described as emblematic of Moses' legacy (34:10–12).

65. For "bread" as a metonym for the Law, see Sir 15:3. For "bread" as a metaphor for Wisdom, see Prov 9:5. For food in general as a metonym for the Law, see Sir 24:19–23. For "eating" as obedience or study of the Law, see Sir 15:3; 24:19–22. Schnackenburg agrees it likely that John has these traditions in mind (Schnackenburg, *Gospel according to St. John*, 2:45). Also, Keener, *John*, 1:679–87.

memory the biblical tradition maintained God, rather than Moses, gave the manna. However, in later extra-biblical reception history, as seen in chapter 2 above, the Law is often portrayed as being given by Moses, though it acknowledged both ultimately originated in God.[66]

In agreement with the biblical tradition Jesus maintains God gave the manna (6:32) but uses the indefinite subject in 6:31 as a starting point for reinterpreting the manna and eating metaphors so they apply to belief in him. Jesus is now the manna (τὸ μάννα), renamed bread (ὁ ἀρτός) in light of the quotation of LXX Ps 77:24.[67] Eating is now belief in Jesus rather than keeping or studying the Law. In John 6:41 initial belief turns to unbelief due to Jesus' reinterpretation of the manna tradition. Jesus maintains continuity as the prophet like Moses, but discontinuity remains in that, as was apparently expected in 6:28, Jesus does not add to the legislative or *halakic* tradition but situates himself as the object of trust and obedience (6:22–58).

The Gospel portrays Moses in three ways. The first is that Moses is an intermediary agent rather than source of the Law. This is seen in John 1:17, where it states ὁ νόμος διὰ Μωϋσέως ἐδόθη (the Law was given through[68] Moses); contextually it is assumed the Law is given by God via Moses. Moses is also presented as an intermediary in John 5:45–46, where on Jesus' behalf he affirms the truth of his message and accuses the opponents in the narrative, tacitly subordinating him to Jesus.[69]

The second depiction is that, as in other Jewish literature, John portrays Moses as the origin of the Law. In John 1:45 there is a passing

---

66. In Nehemiah and Exodus, Moses is the mediator who delivers the Law on behalf of God, while God directly provides the sustaining manna from heaven himself (Neh 9:13–15; Exod 16:15). For Moses as "the legislator," see discussion of the Letter of Aristeas and *Against Apion* in chapters 2 and 4.

67. MT Ps 78:24; Court, *New Testament Writers*, 118.

68. Louw and Nida note that this does not preclude causative agency.

69. Schapdick, "Religious Authority Re-evaluated," 193–95, 205–8. He observes, "It is the distinct intention of the Gospel to absorb the whole biblical tradition of Israel christologically. Any preservation of these traditions succeeds only by believing in Jesus and his revelation of salvation. Thus, Jewish faith in God is realized only by faith in the divine revelation in Jesus. Any knowledge of God's prior actions for Israel and for the world is in the end soteriologically irrelevant without acceptance of Jesus' divine revelation" (208).

reference that Moses wrote the Law; it states that Moses gave the Law and circumcision in 7:19 and 7:22. However, John still reduces the significance of Moses' role, as John 3:13 denies Moses ascended to Heaven to receive the Law.[70] We can conclude that John accepts a degree of Mosaic human authorship of the Law, and also agrees that the Law originated in Moses as a mediator. However, while Jesus argues from the Law's authority,[71] John limits reverence of Moses and the Law. This is because, thirdly, John presents Moses as an apparent rival focus of trust and belief in the narrative, as seen in John 5:45–46 but also in 9:28–29.[72]

The attribution of the manna to Moses in John 6:31 intimates his opponents trust Moses rather than God. Jewish reception history portrayed Moses as a teacher of knowledge of God, a key element in the argument for continued Jewish ethnic difference in the Letter of Aristeas, *Against Apion*, and Philo. As seen in chapters 2 and 4, the Letter of Aristeas describes Moses as an erudite teacher, while Josephus follows in the tradition of Artapanus by claiming that the Greek philosophers borrowed from Moses.[73] These traditions presume the validity of Greek culture's placing value on learning a polity's laws as an expression of virtue since obedience to Laws, being the primary expression of Jewish piety, is something that Jews taught and passed on through religious practices.

For the Gospel's part, John makes no reference to Moses teaching the Law or knowledge of God.[74] John presents Jesus as a teacher,

---

70. Maronde, "Moses in the Gospel of John," 35–38 (citing Meeks, *Prophet-King*); Borgen, *Bread from Heaven*, 56–65. Examples of Moses ascending or being granted god-like status are Philo, *Moses* 1:158, where "he was called god and king of the whole nation [Israel]" (ὠνομάσθη γὰρ ὅλου τοῦ ἔθνους θεὸς καὶ βασιλεύς) on account of his merit (*Moses* 1.155–56; also see *Sacrifices* 10's use of ἐπιθειάζουσαν), possibly building on Exod 7:1 where Moses is made a god: "Look, I have given you as a god to Pharaoh" (NETS; LXX ἰδοὺ δέδωκά σε θεὸν Φαραω). See also Thompson, *God of the Gospel of John*, 33–34.

71. E.g., John 8:17; 7:22–24; 10:34.

72. Discussed below.

73. Also *Ag. Ap.* 2.255, 57; Eusebius, *Praep. ev.* 9.27.4.

74. The closest Moses comes to teaching the Law or knowledge of God is John 1:45, where Moses and the prophets are said to have written prophetically about Jesus. Moses writes (γράφω; 1:45; 5:46–47) or gives (δίδωμι; 7:19, 22) the Law. Discipleship to Moses is claimed in John 9:28–29 because God spoke to him, granting him the status of a revealing agent. However, this is set in the ironic context of John

though this likely reflects his status as a Rabbi,⁷⁵ and places greater emphasis on his being a Revealer in obedience to the Father. Jesus passes on knowledge that he was taught by God, rather than Moses in the Gospel (e.g., John 7:16; 8:28). Just as the Jewish literature surveyed above presents Moses as an erudite teacher and legislator, John presents Jesus as exceptional in his divine knowledge on account of his identity as the Son taught by God.⁷⁶

However, Jesus distances himself from becoming the leader of a messianic revolt or earthly kingdom in John 6:15, 60–71.⁷⁷ Many disciples reject Jesus because they are unwilling to accept his teaching (6:60–61, 66) and, like Moses, Jesus is challenged by unbelief manifested in complaining⁷⁸ among those who initially wanted to follow him (John 6:41).⁷⁹ In 6:61 Jesus asks, τοῦτο ὑμᾶς σκανδαλίζει; (Does this offend you [cause you to stumble]?), suggesting the author is aware of the potentially offensive nature of the Gospel's Christology, as use of the term bears connotations of intense theological controversy.⁸⁰ Jesus

---

9 (see below).

75. John 1:38; 3:2; 11:28; 13:13–14; 20:16 (esp. 1:38; 20:16).

76. Meeks, *Prophet-King*, 286–313; Maronde, "Moses in the Gospel of John," 35–43; Schapdick, "Religious Authority Re-evaluated," 181–209; Borgen, *Gospel of John*, 43–66.

77. E.g., Beasley-Murray, *John*, 88–89; Keener, *John*, 1:669–71.

78. Literally "grumbling" (ὁ γογγυσμός) and cognates. Grumbling is a noteworthy theme, especially in Exod 16:2, 7–9, 12; 17:3–4. Deuteronomy 1:27–32 presents grumbling as a metonym for unfaithfulness that resulted in failure to inherit the Promised Land. It is interpreted thus even in Philo, *Moses* 1.193–196. Hylen, *Allusion and Meaning*, 148–50; Yee, *Jewish Feasts*, 66.

79. Schnackenburg, *Gospel according to St. John*, 2:49; Keener, *John*, 1:684–85. Both citing Exod 16.

80. Avoiding the offense of Torah violation or sin seems to be behind the use of σκανδαλίζω and its cognates in Jdt 5:20 and 12:2, as well as in Wis 14:11; Sir 23:8; 27:23; 32:15; and Pss. Sol. 4:23. Avoiding strife is likely behind its use in 1 Clem. 35:8 and Pol. *Phil.* 6:3. Matthew has Jesus say καὶ μακάριός ἐστιν ὃς ἐὰν μὴ σκανδαλισθῇ ἐν ἐμοί (Blessed is anyone who takes no offense at me [Matt 11:6//Luke 7:23]). Jesus causes a "scandal" when teaching in his hometown of Nazareth, καὶ ἐσκανδαλίζοντο ἐν αὐτῷ (And they took offense at him [NRSV] Matt 13:57//Mark 6:3). Jesus' teachings are also recorded as offending the Pharisees, οἶδας ὅτι οἱ Φαρισαῖοι ἀκούσαντες τὸν λόγον ἐσκανδαλίσθησαν; (Do you know that the Pharisees took offense when they heard what you said? [Matt 15:12]). In Matt 17:24–27 Jesus performs a miracle to avoid causing offense (μὴ σκανδαλίσωμεν αὐτούς) when it is questioned whether

also states that the Father must enable people to believe (6:63, 65). John 6 presents Jesus as like Moses, but not in a way deemed acceptable by the Jews present, meaning previous conceptions of Moses' importance in Judaism continue to present him as a potential obstacle to belief in Jesus.

The above indicates that John challenges categorizations of "pious" that would normally place Israel in a privileged relationship to God on account of the Law of Moses. In John it is Jesus who makes relationship with God possible, mitigating faithfulness to the Law as the salient factor and subordinating it to belief in Jesus (6:61) and thereby also undermining the social categorizations of Jews as "philosophical." The portrayal of Jesus as similar to Moses also implies that the Jews present are like Israel in the wilderness, and the "grumbling" allusion characterizes them as lacking faithfulness or spiritual insight. The confusion over the details of the Exodus tradition on the part of the crowd and the application of the misunderstanding motif to the discussion likewise reduces characterizations of theological insightfulness that could apply to Jesus' discussion partners while positively portraying Jesus as the locus of revelation. This runs strongly to the contrary of depictions of Jewish social identity during this period surveyed in chapters 2 to 4 above, abstracting Jewish relative difference to gentiles in the broader culture and making them very similar to gentiles in terms of perceptiveness, at least when Jesus and his teachings are the salient factor.

John 9

John 9 is another incident that undermines the Jewish social categorization of "philosophical," or having privileged insight into God. It is not uncommon to propose that John 5 and 9 are two reworked versions of the same tradition on the basis of their both being Sabbath-conflicts

---

he bothers to pay the temple tax. In Matt 24:10 σκανδαλίζω is usually translated as "many will fall away," with subsequent mutual hatred and betrayal, although given the context "many will be offended" is perhaps as suitable. In addition, given the honor-shame cultural dynamics in the Hellenistic period, in Matt 26:31–33//Mark 14:27–29 σκανδαλίζω can again denote offense (or a desire to avoid the offence of humiliation through association) rather than desertion. It is likely that one concern of that author was to portray Jesus as a pious Jew in the face of accusations to the contrary (Matt 5:20).

arising from a healing incident (John 9:14).[81] However, John 9 is distinct in its stronger ironic emphasis on the spiritual blindness of Jesus' opponents (9:39–41).[82] For our purposes, the underlying theme is that traditional social positions are not accurate predictors of theological insight, as experts like the Pharisees are not more capable of evaluating Jesus than socially marginal individuals such as the formerly blind man.[83] The story builds on Jesus' claims to be "living water" and "the light of the world" in John 7:37–39 and 8:12 to present Jesus as the promised Messiah.[84] The theme of blindness is cogent, given the previous conflict in John 8:12–59.[85]

In John 9:1–2 Jesus and his disciples encounter the blind man, which prompts a brief discussion of theodicy. Jesus states the purpose of the man's blindness is to demonstrate God's work (9:3–5). Jesus heals the man (9:6–7), and the man's associates and others question him and take him to the Pharisees (9:8–13), who in turn are divided (9:14–16). "The Jews" (οἱ Ἰουδαῖοι) in 9:18 summon the parents, who under threat of the synagogue expulsion refer questions to their son (9:19–23). John 9:24–41 concludes the narrative by illustrating the spiritual perceptiveness of the formerly blind man in contrast to the blindness of the Pharisees.

John presents the narrative in such a way that it is unavoidable to conclude that Jesus is at least a prophet in terms of the narrative world's criteria established in the Prologue, but the narrative also hints that

81. For example, Bultmann who suggests they are drawn from the same piece of signs-tradition and serve similar pastoral needs, though at present they have been transformed into different stories (Bultmann, *Gospel of John*, 237–39). Schnackenburg adopts a similar position (Schnackenburg, *Gospel according to St. John*, 2:243).

82. Kim, "Significance of Jesus' Healing," 315, 318; Brown describes John 9 as the single most skillful use of irony in the Gospel. Brown, *Gospel according to John*, 1:376.

83. This, along with mention of synagogue expulsion in 9:22, 12:42, 16:2, prompted Martyn to read this passage allegorically as a two-level drama (Smith, "Introduction," 6). However, Beasley-Murray is correct that the Martyn-Brown hypothesis is unnecessarily complicated for it to be applicable to the plight of Christian Jews, given testimony in the Synoptics and Paul to persecution by Jewish coreligionists at an early date (Beasley-Murray, *John*, 153; see also Schnackenburg, *Gospel according to St. John*, 2:239).

84. Kim, "Significance of Jesus' Healing," 312.

85. "Blindness" will be discussed in chapter 6.

Jesus is something more. The OT states that God's giving sight to the blind is a messianic activity.[86] Further, Daniel Frayer-Griggs persuasively argues the use of spittle and clay intimates Jesus' identification with God as creator (John 9:6), though mention of the spittle is omitted in the man's testimony in 9:15 to the Pharisees.[87] The sign of the healing of the blind man legitimates Jesus' authority, but Jesus' opponents claim discipleship to Moses because they do not know his origins (9:28–29)[88] and refuse to accept his sign[89] despite Moses' having promised another prophet (Deut 18; John 9:17).

In John 9:28–29 the opponents, here "the Jews" in the Gospel, prefer discipleship to Moses because they knew with certainty that God had spoken to him. The man born blind counters that Jesus had worked a miracle in the restoration of his sight, saying that Jesus is θεοσεβής (God-fearing) and must therefore be in line with God's will (9:31) and "from God" (παρὰ θεοῦ) to perform the healing.[90] Jesus identifies himself as "the Son of Man" (τὸν υἱὸν τοῦ ἀνθρώπου) in John 9:35 and accepts the man's worship in 9:38. Infirmity was associated with "socio-religious marginalization," adding a strong social element to the restoration of the blind man.[91] Therefore traditional authority structures are not reliable when it comes to assessing Jesus' identity. Jesus demonstrates his opponents are blind (9:39–41), undermining the social categorizations associated with theological insightfulness,[92]

---

86. Kim, "Significance of Jesus' Healing," 312. See also Kok, who observes how in the context of honor-shame dynamics, Jesus' healings would, alongside serving as signs of power, function as a symbol of social restoration and refutation of social marginalization (Kok, "Healing of the Blind Man in John," 41–53, 58–59).

87. Frayer-Griggs, "Spittle, Clay, and Creation," 659–70, esp. 264–66. The spittle is a possibly crucial detail, according to Frayer-Griggs, as Qumran evidence indicates that Adam was understood as being formed from both God's spittle and the dust of the ground in 1QS 11.21–22; also 1QH 20:31–32.

88. Keener notes that this would be a "safe" strategy, given the rabbinic belief that Moses was the "father" and teacher of all subsequent prophets. This would situate Jesus' opponents on the correct side, though John ironically refutes this juxtaposition of Moses vs. Jesus (Keener, *John*, 1:790–91).

89. This is ironic given previous requests for a sign in John 2:18; 6:30.

90. John 9:16, 33.

91. Kok, "Healing of the Blind Man in John," 41–42.

92. A similar point also noted by Keener, *John*, 1:789.

again abstracting the social identity of "the Jews" so that it becomes more similar with that of the rest of humanity.

Summary

John twice presents Sabbath healing controversies as *segues* for discussing Jesus' identity as the obedient one sent from the Father. The Johannine trial motif contrasts Jesus and the Jews in the Gospel, giving insight into how the author would socially categorize Jesus, Christians, and non-Christian Jews. The discussion connects Jesus to imagery traditionally associated with the Law of Moses via the Wisdom tradition. Jesus, as God's Wisdom, is granted privileged insight into the will of God, simultaneously undermining several Jewish self-categorizations operative in the contemporary culture. Claims to privileged knowledge of God, intimate relationship with God, and exceptional piety, all of which Jews used to categorize themselves socially vis-à-vis gentiles and which were derived from knowledge of the Mosaic Law, are presented as of little benefit for understanding Jesus or the Father.

However, similar categorizations are applied positively to Jesus to present him as the one in possession of the privileged knowledge of God. In terms of relative difference, when these categories are salient in the context of Samaritans, Jews are presented as more similar to Jesus in terms of knowledge of God compared to Samaritans. It is important for our purposes to see that Jesus, as the revealer in John, is the sole individual in the narrative who possesses theological knowledge and insight into God while his opponents demonstrate imperceptiveness. Yet, while John's Christology may seem all-consuming, the Gospel does recognize that some non-Johannine traditions have more truth to them than others, allowing grounds for recognizing similarity when other social categorizations are salient.

EXAMINATION OF JOHN'S TREATMENT OF OTHER SELECT SOCIAL CATEGORIZATIONS

John interacts with several other key Jewish self-categorizations that served as a basis for comparison with gentiles in order to reduce relative difference while preserving distinct identities. The single most important of these is the self-categorization of Jews as theologically "philosophical," under which can be placed related categorizations found in John such as claims to being "taught by God," knowing God, and claiming unique insight into what God expects from humans. John also interacts with Jewish self-categorizations of being "zealous" for the Law or ancestral customs.

Faithful to Ancestral Customs

As discussed in preceding chapters, part of Jewish social identity included the social categorization of being faithful to ancestral customs. Used by Jews as a means of maintaining ethnic distinction and demonstrating piety, the value placed upon ancestral customs in Greco-Roman culture acted as a point of salience for social convergence with gentiles. We will see below that John does not consider the ancestral customs salient for demonstrating piety, though it presents Jesus as the fulfillment or climax of some ancestral customs such as the festivals. Jesus seems genuinely concerned with the "fulfillment" of Jewish hopes and aspirations and seems to be situating himself as their climax.[93] While it is conspicuous that John does not criticize the practices themselves, faithfulness to ancestral customs nonetheless no longer functions as a salient category for evaluating piety because John introduces belief in Jesus as the new salient category for establishing relative difference.

Jesus' Appropriation and Realignment of Diaspora Jewish Self-Categorizations

We saw above that Jesus presents himself as the truly pious and theologically philosophical one. We shall see here that the Passover fulfillment motif serves two functions in terms of its implications for Jesus' social identity: demonstrating Jesus as zealous for God and showing his faithfulness to the ancestral customs.

---

93. Thompson, *God of the Gospel of John*, 189–225. She is arguing along a line most similar to Hylen, *Allusion and Meaning*. This is a point made by many. For example, Maronde, "Moses in the Gospel of John," 26; Schapdick, "Religious Authority Re-evaluated," 188–89.

Diaspora Jewish Social Identity and John's Portrayal of Jesus

Brave (and Zealous)

"Zeal for God," often coterminous with zeal for the Law or other Jewish symbols,[94] is another Jewish self-categorization applied to Jesus. Jesus' zeal is reflected in the second of seven appearances of the Passover theme in John 2:13–25,[95] when LXX Ps 68 (MT 69) is directly quoted in John 2:17 after Jesus enters the temple precincts, makes a whip of cords, and clears the temple (2:14–16). In John 2:17 Jesus' disciples remember Ps 68:10 (69:9): ὁ ζῆλος τοῦ οἴκου σου καταφάγεταί με (zeal for your house will consume me). John 2:16's condemnation of making the temple a house of trade suggests Jesus' act, at least in the Johannine context, should be understood as some kind of cleansing.[96] When asked for a legitimizing sign for his own zealous behavior, Jesus responds with a veiled prediction of his death and resurrection.

John is alone among the canonical Gospels in placing the temple incident first and its primary purpose appears to be to provide opportunity for the Evangelist to introduce Jesus as the new temple, suggesting the incident had some importance for John.[97] The Psalm citation, referencing the consuming motivation of zeal, serves to provide an explanation for Jesus' action and the nature of the conflict between Jesus and his opponents as stemming from his zeal for the Father. Additionally, John alters the verb to a third person singular future middle, versus LXX's third singular aorist active (κατέφαγεν) so that the quotation is

---

94. Dunn, *New Perspective on Paul*, chapter 3.

95. Porter, *John, His Gospel, and Jesus*, 206.

96. Chilton, *The Temple of Jesus*, 119, 153–55, and Klawans, *Purity, Sacrifice, and the Temple*, 79–89 who argue with an eye to historical Jesus studies that he would have been concerned with verifying the proper ownership of the animal victim due to possible unjust market practices. On the grounds of Ezek 28:18 and Zech 14:21, C. H. Dodd sees this as a rejection of trade in the temple (Dodd, *Interpretation*, 300). Bruce G. Schuchard doubts a portent of destruction according to the OT pattern as this would require provocation and a chance for repentance, neither is mentioned (Schuchard, *Scripture within Scripture*, 24). *Pace* Sanders, who sees the temple act as a portent of destruction (Sanders, *Jesus and Judaism*, 70–71). This may well be true of the Synoptic accounts of the Temple incident due to the cursing of the fig tree in Mark and Matthew (Mark 11:13–14, 20–21; Matt 21:19–20).

97. Dunn, "Let John be John," 293–322; Motyer, *Your Father the Devil*; Hakola, *Identity Matters*; Köstenberger, "The Destruction of the Temple," 205–42; Kerr, *The Temple of Jesus' Body*; Hoskins, *Jesus as the Fulfillment*; Um, *Theme of Temple Christology*.

read as a prophecy that is integrated into the narrative to foreshadow Jesus' destiny—that his zealous behavior will result in his death, which acts as a allusion to characters and examples from the Maccabean literature.[98] This identifies Jesus as a hero similar to the Maccabees, who also "cleansed" and rededicated the temple in 1 Maccabees 4.[99] The result is that Jesus is categorized as "zealous" (and therefore "pious"), while his opponents are categorized negatively.

Through clever use of irony and *double-entendre*, John appropriates the social categorization of zeal, normally used as a Jewish self-categorization based on fidelity to the Mosaic Law and ancestral customs, and applies it to Jesus to the exclusion of his opponents. John presents Jesus as the truly, or at least correctly, zealous one.

Anti-Jewish Categorizations in John

Having completed our survey of John's treatment of some of the positive Jewish social categorizations, we turn our attention to the negative social categorizations ascribed to Jews by non-Jews. We saw above that there is a literary tradition where the so-called "educated elite" of Alexandrian and Roman society categorized Jews in a profoundly negative manner to categorize Jews as violators of the in-group. While writers such as Philo and Josephus categorized their fellow Jews as peaceful, co-participants, and pious, Romans and others categorized them as the opposite: as petty, superstitious, and militaristic. Below we see that John exploits both the positive and negative categorizations applied to Jews, but it does so by using Jewish values as its frames of reference and criteria of evaluation. The result is that John sounds anti-Jewish, but the reasons for this negative portrayal derive from ideas that have their origins in Jewish values and sensitivities.

Petty and Superstitious

There are portrayals of pettiness that appear in John's depiction of Jewish people. These are not nearly as severe as what one finds in

---

98. See Jason J. Ripley, who proposes a similar point (Ripley, "Exploring Ideological Contexts," 605–35).

99. Moloney, *Belief in the Word*, 97–98. I discuss this in more depth in Numada, "Christological Appropriation," 90–110.

anti-Jewish literature of the period but occasionally touch on similar areas of concern. The closest thing to a portrayal of an apparent Jewish *superstitio* is a possibly magical understanding of the pool of Bethesda implicitly criticized in John 5.[100] Another practice likely viewed as petty, at least in terms of how Jesus' opponents regarded it, is John's portrayal of the Sabbath. Many Roman writers considered Sabbath observance an expression of pettiness, superstition, and laziness. Circumcision was deemed just as ubiquitous, the rite being viewed by non-Jews as a permanent marker of their ethnic identity. Juvenal had a poor regard for scrupulous religious practice and sensitivity to religious issues, and Jews as a group were perceived as being notoriously inflexible regarding ethnic and religious practices.

John is notable because, unlike gentile writers, the Gospel never criticizes the observance of the Sabbath or the practice of circumcision, though it portrays Jesus' opponents as inflexible. Partly this is seen in John's lack of concern for propagating a revisionist Sabbath *Halakah*. In John 7:19–24 Jesus argues from lesser to greater that it is wrong for his opponents to kill him, the minor premise being if circumcision is permissible on the Sabbath, then it is permissible to heal. The major premise is if it is permissible to heal, then it is wrong to kill Jesus for his restorative Sabbath violation. Circumcision observances facilitate this argument, though John suggests something not originating in the Law can take precedence over the Law since circumcision originates with Abraham rather than Moses.[101] The narrative assumes that circumcision is valid and it does not betray gentile dislike of the practice because of percieved damage to the body,[102] but uses it as a discussion topic to address issues that prevent belief in Jesus.

---

100. Steven M. Bryan's reading coheres well with the passage's emphasis upon Jesus' dependence on the Father, rather than a mechanistic conception of power that would reflect a magical understanding of how God works (Bryan, "Power in the Pool," 7–22). There is little evidence of an overt, anti-magic polemic in John, though John's Christology clearly excludes magic of any such legitimacy in John's world-view.

101. Huie-Jolly, "Like Father, Like Son," 567–95 (578–79).

102. For example, 1 Macc 1:14–15 claims some Hellenizing Jews attempted to hide their circumcision, while the narrative portrays the Seleucids as forbidding circumcision (1 Macc 1:60–61; also 2 Macc 6:10). Paul, meanwhile, seems to refer to Gentile sensibilities when he refers to circumcision as ἡ κατατομή (mutilation) in

A similar example is the Sabbath controversies in John 5 and 9 discussed above. Jesus is said to violate the Sabbath twice (John 5:10, 16; 9:14–16). Yet in John 5:16–18 the Jews in the Gospel seek to kill Jesus *more* because he self-identifies with the Father, implying they already sought his death for violating the Sabbath. If Philo is any indication, many Jews would probably side with Jesus by accepting the rationale for his infringements as non-threatening to the existence of the Sabbath institution.[103] Mark 2:27–28, on the other hand, presents the most threatening version of Jesus' Sabbath *Halakah*, where Jesus claims lordship of the Sabbath and subordinates Sabbath traditions to human needs. The Synoptic Sabbath controversies provide ample warrant for opposition to Jesus, but John never indicates what Jesus thinks is appropriate Sabbath practice. The Johannine Sabbath controversies in John 5 and 9 serve as *segues* to discussions of Jesus' divinity and authority, but presenting the initial conflict as being over Sabbath observances with more significant claims being made subsequently underscores a certain pettiness on the part of Jesus' opponents, or cynicism on the part of John, when contrasted with Jesus' healing signs. Jews are known to have been flexible with the Sabbath when they thought it was warranted, but John's portrayals present the Sabbath healing conflicts as rooted in pettiness. The use of the pettiness social categorization in turn portrays the conflict as one of willful disbelief and inflexibility on the part of Jewish opponents.

Another Johannine categorization of pettiness is seen in debate over whether Jesus was a prophet or the Messiah because he came from Galilee (John 7:41–43, 52). While the Synoptics maintain Jesus was born of Davidic descent in Bethlehem in Judea, John is silent on this except for the fact that some of his life was spent in Galilee. The

---

Phil 3:2; also see ἀποκόπτω (cut off) in Gal 5:12.

103. Papaioannou, "Jesus and Sabbath Law," 258–59. I disagree that the Johannine Jesus is offering an alternative interpretation of the Sabbath. I do agree with Pappaioannou that it is unlikely that, given the diversity of early Judaism, Jews would seek to kill Jesus over his Sabbath transgressions. Herold Weiss proposes that the Johannine community saw itself as living in a realized, eschatological Sabbath. While it seems John may endorse something of a realized eschatology with eternal life experienced in the present, it remains uncertain that John would disregard Sabbath observance on these grounds (Weiss, "Sabbath in the Fourth Gospel," 311–21).

Diaspora Jewish Social Identity and John's Portrayal of Jesus

Pharisees in 7:49 criticize the crowd for debating Jesus' identity because they do not know the Law, though information from the Synoptics suggests the crowd is correct. Pettiness is suggested when they do not pursue the matter more seriously in the face of Jesus' signs (7:52–53), while the desire to execute Jesus due to his claims to sonship is petty due to similar self-ascriptions at times being granted to Israel.[104] Further, the statement in John 11:48 could reflect a petty fear of the loss of political power due to Roman political intervention instead of a national existential threat,[105] while in John 10:41 people believe Jesus on account of John the Baptist, even though the Baptist gave no legitimating signs. Above all, in John's mind at least, it seems that pettiness is seen in the inability to exercise what John's Gospel considers right judgment.[106]

Social categorizations of Jesus' opponents in the Gospel as "petty" still assume Judaism's validity, with the disagreements being over one's priorities and which source of authority is more salient. In no way does John use the pettiness motif to reflect Roman categorizations of Judaism as a *superstitio*. Rather, in conjunction with the misunderstanding and irony devices, pettiness undermines Jewish social categorizations of being theologically "philosophical" because the Gospel's Jews fail to perceive his true nature and accept the content of his revelation due to their incorrect preconceptions.

Militaristic or Violent

It is very ironic that conquerors such as the Romans categorized Jews as militaristic, though it could be said this is merely the negative correlate to zeal for the ancestral customs. As we saw in chapter 4, Roman writers variously characterized Jews as militaristic or violent. Romans also depicted Jewish resistance to their power as irrational, and violent resistance as resulting from supposed xenophobia. Tacitus uses Jewish militarism as a lens to interpret nearly every positive aspect of Jewish social identity negatively. Horace, meanwhile, classifies Jews as

---

104. See the discussion on "sonship" and Ps 82:6 below.

105. An observation made by Haenchen, *John*, 2:75; Beasley-Murray, *John*, 196; Hakola, "Counsel of Caiaphas," 146.

106. John 7:24; 8:15. Euphemistically, this may be what John means in John 1:11; 3:11.

members of the Roman mob who are easily affronted, coercive, and prone to violence. Outwardly John appears to allude to some of these categorizations, though it is uncertain if it is because Jesus is dealing with the Jewish leaders on the one hand, or the Jewish "mob" (ὁ ὄχλος) on the other.[107] It is more likely that John has entirely different, Christological motives for portraying Jesus' adversaries and discussion partners in this manner.[108]

Jesus hides himself out of fear of violence in John 8:59. In John 12:36 hiding was likely taken as a precautionary measure, while in John 6:15 Jesus evades an unruly attempt by οἱ ἄνθρωποι (the people) to crown him the national king by force. Attempts to kill Jesus are responses to his claims of divine identity and violation of the Sabbath, made known by the *Shaliach* and Wisdom Christology discussed above. The closest John comes to the Roman categorization of Jews as militaristic is in 11:50, where it describes fear of Roman military intervention in response to a Jewish popular uprising.

The rationale given for executing Jesus, at least as far as the narrative is concerned, ironically hints that the leadership assumes Jesus possesses prophetic legitimacy, connecting his death with the Jewish cultural memory of the rejection of the prophets. In the narrative many think that Jesus' words and actions reflect prophetic rather than demonic content. John the Baptist self-identifies as not being "the prophet" (1:21–23), while in John 4:44 the narrator indicates that Jesus thought of himself as a rejected prophet.[109] Some of the people conclude that Jesus is a prophet in 6:14 and 7:40, as does the man born blind in John 9:17. Each affirmation is presented as part of a debate stemming from misunderstanding of Jesus' significance. In John 11:47–53, the Jewish leadership decides to have Jesus executed, further in keeping with the

107. Pharisees and Jewish opponents seek to kill Jesus in 5:18, 7:1 (and probably 7:25), 8:57–59 and 11:47–52, but they are not the only party to do so. For example, in John 7:19–20 the crowd is alleged to be seeking to kill Jesus. In 8:37–40 it is believing Jews in the narrative (see 8:30) who want to kill Jesus.

108. Culpepper characterizes "the crowd" as receptive to Jesus, though they do not respond in belief (Culpepper, *Anatomy of the Fourth Gospel*, 125, 131–32). Meanwhile, Brant likens the function of the Johannine "crowd" and "Jews" alike to that of a chorus in a Greek drama (Brant, *Dialogue and Drama*, 178–87).

109. For similar comments made by Jesus in the Synoptics, see Matt 13:57; Mark 6:4; Luke 4:24.

prophetic-rejection cultural memory. Paradoxically, the rejection of Jesus refutes the Roman categorization of Jews as militaristic because these actions are taken due to fear of Rome.[110] John does not consider militarism a salient categorization of Jews in John, as no one in the narrative thinks they are able to militarily withstand Rome, and it is the Romans who execute Jesus as the rejected prophet and king on behalf of the Jewish leadership.

There is also the implicit rejection of God as Israel's king in John 19:15's assertion of loyalty to Caesar by the chief priests.[111] If composed after the destruction of the temple, this is extremely ironic, though the irony would still remain if John were composed prior to the Revolt of 66–73 CE. The statement οὐκ ἔχομεν βασιλέα εἰ μὴ Καίσαρα (we have no king except for Caesar) excludes all other messianic claimants, effectively rejecting any intervention by God as their ultimate king.[112] This is made more apparent in John 19:12, where "the Jews" equate release of Jesus with treason against the emperor. In these instances the Jewish leadership aligns itself with "the world," represented in the person of the emperor.[113] Socio-politically, this runs against social categorizations where Jews are solely concerned with worship of YHWH, but remains consistent with Jewish self-categorizations of being loyal participants. This furthers the prophetic rejection motif found in Jewish cultural memory, as it excludes the necessity of their being sent to God's people on account of their holding different allegiances.

Attempts to kill Jesus are presented as responses to perceived violations of the Law, his threat to the established religious and political authority, and social stability. From John's perspective, Jesus' prophetic status is not evaluated objectively by his opponents and serves as part of the backdrop for the decision to have him executed. Such behavior is more consistent with the Jewish cultural memory of the rejection of the prophets than categorization of Jews as militaristic or

---

110. For a discussion of John's approach to messianism in light of the consequences of the violence of the Jewish revolt, see Trost, *Who Should be King in Israel*, 76, 219–25.

111. Meeks, *Prophet-King*, 76.

112. Beasley-Murray, *John*, 343.

113. Schnackenburg, *Gospel according to St. John*, 3:266; Keener, *John*, 2:1132; Dahl, "Johannine Church," 124–38, esp. 135.

violent. Anti-Jewish prejudice resulting from the revolt in 66–73 CE (if John post-dates the revolt) or a growing anti-Semitic *Zeitgeist* (if it pre-dates the revolt) do not adequately explain use of this motif. It is highly unlikely that Jewish militarism is a salient category that John seeks to exploit; it is more likely that John is making connections with Jewish cultural memory's normally exhortatory interpretive tradition of Israel's rejection of the prophets, the prophet-king *par excellence* being presented ironically. This would reduce the saliency of social categorizations predicated upon privileged knowledge of God frequently seen above.

SOCIAL PROCESSES IN JOHN
Implications for Jewish Self-Categorizations

In the above discussion, it is notable that the Johannine Jesus scarcely comments on circumcision or the Sabbath given that circumcision and Sabbath were considered the most significant markers of Jewish ethnicity. There is no *halakic* reinterpretation of the Sabbath similar to that of Mark, nor is there any mention of a need for circumcision of the heart as a replacement (Jer 4:4; Deut 10:16). This indicates that John has little to no interest in undermining Jewish ethnicity for its own sake, but ethnicity as an obstacle to the Gospel. Appropriations and reinterpretations of social categorizations that reflect negatively on Jews as a group, as well as the prophetic-rejection cultural memory, likely exemplify a form of group self-criticism on the part of John to underline Jesus' theological significance.

John's treatment of the Jewish social categorization of "faithful to ancestral customs" has little significance for Jewish ethnicity, but its portrayal of the non-believing Jews' reception of Jesus undermines Jewish self-categorizations of being theologically "philosophical" or insightful in religious matters. Through use of irony, *double-entendre*, and misunderstanding, John frames the debates of John 3–9 so that these social categorizations can no longer apply to Jews generally as a group, but it applies similar social categorizations to Jesus. Jewish self-categorizations made possible through knowing God and conducting oneself as God desires, such as zeal for God and piety, are also applied to Jesus. The audience of the Gospel knows, on account of information in the Prologue, that it is Jesus who obeys the Father, who establishes the criteria for evaluating piety or worship, and teaches the importance of belief in God by believing in Jesus. Jesus' Jewish opponents in the Gospel are not superstitious but are inflexible, and perhaps petty, due to a lack of spiritual perceptiveness. Similarly, Jews are not militaristic or violent by nature but, according to a distinctly Jewish cultural memory, tend to reject God's faithful messengers.

Application of these categories to Jesus consequently makes the social categorizations discussed in earlier chapters less relevant for the formation or maintenance of a social identity. It reduces relative difference between Jews and non-Jews, since belief and worship of Jesus are now the salient factors for determining who is obedient to God. The result is John leaves ethnic practices intact as social identifiers on the genetic-kinship level, but their lack of influence on relative difference when theological or religious matters are salient renders Jews a part of "the world."

6

Interpreting John's Portrayal of Jewish Origins and Collective Destiny

INTRODUCTION

IN THE PREVIOUS CHAPTER we saw that John engages a number of Jewish social categorizations that Diaspora literature suggests were considered prototypical. John uses debates and controversies to demonstrate that Jesus either represents some positive social categorizations that constitute Jewish social identity on the one hand, or to undermine their fit for his opponents on the other. This strategy seems to serve as part of John's case that Jews should be categorized as members of "the world" in the Johannine narrative. Likewise, John seems to consider inapplicable the negative Roman categorizations of Jews resulting from the Jewish revolt against Rome in 66 to 73 CE. This suggests that understanding Johannine anti-Judaism as directed against all Jews, but from a gentile perspective, is also incorrect. The absence of *Halakhic* disputation in John reinforces this point; John leaves the matter of distinctively Jewish ethnic practices virtually untouched. This suggests but does not prove a Jewish authorship behind the Gospel that has little concern for undermining Jewish ethnic identity, at least as far as it involves rejecting circumcision or Sabbath observance in their totality. John devotes far more attention to debates concerning Jesus' identity and provides explanation for why Jesus was misunderstood and rejected.

Interpreting John's Portrayal of Jewish Origins and Collective Destiny

As seen above, and particularly important to A. D. Smith's arguments concerning ancient nationalism, here labelled under the less-political term "cultural identity," a group's common progenitors can serve as resources for establishing derivative social categorizations used to formulate the group's social identity vis-à-vis other social groups. In chapters 2 and 4 it was seen that in reception history Moses, and to a lesser extent Abraham, formed important foundations for asserting Jewish social identity within a Hellenistic gentile context through retrospective attribution of shared values to these Jewish progenitors. Furthermore, the Mosaic Law was interpreted as fostering that which was best about Hellenistic culture. It is therefore necessary to interpret John's treatment of Moses, the Law, and Abraham in light of their significance for Jewish cultural and social identity, and how this influences the author's formation of social categorizations. These social categorizations must then be understood within the Gospel's system for establishing relative difference or similarity as a basis for facilitating social convergence or divergence.

This chapter will examine John's treatment of Abraham and Moses, as well as the Law, and its implications for social identity by examining social categorizations derived from self-identification with these progenitors and the Law, which was treated by some as Moses' workmanship. As in chapter 5, in this chapter I will argue that the manner in which John appropriates these symbols indicates that the author is seeking to disassociate core elements of Jewish social identity from Jews in the Gospel. This abstracts the distinctive features of their social identity and increases their similarity to "the world," further indicating that they symbolically serve as representatives of its unbelief. This chapter will examine the roles played by Jewish cultural memories of Moses and Abraham, and their influence in the formation of Jewish identity, and what this could mean for our understanding of how the Gospel wants its audience to evaluate relative difference and similarity among people.

ABRAHAM

Reception History

While Moses is much more prominent in Hellenistic Jewish literature than Abraham, Abraham still receives significant attention in the canonical and deuterocanonical tradition, as well as literature usually considered to originate in Palestine. In addition, Philo devotes two treatises to interpreting Abraham for his Greek context. The result is that in Hellenistic Jewish biblical and interpretive tradition, Abraham can function as a metonym for elect status or Jewish faithfulness. Abraham therefore had a significant role in the Jewish cultural identity of the Diaspora which John engages directly.

Among these is the importance Jewish reception history placed upon Abraham's faithfulness. In 1 Macc 2:52 Abraham's faithfulness is considered warrant for defending the Law, as seen when it quotes Gen 15:6 as warrant for demonstrating zeal. In 1 Macc 2:50 Mattathias gives instructions on his brand of faithfulness, which takes the form of a doublet where remaining within the Jewish biblical tradition of Abraham's faithfulness to demonstrate the applicability of the corresponding social categorization is expressed through zeal and accepting death for the sake of the Law. The noun phrase in 1 Macc 2:50 διαθήκης πατέρων ἡμῶν (covenant of our ancestors) adds an ethnic connotation by stating that what sets Jews apart religiously also sets them apart ethnically. Manfred Oeming describes Gen 15:6 as a quintessential Deuteronomic history proof text, where God graciously expresses his choice, the chosen acts in faithfulness, which prompts God to confer blessing.[1] In each case presented in Mattathias's exhortation, the righteous God responds to their faithfulness.[2] Perseverance results in reward, and

---

1. Oeming, "Glaube Abrahams," 16. The Deuteronomistic history's covenant theology arose as an explanation for Israel's political troubles. The main tenets are the people's faithfulness would be reciprocated by God, and national misfortune was to be understood as testing or punishment (Millar, "Deuteronomy," 159–61; Noth, *Deuteronomic History*). Noth held a pessimistic interpretation, while Von Rad saw it as an expression of God's grace. Either way, its theology was intended to encourage fidelity to YHWH (Fretheim, *Deuteronomic History*, 19–22), influential in works such as Sirach, Jubilees, and Wisdom of Solomon.

2. The list of persons discussed includes: Abraham (2:52), Joseph (2:53), Phinehas (2:54), Joshua (2:55), Caleb (2:56), David (2:57), Elijah (2:58), Ananias, Azariah,

these examples are described as τὰ ἔργα τῶν πατέρων (deeds of the ancestors). It is in this context that the quotation of Gen 15:6 appears:

> Αβρααμ οὐχὶ ἐν πειρασμῷ εὑρέθη πιστός καὶ ἐλογίσθη αὐτῷ εἰς δικαιοσύνην;
> Was Abraham not *found faithful in temptation* [testing], and it was accounted[3] to him as righteousness? (1 Macc 2:52)
> Ἐπίστευσεν Αβραμ τῷ θεῷ καὶ ἐλογίσθη αὐτῷ εἰς δικαιοσύνην.
> *Abram trusted in God*, and it was accounted to him as righteousness (Gen 15:6).[4]

The italicized texts show the discrepancy in the above quotations. The reason for the difference is likely a conflation of interpretive options. The consonantal text of Gen 15:6 can be rendered differently, where והאמן can be alternately read either as "he was faithful" or as "he believed/trusted in" (LXX's reading).[5] The former option corresponds with how Gen 15:6 could be read in light of the near-sacrifice of Isaac in Gen 22 as the ultimate test.[6] Both of these interpretive elements are consistent with reception history, where Abraham is accounted righteous because he had passed God's testing and acquired God's approval.[7] Such causality implies that the righteousness accounted to Abraham is a result of Abraham's perseverance in response to God's pledge, and so God does not impute righteousness to him without merit.[8] LXX Neh 9:7–8 depicts the covenant as a result of both Abraham's faith and God's righteousness:

> You are the Lord God. You made a choice in Abram and brought him out of the country of the Chaldeans . . . *you found his heart faithful before you* (εὗρες τὴν καρδίαν αὐτοῦ πιστὴν ἐνώπιόν σου) and made a covenant with him . . . and you have established your word, because you are righteous (NETS).

---

and Mishael (2:59), and Daniel (2:60).

3. NETS translates ἐλογίσθη as either "accounted" or "reckoned," depending on the preceding context. I have harmonized them here.

4. This is an adaptation of Brayford's translation (Brayford, *Genesis*, 73).

5. Longenecker, *Triumph of Abraham's God*, 131.

6. Harrisville, *Figure of Abraham*, 127.

7. Hieke, "Role of 'Scripture,'" 65.

8. Oeming, "Glaube Abrahams," 32.

Abraham was deemed faithful, making him worthy of God's gracious act of establishing a covenant with him. Abraham acted on faith, and God in his righteousness responded to that faith, reflecting somewhat the logic of 1 Macc 2. The contention that Abraham was on some level righteous because of his trust is made even more explicit in Sir 44:19-21's summary of the Abraham narrative in Genesis, especially in the italicized phrases:

> Abraham was a great father of a multitude of nations, and no blemish was found on his glory, *who kept the Law of the most high* (ὃς συνετήρησεν νόμον ὑψίστου), and he entered in a covenant with him; in his flesh he established a covenant, and *in a trial he was found faithful* (ἐν πειρασμῷ εὑρέθη πιστός). *Therefore* (διὰ τοῦτο) [God] established by means of an oath with him that nations would be blessed by his seed ... and give to him an inheritance ... (NETS).

Like Neh 9:7-8, in Sir 44:19-21 Abraham is first chosen by God. He is called with the promise of a covenant that is established after he has been successfully tested by God. In Neh 9:7-8 only God is righteous, but in Sir 44:19 Abraham is "glorious" because he faithfully kept the Law of God, an idea which is likely part of Sirach's response to the increasing influence of Greek culture.[9] As the Law had not yet been given, Torah-piety is retrospectively attributed to Abraham, who is the prototype of the future Israel and an example of the prototypical Jew who keeps the Law.

Jubilees 17:15-18 expands the trial motif to encompass more than the testing involved in the near-sacrifice of Isaac. In the process, it almost equates Abraham's patience with that of Job, which entails a superhuman, meritorious fidelity:

> ... words came in heaven concerning Abraham that he ... was faithful in all affliction. And Prince Mastema came and he said before God, "Behold, Abraham loves Isaac, his son. And he is more pleased with him than everything. Tell him to offer him [as] a burnt-offering upon the altar. And you will see whether he will do this thing. And you will know whether he is faithful

---

9. Oeming, "Glaube Abrahams," 25.

in everything in which you test him." And the Lord was aware that Abraham was faithful in all his afflictions . . . everything in which he tested him, he was found faithful and a lover of the Lord.[10]

In the biblical narrative Abraham is not yet a prototypical Jew in terms of being a Torah-observant Jew. This made interpretive expansions necessary, especially as evidenced in Jubilees,[11] but also in writers such as Philo and Josephus, to turn Abraham into an exemplar of what it meant to be Jewish.[12] It also prompted other rhetorical strategies, such as in the Letter of Aristeas, where Abraham is almost ignored and much greater emphasis is placed upon Moses' role in the formation of Israel and its Law.

Elsewhere, according to literary evidence, σπέρμα Ἀβραάμ acts as an ethnic title bearing connotations of divine election. The first canonical appearance is in Gen 15:3–5, where God promises Abraham his descendants (σπέρμα) will be numerous. The promise of its fulfillment is repeated to Isaac on account of Abraham (Gen 26:24). LXX Ps 104:6 urges remembrance of God's past deeds among σπέρμα Αβρααμ δοῦλοι αὐτοῦ υἱοὶ Ιακωβ *ἐκλεκτοὶ αὐτοῦ* (offspring of his servant Abraham, children of Jacob, *his chosen ones*).[13] Psalm 104 understands the descendants of Abraham as God's elect, and the σπέρμα Αβρααμ are similarly understood in Isa 41:8. A more developed refrain appears in Pss. Sol. 9:9, which maintains the chastisement of Israel is never permanent because "you chose the offspring of [Abraham] (τὸ σπέρμα Αβρααμ) above all the nations, and you placed your name upon us (ἔθου τὸ ὄνομά σου ἐφ᾽ ἡμᾶς), O Lord, and you will not reject us forever" (NETS). The passage understands Israel's election as permanent (οὐκ ἀπώσῃ εἰς τὸν αἰῶνα) and unique (παρὰ πάντα τὰ ἔθνη), and that God's reputation has a stake in Israel's welfare. In Pss. Sol. 18:3

---

10. O. S. Wintermute's translation in Charlesworth, *Pseudepigrapha*, 2:90.

11. VanderKam, "Biblical Interpretation," 121–22.

12. For discussion of Philo on Abraham, see chapter 2. In Josephus' account of the sacrifice of Isaac in *Ant.* 1.224–235, Isaac and Abraham are both portrayed as willing and obedient participants in the sacrifice.

13. NRSV. Italics mine.

Israel continues to enjoy God's partiality, though subject to his caring discipline.

This ideal of the special election of the σπέρμα Αβρααμ is developed further in 3 Macc 6:3, where Eleazar asks God to "look upon the seed of [Abraham], upon the children of sanctified (ἡγιασμένου) [Jacob], the people of your sanctified (ἡγιασμένης) inheritance" (NETS). Notable here is the double use of ἁγιάζω in relation to Jews as an ethnic group, "the children of sanctified Jacob" and "the people of your sanctified inheritance." The author of 3 Maccabees was aware not all Jews were faithful (1:3; 2:31; 7:12), but nonetheless uses idealized ethnic terminology.

1 Maccabees' adherence to the precedent of Phinehas in Num 25:7–13 prompts a greater interrelationship of faithfulness to YHWH and ethnic identity. The reference to Abraham's faithfulness in 1 Macc 2 is the first of a series of references to characters who had been faithful to God, suggesting the reader too must be faithful to God while resistant to imperial authorities. 1 Maccabees 2 uses Gen 15:6b in a manner consistent with its original context, but it creatively manipulates the meaning of Gen 15:6a by capitalizing on a singular reading of the Hebrew text, further conflating it with the testing motif in Gen 22. This portrays the persecution of Judaism by Hellenistic rulers as another test by God. Along with others in the "covenant of the Fathers," as a symbol of fidelity to God, Abraham serves ethnic identity as a nationalistic symbol. In 1 Maccabees the use of Abraham helps underline the importance of obedience to the Hasmoneans, as well as validates national retribution against the gentiles.

In Jewish biblical tradition, Abraham, as the progenitor of the people, bore symbolic connotations prototypical of Jewish social identity. Among these is above all religious faithfulness. As the progenitor, Abraham could also symbolize ethnic identity. Taken together, these form part of a tradition in Jewish cultural memory that touches on many aspects of Jewish social identity reviewed above. Jewish cultural memory treated Abraham as the epitome of faithfulness, prototypical of his descendants.

While John accepts the former, he denies that ethnic descent, or even adherence to the Law, *automatically* results in the latter. This is usually suggested indirectly through discussing such topics as those related to the historical or spiritual significance of Abraham or Moses. One of the more direct critiques of overvaluing Jewish ethnicity is John's treatment of the σπέρμα Ἀβραάμ (descendants of Abraham). What prevents this from becoming a direct critique on ethnic identity itself is the lack of criticism directed towards God's covenant with Abraham or his immediate descendants (Gen 15:18; 17:4–19). The Gospel juxtaposes σπέρμα Ἀβραάμ (descendants of Abraham)[14] against τέκνα θεοῦ (children of God),[15] and the distinction between σπέρμα and τέκνα is significant in John 8. The phrase τέκνα τοῦ Ἀβραάμ (children of Abraham) appears once in John 8:39, but in the context of a self-made claim that is denied by Jesus.[16]

The Johannine controversies with "the Jews" are notable for the repeated use of the demonym rather than reference to specific parties, but in John's Gospel the shortcomings of "the Jews" are not purely Jewish failings. In John 3:27 the Baptist says human helplessness and reliance upon God applies to all people. In John 5:42 Jesus asserts his opponents are obdurate because they do not have God's love in them, not because of some ethnic or religiously unique failing. In the previous verse (5:41) Jesus states he does not seek glory from *humans*, "I do not accept glory from human beings" (Δόξαν παρὰ ἀνθρώπων οὐ λαμβάνω). Here, Jesus does not use οἱ Ἰουδαῖοι, which universalizes the scope of the applicability of Jesus' declaration. The perceived problems with Jesus' opponents are universal and human. Meanwhile, John describes those who do believe in Jesus as those whom God has given him from out of "the world" (John 17:6).

The Gospel describes Jesus as the true light for all people (John 1:4, 9). In John 2:23 many (Jews) believe in Jesus, as "many believed in his name" (πολλοὶ ἐπίστευσαν εἰς τὸ ὄνομα αὐτου) on account of his signs, but John 2:25 says Jesus does not trust them because he knows *human nature* (τί ἦν ἐν τῷ ἀνθρώπῳ). In John 3:19 the judgment of

---

14. John 8:33, 37.

15. John 1:12; 11:52.

16. Nicholson classifies this as an example of misunderstanding based on an ambiguous word. He claims the misunderstanding ends at John 8:36, but the reference to Abraham in 8:33 suggests that the same topic is still under discussion in 8:39 (Nicholson, *Death as Departure*, 35).

the world is described as its rejection of Jesus,[17] because "people" (οἱ ἄνθρωποι) prefer darkness over the light.[18] There are also the numerous participial constructions where Jesus makes generalized statements that stress the importance of belief and the danger of sin without regard for ethnic background, be it Jewish or otherwise.[19] Though the controversies between Jesus and his people (τὰ ἴδια, John 1:11)[20] are placed in a Jewish setting, the reasons for the conflict are applicable to humanity in general. Taken with the fact that Jesus does not exhort his followers to be more pious or virtuous, and Jesus never pronounces active judgment on "the Jews" as Jews, it seems John has little interest in condemning Jews for being Jews. Instead, John generalizes everyone as subject to the same spiritual dynamics.

The preceding overview shows that John dissociates Jewish ethnicity from a salient factor introduced in the narrative, eternal life, through the use of irony and treatment of related topics. The cumulative result is the reader is to infer that Jewish ethnicity does not automatically, in and of itself, place one in the spiritual in-group as one who has eternal life. This universalization of spiritual failings to include Jews would not necessarily have been offensive to someone whose outlook is reflected in documents such as the Letter of Aristeas or 2–3 Maccabees, but it

---

17. While Satan as ruler of the world seems to be an object of God's active judgment (16:11), the world itself is the object of passive judgment in being left to its own condition of unbelief as expressed in the rejection of Jesus (1:18–19; 3:19; 8:15–16; 9:39; 12:31–32; 12:47–48). C. H. Dodd writes, "Christ came into the world as life and light, to save the world and not to condemn it. But what happens when light shines into dark places? . . . by an inevitable reaction the manifestation of the light brings into view the ultimate distinction between truth and falsehood, between good and evil. Hence it is κρίσις, discrimination" (Dodd, *Interpretation*, 210).

18. See Dodd's discussion on the interrelationship between light, glory, and judgment (Dodd, *Interpretation*, 201–12).

19. I am referring to the "whoever" statements. Often these are part of the "I am" or "amen" sayings, but not always (See John 1:18; 3:4, 15, 16, 18, 20, 21, 31, 36; 5:23, 24; 6:35, 40, 47, 51, 54, 56, 57, 58; 7:38; 8:12, 34, 47; 10:2; 11:25, 26; 12:25, 35, 44, 45, 46, 48; 13:20; 14:12, 21, 24; 15:5, 23; 18:37).

20. La Marche, "Prologue of John," 48; Barrett, *Prologue*, 9; Elizabeth Harris takes it to be all humanity, given the universal scope of the Logos (Harris, *Prologue and Gospel*, 63), while David Granskou observes that while "his own" are more receptive, generally there is little difference between Israel and "the World" (Granskou, "Anti-Judaism," 204).

could be deemed confrontational by those who adhered to some of the ideologies concerning Abraham discussed above in this chapter and felt that they met the criteria. John does not confine this dissociation to matters of theology but addresses challenges from Diaspora Jewish social identity in a manner consistent with the Gospel's general attitude to the relative importance of ethnicity compared to belief in Jesus. Having examined this issue thematically in chapter 5 and surveying Moses' significance and the significance of Abraham's faithfulness in reception history, below we will see the same point made in the passages that discuss the relative significance of Moses and Abraham in John's Gospel.

John 8:21–59

John 8:21–59 offers some of the best evidence that the Gospel is challenging Jewish self-categorizations derived from the reception history of Abraham surveyed above. The topic is set in John 8:12–20, where in 8:12 in an "I Am" statement Jesus asserts he is "the light of the world" (τὸ φῶς τοῦ κόσμου) and those following him "will have the light of life" (ἕξει τὸ φῶς τῆς ζωῆς). This prompts dispute over the validity of Jesus' testimony, and in a veiled "I Am" statement Jesus claims the right to testify on his own behalf alongside the Father to establish the validity of his witness (8:18), but this also leads to Jesus' claim that his opponents do not know either himself or God (8:19). John 8:12–20 introduces themes discussed in the rest of the chapter: Jesus' authority to make pronouncements, knowing God, and spiritual identity. The themes of dualism, Jesus' heavenly origins, and his return to the Father are reintroduced in John 8:21–29.

Ball and Porter note the "I Am" saying in John 8:12 (repeated in 9:5) is a continuation of the discussion of the validity of a Galilean provenance for a prophet from 7:52 that is interrupted by the insertion of the *pericopae adulterae* in 7:53—8:11.[21] Ball comments that the motif of "Light" has no direct specific parallel in the Hebrew Bible,[22] though he connects it to the metaphor of light in Isaiah.[23] Light itself func-

21. Porter, *John, His Gospel, and Jesus*, 135; Ball, *"I Am" in John's Gospel*, 221.

22. Ball, *"I Am" in John's Gospel*, 215.

23. Ball notes the statement, in light of its allusions to the theme of light and the reference to Galilee in Isa 9:1–2 would be an ironic retort to the claim that a prophet

tions as a metaphor for revelation (in the Law), life, the Logos, and God himself.[24] Williams notes that Jesus' testimony itself becomes judgment because it forces a choice between belief and unbelief.[25] In so saying, Jesus is "claiming to mediate the Word of God . . . in an authoritative way"[26] to establish his life-giving role.[27] The corresponding "I Am" statement in 8:18 (ἐγώ εἰμι ὁ μαρτυρῶν περὶ ἐμαυτοῦ) means that Jesus sees the validity of his own testimony as self-evident since he is the truthful light.[28] The metaphorically global scope "of the world" (τοῦ κόσμου) indicates his message is relevant for Jew and gentile alike.[29] The following use of the absolute "I Am" statement in the context of John 8:24[30] reflects the logic that it is not possible to believe the Scriptures but not God's agent, and yet still have eternal life.

The discussion pertaining to Abraham begins in John 8:30 when the narrator says many believed in Jesus in 8:12–20 and 8:21–29.[31] In 8:31 Jesus directs his speech towards "the Jews who believed in him" (τοὺς πεπιστευκότας αὐτῷ Ἰουδαίους). Jesus informs his dialogue partners that freedom is contingent on obedience and faithfulness to his teachings (8:31).[32] It is important to stress here that the following dialogue involves those Jews who had believed in Jesus. What follows is confusing if one forgets the conditional dualism presented in John 8:23 where the discussion partners are "from below" and Jesus is "from

---

cannot come from Galilee (Ball, *"I Am" in John's Gospel*, 215–21).

24. Dodd, *Interpretation*, 202–5.

25. Williams, *I Am He*, 273–75. This perhaps reflects the "distinction" connotations of κρίσις and κρίνω.

26. Dodd, *Interpretation*, 205.

27. Williams, *I Am He*, 274.

28. Dodd, *Interpretation*, 205; similarly Porter, *John, His Gospel, and Jesus*, 136.

29. Ball, *"I Am" in John's Gospel*, 216–17.

30. The misunderstanding and irony reappear in 8:24–25 where Jesus stresses the importance of believing that he is "I Am," followed by the response "Who are you?" (Williams, *I Am He*, 267).

31. The phrase in 8:21, εἶπεν οὖν πάλιν αὐτοῖς (And again he said to them) indicates the transition to a new section, though it relates to the preceding one. John 8:30, 31 lack similar transitions.

32. "If you continue in my word, you truly are my disciples" (ἐὰν ὑμεῖς μείνητε ἐν τῷ λόγῳ τῷ ἐμῷ, ἀληθῶς μαθηταί μού ἐστε).

above."³³ The Gospel portrays Jesus' discussion partners as "believing" because they want to be "from above." This self-categorization is central to Jewish social identity—Diaspora Jewish writers categorized themselves as understanding God's wishes and remaining faithful to him in a manner superior to that of gentile philosophical monotheists. Hans Förster maintains that in John 8:47 the διὰ τοῦτο does not signal causality but introduces a conclusion.³⁴ The translation would be something like, "He that is of God hears (obeys) God's words. From this follows: you do not hear (obey). Thus, you are not of God."³⁵ Such a translation is consistent with the function of Johannine dualism here as well as Johannine theology³⁶ attested elsewhere.³⁷ Thus, even when John sounds deterministic, the language is intended to function persuasively.

In John 8:24 Jesus claims the key to deciding one's status is belief in himself, specifically that "I am he" (ὅτι ἐγώ εἰμι). Misunderstanding is revealed when his discussion partners respond by asking, "who are you?" (σὺ τίς εἶ;) in 8:25. The misunderstanding of John 8:23–24 that emerges in 8:25 escalates until it comes to a head in 8:44. The misunderstood topics are the status of those who believe in Jesus contrasted with the identity of Jesus himself, and the need for belief in Jesus. Much of John 8:26–59 is devoted to Jesus establishing that his dialogue partners need him for their salvation, which is most bluntly stated in John 8:44 by labelling them children of the Devil, contrasted with Jesus' identity in John 8:45–59. This climaxes in an "I Am" statement in John

---

33. Von Wahlde observes that John 8 has six bases for comparison in its dualism: (1) knowing origin and destination (8:14), (2) judging by the flesh or note (8:15–16), (3) knowing God or not (8:18–19), (4) being from below or above (8:23), (5) being from this world or not (8:23), or (6) being slaves for freed-persons (8:32–37). The point of all of the above is whether or not one truly knows God, with Jesus arguing the believing Jews do not know God. Wahlde, "You are of Your Father the Devil," 421.

34. Förster, "Die syntaktische Funktion von ὅτι in Joh 8.47," 158.

35. Förster's translation (Förster, "Die syntaktische Funktion von ὅτι in Joh 8.47," 157). Parentheses mine.

36. Förster connects it to the importance of making a decision in favor of Jesus (Förster, "Die syntaktische Funktion von ὅτι in Joh 8.47," 165).

37. See, for example, the contingency of one's spiritual status in John's ethical dualism on belief, obedience, and corresponding behavior, as displayed in the logic of 1 John 3:23–24; 4:6; 4:7–8; 4:12; 4:20.

8:58,[38] "before Abraham was, I am" (πρὶν Ἀβραὰμ γενέσθαι ἐγὼ εἰμί), that is followed by an attempt to stone him.

The basis for comparison is not Jesus versus Abraham, but heavenly versus earthly as demonstrated through hearing and obedience. Abraham appears in the discussion to represent those who are "from above," faithful and obedient to YHWH. Jesus' "I Am" saying in 8:58 functions as the ultimate claim to the authority to make pronouncements as to who is "from above" or "below," on the basis of his preexistence and superior status.[39] The main area of disagreement lies in whether the "Jews who believed in him" are *already* "from above." Jesus informs them that belief and discipleship will result in knowledge of the truth and freedom,[40] implying that they do not already have them. The promise of knowing the truth is what drew these people to belief, but the discussion indicates they held to a self-understanding that, like Jesus, they were already "from above" because of their descent from Abraham. Jesus, however, considers them "from this world" (ἐκ τοῦ κόσμου τούτου) (John 8:23), which in the Johannine conception is "from below" (ἐκ τῶν κάτω) and subject to the rule of the Devil.

In John 8:32 Jesus introduces what are perceived as two promises but are really a single promise. Jesus is misunderstood as saying that if the believing Jews follow him, they will (1) know the truth, and (2) be made free. The believing Jews question the promise of "freedom," which at first is queried on a social-political understanding of freedom (8:33) but then demonstrated by Jesus in the following conversation to

---

38. The phrase appears ἐγώ εἰμί appears 5 times in John 8 (vv. 12, 18, 24, 28, 58). Three of these are absolute "I Am" statements (8:24, 28, 58), all of them appearing in the discourse under examination here.

39. Porter, *John, His Gospel, and Jesus*, 139–40; Freed, "Who or What was before Abraham," 52–59. As Edwin D. Freed puts it, the "I Am" statement here means: "Before Abraham was, I, the Christ, the Son of God, existed" (52). Use of "I Am" reflects the Jewish convention that the "Name" refers to the Messiah, but John is unique in employing God's name, "I Am," in reference to Jesus (56).

40. Brown regards 8:30–31 as serving organizational and transitional functions, rather than serving a substantive role in the narrative. This allows him to disregard the importance of 8:30–31 as editorial insertions, though he does posit the possibility that Jews would believe in Jesus, though in an incorrect type of belief (Brown, *John*, 1:351–54; Keener, *John*, 1:746).

be an apocalyptic-dualist ontological issue (8:34, 44).[41] B. F. Westcott comments that in John 8:33 the Jews in John's Gospel were disregarding preceding episodes of subjugation as abnormal in a general pattern of freedom.[42] Warren Carter suggests that the Jews in John are collaborationists attempting to preserve their rights.[43] Carter's diachronic scenario is tentative and hypothetical and is built around the fact that John opposes the Roman Empire. Craig Keener proposes a more metaphorical and spiritual understanding, where Jews in the narrative have freedom from sin, as this is what Jesus speaks about in 8:34.[44] The context is misunderstanding and debate, indicating a recurrence of Johannine *double-entendre*.

Westcott's comment, while not expressing the full depth of the social categorizations behind this assumption, is likely closer to the truth. As seen in chapters 2 and 4, Jews in Egypt assisted the Ptolemaic imperial establishment and were considered "Greeks" by the Ptolemaic rulers, but in the Roman period these Jews were deprived of upward social mobility and placed in a similar position to the local Egyptians. In this arrangement the Judean state operated quasi-independently as an "ally" under the Ptolemies and later the Seleucids, and a similar arrangement continued to exist under the stewardship of the Herodians in the Roman period, at least in name. This allowed Egyptian Jewish literature to categorize Jews as citizens of an allied state ruled from Jerusalem to attribute Jews the dignity of citizenship. The ascription of importance to Jewish service to the Ptolemaic and Roman empires, which generally followed the participationist cultural memory exemplified in Daniel, the patriarch Joseph in Egypt, or Esther and Mordecai

---

41. Wahlde, "You are of Your Father the Devil," 418–44. Motyer argues for the presence of an ethical rather than ontological dualism (Motyer, *Your Father the Devil*, 192–94). Von Wahlde shows that in apocalyptic literature, dualism functions ethically. That is, while presented in apocalyptic ontological terms, it is designed to promote ethical change.

42. Westcott, *John*, 134. Also in general agreement with Carter, though I would dispute the idea that this claim refers to relative Jewish freedom under the Romans (Carter, *John and Empire*, 101–5). Brown holds a similar view (Brown, *John*, 1:355).

43. Carter, *John and Empire*, 157–58.

44. Keener, *John*, 1:749–51. Also Beasley-Murray, *John*, 134.

in Persia, established precedent for the reinterpretation of the embarrassment of conquest and political subordination along similar lines.

Josephus, writing from Rome, also repeatedly states that Jews were Rome's "allies," despite his first-hand knowledge of Roman destruction, conquest, and domination. Alongside the more militant nationalism of Jews expressing zeal, categorization as allies and participants in the imperial enterprise provided resolution for subjugated status of Jews under imperial powers. This was aided by the fact that there were many other such "free cities" in the Roman Empire that were "free" to obey everything Rome instructed. The perplexing overstatement in 8:33 likely refers to this tradition of Jewish cultural memory that relabeled foreign domination as participation.

In John 8:33 the Jews in the narrative protest to ever being slaves to anyone (οὐδενὶ δεδουλεύκαμεν πώποτε). They state they already are free by claiming the participant social categorization discussed in chapters 2 to 4 above. Such a categorization given the political situation of the time may seem odd to modern readers accustomed to understanding Judea as under Roman domination, but as seen in preceding sections of this study, Jewish social identity and self-categorizations labelled Jews as free partners and allies in the imperial systems of the Ptolemaic and Roman empires. While Judea had been conquered and the Herodian monarchy was installed and controlled by Rome, the fact that Herod and his sons enjoyed the title "king" reflected vestiges of national sovereignty. Both Philo and Josephus portray Herod Agrippa positively, and the origins of the Alexandrian riots under Flaccus suggest some Alexandrians may have resented the visit by Antipas and a possible royal reception put on by the local Jewish community, in which Alexandrian Jews may have taken pride.[45] Jewish kings were proactive in furthering the interests of Diaspora Jews, and Jews in general, within the Roman Empire, indicating a continued national consciousness among the Diaspora.

In John 8:33 the Jews in the narrative also respond to (1), Jesus' assertion that they do not know the truth by asserting they are Abraham's descendants (σπέρμα Ἀβραάμ). We saw above that σπέρμα

---

45. This is a skeptical reading of *Flaccus* 25–31 in light of 36–40. Horst, *Philo's Flaccus*, 3, 33.

Jesus' opponents again attempt to realign themselves with the correct side of John's cosmological dualism, "from above" (ἐκ τῶν ἄνω), in their direct claim to God as father in 8:41: "we are not illegitimate children; we have one father—God himself!" (ἡμεῖς ἐκ πορνείας οὐ γεγεννήμεθα, ἕνα πατέρα ἔχομεν τὸν θεόν). Jesus counters this not by appeal to belief or descent, but through evaluation of the actions involved in their response to him in 8:42–44. These believing Jews, according to the Gospel, do not love Jesus and are incapable of understanding or accepting his claims. The reference to the Devil as being the father of the believing Jews is metaphorical—it means they are mistaken in their perception of which side they belong to: they belong to "the world" and are presently outside the scope of salvation. It becomes clearer that his opponents are on the wrong side of the dualism operative in the chapter in 8:54b–55a: "It is my Father who glorifies me, he of whom you say, 'He is our God,' though you do not know him." Jews are not inherently Satanic, but such an ascription is the logical result of comparison in a dualistic schema where it equates belief in Jesus with faithfulness to YHWH, and it comes into conflict with a conflation of biological and spiritual descent from Abraham.

The Gospel also presents the faithful Abraham as taking Jesus' side. Abraham operates in the discussion at two levels: as the representative of a faithful ethnic Israel, and as the individual Abraham, reputed for his faithfulness. Jesus never denies Abraham's faithfulness, but presumes it in his statements in 8:39 and 8:56. John uses it as a point of contrast with Jesus' opponents to demonstrate that faithfulness is an ontological state derived from God himself on account of belief in Jesus, rather than socialized through ethnic kinship or ingrained into a person's character through ancestral customs, as previously understood by Diaspora Jews.

An additional interpretive tradition that John employs is that of Abraham's hospitality, described in the largesse Abraham presents in his reception of the three visitors in Gen 18. Philo considered this a by-product of Abraham's piety,[49] the grounds for the divine visit to Abraham being that his faithfulness made him an acceptable host (116). Testament of Abraham 1:1–2 describes Abraham as welcoming to

---

49. Sandmel, "Philo's Place in Judaism," 227. Philo, *Abraham* 114.

Interpreting John's Portrayal of Jewish Origins and Collective Destiny

Ἀβραάμ served as an ethnic slogan denoting the unique elect statu of Jews on account of the covenant and their relation to YHWH. Jew understood themselves as knowing the truth about God, so in prote; in the narrative they identify themselves with Abraham, the exempla *par excellence* of faithfulness to God. Jews were perfectly aware that n(all of their in-group were faithful and so spiritually did not qualify 1 be identified with Abraham, but it was something held to be general true of most Jewish people.

However, in John 8:34–36 Jesus re-interprets Abraham's fami situation in a manner similar to Paul's interpretation of slave laws Gal 4:21–31 to assert that not all born of Abraham are the patriarcl spiritual descendants.[46] Paul Miller points to a distinction betwee "descendants" (σπέρματα) and "children" (τέκνα) of Abraham, whe it is those who are recognized as children (τέκνα) who imitate the father (8:33, 39), rather than all his descendants (σπέρματα).[47] John 8:33 Jesus' opponents first assert they are Abraham's biologic and therefore spiritual, descendants (σπέρμα Ἀβραάμ ἐσμεν). This recognized by Jesus in John 8:37 (οἶδα ὅτι σπέρμα Ἀβραάμ ἐστε) a the opponents never claim to be Abraham's τέκνα. In John 8:34– Jesus then correlates sinful behavior with slave status. Behavior, be sinful or otherwise, is used to determine the validity of claims to (scent from Abraham. In John 8:39, Jesus denies that his opponents : Abraham's children (τέκνα) on grounds that they do not imitate th progenitor's hospitality, but rather seek to perpetrate sin by killing h (John 8:37), therefore logically placing them on the wrong side o cosmological-dualist divide in John 8:44 and invalidating their clairr spiritual descent from Abraham. Jesus' rejection is a prominent the in John (1:11) while positive reception results in life (1:12).[48] Je does not disparage the value of descent from Abraham, but mainta his discussion partners' impending response is inconsistent with claimed character they seem to consider derivative of their ethnic s tus (8:37–41).

46. In agreement with Keener, *John*, 1:752; Westcott, *John*, 134.
47. Miller, "They Saw His Glory," 142. Citing John 8:37, 39.
48. Hunt, "Word became Flesh," 85.

Interpreting John's Portrayal of Jewish Origins and Collective Destiny

everyone. According to Steven A. Hunt, John 8 reflects these ideas, which has several references to a lack of hospitality towards Jesus on the part of his Jewish opponents. The most convincing example presented by Hunt is Jesus' complaint in 8:39 that his opponents do not emulate their progenitor's behavior in Gen 18.[50]

Abraham's faith, as exemplified by his hospitality, is further underlined by a diverse range of interpretive traditions that God had given Abraham visions of the future fulfillment of his promises. Jesus would then be implying the veracity of these traditions by claiming Abraham had witnessed Jesus' coming.[51] John presents Abraham as anticipating Jesus, with the appropriate response being acceptance of him. Failure to do so demonstrates a lack of perception, faith, and discontinuity with Abraham.[52] Jesus repeats a similar point in John 8:43 and 8:45. His opponents do not understand him ("why do you not understand what I say?"; τί τὴν λαλιὰν τὴν ἐμὴν οὐ γινώσκετε) because they cannot listen to him ("it is because you cannot accept my word"; ὅτι οὐ δύνασθε ἀκούειν τὸν λόγον τὸν ἐμόν) (8:43), in turn because, as per John 8:45, they do not believe (obey) Jesus (οὐ πιστεύετέ μοι).

That an over-valuing of ethnicity can be a barrier to belief in John 8 is seen in the Jews' protests that Abraham is their father (John 8:33, 39). In John 8, ethnic descent from Abraham prevents the Jews in John from perceiving the barriers that keep them on the wrong side of the dualistic divide (8:47) and stop them from engaging in corrective action because they presume they already know God (8:54b–55a). In all likelihood, Jesus' Jewish discussion partners think they are predisposed to righteousness on account of socialization derived through being raised up in their ethnic heritage, and therefore do not believe in Jesus in the way that John thinks is necessary.[53] They want to *join* Jesus in

---

50. Hunt, "Word Became Flesh," 89, 91–92.

51. Precisely which literary tradition is alluded to is unknown. There are examples seen mostly in apocalyptic literature, which is typically attributed a "Palestinian" provenance, such as Apoc. Ab. 9:6–7; 4 Ezra 3:14; 2 Bar. 4:4, as well as numerous possible rabbinic sources of uncertain date (Miller, "They Saw His Glory," 142; Hunt, "Word Became Flesh," 98). Also see Brown, *John*, 1:360; Keener, *John*, 1:767 for rabbinic sources.

52. Miller, "They Saw His Glory," 141–42; Hunt, "Word Became Flesh," 97.

53. Hoskins interprets this passage as primarily a warning on the need to imitate

his cause because of his statements in 8:12–30, such as the reference to the "Son of Man" in 8:28, and hopes for a, probably apocalyptic-like, national restoration. In John's mind *joining* Jesus is not necessarily the same as *following* him, welcoming him, or accepting his claims.

PATTERNS OF INNOVATION

In one trend in Jewish cultural memory found in Ptolemaic Egypt, Abraham served as one of the founders of human civilization and technology to facilitate social convergence with the gentile dominant-cultures in which Jews lived. Gentiles often saw Jews as similar to Chaldeans, with whom Jewish writers alternately used Abraham as a means to align or differentiate themselves.[54] As discussed in this chapter, the more zeal-oriented traditions of Judaism used Abraham as a symbol of ethnic and theological identity. Just as Abraham's background could speak to Jewish intellectual and cultural sophistication to facilitate social convergence, they also used Abraham to maintain Jewish ethnic distinctiveness. In this capacity, Abraham's legendary faithfulness served as an example for Jews seeking to be obedient to the Law. Abraham, therefore, served in this latter cultural memory as a metonym for piety and faithfulness.

John appears unaware of traditions that portrayed Abraham as intellectually sophisticated, though John does seem to know cultural memories where Abraham was an exemplar of what should be prototypical of Jewish social identity and assumes some of these traditions are true. The Johannine Jesus presumes Abraham was indeed faithful and just, and uses this as warrant to complain that his discussion partners are not (8:39–40) and place his opponents on the wrong side of a dualistic divide.[55]

Jesus' discussion partners appear to follow a conventional Hebrew reading of Gen 15:6 that describes Abraham as being accredited

---

the example of Abraham's faith, which is similar to my interpretation (Hoskins, "Passover Theme," 56–60).

54. For Jewish use of Abraham for the purpose of self-differentiation, see chapter 2. For discussion of perceived similarity between Jews and Chaldeans, see chapters 2 and 4.

55. Hoskins, "Passover Theme," 57.

Interpreting John's Portrayal of Jewish Origins and Collective Destiny

righteousness for being faithful, while John assumes the Septuagintal reading where the same is due to Abraham's belief, which is expressed by his faithfulness. Both interpretive traditions, however, maintain Abraham welcomed God when he visited, something which the Jews in the narrative, Jesus' "own," fail to do.

This failure to welcome Jesus deconstructs social categorizations derived from the Jewish common progenitor Abraham that symbolized the ideal for his descendants. Abraham was indeed righteous, believed in God, and "saw" Jesus. The discussion between Jesus and the believing Jews in John 8 demonstrates that, in John's mind, biological and spiritual descendants of Abraham are two different groups of people. While Abraham was faithful and believed God, the social categorization of "pious" cannot be imputed on the grounds of ethnic descent alone because it is not salient; the salient factor in the narrative is that one must also be a member of a Jesus-centered "spiritual Israel"[56] in order to establish relative similarity between Jesus and his discussion partners. The failure to realize this in the narrative again undermines the normative fit of the social categorization in question. As a result, the inability to use Abraham as a support for this social categorization removes it of its salience. The result is that the identity of the Johannine Jews become more abstract, making them a local manifestation of "the world" in the narrative.

MOSES AND THE LAW

In John, there is much engagement with cultural memories of Moses: whose side is Moses on? Is Jesus greater than Moses? Who will the people choose to follow? There is good reason for this, as Moses is a central figure in Jewish reception history and social identity. How John interacts with previous cultural memories concerning Moses bears significance for interpreting John's approach to Jewish social identity.

Moses in Reception History

As noted in earlier chapters above, especially chapter 2, Moses was central to constructing Diaspora Jewish identity. It is not uncommon

---

56. Dennis, *Gathering of True Israel*, 341–51.

for Moses to be presented as the greatest leader and thinker in Jewish history. In the Letter of Aristeas the Law is the medium of God's instruction, and Moses is the teacher of the Law. The "legislator" (ὁ νομοθέτης) in the Letter of Aristeas is Moses, and it is Moses who is lauded for the Law's grandeur. The Letter of Aristeas understands that the Law originates with God himself, but God is placed at one remove due to Moses' involvement in order to depict him as a *polis*-founding Greek-styled philosopher-king.[57] Furthermore, in Plato's political philosophy one purpose of a polity's legislation is to serve as instruction that comprehensively governs and regulates life to produce an orderly and just society. The Letter of Aristeas praises the Mosaic Law as the most comprehensive and perfect form of legislation.

The Letter of Aristeas categorizes Jews as philosophical on account of the Torah being God's wisdom. Josephus provides further evidence that Jews categorized themselves as "taught by God" through Moses' Law,[58] and makes the claim that Plato imitated Moses in proposing the need for comprehensive systems to preserve the obedience of a population to the laws of its polity (*Ag. Ap.* 2.257). Philo indicates that Jews considered themselves "taught by God" through Moses' career.[59] It is central to the Jewish worldview of the time that Jews were uniquely granted privileged instruction by God himself through the Law given by Moses.

Jesus, Moses, Law Codes, and Revelation in John

Another consideration at play is that law codes in antiquity were viewed as a means of blessing because they provided order and security. The

---

57. For Moses as a philosopher-king, see Clifford, "Moses as Philosopher-Sage in Philo," 151–67, drawing on Philo's exposition of Moses' career, especially *Moses* 2.2, 66–67.

58. For more, see the discussion of *Against Apion* in chapter 4.

59. In *Creation* 1.170–171, Moses is the teaching agent who grants knowledge of God's nature and character. In *Good Person* 1.43, Philo claims that ὁ τῶν Ἰουδαίων νομοθέτης (the Jewish Legislator; Moses) teaches that those who fully love God can participate in his nature. In Philo, Abraham finds himself used as a moral example, where in *Abraham* 1.52, Abraham, Isaac, and Jacob stand in as symbols for taught, natural, and practiced forms of virtue.

Interpreting John's Portrayal of Jewish Origins and Collective Destiny

Law was God's conduit of grace[60] because it taught God's character and how his creatures should live. This has interesting consequences for the Johannine Jesus' relationship to the Law in John 1:16–18:

> From his fullness (ὅτι ἐκ τοῦ πληρώματος αὐτοῦ) we have all received, grace upon grace (χάριν ἀντὶ χάριτος). (ὅτι) The law was given through Moses; grace and truth came through Jesus Christ. No one has ever seen God. It is God's only son, who is close to the Father's heart, who has made him known.

Treatment of the Prologue at times results in examining 1:16–18 as separate theses because they are read as different stanzas in a song or hymn, which tends to result in dropping the conjunction ὅτι in translation. If we include these conjunctions in the translation, we see John explaining what he means in 1:17. Jesus is a fulfillment, or fullness (πληρώματος), of some kind. The χάριν ἀντὶ χάριτος (grace upon grace) of 1:16 is paralleled in 1:17, meaning both Jesus and the Law are described as media of grace.[61] John is explicit that "grace and truth came through Jesus Christ."

As the climax of the Prologue,[62] John claims in John 1:18a that Jesus' revelation is qualitatively superior because Moses had not seen God.[63] John 1:18b elaborates that God himself, here Jesus, gives expla-

---

60. Dumbrell, "Grace and Truth," 116.

61. Moloney holds that "upon" is the correct translation given the context (Moloney, *Belief in the Word*, 47), citing Edwards, "Grace and the Law," 5–10. Edwards notes that literary testimony from the Early Church understood ἀντὶ as meaning "instead of," in the sense of replacement (7), though Edwards favors the rendering "upon" as an example of progressive parallelism (5). Edwards thinks it possible that John is being deliberately ambiguous (11). Bultmann argues for a translation of "grace upon grace" as well, reflecting the blessing in Jesus as incarnate revealer, though in the following verse he sees a contrast between the Law and Moses on the one hand, and grace and Jesus on the other (Bultmann, *Gospel of John*, 78; see also 78n2). Dumbrell, too, favors translating ἀντὶ with "upon," though suggests a qualitative distinction on account of the Law as a medium of grace being inferior due to its being mediated through Moses, while the grace granted through Jesus is unmediated ("Grace and Truth," 117). Similarly, Evans, *Word and Glory*, 80. The above discussion shows the question of John's relation to the Law is not to be answered on the translation of a single word, but in the broader context of its theology as a whole.

62. Harris, *Prologue and Gospel*, 92.

63. A likely polemical statement against cultural memories that exemplary ancestors such as Moses had ascended to Heaven to experience theophanies. Detecting

nation (ἐκεῖνος ἐξηγήσατο) and communicates what God is like and expects.⁶⁴ Jesus fulfills the revelatory function performed by the Mosaic Law because Jesus is from the Father and is qualified to act as a revealer. Jesus does not function as a sort of antithesis to the Law but reveals it in a new and unique way. Given the explanatory function of the prologue, this insight influences the understanding of Jesus for the remainder of the Gospel.⁶⁵ This reduces singular significance of the Mosaic Law in comparison to Jesus, but it does not completely dismiss it or consider it antithetical.⁶⁶

In the Johannine conception, the Law and scriptures do not merely serve as testimony to Jesus. From a surface reading it seems that Jesus replaces the Law, but this ignores Johannine polemic against interpretive traditions where Moses ascended to receive the Law (John 3:13).⁶⁷ Further, an implication of Wisdom Christology is that John views Jesus as the origin of the Law in a capacity that gives him priority, not subsequent superiority, over Moses.⁶⁸

Both the Law and the Scripture are treated as authoritative documents employed by both Jesus and his opponents.⁶⁹ In general there

---

Johannine polemic against Mosaic ascent traditions is not uncommon in Johannine scholarship. See, for example, Meeks, "Man from Heaven," 53, 67; Borgen, *Gospel of John*, 60–65; Maronde, "Moses in the Gospel of John," 35–43.

64. Moloney notes the verb is often used in Hellenistic literature of "making known of divine secrets, and it is often the gods themselves who do this" (Moloney, *Belief in the Word*, 50).

65. While many suggest the Prologue has an independent pre-history, it is common for commentators to understand the prologue as influencing how one reads the rest of John. Recently, Moloney, *Belief in the Word*, 23 (also Bultmann, *Gospel of John*, 13); Kierspel, *Jews and the World in the Fourth Gospel*, 113–23. Evans firmly connects the Prologue to biblical interpretive traditions, particularly Wisdom traditions (Evans, *Word and Glory*, 77–186).

66. Maronde, "Moses in the Gospel of John," 29; also see Loader, "Jesus and the Law in John," 148, though Loader maintains it is "replaced" by Jesus though it continues to be respected by John (141–42).

67. For discussion, see Meeks, *Prophet-King*, 295–313; Maronde, "Moses and the Law in John," 35–38; Borgen, *Bread from Heaven*, 60–65.

68. See also Thompson, "Wisdom and Theology in John 6," 228–30, 246; Maronde, "Moses in the Gospel of John," 37, 43.

69. "The Law" (ὁ νόμος) in John 7:19, 23, 51; 8:5; 10:34; 19:7; "the Scriptures" (αἱ γραφαί) in John 5:39; 7:42; 10:35.

Interpreting John's Portrayal of Jewish Origins and Collective Destiny

is some difference in how "the Law" (ὁ νόμος) and "the Scriptures" (ἡ γραφή) are treated. Normally the Scriptures are fulfilled[70] while the Law establishes conformity of conduct.[71] However, the two are blended in John 1:45 when Phillip tells Nathanael, "We have found him about whom Moses in the law and also the prophets wrote (Μωϋσῆς ἐν τῷ νόμῳ καὶ οἱ προφῆται)." There are three clear exceptions to the rule in John 10:34–35, 12:34, and 15:25. In John 10:34–35 Jesus refers to Ps 82:6 as part of "the Law," and Jesus then presses his point with the statement that Scripture cannot be annulled.[72] This is significant because elsewhere the Psalms are treated as prophecies that are fulfilled.[73] In the second example in John 12:34, "the crowd" (ὁ ὄχλος) refers to a promise "from the Law" (ἐκ τοῦ νόμου) that the Messiah will remain forever.[74] The third appears in John 15:25, where Psalm 69:4 is fulfilled when Jesus' opponents are said to hate him without cause. Normally "the Law" is used in contexts of dispute over practice, and "the Scriptures" in contexts of prophetic fulfillment, but at times the Law, as does the Scripture in general, performs a prophetic function that would normally seem to be assigned to the Scriptures.[75]

In the treatment of the motif of Jesus as the "light of the world," most scholars see allusions to the Law of Moses by means of John's Wisdom Christology and its connections to the Wisdom tradition.[76] Af-

---

70. Formulaic fulfillment statements are found in John 13:18; 17:12; 19:24, 28, 36.

71. See John 7:19, 23, 51; 8:17; 19:7.

72. I question Loader's contention that Jesus is mocking his opponents here (Loader, "Jesus and the Law in John," 145). It is more likely that Papaionnaiou is correct that Jesus is challenging what John would consider are his opponents' presumptions (Papaioannou, "Jesus and Sabbath Law," 254–55).

73. For example, Ps 69:9 in John 2:17; Ps 41:9 in John 13:18; Ps 22:18 in John 19:24; Ps 69:21 in John 19:28–30; Ps 34:20 (and perhaps also Exod 12:46; Num 9:12) in John 19:36.

74. For example the promises of permanent restoration by the Son of Man or a similar figure in Dan 7:14; Ezek 37:25; Isa 9:7; Ps 110:4. Brown also gives the possibility of the emergence of a "hidden" Messiah who would remain forever, as per the Son of Man in 1 En. 62:5–16 (Brown, *Gospel according to John*, 478–79). However, none of these examples are found in the Law proper.

75. Compare John 2:22; 7:38; 13:18; 17:12; 19:24, 28, 36–37; 20:9 with 1:45; 7:49; 12:34; 15:25.

76. Light as symbol for the Law: Pss 43:3; 119:105, 130; Prov 6:23; Sir 24:27 [32];

John and Anti-Judaism

ter Jesus states the necessity of his impending death and the judgment of "the world" in 12:31–33, the crowd contradicts him stating that "we have heard from the Law (ἐκ τοῦ νόμου) that the Christ remains forever." They then equivocate the Son of Man and Messiah in John 12:34. Jesus unites these symbols with the Law in his own person and speaks about all of them at once in John 12:35–36. Dodd also notes that Rabbinic tradition categorized Israel and Jerusalem as the "light of the world," a status derivative of God himself,[77] mediated through the revelation contained in the Law of Moses. In John 9:5 Jesus claims to be "light of the world," while in 12:35 Jesus implores his audience to "walk while you have the light" (περιπατεῖτε ὡς τὸ φῶς ἔχετε). Walking in the light is a metaphor for knowing God or keeping the Law in obedience to YHWH.[78] The exhortation to become "children of light" (υἱοὶ φωτὸς) in 12:36 implies that this status does not apply *tout court* to Israel. This would not be the first time one Jew made this accusation against another, since Isaiah is quoted as a precedent and prophecy for the rejection of Jesus.[79] John holds that possession of the Law does not automatically result in privileged knowledge or access to God, illustrated in the chart below.

Figure 3: Chain of Revelation

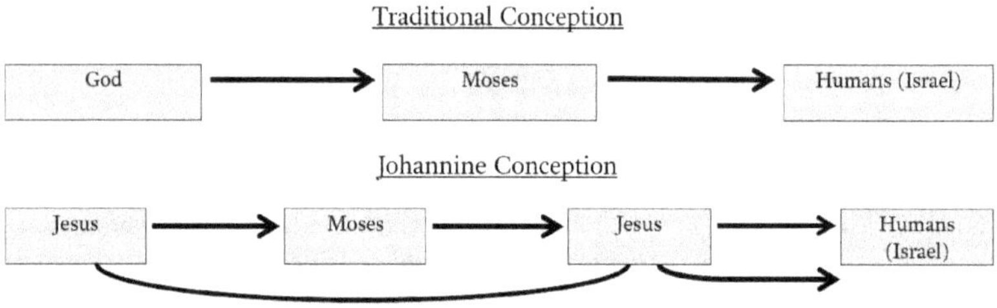

Traditional Conception

God → Moses → Humans (Israel)

Johannine Conception

Jesus → Moses → Jesus → Humans (Israel)

Wis 18:4; Bar 4:2. Though Pancaro remains skeptical due to uncertainty of John's theological provenance (Pancaro, *Law in the Fourth Gospel*, 485–87). Light also serves a similar function for truth, reality, and life (Dodd, *Interpretation*, 201–4).

77. Dodd, *Interpretation*, 204.
78. Ps 56:13; 89:15; and Isa 2:5; Bar 4:2.
79. John 12:38–40, quoting Isa 53:1 and 6:10.

Interpreting John's Portrayal of Jewish Origins and Collective Destiny

Moses and Jesus in John

There have been previous studies on the importance of Moses in the Fourth Gospel, especially in terms of how cultural memories pertaining to Moses and the Law influence the Gospel's Christology.[80] The following section will focus on the treatment of Moses in John according to A. D. Smith's ethnosymbolic cultural-nationalist paradigm discussed in chapter 1. We will briefly examine the role of Moses as a common progenitor and founder of the Jewish people in John, on the premise that he functioned as such in Hellenistic Jewish literature. While in the Synoptic Gospels Jesus engages in *Halakhic* disputes, John uses these kinds of debates as a pretense for discussing Jesus' significance and are secondary to discussions of his identity and authority.

Moses in John 5:45–46

The continued relevance of Moses' revelatory function to Jewish social identity can be seen in the debate in John 5:30–47, where "Moses" serves as the climax regarding valid witnesses who testify in Jesus' defense. Jesus accuses his opponents of trusting in the scriptures for eternal life in 5:39, while in 5:45 Jesus makes the comment that they had put their trust in Moses when he was their accuser. The two statements in 5:39 and 5:45–46 demonstrate the near equivalency between Moses and the Law frequently found in Diaspora Jewish literature. While God gave the Law, it was often described as Moses' Law.

Jesus exploits this distinction to separate the Law, central to Jewish identity, from being coterminous with faithfulness and worship of Judaism's God. This divides Jewish social identity into three parts where (1) maintaining piety, (2) keeping the Law, and (3) pleasing God were so closely associated they at times became synonymous in the literature examined in chapters 2–4. In John's Gospel, Jesus distinguishes these from one another so that 1, 2, and 3 are no longer coterminous:

---

80. Recent studies include Boismard, *Moses or Jesus*, 68–84; Scott, *Sophia and the Johannine Jesus*, 83–173; Sharon Ringe, *Wisdom's Friends*, 46–63; Thompson, "Wisdom and Theology in John 6," 221–46; Thompson, *God of the Gospel of John*, 101–33; Cory, "Wisdom's Rescue," 95–116; Fletcher-Louis, "Wisdom Christology," 52–68; Glasson, *Moses in the Fourth Gospel*; Evans, *Word and Glory*, 135–45. For a literature review, see Harstine, *Moses as a Character*, 3–11.

it is possible to seemingly behave piously and keep the Law that Moses gave, but no longer please God or be truly pious if they reject Jesus. This establishes belief in Jesus as the basis for establishing relative difference, and whether one should be categorized as truly pious, virtuous, or philosophical.

Moses in John 6:30–32

After the feeding of five thousand in Galilee, the crowd pursues Jesus across the lake (John 6:24–25). Jesus urges them to trust him as the Son of Man (6:27). In keeping with the theme of desert provision of the feeding,[81] in 6:28 the crowd asks τί ποιῶμεν ἵνα ἐργαζώμεθα τὰ ἔργα τοῦ θεοῦ; (what must we do to perform the works of God?). This question mirrors the assumption that the Law gives instruction on what is necessary to please God, which God gave in the wilderness at Sinai through Moses. By asking this question, the crowd effectively expects Jesus to respond as Moses had in the wilderness. Jesus responds that belief in him is the necessary work (6:29).

In further comparison to Moses, the crowd proceeds to tell Jesus that provision of manna was Moses' ongoing legitimating sign (6:30–31). As we discussed in the previous chapter, Jesus counters that the manna was not a legitimating sign, but God's gift—therefore a sign of God's power rather than Moses' legitimacy. This downplays Moses' role and emphasizes God's role. Reconnecting both the Exodus and the Law with God himself provides Jesus' warrant for his self-identifications as the Bread from Heaven.

This is not necessarily theological correction: Jews were well-aware that the scriptural record said it was God who had delivered them from Egypt, that Moses was his human agent, and that it was God who had provided the Law and provision in the wilderness. However, John is concerned about cultural memories that could over-glorify Moses or the Law at the expense of Jesus, who in the Johannine view serves as God's agent and has revelatory and salvific priority, and in whom they must accept as the bread of life. Again, the truth of the Law and the

---

81. Exod 12, 16. Glasson, *Moses in the Fourth Gospel*, 45–47; Thompson, "Wisdom and Theology in John 6," 245; Schapdick, "Religious Authority Re-Evaluated," 195–98.

Exodus led by Moses that it narrates is accepted and, by means of the bread metaphor, extended to embrace Jesus as its symbolic representative that establishes whether or not one has eternal life. This relativizes and subordinates the importance of ethnicity, or being pious or philosophical about God, to faith. It undermines the salience of these social categorizations so that they cannot serve as a basis for determining who belongs to the spiritual in-group. It makes belief in Jesus as the true bread become a salient category for establishing the identity of members of the spiritual in-group.

Moses in John 7:19–23

Moses again appears in John 7:19–23, where the Johannine Jesus states that since circumcision is permissible if the eighth day of life for a male is a Sabbath, it should be permissible to heal an entire individual on the Sabbath. The permissibility of circumcision, which affected part of an individual, was regarded as justification for saving an individual's life (a person's whole).[82] It was also understood as a way of making a male complete.[83] According to John, it is therefore acceptable for Jesus to heal lesser ailments or dangers on the Sabbath in John 7:23. This supports Jesus' claim in 7:19 that none of his opponents obeyed the Law because they were violating the command not to murder by seeking his death (Exod 20:13). Further, since circumcision took priority over the Sabbath, it was not unreasonable for Jesus to decide that healing an individual's well-being took priority over the Sabbath. This reflects the Markan Jesus' *halakah*, though it remains unstated, a conclusion arrived at through Jesus' reading of Genesis and the Mosaic Law. Moses is used as the standard of judgment for determining the acceptability of an act, an act of reasoning of which Jesus' opponents are portrayed as being incapable, undermining social categorizations pertaining to theological acumen.

---

82. This legal interpretive precedent is discussed in Beasley-Murray, *John*, 109; Keener, *John*, 1:716–18; Brown, *John*, 1:312–13.

83. Discussed in Hakola, *Identity Matters*, 137. Citing *m. Ned.* 3:11, where Abraham is not called "perfect" until after he was circumcised. It should be noted that Hakola doubts the relevance of this position for interpreting John; the previous possibility, the legitimacy of breaking the Sabbath to save a person's life, is more likely and is noted by many commentators.

Moses in John 9:28–29

One of the functions of John 9 is to paint a contrast between those who accept and reject Jesus, while providing a venue for Jesus to discuss his own significance. The ironic contrast between spiritual sight and spiritual blindness, together with the appearance of ἀποσυνάγωγος in John 9:22, led J. L. Martyn to propose John 9 was an allegory for the Johannine community or its leader(s). John 9 opens with the discussion leading to the blind man's being given sight (9:1–7), the Pharisees' investigation (9:8–34), and Jesus' discussion of spiritual blindness (9:35–41). Key themes are sin, denial, and social sanctions for belief in Jesus.[84] Again, the pretense for the conflict is Sabbath observance,[85] though the real topic of discussion is Jesus' identity.[86]

The Pharisees initiate their investigation at the request of the man's associates (9:8, 13). Jesus' status as a prophet (9:17) is rejected in favor of preference for Moses' well-established prophetic status (9:28–29),[87] and who in reception history was portrayed as the teacher of all subsequent prophets.[88] This occurs after John steers the discussion so there is no logical alternative to the conclusion that Jesus was sent by

---

84. Schnackenburg characterizes the allusions between the Gospel and the problems faced by its contemporary audience as particularly transparent, though he does not fully subscribe to Martyn's two-level reading. Schnackenburg, *Gospel according to Saint John*, 2:238–39.

85. In this instance, Loader sees no disparagement of Sabbath practice (Loader, "Jesus and the Law in John," 142).

86. Papaioannou, "Jesus and Sabbath Law," 258–59.

87. Schnackenburg characterizes this as a common Pharisaic position testified to in later rabbinic literature, while also demonstrating that Jesus' opponents do not understand his revelation (Schnackenburg, *Gospel according to St. John*, 2:251). Beasley-Murray, *John*, 158, cites the primary source as *b. Yoma* 4a. This is credited to Barrett by Brown, *John*, 1:374 (citing Barrett, *Gospel according to St. John*, 300 [2nd ed. = 362]). Meanwhile, Haenchen sees it as simply demonstrating that they see Jesus as lacking legitimation (Haenchen, *John*, 2:40).

88. Keener, *John*, 1:791. Keener traces this idea in Philo, where in *Cherubim* 49 Philo claims to have been initiated into mysteries by Moses and taught by a disciple, who had also been initiated into the same mysteries. In *Confusion* 39 it is implied the psalmist of Ps 30:19 learned from Moses, and of Zechariah in *Confusion* 62. In *Virtues* 66, Joshua is described as Moses' pupil, and in *Prelim. Studies* 177 Solomon is classified thus. Particularly important for this passage, in *Spec. Laws* 1.345 and 2.88, Philo labels Jews generally under this category.

God (9:30–33). The man responds positively and worships Jesus when informed of Jesus' identity (9:35–38), while spiritual blindness is pronounced on the observing Pharisees (9:39–41).

In 9:28–29 Jesus' opponents reveal that they choose to be disciples of Moses because they remain agnostic about Jesus' identity. This statement is used to demonstrate spiritual blindness because the preceding miracle and discussion lead the reader to conclude there is no other alternative to the conclusion that Jesus is sent from God. In this example, discipleship to Moses is "playing it safe" because it is known for a fact that Moses is a revelatory agent, though the Gospel's Wisdom Christology, unknown to the opponents, shows that the source of Moses' revelation is Jesus himself. Again, John is in part criticizing a failure to distinguish Moses as the intermediary, and God (as represented in Jesus) as the source of revelation. The tradition that Moses ascended to Heaven to receive the Law rendered Moses as effectively the source of revelation in itself, placing him in competition with Jesus.[89]

In John 5 the Jews in the narrative are accused by Moses, who in the lawsuit motif serves as a prosecuting attorney.[90] In the Johannine conception, Moses would have recognized Jesus as the embodied Wisdom in which the Law originated.[91] In John 9:29, the Jews in John make a conservative decision and decide to reject Jesus in favor of discipleship to Moses. However, the miracle in 9:1–7 is intended to make Jesus' origins apparent in his use of elements symbolic of creation (9:6).[92] Jesus states one of his functions is to take away sight from those who can see (9:39); Jesus' statement that the Pharisees are in sin is a reference to 9:30–33, where there is no logical alternative to acceptance

---

89. Meeks, *Prophet-King*, 295–313; Maronde, "Moses and the Law in John," 35–38; Borgen, *Bread from Heaven*, 60–65.

90. Harstine, *Moses as a Character*, 60, 72; Schapdick, "Religious Authority Re-Evaluated," 206.

91. On the Law as the expression of wisdom, see Thompson, "Wisdom and Theology in John 6," 246; Boismard, *Moses or Jesus*, 70–73.

92. Frayer-Griggs, "Spittle, Clay, and Creation," 659–70. Frayer-Griggs points to Jewish exegetical traditions where God created humans out of the dust, using his spittle to hold the dust together. For Frayer-Griggs, the use of spittle by Jesus to create mud to cover the man's eyes is an allusion to Jesus' (and God's) creative activity alluded to in the Prologue.

of Jesus' claimed identity. Jesus' opponents are therefore in contravention of Deut 18:19.

The significance of this is that it reduces the relevance of Jewish self-categorizations that involve knowing through the Scriptures what God is like, such as being philosophical or theologically-informed, maintaining piety, and living in obedience. This relativizes the benefits of Moses serving as a symbolic common progenitor by giving Jesus theological and revelatory priority. Especially important is Jesus' statement that his opponents "see" yet remain in their sin, thereby demonstrating their spiritual blindness (9:39, 41).[93] This likewise lessens the salience of a number of Jewish self-categorizations because belief in Jesus is now the most salient factor for determining the identity of the spiritual in-group.

Summary

In John Jesus does not supersede the Law as something subsequent and superior—Jesus precedes the Law and is its origin, and therefore has the right to emend how his opponents read the Law, interpret it, or decide which issues take priority over others. Further, since Jesus is treated as the origin of revelation, which is inclusive of the Law as written revelation, John is therefore not "anti-Law." The references to "your Law" in John 8:17 and 10:34 are at least partially rhetorical. Both occur in proximity to predictions or attempts to implement his death;[94] John 8:17 occurs in a context where Jesus arguing against placing too much value on a biologically-centered ethnic identity at the expense of belief, which in John's mind is equated with faith in Jesus. Meanwhile, John 10:34 occurs in the context of a rejection of Jesus before the performance of his climactic seventh sign, and where he faces rejection and death. In the Johannine presentation Jesus is the revealing agent who has priority over Moses in the process of revelation. Moses wrote

---

93. Borgen, *Bread from Heaven*, 176–78; Lieu, "Blindness in the Johannine Tradition," 88–89.

94. According to J. Augenstein, the phrase "your law" does not suggest psychological distance on the part of the author from Judaism because it follows biblical speech conventions. A second issue is that in John's perception, the Johannine Jews do not accept Jesus' priority over the Law in terms of his eternal preexistence or divinity, prompting Jesus to use this pronoun (Augenstein, "'Eur Gesetz,'" 311–13).

the Laws, legislation, and wisdom that he was taught. In short, Moses was writing about Jesus. From John's point of view, anything positive attributed to Moses can also be ascribed to Jesus to a greater degree, which means true piety and worship must be centered in Jesus.

Johannine Attitudes to the Common Progenitors

John does not disregard the significance of Abraham or Moses lightly, and maintains much of their previous significance in Jewish cultural memory while incorporating them into the new salvific paradigm under Jesus. However, it deconstructs Jewish prototypicality to the extent that maintaining the ancestral customs inherited from Moses and Abraham no longer serves as a means for situating a person as God's child. That said, these failures are due to what John considers to be the inability to live up to what John presents as the prototypicality of Moses or Abraham. The Jews in John's Gospel do not welcome or believe Jesus, as it maintains the faithful and hospitable Abraham would have. Likewise, they do not keep the Law that Moses wrote or have Moses' insightfulness, evidenced in that they do not accept Jesus, whom John maintains Moses would have recognized. Moses and Abraham remain prototypical of Israelite heritage, but John reinterprets this prototypicality so that it severs any derivative status Jewish members of the audience may have attempted to claim on account of ethnic background or biological descent. Instead, John presents them as ideals to aspire to because they correctly understand who Jesus is.

John also claims God himself as the common progenitor of Christians. John situates Moses and Abraham in its cosmic dualism to defend this assertion from Jewish claims to God as father to explain the rejection of Jesus by many Jews in the first century. The result is that the progenitors Moses and Abraham are accepted, but their importance in determining ontological status deriving from ethnic descent before God is reinterpreted in light of Jesus. Von Wahlde argues that even though "stereotyped apocalyptic polemic" uses deterministic language, writers in fact are aware that individuals can make choices and be persuaded to change. While the reasoning sounds circular, in fact John categorizes an individual as "children of God" or part of "the world" on the basis of response to Jesus.[95]

The Johannine treatment of Moses is more faithful to the biblical account of his role in the Exodus and giving of the Law than some material derived from Jewish reception history. Meanwhile, John seems to allude to similar laudatory reception history material that exalts Abraham's faithfulness, hospitality, and prophetic knowledge of God's future fulfillment of his promises. This allows Abraham, as biological progenitor, to continue to act as an exemplar and metonym for those who are faithful to God. Simultaneously, while Moses' revelatory function allows him to be used as a witness to Jesus, his status is derivative of Jesus' role as the revealing Logos/Wisdom. This permits John to reorder the chain of revelation and assign significance to obedience to the Law as an expression of faith that is secondary to belief in Jesus. The chart below illustrates how the Fourth Gospel can sanction Moses and Abraham as common progenitors, yet still maintain that belief in Jesus has priority over both.

Figure 4: Progenitors in John

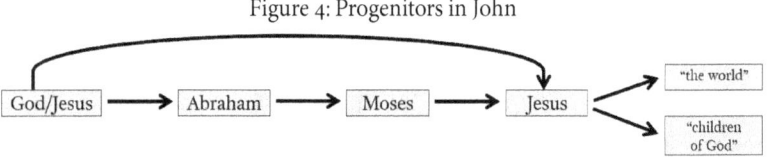

Children of God under God as Father

John reinterprets the divine kinship of Israel with God in cosmic-dualist terms. As seen above, Jews categorized their close relationship to God vis-à-vis gentiles as an ethnic trait. Jews described it as such under the assumption that the Mosaic Law and Jewish lifestyle socialized individuals in this character trait, though Jews were aware that their fellows could choose to be unfaithful and Second Temple literature demonstrates they disputed accordingly.

John 1:12–13 states children of God are "born from God." John 1:13 specifically denies this status is derivative of a common human progenitor. Most would probably have claimed it was partially a

---

95. Wahlde, "You are of Your Father the Devil," 418–44.

Interpreting John's Portrayal of Jewish Origins and Collective Destiny

spiritual status and partially an ethnic status, the two being different sides of the same coin. The status of "born from God" is carefully distinguished from that of Jesus in 3:16, so that humans may enjoy a status similar to that of Jesus, though of a lesser order, where humans are τέκνα θεοῦ (children of God) while Jesus enjoys the singular status of "son" (τὸν υἱὸν τὸν μονογενῆ). The special status of the Son in John 8:35 underscores this further: there is only one son of God, but also many children. John understands "children of God" in a metaphorical and theological sense as a sign of election.

In John 11:47–52, the author alleges that the Jewish leadership shift their allegiance from God to "the world." In this passage, the chief priests and Pharisees call a meeting of the national council to decide to seek Jesus' death. The dialogue as portrayed in John reflects concerns both for the existential survival of Judea and a desire to continue Jewish participant status within the empire. In the Johannine depiction, no mention is made of earthly monarchs and Judea is ruled by the Roman procurator and the Temple establishment. This may be due to refusal to recognize the political legitimacy of these rulers or reflect a desire to position Israel as a nation waiting for its king. This convenient absence allows John to portray Jesus' opponents as loyal to "the world" as symbolized in Caesar as the human world-ruler in 19:12, carrying with it an implicit allusion to Jewish self-categorizations as loyal participants. John portrays the Sanhedrin in John 11 and "the Jews" in John 19:12 as though they categorize themselves as a "free" nation under the Romans—albeit wary of any Roman intervention. This is not inconsistent with Jewish self-categorizations of being "participants" and "allies" of Rome.

John 11:47–52 is replete with ethno-national language. The meeting involves the Sanhedrin, and they decide to execute Jesus to preserve the populace (ὁ λαός) from destruction (11:50). There is also concern for the destruction of the nation (τὸ ἔθνος) as a whole (11:48, 50), and its national symbol, the Temple. The sentence, ἀροῦσιν ἡμῶν καὶ τὸν τόπον καὶ τὸ ἔθνος (they will destroy our place and our nation) in 11:48 may also be another instance of *double-entendre*, as the use of αἴρω (destroy, take) could denote either destruction of the Temple or the imposition of direct Roman rule (taking their place and their

John and Anti-Judaism

nation from *them*). John phrases 11:48 so that the execution of Jesus is not entirely altruistic.⁹⁶ The decision to execute Jesus, even though it is a decision made by the leadership and not all Jews as a group, nonetheless undermines Jewish self-categorizations of being just or faithful to the Law. This is especially apparent because the decision is presented as a political rather than judicial decision, and the language implies the leadership thinks the people are theirs to govern, rather than God's people. This is further reflected in continued demands for Jesus' execution (11:38–12:15) and Pilate's description of its injustice being re-labelled a demonstration of loyalty to Caesar (19:12).⁹⁷ However, in John 11:51–52 Caiaphas "prophesies" that Jesus dies for both the "nation" (ἔθνος) but also "the dispersed children of God" (τὰ τέκνα τοῦ θεοῦ τὰ διεσκορπισμένα).

John A. Dennis maintains this statement is reflective of restorationist theology in John where the Johannine community is to be seen as "True Israel" vis-à-vis "Jews" and the leadership in the narrative.⁹⁸ The mention of "the people" (τοῦ λαοῦ) and "the nation" (τὸ ἔθνος) in 11:50, according to Dennis, makes it explicit that there is not a strong distinction between the Judean people and their nation in this context.⁹⁹ John 11:52 further explains that the members of an ethnic group, the nation, and God's elect are not synonymous because Jesus dies for the nation, its people, but also to gather "the children of God."¹⁰⁰ Gentile Christians reading retrospectively typically take this to be gentiles, though Dennis is likely correct that John, like Paul in Rom 9–11, is

---

96. In addition to a lack of altruism, Keener also detects irony in Caiaphas' statement in 11:49, ὑμεῖς οὐκ οἴδατε οὐδέν (you know nothing at all!). Keener, *John*, 2:855–56; also, Beasley-Murray, *John*, 340–41. For how this passage speaks to the motif of the restoration of Israel, see Dennis, *Gathering of True Israel*.

97. Keener notes that Pilate, as a client of Sejanus (and therefore the emperor), would have been politically vulnerable to charges of misconduct (Keener, *John*, 2:1128). As seen in chapters 2 and 4, similar charges were laid against governors in Cicero's *Pro Flacco* and Philo's *Against Flaccus* and *On the Embassy to Gaius*.

98. Dennis, *Gathering of True Israel*, 351.

99. Dennis, *Gathering of True Israel*, 249.

100. Dennis, *Gathering of True Israel*, 318.

probably employing the Jewish notion of a "True Israel" that believes in Jesus.[101]

SUMMARY: THE COLLECTIVE DESTINY OF JEWS AND THE JOHANNINE AUDIENCE

Beginnings often influence how people interpret the end, an idea that the Gospel of John apparently assumed to be true. Accordingly, John does not sever itself from the progenitors Abraham and Moses but claims these progenitors as its own in order to reinterpret their legacy. Previously in Jewish reception history Abraham had functioned as a symbol for faithfulness. John alters this so that Abraham is now a symbol for belief—that is, belief in Jesus. John portrays Abraham's belief in God, his welcoming of the heavenly visitors, and his justice as testimony to Jesus.

John likewise reinterprets Moses' significance in light of Wisdom Christology in John's Gospel. The Law and Scriptures continue as authoritative standards by which Jesus and his opponents spar. John theologically subordinates their legislative function due to the Logos's theological authority, but it does not abolish or set them aside. Prophetic and predictive functions are applied to the entire canon. The previous ascriptions of wisdom to Moses and his legislation, and Abraham's faithfulness, are assumed in the background, though not discussed because the focus is on the exposition of Jesus' identity. As symbols embodying prototypical Jews, Moses and Abraham do not change much in substance, but most significantly in their application; it ascribes to these characters the ideal responses to Jesus, and contrasts these with the dialogue partners in the narrative who do not believe (or are confused).

The result is that John creates a division between Abraham and Moses on the one hand, and the major contours of Jewish social identity surveyed in chapters 2 to 4 on the other. While Jews were well-aware that not all their brethren were faithful, pious, or knowledgeable about God, they felt free to make generalized ascriptions attributing these categories to their ethnic group as a whole. John, however, uses Jesus

---

101. Dennis, *Gathering of True Israel*, 342.

and the progenitors to separate Jews generally from these attributes in likewise generalized manner, while stressing the need for individual belief. The result is that Jews are no longer portrayed as prototypical of their social categorizations. These, instead, are applied to the Johannine Jesus directly, and through inference it is also applied to those who believe. John does not portray Jews in the Gospel negatively for its own sake; he systematically separates these characters from the social identity associated with the demonym in order to elevate the credibility of Jesus in the eyes of the audience.

However, simple social re-categorization is not enough for these claims against the opponents to hold. John also appropriates Jewish destiny as God's metaphorical children for the Johannine community and Jesus. The application of Wisdom-Torah imagery to Jesus appropriates benefits of Torah observance to reapply its salience for social categorization. Disbelief in Jesus is described as breaking one of God's commands: the embrace of eternal life. Those who do not believe in Jesus are now those who break his commandments, his Law. This characterization of Jesus' opponents effectively reduces the normative fit of their Jewish social categorizations as presented with the values of Greco-Roman culture in part one of this study, rendering them as just as in much need of Jesus as revealer and savior as anyone else, categorizing the Jewish characters in the narrative as members of the same spiritual grouping as the rest of humanity.

7

Interpreting John's Relationship to Jews and Judaism

INTRODUCTION

THE FIRST PART OF this study surveyed important Jewish social-categorizations derived from Judaism's cultural memory and their influence on the construction of a Jewish social identity in majority-gentile contexts. In chapters 5 and 6 I attempted to show that John takes issue with certain aspects of Jewish social identity and treatments of Jewish cultural memory. It relativizes the importance of these in order to make believing in Jesus the salient factor. The result is that Jews in the narrative are, generally, little different from unbelieving non-Jews so that in terms of their social identity as presented in the Gospel, Jews blend in with the rest of humanity. In the present chapter, we examine some more of the implications for John's treatment of Jewish social categorizations.

One consequence of John's treatment of social categorizations is that it increases relative difference between the Gospel's audience and the broader Hellenistic Jewish culture. A result would be that it reduces the attraction of Judaism and Jewish social identity for the Gospel's audience, given that Christianity has its origins as a movement within Judaism. Here I will attempt to show that the purpose of this is to use Jesus and the fulfillment motif to essentialize Jewish symbols to incorporate them into John's Christology, so that a new identity can be based on the Gospel's Christology. The function of the fulfillment motif is to maintain continuity, so that theological continuity can be maintained between Judaism and the Christian movement, even while planting the seeds for the development of a new religion. John's theological and social agendas are therefore two sides of the same coin.

PATTERNS OF INNOVATION AND OVER- AND UNDER- COMMUNICATION

In chapter 1 we explored how presentist views of collective memory can serve a heuristic function for understanding historical social identities. Also introduced in chapter 1 was the concept of memory "distortion," renamed with the less pejorative term "innovation."[1] Memory innovation can be a point of contact between SIT and SCT on the one hand, and collective memory theory on the other, because it evidences the social-psychological mechanisms of over-communication and under-communication, roughly analogous to the processes of *remembering* and *forgetting* in collective memory theory, which provide insight into an author's strategies for increasing or decreasing relative difference. In chapters 2 to 4 we saw how Jews creatively used their past to further integrate into the larger Greco-Roman culture. In chapters 5 and 6 I sought to demonstrate that John disagreed with how some Hellenistic Jews treated Jewish cultural memory in interpretive and biblical traditions and specific events, particularly the significance of Moses and Abraham. We also saw that the Gospel of John appropriates for Jesus most, but not all, major Jewish social categorizations that were operative in the Jewish communities of Egypt, Asia Minor, and Rome. Patterns of over- and under-communication and memory innovation of cultural memory in John will be discussed in greater detail below.

SOCIAL CATEGORIZATIONS

We saw in chapters 2 to 4 that Jewish self-categorizations were compatible with those of the broader Greco-Roman cultural context and

---

1. Misztal, *Theories of Social Remembering*, 17; Schudson, "Distortion in Collective Memory," 346–61.

allowed for social convergence between Jews and gentiles. Social integration, accommodation, or marginalization do not appear to have occurred along class lines but were due to local political or social phenomena. The contention of Joseph Mélèze Modrzejewski and Sylvie Honigman that Greek and Jewish identities were fully compatible with one another coheres with evidence surveyed in chapters 2 to 4 above.[2] In most cases, Jews appear to have socially converged with the gentile social groups that were socially accessible to them. Jews in Asia Minor, over the longer term, appear to have integrated successfully.[3] Evidence from Rome suggests social integration with the upper classes was an aspiration, though on the whole was not as successful as it had been in Ptolemaic Alexandria. Opposition to Jews, when detectable, appears to have usually originated among the upper classes. It is likely that Jews had little difficulty integrating with lower social strata at Rome.

We saw above that Jewish writers (and perhaps Jews generally) used theological aspects of their ethnicity to maintain ethno-religious distinction while permitting integration at the social level. In the first century Judaism was understood as an ethnicity, though gentile proselytes may have contributed to the development of the modern understanding of "religion" by assenting to theological beliefs but not adopting ethnic customs such as circumcision or food laws.[4] Notably, social categorizations presented in Jewish writers are remarkably conducive to the four cardinal virtues.[5] The role of the Mosaic Law in preserving ethnic identity and promoting virtue is presented as analogous to the function of laws in broader Hellenistic culture, at least as presented in Plato. It was usually to their advantage for Jews to socially integrate as much as possible,[6] and so we can assume that day-to-day interactions followed the general pattern of the literary evidence where they presented themselves positively, as, in the words of Honigman,

---

2. Modrzejewski, *Jews of Egypt*, 56; Honigman, "Jews as the Best of All Greeks."
3. Trebilco, *Jews of Asia Minor*, 164–66.
4. In agreement with Miller, "Ethnicity," 216–65.
5. Sandmel, "Philo's Place in Judaism," 158; Rajak, "Against Apion," 231–32.
6. Hughson T. Ong, citing Grabbe, makes a similar observation (Ong, *Multilingual Jesus*, 145–46).

"the best of the Greeks" (and Romans).[7] Below we will briefly summarize the dialogue between John and Hellenistic Diaspora social identity to show that John's anti-Judaism is best seen as reflecting religious competition.

Status as Participants

The Jewish literature written in Greek that we surveyed is strong on assertions of participant status, loyalty, and dignity for Diaspora Jews. Documents such as 3 Maccabees and the Letter of Aristeas acknowledge what is at times a disenfranchised foreign status but ascribe Jerusalem citizenship to compensate by asserting Jewish equality. Likewise, God as ruler through the Law of Moses, and the importance of Jewish leaders such as the high priests or Herodian kings, are used to ascribe a positive interpretation of their country's relationship to the imperial power as an allied nation.

John offers a very different interpretation by emphasizing the subjugated status of Jews. The subordinate, proxy-government status of the Sanhedrin is acknowledged and the Herodian kings are ignored in John 11:47–52. It is unlikely this is accidental, and it is questionable that this is meant to contemporize the Gospel to a post-70 CE context. The omission of the Herodian kings is probably an act of "forgetting" or "under-communication" of the monarchy as part of the Gospel's emphasizing the conquered status of Judea, thereby depriving Jews of ascriptions of national dignity and subverting social claims to loyalty and participant status as allies of the Romans. This argument would hold regardless of whether John was composed pre- or post-70 CE.

Yet even with this remnant symbol of nationhood absent from the narrative and John's emphasis upon fear of the Romans, Jesus' opponents still assert their freedom in John 8:33. Meanwhile, in John 6:15, the audience attempts to crown Jesus as their national king, suggesting a desire for liberation. The cumulative effect is that John denies these Jewish social categorizations: the Jewish people are not free, allies, or participants. The application of dualism in John 8 further underscores enslavement in spiritual terms: the Jewish people are members of "the

---

7. Honigman, "Jews as the Best of All Greeks," 207–32; for discussion of similarities between Jews and Romans, see Barclay, *Against Apion*, 362–69.

world," subject to the Devil, and placed in opposition to God.[8] Freedom is only found in liberation through believing in Jesus as their king; those who do not believe are subjected to the status of slavery to sin.[9]

Pious/Faithful

In chapters 2 to 4 I attempted to show that one of the most important Jewish social categorizations is that of being faithful or pious before God, at least relative to their gentile counterparts. Much of the literary testimony from the Diaspora suggests Jews saw this as on a continuum rather than a dualism, with some gentiles being considered more pious than others, and Jews evaluating both themselves and gentiles according to similar criteria, though a prototypical Jew would occupy exemplar status. While philosophical monotheism was appreciated by Jews,[10] the rhetoric of one such as Josephus suggests such beliefs were not of the same qualitative level as the beliefs held by a Jewish prototype. Positively, the spectrum can be seen in Letter of Aristeas 15–16 where some Greeks are pious like Jews and the Ptolemaic courtiers use universalistic language. Negatively, this can be seen in 3 Maccabees, where some Jews are, along with gentiles, categorized as disloyal to the Law and impious. Even 2 Maccabees' account of the Hasmonean revolt places people on a continuum that partially ignores ethnic boundaries, though in general Jews are more pious.

In contrast to much Hellenistic Diaspora literature, John employs a conditional dualism that incorporates a spectrum of relative difference within the Gospel to emphasize the need for belief in and obedience to Jesus. Within the Gospel's dualism Jews continue to be categorized as more pious than gentile members of "the world," such as the Samaritans, and are still considered Jesus' "own" (John 1:11). Ultimately, though, the Gospel thinks Jews are still "from below" (John 8:23) and children of the Devil (John 8:44), even though to the normally out-group Samaritans Jesus asserts that salvation is from the Jews (John 4:22). This suggests Johannine dualism is not a reflection of social divisions but serves a literary and rhetorical function that relies on

---

8. Painter, "Monotheism and Dualism," 228.
9. Hoskins, "Passover Theme," 48–60.
10. Horbury, "Jewish and Christian Monotheism," 27–31.

the spiritual consequences of belief or unbelief to persuade change in the audience.[11] This reflects the observation above—that ethnicity or concurrent social categorizations are not a salient factor for determining where one belongs in terms of spiritual identity, and one cannot derive authority, prestige, or security from historical figures such as Abraham or Moses, or an identity as a spiritual in-group member apart from Jesus.

Philosophical

We saw above that Hellenistic Diaspora Jews categorized themselves as theologically "philosophical" or insightful relative to gentiles because of the importance ascribed to the teachings of Moses and the Law. As with the social categorization "pious," Jews did not consider themselves entirely alone in this category. Diaspora Jews did not consider knowledge of God their sole purview, though Jews considered themselves, generally as a group, to be the best-informed on God's nature and expectations. While Jewish knowledge of God remained exceptional, the presumption of this social categorization is that knowledge of God is like any other form of knowledge in the sense that it can be taught and learned.[12]

John continues to emphasize the privileged status of Jews as recipients of God's written revelation but under-communicates the significance of possessing this revelation. The Gospel concurs that Jews are among the best informed in Jesus' conversation with the Samaritan woman (John 4:22a). However, the controversies of John 2–12 appear to have two main purposes at the socio-cultural level: (1) using the misunderstanding motif to demonstrate many Jews were mistaken as to Jesus' identity, and (2) to counter claims to Jewish theological authority because of the historical significance of their stewardship of the Scriptures. John partially deconstructs the Jewish self-categorization of "philosophical" in a way that preserves the authority of the Scriptures but encourages belief in Jesus. Soteriologically, this significantly reduces the relative difference between Jew and non-Jew while increasing it

---

11. Wahlde, "You are of Your Father the Devil," 426–37.

12. Scott, "Epistemology and Social Conflict," 195–213; Scott, "Revelation and Human Artefact," 1–28.

Interpreting John's Relationship to Jews and Judaism

between Christians and everyone else. While John depicts Jews as less ignorant than their gentile neighbors, the Gospel reduces the normative fit of their identity because they remain a part of "the world" that, while loved by God, is in opposition to him.

God's Elect

There are multiple metaphors that present belief in Jesus as the marker of election in John. In intra-Jewish conversation, where salient factors are faithfulness or worship of YHWH, Jews and Israelites have always viewed themselves as a diverse group, meaning the notion of a faithful remnant situated within a larger group is not new. John separates this category of Jewish social identity from its links to Abraham and Moses and re-centers it on positive reception to Jesus. Since John's interest is in categorizing Jews as members of "the world," it is must address the issue of comparative fit because Jews still knew more about God than gentiles did. John over-communicates the importance of Jesus and under-communicates the legacy of Jewish faithfulness to present Jews as part of "the world." Like the above, this reduces the salience of key unique aspects of Jewish self-categorizations seen in chapter 2 through 4 used in constructing Jewish social identities. The result is that if one holds an identity that does not include belief in Jesus, they are grouped in with "the world."

Brave and Zealous

In terms of the social categorization of being zealous for God, John is faced with the problem that many who opposed Jesus were zealous for the Law. In chapter 5 we saw that John counters by categorizing opponents who would otherwise be labelled as zealous as consumed with pettiness and self-interest. This is achieved through over-communication of the Law's significance to Jews at the expense of obedience to God himself in the person of God's agent, Jesus, thereby stereotyping Jews as petty in being totally Law-centered rather than God-centered. John under-communicates that, for Jews, fidelity to their God was motivation for obedience to the Law as an expression of reverence, faithfulness, and zeal. This is further supported through John's emphasizing

Jesus' unique relationship and faithfulness to the Father while portraying resistance to Jesus' claims, miracles, and teachings on account of the Law as unfaithfulness to God. Jewish bravery is further mitigated though the leadership's decision to have Jesus executed out of fear of the Romans in John 11:47–53, and the pledge of allegiance to Caesar at the expense of their God-sent king in John 19:15. Meanwhile, Jesus' singular devotion to the Father in the face of opposition and misunderstanding further categorizes Jesus as brave and zealous relative to his opponents.

John emphasizes the application of the social categorizations of bravery and zeal to Jesus while deemphasizing their comparative fit for Jewish characters, and by implication, Jews in general, though opposition to Jesus could be understood as zeal for the Law. While zeal for the Law contributed to the death of Jesus, John seeks to show that it was the correctly zealous one who was executed. This compounds Johannine irony so that zeal results in the death of the zealous one. John emphasizes its presentation of Jesus as the brave and zealous one to reduce the salience of the categorization as applied to Jews in the narrative, and reduce its normative fit with John's presentation of Jewish social identity in the Gospel.

Evaluation

The pattern of social categorizations above indicates John is construing Jewish social identity as a purely human-centered, or "world"-centered, social identity. Meanwhile, in aligning Jesus so closely with the Father, John is attempting to present an alternative theocentric identity focused upon belief in Jesus. This identity decenters the significance of both the ethnic group and the individual and puts the symbols Jesus and God's work in their place. This is especially seen in that while people may have access to life via Jesus and his teachings, believers are only "from above" (ἐκ τῶν ἄνω) in a derivative sense. Jesus labels believers in him as "from out of the world" (ἐκ τοῦ κόσμου), meaning they have a realigned form of the world's identity (John 6:37; 17:6) which is from "below," (ἐκ τῶν κάτω; John 8:23). Being born "from above" (ἄνωθεν) is the result of the Spirit's work, not the effort or virtue of the individual (John 3:3–8). Any laudatory character trait, be it zeal,

Interpreting John's Relationship to Jews and Judaism

theological insightfulness, or faithfulness is either applied directly to Jesus or is a result of belief in him.

Politically, one implication is that the refutation of the "participant" social categorization, as well as dignity and loyalty, is that nonbelief becomes a form of bondage to the sinful world system under the rule of the Devil. While these social categorizations were used to assert Jewish freedom within gentile-run empires, John asserts that Jews were in reality a subjugated people.[13] For the more important religiously oriented social categorizations, the implications are even more significant. Jews understood piety and faithfulness as traits partially socialized through being taught the Law. Likewise, Jews saw themselves as the elect people but considered obedience necessary in order to maintain this status.[14] Zeal is demonstrated by, if necessary, the taking of extraordinary steps to preserve piety and faithfulness to God, usually by expressing fidelity to the Law and ancestral customs.[15] This is inconsistent with Johannine theology, where one's status of being in obedience to God is dependent on Jesus as the True Vine, the Door, the Light of the World, or "the way, the truth, and the life." Porter writes:

> . . . to accept what Jesus says is to tacitly affirm that God is true or truthful, and also that what God says is true or truthful . . . It is something of the sort that, if a = b and b = c, then a = c. That is, if one accepts Jesus and what he says, and if Jesus speaks on God's behalf, then to accept Jesus' words is to accept what God says.[16]

According to this logic one can keep the Law and ancestral customs and believe in Jesus at the same time. That is, for John it is possible to be a Christian Jew. However, this does not demonstrate one's elect status if

---

13. As Rensberger states, "The Roman prefect is thus by no means a man of just intentions but weak character in this gospel. He is callous and relentless, indifferent to Jesus and to truth, and contemptuous of the hope of Israel that Jesus both fulfills and transcends . . . Pilate is thus in fact a hostile figure second only to 'the Jews' themselves." Rensberger, *Johannine Faith*, 95 (see 92–100 for discussion).

14. Sanders, *Paul and Palestinian Judaism*, 85–101; Das, *Paul, the Law, and the Covenant*, 13–15; Watson, *Paul, Judaism, and the Gentiles*, 11–13; 301–43.

15. Dunn, *New Perspective on Paul*, 361.

16. Porter, *John, His Gospel, and Jesus*, 178.

the basis for this identity is the revelation found in the Law and ancestral customs. In the Gospel, being an elect member of God's people, at least in terms of eternal life, is solely established by a positive response to Jesus' claims; otherwise an individual is considered "from below."

The Common Progenitors

John treats the Jewish common progenitors, Abraham and Moses, in a respectful manner but reinterprets their significance for the human sphere. That is, their previous roles and elements of their importance are retained but in John's formulation they cannot be used, in and of themselves, as tools to establish a social identity. Egyptian Jewish literature emphasized the importance of Moses as a common progenitor, to the relative neglect of Abraham, because as the human originator of the Law he most closely resembled the ideal founder of a state in Greek culture. Treating Moses as the founder also served well the idea that Judaism was an ethnicity with a divinely-created Law code and belief system. For its part, the Gospel of John accepts the revelatory *function* of the common progenitors but plays down the significance *of the progenitors themselves* on account of these functions that they performed. Moses' role in revelation is respected but he is said to be the mediator of a revelation that originates in Jesus. Likewise, Abraham's exemplary faith and hospitality are made the standard of judgment in John 8:37–40 so that rejection of Jesus can be framed as their antitheses.[17] John accepts the importance of the common progenitors, but denies that which they exemplify can be applied derivatively to those who come after apart from belief in Jesus.

Summary

At first glance John's treatment of Judaism may appear to be grounded in emotion, but a systematic study of the scope to which John deconstructs Jewish social identity suggests a theological program on the part of the author. Emotions may be operative in the background, but John's strategy of framing Jews as needing to believe in Jesus as much as anyone else appears quite systematic and intentional. It is important

---

17. Hunt, "Word became Flesh," 88–97.

to note that John never applies prototypical Jewish social categorizations directly to himself or to Christians but either only to Jesus, or derivatively through belief in Jesus. Likewise, the Jews are never rejected by Jesus; rather they reject him through being inhospitable, pledging allegiance to Caesar, and embracing a murderous "son of the father" (Barabbas) over the "Son of the Father" that is murdered (John 18:40). The apparent Johannine self-categorization of "true worshippers" (John 4:23–24) is only applied to believers derivatively because of the Spirit and Jesus, and it is not a quality that is innate to them. Diminutive language is used of the disciples in John 13:33.[18]

Use of the Second Exodus/Passover motif of the Fourth Gospel and its Moses imagery[19] presupposes the greatness of the Exodus and Moses in Jewish cultural memory. Yet John disagrees that obedience to the Law socializes one in the high principles that the Law teaches (John 7:19), meaning those who obey the Law are not necessarily like the prototypical Moses or Abraham. While the honor-shame dynamics of Hellenistic culture[20] motivate some Jewish writers to "forget" to mention some of the human failings demonstrated by certain historic forebears in their writings, John "remembers" the people's grumbling in the wilderness (John 6:41) and that the first generation died because of their unbelief (6:49, 58). Like the social categorizations discussed above, John's treatment of the symbols of cultural memory in reception history and interpretive tradition appears intended to challenge an attractive social identity that might prevent belief in Jesus.

The above discussion shows that when Johannine anti-Judaism towards Jewish symbols and the demonym is interpreted considering contemporary Hellenistic Diaspora Jewish social identity and patterns of over- and under-communication found in its cultural memory, one can see a pattern where Jewish identity is rendered a solely human identity that is in need of redemption when compared with the new theocentric identity presented in Jesus. Bultmann notes:

18. Note the use of τεκνία instead of τέκνα for children in this passage.

19. See above. Also Hylen, *Allusion and Meaning*; Porter, *John, His Gospel, and Jesus*, 214–16, citing Hoskins, "Passover Theme," 47–63; Harstine, *Moses as a Character*; Boismard, *Moses or Jesus*; Maronde, "Moses in the Gospel of John," 23–44.

20. Neyrey, "Trials (Forensic)," 107–8; Neyrey, "Despising the Shame of the Cross," 113–37; Moxnes, "Honor and Shame," 167–76.

> [The Gospel of John] makes it seem as if mankind falls into two classes[,] each of which is from the outset determined as to its essence and its fate by its specific nature. Is not each [person] stamped by his origin? Does not his origin determine the direction of [their] way? . . . And the assertion that they are stuck in darkness and blindness and stand under God's wrath applies to all [people]. And [people] are asked, one and all, whether they want to *remain* in this situation. But Jesus' words are not didactic propositions but an invitation and a call to decision.[21]

Rhetorically, John's treatment of Jewish social identity is meant to simplify the audience's decision to be "pro God" by narrowing their options to being "pro Jesus" or "anti-God." It separates this decision from other historical or cultural considerations in order to make it easier for one to choose the status of becoming a Christian, something which, historically-speaking, was potentially dubious on a theological basis. Positive portrayal of Jesus and negative portrayal of Jews in light of the cultural values at the time may also be a means for the Gospel author to confirm the audience in decisions already made.

IMPLICATIONS FOR JEWISH CULTURAL NATIONALISM IN JOHN

The preceding discussion in this chapter has implications for Hellenistic Jewish cultural identity. As noted in chapter 1, A. D. Smith lists what he has identified as the major features of ancient nationalism. The subjective elements investigated in this study are: (1) authenticity (analogous to prototypicality), the (2) dignity of the group (the belief that members of the group should enjoy a certain level of prestige or status), (3) continuity with a common progenitor, and (4) collective destiny.

At least within the context of the Johannine narrative, the Gospel presents Jewish (1) authenticity as "pettiness" or a lack of theological insightfulness. John does not recognize the reality of (2), the dignity of the Jewish people because of the subjugation of the Jewish people to the Roman Empire and its enslavement to the spiritual powers of the world. Criterion (3), continuity with a common progenitor, is genetically and

---

21. Bultmann, *Theology of the New Testament*, 2:21. The brackets are mine and are inserted for gender inclusivity and grammar.

Interpreting John's Relationship to Jews and Judaism

historically recognized but bifurcated of its spiritual benefits. Situating Jesus as the source of "life" likewise denies (4), aspirations of political, national, or social restoration in prophetic eschatology.[22]

Figure 5: John, Jews, "the World"

Different (stereotype)				Similar (prototype)
	Salient Category: Revelation			
"the world"		"the Jews"	Receptive Audience	Jesus
	Salient Category: Belief in Jesus			
"the world"	"the Jews"		Moses & Abraham	Receptive Audience	Jesus

As can be seen in the chart above, the cumulative result is that Jews are stereotyped in a category that is similar but not identical with gentiles. John preserves enough elements of Jewish cultural memory and identity to allow Judaism to be embraced by Christian Jews as an ethnic identity, but it undermines many of the theological presuppositions for Jewish cultural identity as the chosen people.

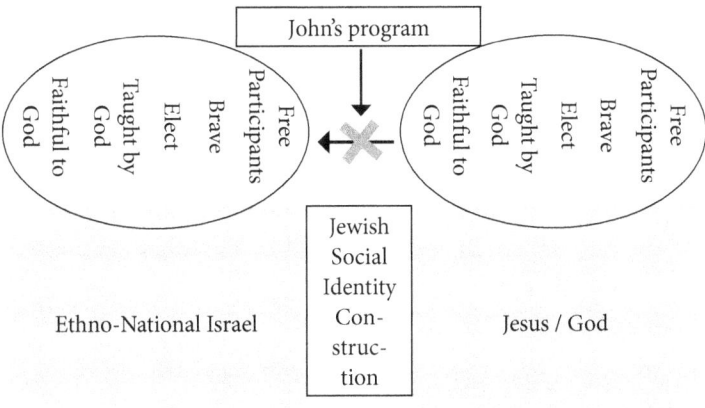

Figure 6: Social Identity of Diaspora Jews and the Johannine Jesus

---

22. Prophetic eschatology more closely concerns the fate of the nation of Israel in history, while apocalyptic eschatology concerns the final resolution of the course of history in general (Plöger, *Theocracy and Eschatology*, 10–50; Hanson, *Dawn of Apocalyptic*, 6; 134–204).

In the chart above, we see that John challenges the comparative fit and normative fit of social categorizations for the majority of Jews so the character's identity become more abstract and generalized. While Wayne Meeks correctly states the Johannine Jesus exemplifies the stranger *par excellence* rather than a hero,[23] my analysis has shown that Jesus still bears many characteristics which, if not heroic due to consistent misunderstanding as precursor to hostility in the narrative, would nonetheless resonate positively with the values of the broader culture. This assessment is amenable to Davies's assertion that the Johannine Jesus is an exemplar of "representative humanity." The primary difference is Davies uses theological frames of reference, while I use social and cultural frames of reference. I believe these two systems may be mutually inclusive.[24]

While I agree with scholars such as Tobias Nicklas and Lars Kierspel regarding the literary function of the Johannine Jews in the narrative, this study suggests that Kierspel's contention that as representatives of "the world" the Johannine Jews signify a context of persecution of Christians by the Romans may be an overstatement.[25] This study more directly supports Nicklas's argument that their function is to serve as a narrative foil that acts as a basis for a contrast that encourages belief in Jesus.[26] Hakola may be correct that there was some sense of Johannine "collective victimhood" where a universalistic *portrayal* of perceived persecution is evidenced[27] rather than Kierspel's description of "universal hate and persecution."[28] Whether or not Hakola is correct on this point, the cultural evidence above suggests that Johannine dualism serves either evangelistic or pastoral ends that help establish the social cohesion of the audience through prompting decision for Jesus.[29] In this context it is also notable that John does not place salva-

23. Meeks, "Man from Heaven," 50.
24. Davies, *Rhetoric and Reference in the Fourth Gospel*, 188–208.
25. Kierspel, *Jews and the World*, 213.
26. Nicklas, *Ablösung und Verstrickung*, 399–401.
27. Hakola, *Reconsidering Johannine Christianity*, 96–117.
28. Kierspel, *Jews and the World*, 213.
29. Hakola, *Reconsidering Johannine Christianity*, 120–28; Ashton, *Understanding the Fourth Gospel*, 397, citing Bultmann, *Theology*, 2:21.

tion in Heaven, in the way that 2 Baruch or 4 Ezra situate God's real temple in Heaven, where relief is out of reach of imperial conquerors or persecutors.[30] Some would probably draw comfort from the Gospel's use of dualism, though this may be a secondary function.

Since a secure social identity is very often just as important as theology in community maintenance,[31] this suggests two possibilities that are not mutually exclusive. The first is a context of social competition where the positive aspects of Jewish social identity and its cultural legacy are interfering with witness and maintenance of a Christian community. A second possibility is the more common position that the social cohesion of the community is under threat due to attachment to Judaism, possibly due to the attractiveness of some of the Jewish social identities used by Jews in the Greco-Roman world discussed above.

In this light, Johannine anti-Judaism in John's treatment of social categorizations should be interpreted as a reaction against the perceived threats of a Jewish cultural identity and cultural nationalism that are still attractive for John's audience. As a new movement, the credibility of Christianity's interpretations, teachings, and leadership were probably challenged to a degree not faced by those of Judaism. Putting Jesus in conflict with "the world," and making Jews a part of this world, would facilitate an agenda that seeks to reduce the threat from the kinds of competition early Christianity would have faced. On balance, such a conclusion would best support an altered version of Frey's hypothesis of a local Christological conflict between Christian

---

30. Käsemann, *Testament of Jesus*, 6–7, 52, esp. 73.

31. Presuming a synagogue expulsion, Whitacre makes a similar point (Whitacre, *Johannine Polemic*, 11–12); Abby Day's social-psychological study attempts to empirically demonstrate this point (Day, *Believing in Belonging*, 5, 157–81). Wayne O. McCready makes a similar point, though rejecting a synagogue expulsion as speculative (McCready, "Johannine Self-Understanding and the Synagogue Episode of John 9," 152–63).

Davies, for example, proposes John was composed by a Gentile with a thorough knowledge of Judaism. She comes to this conclusion on the basis of a "mistake" in John's presentation of Jewish practice (312) and the presentation of the Pharisees (293–99). The former may be the result of a plurality in *halakhic* practice, the latter may be addressing *pragmatic* concerns. That said, I do not see my argument as inimical to her thesis that John is written to extrapolate the significance of its Christology (Davies, *Rhetoric and Reference*, 348). Davies presumes a division between Jewish communities and Christian communities.

and non-Christian Jews.[32] The data surveyed in this study suggests this would not necessarily stem from anger over rejection but a danger of community members returning to a non-Christian form of Judaism. While there are some differences, Frey's proposal and that suggested here are not mutually exclusive because they could be two sides of the same coin, and the conclusions reached here could complement other historical reconstructions as well.

What kind of context could such dynamics reflect? Given the vitriol that is often perceived in John's presentation of Jews in the narrative it is perhaps ironic that a theological consequence of ascribing non-Christian Jews a more abstract social identity is to emphasize everyone's shared common humanity. The irony and sense of historical tragedy increases all the more when we consider that emphasizing shared values and common humanity is a primary social strategy that appears in the evidence from the Jewish Diaspora literature that we surveyed in chapters 2 through 4.

Likewise, in chapters 2 through 4 we saw that relations between Jew and gentile, while at times very problematic, could also be very positive and foster the thriving of Jewish communities in Asia Minor. If John were written in a major diaspora center such as Ephesus, or any other Greco-Roman city where Jews were successful in integrating with the broader civic community, Jews and Judaism may have enjoyed a great amount of prestige among some gentiles and members of a Christian community where a significant number of members were either Christian Jews or their descendants. In such a case a writer such as John might feel the need to reduce the attractiveness of Jewish social identity because if John had made use of diverse titles such as scribes, priests, and elders in the narrative, a Christian may say "well, the ones I know are not like that!" Such a person might have been tempted to return, join, or divide their allegiance with a Jewish community, as in the case noted by John Chrysostom in *Adv. Jud.* 8. The reading presented here does not definitively prove this is indeed what happened, but it increases the plausibility of such a scenario where Jews and Judaism are an attractive option for the audience, given the effort the Gospel

---

32. Frey, "'Die Juden' im Johannesevangelium," 339–77

MAKING JUDAISM "PORTABLE" IN JESUS: THE FULFILLMENT OF JUDAISM?

John appears to try to maintain continuity with Judaism in the face of competition with Judaism, at least at an abstract level.[33] Likewise John, according to the Wilsonian taxonomy of sects, sounds like it is introversionist, but if broader social and cultural data and John's interaction with these are borne in mind we can see that the Gospel pursues conversionist goals.[34] This is especially seen in how John appropriates Judaism for its audience by applying its symbols to Jesus, but the question remains as to whether this is an expression of supersessionism or fulfillment.

John's contextualization strategies, exemplified in the Johannine Jesus' various "I Am" statements, at first glance suggest the one-to-one correlation of a "translation" paradigm of theological contextualization. However, it is more likely that John is using a "synthetic" model that synthesizes Judaism and the Jesus tradition on the levels of Jewish culture, Hellenistic culture, and their respective intellectual heritages.[35] A growing number of scholars are adopting the position that the fulfillment motif in John involves the use of metaphor.[36] Dennis contends, ". . . John did not think in a category such as 'supersessionism' or 'replacement theology'; rather, he believed that his community was the true

---

33. According to Bryan R. Wilson, maintaining continuity with an originating religion is common among new religious movements (Wilson, *Religion in Sociological Perspective*, 105–6).

34. Wilson, *Magic and the Millennium*, 22–24.

35. Bevans, *Models of Contextual Theology*, 30–35; 81–86 (esp. 86).

36. Spaulding describes it as "layering" a new meaning onto an existing practice (Spaulding, *Commemorative Identities*, 162. The most explicit application of metaphor to the fulfillment theme is Hylen, *Allusion and Meaning*. See also Beth Stovell's discussion of the fulfillment of prophecy and application of multiple metaphors to the theme of Jesus' kingship in the Gospel. Though it does not deal with the issue of fulfillment specifically (Stovell largely assumes it in her discussion of prophecy, but does not deal with the issue of supersessionism), her treatment discussion of metaphor mapping is helpful for elucidating the fulfillment theme and how it is presented (Stovell, *Mapping Metaphorical Discourse*, 268–303).

or *genuine* Israel."[37] Marianne Meye Thompson makes a similar point. Describing the concepts of theological replacement and supersession as "awkward," "highly compressed," and "not particularly helpful" for discerning the character of John's theology, she notes the basis for comparison is an individual person versus a festival that people perform to commemorate the past.[38] Thompson continues:

> . . . it would be more precise to argue that even as the great pilgrim festivals celebrate God's work, so too Christians commemorated God's act of salvation—here, the act of eschatological salvation in Christ. When the issue is framed in this way, it also becomes apparent that Jesus does not "supersede" or replace the action of God through Passover; rather, Passover clarifies and illumines the nature of Jesus' own work.[39]

Similarly, this time speaking of person-to-person comparison, Susan Hylen explains further:

> The identification of multiple metaphors in John affects the question of Jesus surpassing Moses. In this interpretation, Jesus' greatness may be seen as a function of the literary effect of these multiple metaphors. Jesus does not surpass Moses by rejecting him, or because John explicitly identifies Jesus as Moses' superior. Through the metaphorical associations with manna, Wisdom, Passover, and God, Jesus takes on functions that go beyond those associated only with Moses. If Jesus is more than Moses, it is not a result of John's rejection of the figure of Moses but of relating Jesus to other aspects of the Exodus tradition as well.[40]

The exclusive nature of Jesus' claims in John suggests John is essentializing Judaism. To essentialize something means to make the features A1, A2, or A3 necessary for the definition of A as A. The many discourses in the Gospel show John clearly sees belief in Jesus as central to being categorized as a spiritual in-group member.

37. Dennis, *Gathering of True Israel*, 351.
38. Thompson, *God of the Gospel of John*, 218.
39. Thompson, *God of the Gospel of John*, 219.
40. Hylen, *Allusion and Meaning*, 190.

Interpreting John's Relationship to Jews and Judaism

The clearest example of this is in the predicative, or metaphorical, "I Am" statements.[41] All of these pertain to Jewish cultural identity in some way, be it retrospective in terms of cultural memory and history, or as anticipating eschatological resolution. In the use of metaphor, the Gospel essentializes Jewish cultural identity by associating key elements of the culture with Jesus, so that belief in Jesus becomes the basis for understanding what it means to value these symbols.[42] In this way, Jesus is made a part of the Passover and given the salvific connotations of Passover. Likewise, the value placed on the Law expressed by Wisdom traditions is incorporated into Jesus by means of the Logos doctrine and Wisdom Christology, allow Jesus to grant the benefits previously granted by the Law. John's Christology makes Judaism "portable," at least according to Daniélou's idealist approach to Jewish Christianity. This allows the theological and historical heritage of this ethnic group to remain applicable through their new associations with Jesus. Jesus is thus presented as a proposed means for meeting many of the needs of Jewish believers and portrays faith in him as a natural development of Judaism.

How essential is Judaism compared to belief in Jesus? The implication of John's theology is a Jew must believe in Jesus to have life, but a gentile who believes in Jesus does not have to become a Jew in order to enjoy the same.[43] John's theology is derived from Jewish theology using Jewish theological tools, values, and frames of reference, but the nature of its being synthesized with the incarnation essentializes this Jewish-Christian theology so that it takes on a mostly intellectual-historical character. In this sense John reflects a Jewish Christianity similar to Jean Daniélou's idealist definition, or what Kraft terms an "idealist abstraction," that focuses mostly on Jewish theological ideas and motifs but relativizes some of the markers and practices necessary

---

41. Ball, *"I Am" in John's Gospel*, 204–5.

42. This is in general agreement with Dennis, though I do not think he sufficiently accounts for the implications of belief in Jesus upon Jewish identity (Dennis, *Gathering of True Israel*, 247–318).

43. Kåre Sigvald Fuglseth writes, "The temple, festivals, and other institutions mentioned in the Gospel are reinterpreted in a way that may have *prepared for* a replacement at a later stage" (Fugelseth, *Johannine Sectarianism in Perspective*, 161). Italics original.

for maintaining an ethnic identity through relative difference with other groups.[44] Motyer has argued that the appropriation and reinterpretation of Jewish theology would be amenable to evangelistic aims.[45] In this light, Johannine anti-Judaism, its treatment of Jewish social identity and cultural memory in regards to "the Jews," and its patterns of theological innovation all appear to serve more a pastoral function, preventing the defection of Jewish Christians while making the belief system practical for non-Jews by demanding minimal adaptation in terms of lifestyle adjustments.

JEWISH CHRISTIANITY OR NEW RELIGION?

Proposed in the 1960's, the hypothesis of the synagogue expulsion as occasion for John's Gospel has been in circulation for half a century and is probably the closest thing to a consensus in Johannine studies.[46] Additionally, Meeks's work has been very influential on Johannine scholarship, especially in terms of the purported Johannine community's isolation and introversion.[47] However, this characterization of John's Gospel has been questioned over the last twenty years, and interpreting Johannine Christology as exemplifying a socially-isolated, introversionist sectarian community has been persistently questioned.[48]

---

44. Kraft, "Problems of Definition and Methodology," 86–89; Daniélou, *Theology of Jewish Christianity*, 9–21. See also Edwin K. Broadhead who adopts a more middle-road approach to the alternatives to the intellectual approach presented by Daniélou and the minimalist approach of Matt A. Jackson-McCabe (Broadhead, *Jewish Ways of Following Jesus*, esp. 31–58; Jackson-McCabe, "The Problem of 'Jewish Christianity,'" 24–37).

45. Motyer, *Your Father the Devil*, 145–50; 212–13; Porter, *John, His Gospel, and Jesus*, 37–62; Klink, *Sheep of the Fold*, 254–55.

46. Despite his own proposals that the Johannine community bore many features of an ancient school that became self-isolated in its later history, Culpepper's assessment in 1975 that there is no consensus regarding its character continues to hold true (Culpepper, *The Johannine School*, 34).

47. Meeks, "Man from Heaven," 68–70.

48. Schnackenburg, *Gospel according to St. John*, 2:239; Beasley-Murray, *John*, 153; Klink, *Sheep of the Fold*, 185–247. Meeks arrived at his proposal before taxonomies of sectarian communities were well-known (Meeks, "Man from Heaven," 70). Reading retrospectively, Meeks' proposal roughly corresponds to Wilson's seven-fold taxonomy that includes "introversionist" sects (Wilson, *Magic and the Millennium*, 23–24). However, a key weakness in Wilson's typology is its breadth of responses to

The reading presented in this study, assuming there was some sort of synagogue expulsion of a Christian Jewish group, questions whether such a community would have been introversionist in nature and would better fit with Brown's depiction of the community's character.[49]

Further, alternate hypotheses taking the form of less-localized responses to social conflict have been proposed. Among these are proposals that John is responding to issues in the public sphere, such as political and social ideologies relating to the Roman Empire. Implications at the socio-political level are helpfully elucidated by Carter, who along with David Rensberger, Lance Byron Richey, and Tom Thatcher argues that John may be writing to challenge some of these ideologies.[50] Others have presented John's theology as a Jewish response to the revolt against Rome and the destruction of the temple.[51] What is important is that there are plausible proposals that do not interpret the Gospel of John as solely a response to a traumatic social conflict in the author's local Jewish community.[52] Implicit is that John was not composed for

---

"the world" (He lists: 1. "conversionist," 2. "revolutionist," 3. "introversionist," 4. "manipulationist," 5. "thaumaturgical," 6. "reformist," and 7. "utopian" sects), the result being that a group can belong to more than one category at a time. Wilson, for his part, maintains that all models have weaknesses but their function is heuristic rather than descriptive (Wilson, *Magic and Millennium*, 18).

49. Brown has argued for a Johannine community that is separate from but sharing important characteristics with the broader Christian movement. Brown notes that the broader Church accepted John's Gospel as canonical and adopted its Christology as its own. For Brown, this suggests that a Johannine community did not adopt isolationist or sectarian tendencies detected in its literature but was in fact broadly engaged with the issues of its time. Brown regards his own proposal as very tentative (Brown, *Community of the Beloved Disciple*, 7; 90–91; also Cullmann, *Johannine Circle*, 15, 55).

50. Rensberger, *Johannine Faith*, 87–100; Carter, *John and Empire*, 19–20; Richey, *Roman Imperial Ideology and the Gospel of John*, 33–86; Thatcher, *Greater than Caesar*, 6–16.

51. Dunn, "Let John be John," 293–322. It has been elaborated upon by Motyer (*Your Father the Devil*), Hakola (*Identity Matters*), Köstenberger ("The Destruction of the Temple," 205–42), Kerr (*Temple of Jesus' Body*), Hoskins (*Jesus as the Fulfillment*), Um (*Temple Christology in John's Gospel*).

52. There are many refutations of the Martyn-Brown hypothesis of late. Especially convincing is Klink, *Sheep of the Fold*, 185–247. Klink retains some form of "community" by allowing for extended networks of social relationships between individual Christians. Jonathan Bernier's discussion traces its numerous forms. Especially see the terminology used in his table of contents (Bernier, *Aposynagōgos*

use solely by this local community but the broader Christian movement and should be interpreted with this readership in mind.[53] While a localized conflict remains a possibility, the reading presented here could also support proposals that John is responding to issues in the public sphere because of its reliance on SCT.

According to some sociologists of religion, new religious movements typically seek to maintain as much continuity with the parent faith as is practical. It is common for new religious groups to be both radical and conservative in their tendencies—different in terms of introducing theological innovations but demonstrating overall theological continuity so as to maintain plausible acceptability on the part of individuals from the preexisting religious background.[54] Typically, deviant religious groups have been labelled "sects," but an alternative three-fold model of "church," "cult," and "sect" has been proposed by Rodney Stark and William Sims Bainbridge,[55] and utilized by Kåre Fuglseth in his study of John's attitude to the temple.[56] In this model a so-called "church" is a socially-accommodationist group, emblematic of the Jewish social categorizations surveyed here. Meanwhile, a "cult" is, according to Fuglseth:

> ... the social group that *de facto* is the beginning of a new religion. 'Cults' claim to be different and justify the difference by a new revelation or new insight that changes the original tradition" and a "sect" "splinters [from] the indigenous tradition, it is the social group that left the parent body not to form a new faith, but to re-establish or regenerate the old one. 'Sects'

---

and the Historical Jesus in John). See also David A. Lamb's evaluation for the failure of the community hypothesis (Lamb, *Sociolinguistic Analysis*, 1–27). He engages in a sociolinguistic analysis that refutes the notion that John employs the Hallidayan concept of "anti-language" by arguing that many arguments in favor of the community hypothesis are circular or lack extensive use of textual evidence. He concludes the Johannine literature was intended for a broad audience, perhaps consisting of a loose network of churches (Lamb, *Sociolinguistic Analysis*, 1–28; 103–205).

53. Bauckham, "For Whom were the Gospels Written," 9–48.

54. Wilson, *Sociology of Religion*, 105; Bainbridge, *Sociology of Religious Movements*, 411.

55. Stark and Bainbridge, *Future of Religion*.

56. Fuglseth, *Johannine Sectarianism in Perspective*, 55–61.

therefore claim to be the authentic, purged, and refurbished religion.[57]

In my reading, the Johannine Community, insofar as it can be discerned through the Gospel of John, appears to be a "cult" rather than a "sect." So-called "cultic" religious groups may have insular *theological* tendencies as part of their response to "the world," yet on a *social* level may be surprisingly well-integrated with the broader culture, in part for recruitment purposes.[58] They use isolationist language but are not isolationist; they present themselves as in *de jure* theological continuity with the parent religion, but are *de facto* the beginning of a new religious movement. In this case John appears radical in terms of Christological claims, and Jesus' claims regarding his faithfulness to the true nature of the ideals and values held dear by antecedents in Judaism.[59] There are limitations to the use of sociological typologies for religious movements[60] but in light of the present study's assessment of John's treatment of ethnicity, Judaism, and the fulfillment motif, the Stark-Bainbridge classification of "cult" seems to fit.

If this is assessment is correct, it would fit well with the argument that ethnicity was the determinative factor in initiating the "Parting

57. Fuglseth, *Johannine Sectarianism in Perspective*, 55. Bainbridge, like Wilson, hesitates to present his model as definitive (Bainbridge, *Sociology of Religious Groups*, 25).

58. Onuki, *Gemeinde und Welt*, 213–18; Consistent with arguments for the proselytizing nature of new religious movements made by Stark and Bainbridge, *Future of Religion*, 348, 359–63; Bainbridge, *Sociology of Religious Groups*, 411.

59. Wilson, *Sociology of Religion*, 106.

60. Here one should also note Ruth Sheridan's protest against the use of the Stark-Bainbridge typology as nomothetic (Sheridan, "Johannine Sectarianism," 142–66). She favors a more social-descriptivist approach using sociolinguistics, namely Halliday's concept of anti-language" (159–66). However, it should be noted that Bainbridge intended his typology to serve as a heuristic tool rather than provide definitive categorizations, and stressed that models were by nature limited (Bainbridge, *Sociology of Religion*, 25). One should note also the similar caveat made by Wilson mentioned above (Wilson, *Magic and Millennium*, 18), and the discussion concerning the importance of social description made in chapter 2. Along this line of reasoning, then, the sociologists who produce these typologies seem to presuppose the accessibility of the religious community in question for further study, of which their typologies would serve as a starting point. Accordingly, these typologies are not necessarily "positivistic" in nature (as per Sheridan, "Johannine Sectarianism," 166). Rather, the error lies in Biblical scholars who use them without due caution.

of the Ways" between Christianity and Judaism.[61] Though in the past Johannine scholars understood John as being influenced by Pauline theology,[62] we lack a clear picture of the relationship between John and Paul, meaning that we cannot necessarily rely on parallels in Paul to interpret John's Gospel, even if similar social dynamics are operative. For example, on the basis of the Church's adoption of the Alexandrian canon (LXX) and that no Pauline missionary activity in Alexandria is known, Modrzejewski holds that Alexandrian Christianity likely originated as a form of Judeo-Christianity under Jerusalem's influence until it was annihilated during the Kitos War, thereafter being re-founded (or its remnant continuing) as a gentile-Christian community. If his reconstruction is accurate, then a social transformation eventually came about in Alexandria that looks outwardly similar to what happened in Galatia, though with different historical causes.[63] John may therefore reflect a parting of the ways of its own, but it may have been less schismatic or more understated than has been previously understood.

The Gospel's theological program of rendering Judaism "portable" by re-centering it on ideas such as Christology to preempt religious defection or competition suggests a pastoral goal of solving the problem of its audience's relationship to Judaism. The Gospel's *de jure* continuity with Judaism but the *de facto* effect of promoting development of a new religion likewise reflects such a purpose because it attempts to provide stability while also initiating change.

Finally, its treatment of Jewish social and cultural identity may reflect this purpose as well because it attempts to lessen the attractiveness of Judaism. We can therefore conclude that John's anti-Judaism and "the Jews" is grounded in the conflict-competition paradigm advanced by scholars such as James Parkes, Marcel Simon, and Jules Isaac, discussed in the introduction, though this study does not claim to come to definitive conclusions regarding its nature beyond the Gospel possibly

61. Porter and Pearson, "Why the Split," 114.

62. For example, see examples of arguments drawing connections between Johannine theology to Pauline theology in the following late nineteenth- to early twentieth-century works, usually assuming some sort of a developmental relationship in Scott, *Fourth Gospel*, 14–33; Baur, *Das Christenthum*, 148; Gardner, *Ephesian Gospel*, 220–34; Bacon, *Fourth Gospel*, 283–87; Bacon, *Gospel of the Hellenists*, 104–9.

63. See Modrzejewski, *Jews of Egypt*, 228–30.

being a response to the positive and attractive elements of Jewish social identity and Judaism's historical and theological legacy.

Conclusion

Where Do We Go from Here?

INTRODUCTION

THIS STUDY OPENED WITH the illustration of the *Komagata Maru* and its passengers of unwanted race who were perceived as a threat to a country's British identity. Almost a century later there now stands a memorial on the shore near where the conflict occurred which symbolizes what many today would just as soon forget: the mistreatment of Indian immigrants because of the perceived challenge they posed to a racial and cultural identity. The present irony is that neither Canadians nor Indians consider themselves particularly British. Like Indians and Canadians, Judaism and Christianity have both changed significantly since the first century, and modern Jews or Christians may not be so quick to identify themselves with the same things as their spiritual forebears.

Since the Holocaust a vast scholarly literature continues to be produced, much of it written by scholars of Christian background, that explores John's Jewish culture and Jewish thought-world. Like the memorial, Christian scholarship symbolizes remorse for past wrongs done in the face of much pre-war scholarship. Ultimately, it seems the problem lies not with the reflective activity of scholars but with actions stemming from a need for identity that has not been subject to adequate reflection or introspection. When it comes to John's Gospel, regardless of almost every interpretive option there is, the question remains: if we accept John's Jewish intellectual and cultural heritage, why

Conclusion

does John so frequently use the term "the Jews" (as in, "all of them!")? Providing a durable answer to this question has been the goal of this study so that churches can take appropriate action to remedy traditions of misconstruing Jews and Judaism without comprising their convictions, or blithely explaining away the problem.

SUMMARY

In the introduction I tried to show that there are four major strategies for interpreting Johannine anti-Judaism: (1) understanding the Johannine Jews as a specific group of Jews, (2) interpreting the Johannine Jews as representative of all Jews but in a specific historical context, (3) an ontological reading of the Jews as symbols for unbelief, and (4) the cathartic approach of ecclesial and hermeneutical-theological disavowal of anti-Judaism. I concluded that the *Ontological Approach* demonstrates the greatest stability and utility as a starting point for understanding Johannine treatment of "the Jews" in terms of its origins and intent.

In chapter 1 I proposed that employing SIT and SCT paradigms in conjunction with presentist approaches to Social Memory provided adequate means for establishing a secure historical perspective for interpreting Johannine anti-Judaism and its treatment of "the Jews." I developed a procedure for delineating Jewish social identity and for interpreting how John dialogues with contemporary Jewish social identity and Jewish cultural memory.

In chapter 2 we saw that Jews in Ptolemaic Egypt pursued socially convergent, integrationist and participatory strategies for adapting to life in the Egyptian Diaspora. Literary and archaeological evidence suggests that this was a very broad trend until troubles emerged in the early imperial period, when Jewish writers again reasserted these strategies. The Egyptian Diaspora offers the earliest and best evidence of participatory social categorizations, where the religious aspects of Jewish cultural identity were used to simultaneously maintain social distinction and foster social integration. This would be very influential on the collective memory of the Hellenistic Western Diaspora, much of which seems to have used similar language and social strategies.

In chapter 3 we surveyed Jewish social identity in Asia Minor. While the remaining literary and archaeological evidence is far less extensive, enough remains that we can deduce that social strategies and attitudes in Asia Minor among Jews were broadly similar to those of Egpyt. Jews self-categorized themselves as participants in the local cultures, though again using their religion to alternately foster social convergence while also maintaining their distinctiveness. Most evidence for memory distortion and innovation in Asia Minor among Jews comes from evidence preserved in Josephus, which indicates maintaining ethnic distinctiveness continued to be a major social goal of Asia Minor Jews, though as in Egypt it was portrayed as a positive characteristic using Hellenistic ideals.

Chapter 4 reviewed Roman social categorizations of Jews and Josephus's response in *Against Apion*. I offered some suggestions as to how Jews in Rome would have likely categorized themselves. Josephus and his Roman contemporaries both innovated upon collective memory for their own ends—the Romans had the goal of preserving their self-image as those who brought order and justice to the world, while Josephus had the goal of overcoming the negative social consequences caused by the Jewish revolt and restoring Jews to a positive social location similar to that enjoyed in pre-Roman Egypt. Other evidence suggests this was part of a broad trend among Jews in Rome and Italy, where Jewish religion was alternately used to maintain ethnic distinction while fostering integration.

In chapter 5 we saw that John engages the positive social categorizations found in Egypt, Asia Minor, and Rome. However, in the Johannine portrayal Jews do not enjoy these positive social categorizations when in interaction with Jesus. When Jewish social identity is salient in the presence of the Samaritan woman, John still categorizes Jews as having privileged knowledge of monotheism in a manner consistent with other Jew-gentile contexts. Negative categorizations of Jews in John have little if anything to do with how contemporary gentile writers at Rome negatively categorized Jews. The result is that Jews are portrayed, in terms of religious and theological perceptiveness, as much more fallible than in Greek Diaspora literature. That said, discussions of ethnic markers such as the Sabbath or circumcision serve as

Conclusion

the pretense for exposition of Johannine Christology and *Halakhic* issues are ignored. This demonstrates John's lack of interest in nullifying Jewish ethnic identity directly, though John relativizes its importance to belief in Jesus in order to undermine the comparative fit of Jewish social identity so that Jews are grouped in with "the world" even though they possess divine revelation in the Scriptures.

Chapter 6 attempts to confirm and build upon the data explored in chapter 5 and show that John assumes the validity of Abraham's portrayal in reception history as one who was exceptionally faithful to YHWH. However, through application of a dualistic motif contingent on belief in Jesus, John denies that this virtue is passed on to Abraham's descendants automatically. John employs a similar strategy in relation to Moses. Moses functions as a revealer, though his status, and any status attributed to Jews derivatively on account of obedience to the Mosaic Law, is relativized in light of the need for belief in Jesus. This reduces the salience of social categorizations derived from this cultural memory symbol that helped to maintain relative difference vis-à-vis gentiles. The Johannine portrayal is interested in maintaining a less exalted, human Moses, whose laudatory features as an authoritative revealer ascribed to him through reception history are more suitably modelled in Jesus. This subordinates Moses, and therefore the Law, to Jesus, again rendering elect status conditional to response to Jesus. Likewise, an Abraham-like identity as one who is faithful is also contingent on belief in Jesus.

In chapter 6 we saw that the result of Johannine treatment of Jewish symbols and "the Jews" together is to reduce reduce relative difference between Jews and gentiles so that Jews, like gentiles, are members of "the world." In chapter 7 we also saw that, from a sociological perspective, this is typical of new religious movements and is consistent with much recent Johannine scholarship where John produces a theology that is in continuity with Judaism and could be accepted by Jewish Christians, but ultimately undermines the imperative of maintaining a Jewish ethnic identity and *de facto* starts the foundation of a new religion. It explains why, as Meeks puts it, " . . . the Fourth Gospel is most anti-Jewish just at the points it is most Jewish."[1]

---

1. Meeks, "Johannine Christianity and Judaism," 172.

John and Anti-Judaism

This study has been primarily concerned with understanding the nature and function of the Johannine "Jews" in light of its cultural context. Establishing the precise causes of the challenges John faces, or a complete description of how Johannine Christians saw themselves in light of Jewish ethnic identity, be it current or former, are beyond the scope of this study and require further investigation. However, we do get a strong picture of what John is trying to do. The social categorizations and treatment of the common progenitors above probably reflects a *Sitz im Leben* of cultural and religious competition where the social cohesion of a group is at stake due to the continuing *attractiveness* of Judaism. John is therefore probably trying to downplay, but also capitalize upon, elements of Judaism's attractiveness. Given that John does not attact Sabbath observance, circumcision, or defame Moses or Abraham, the Gentilizing tendencies in the Gospel that undermine key ethnic markers are best understood as the theological consequences of reducing their salience for determining the social identity of the spiritual in-group. The complete abandonment of Judaism was probably not John's goal, but it is a logical result of portraying the Jews in the narrative as part of "the world."

THEOLOGICAL REFLECTIONS: LUTHER, ANTI-JUDAISM, AND JEWS AS PART OF THE WORLD

Historically, Christianity and Judaism have had a difficult relationship, and, historically, the love-hate relationship between Christianity and Judaism is perhaps best illustrated in the works of Martin Luther. Early in his career, Martin Luther was quite sympathetic towards Jews.[2] Although he nonetheless wished to see them convert to Christianity, he also saw little point in their social isolation or persecution. While a careful reader will detect considerable distance between Luther and Judaism, he nonetheless appears to have recognized injustice when he saw it:

> I hope that if one deals in a kindly way with the Jews and instructs them carefully from Holy Scripture, many of them will become genuine Christians . . . They will only be frightened

---

2. Bertram, "Introduction to 'On the Jews and their Lies,'" 124.

Conclusion

further away from it if their Judaism is so utterly rejected that nothing is allowed to remain, and they are only treated with arrogance and scorn.³

Later in life as Luther suffered an increasing number of health problems, and perhaps tired from controversy, his famously vigorous temperament took a turn for the worse. Using John 8:44 as support Luther writes:

> . . . if their Messiah, for whom they hope, should come . . . they would crucify and blaspheme him seven times worse than they did our Messiah; and they would also say that he was not the true Messiah, but a deceiving devil.⁴

As if this were not enough, in a particularly virulent tirade (even by late medieval standards) Luther advocates a six-step systematic persecution to convert Jews to Christianity. This involved burning synagogues, destruction of homes and property, the burning of religious literature, prohibition of religious instruction, restrictions on movement, and confiscation of financial assets.⁵ Such a turn by a hero of the Reformation is quite shocking, especially when he earlier felt it necessary to polemically remind the Catholic Church that Jesus himself was a Jew. Luther's failing health, among other factors, seemed to allow for the re-emergence of a traditional anti-Judaism and antisemitism that was latent in the culture. Challenges, be they theological, social, or the emotional and psychological states of leaders and other communicators, can significantly influence what and how one communicates.

In a politically correct era, using the Gospel of John in preaching or witness can be complicated by several theological considerations. The most significant among these is John 8:44–45. I attempted to explain some of these challenges above in terms of Jewish social identity and religious or cultural competition, but repeated affirmation of historically-sensitive readings does little to soften this so-called "embarrassment of history." In fact, it makes it even worse because of the misreading and abuse of the text. It seems the best one can hope for is to pre-empt the

---

3. Luther, "That Jesus was Born a Jew," 200–201.
4. Luther, "On the Jews and their Lies," 141–42.
5. Luther, "On the Jews and their Lies," 47, 268–70.

embarrassments of the future and provide the Church some cathartic explanation as, over a prolonged period, it works to alter the paradigms it teaches its laypeople for understanding their Jewish predecessors in the Judeo-Christian tradition. Like Johannine anti-Judaism, putting latent Christian anti-Judaism in its proper context "cuts both ways." It solves one issue but creates another by demonstrating the follies of the past and further publicizing ecclesial embarrassment.

Along with many others I think John's Jewish background is now beyond question. When compared to the likes of Petronius, Suetonius, Manetho, Tacitus, or Apion, John's anti-Judaism is scarcely recognizable if it is ascribed gentile origins. In later history John appears to have been read along the lines of Tacitus, depicting normal Jews as willfully superstitious, petty, and prone to violence and vengefulness. However, this was not John's intent. As Kierspel notes, speaking of John 3:16 and 3:19:

> An author with anti-Jewish motives would not have missed the opportunity to use this pictorial and forceful metaphor and apply it to "the Jews." But the author of the Fourth Gospel had another interest and we see him creating powerful rhetorical monuments which display the universality of sin.[6]

John is intent on presenting Jews as like gentiles in terms of bondage to sin and the need for redemption and revelation, but in reception history what happened is, at a later date, John's agenda was conflated with existing gentile stereotypes and prejudices against Jews. The connotations of the two different cultural streams converged to create a new reading made possible by John's use of indeterminate, multivalent language: wit becomes controversy, *double-entendre* and misunderstanding become obduracy, and "stereotyped apocalyptic polemic" becomes antisemitism. Meanwhile, portraying Jesus as expressing the ideals of Jewish social identity and cultural memory is turned into a form of theological supersessionism.

This study supports the idea that John marks a change of course for a Christian Jewish party's identity. The uniqueness of this identity set the stage for a parting of the ways, yet the way taken looks far more

---

6. Kierspel, *Jews and the World in the Fourth Gospel*, 149–50.

Conclusion

Jewish than is often recognized. John's social-theological strategy resembles that of Paul, where Jews and gentiles are equally fallible. John's treatment of ethnicity and Jewish cultural identity, then, has a remarkable affinity with some positions taken in the discussion around the New Perspective on Paul. Separating adherence to Judaism from eternal life appears to be the motivator behind portraying the Johannine Jews as local manifestations of "the world."

The most direct theological solution to anti-Judaism for Christians is, rephrasing Kosuke Koyama, to admit "there is no handle on the Bible."[7] That is, Christians are not masters of the Bible and must teach hermeneutical humility in our readings and applications of Scripture. With texts being regarded as a *medium* of revelation, it is easy to fall into the trap of thinking that humans transcend the ideas they own and read, and that they can use these ideas as a source of power over others. However, the purpose of revelation is to communicate ideas that explain but also transcend the human condition, necessitating a degree of hermeneutical humility.

A second solution, to quote Koyama directly, is to recognize "there is no handle on the cross."[8] In making this statement Koyama is discussing Luther's *theologia crucis* (theology of the cross) and contrasting it with the *theologia gloriae* (theology of glory). These two theologies are contrasted in that a "theology of glory" seeks power over others—and God!—and thinks it grants us the final say over the destiny of the world. Meanwhile, a theology of the cross condemns intellectual and social idols that humans are sometimes inclined to put in place of the divine. In terms of knowledge of God, Luther argues for the existence of a "hidden" God on the one hand, and a "revealed" God on the other, due to the logical implications of omniscience, omnipotence, and transcendence.[9] For Luther, this forced the qualitative distinction between the "Word of God" and Scripture where Jesus represented the true Word of God; Scripture was not the Word of God in itself because

---

7. Koyama, *No Handle on the Cross*, 3–12.

8. Koyama, *No Handle on the Cross*, 3–12.

9. McGrath, *Luther's Theology of the Cross*, 166–67; Lohse, *Martin Luther's Theology*, 215.

it could not contain the transcendent God.[10] Whether or not one agrees with Luther on this point, it remains that the *theologia crucis*, the rejected and crucified God in Christ, is the picture of himself that Christians believe God has chosen to reveal and wants created beings to take to heart:

> To the crucified Christ one finds no equivalents, no analogous knowledge of God. God's nature reveals itself in the suffering of the cross in that the 'fullness of God's power' is seen not in the pompous, powerful and the proud, but in the shameful, weak and lowly. Consequently, that God is identified with the crucified Christ not only reverses all human concepts of God but also refuses any understanding of the crucified Christ on the presupposition of a concept of God imported from elsewhere.[11]

The importance of the above is that the primary outward social expression of antisemitism, or prejudice in general, reflects a "theology of glory" that asserts dominance over or persecutes another group of people. Such behavior contradicts the Fourth Gospel, where misunderstanding and rejection manifest Jesus' "glory," and his crucifixion is an act of love on behalf of his friends and the world. As the Word of God, Jesus serves as the revelation of *Deus pro nobis*, or "God for us." The "us" is sinful humanity, or "the world," and though Christians are born "from above" we are given to Jesus by the Father from "out of the world." If this study is correct in its explanation for how John appropriates Jewish social identity, then its purpose is to demonstrate in Jesus the idea that *God is for us*, the world to which the Johannine Jews belong. Johannine anti-Judaism is intended to demonstrate that even the most informed can be mistaken in their perceptions of God, a lesson John would have all readers learn, regardless of their ethnic or religious background.

---

10. Ngien, *Suffering of God*, 58.
11. Ngien, *Suffering of God*, 67–68.

Bibliography

Ackerman, James S. "The Rabbinic Interpretation of Psalm 82 and the Gospel of John." *HTR* 59 (1966) 186–91.
Ager, Sheila. "The Power of Excess: Royal Incest and the Ptolemaic Dynasty." *Anthropologica* 48 (2006) 165–86.
Ameling, Walter. *Inscriptiones Judaicae Orientis. Volume Two: Kleinasien.* Texts and Studies in Ancient Judaism 99. Tübingen: Mohr Siebeck, 2004.
Anderson, Paul N. "Gradations of Symbolization in the Johannine Passion Narrative: Control Measures for Theologizing Speculation Gone Awry." In *Imagery in the Gospel of John: Terms, Forms, Themes, and Theology of Johannine Figurative Language*, edited by Jörg Frey et al., 157–94. WUNT 200. Tübingen: Mohr Siebeck, 2006.
———. "John and Qumran: Discovery and Interpretation over Sixty Years." In *John, Qumran, and the Dead Sea Scrolls*, edited by Mary L. Coloe and Tom Thatcher, 15–50. EJL 32. Atlanta: SBL, 2011.
Armstrong, John A. *Nations before Nationalism*. Chapel Hill, NC: University of North Carolina Press, 1982.
Ashton, John. "The Identity and Function of the Ἰουδαῖοι in the Fourth Gospel." *NovT* 27 (1985) 40–75.
———. *Understanding the Fourth Gospel*. 1st ed. Oxford: Clarendon, 1991.
———. *Understanding the Fourth Gospel*. 2nd ed. Oxford: Oxford University Press, 2007.
Assmann, Jan. "Collective Memory and Cultural Identity." *New German Critique* 65 (1995) 125–33.
———. "Egyptian Anti-Judaism: A Case of Distorted Memory." In *Memory Distortion: How Minds, Brains, and Societies Reconstruct the Past*, edited by D. L. Schacter et al., 365–78. Cambridge, MA: Harvard University Press, 1997.
Augenstein, J. "'Euer Gesetz'—Ein Pronomen und die johanneische Haltung zum Gesetz." *ZNW* 88 (1997) 311–13.
Aune, David E. "Magic in Early Christianity." *ANRW* 2.23.2 (1980) 1507–57.

Bibliography

Bacon, Benjamin W. *The Fourth Gospel in Research and Debate.* New York: Moffat, Yard & Company, 1910.

———. *The Gospel of the Hellenists*, edited by Carl H. Kraeling. New York: Henry Holt, 1933.

Baehrens, Aemilius. *Poetae Latini Minores.* 5 vols. Leipzig: Tuebner, 1883.

Bainbridge, William Sims. *The Sociology of Religious Movements.* New York: Routledge, 1997.

Ball, David Mark. *'I Am' in John's Gospel: Literary Function, Background and Theological Implications.* JSNTSup 124. Sheffield: Sheffield Academic, 1996.

Barclay, John M. G. *Against Apion.* FJTC 10. Leiden: Brill, 2007.

———. *Jews in the Mediterranean Diaspora.* Edinburgh: T. & T. Clark, 1996.

———. "Josephus v. Apion: Analysis of an Argument." In *Understanding Josephus*, edited by Steve Mason, 194–221. Sheffield: Sheffield Academic, 1998.

———. "The Politics of Contempt: Judeans and Egyptians in Josephus' *Against Apion*." In *Negotiating Diaspora: Jewish Strategies in the Roman Empire*, edited by John M. G. Barclay, 109–27. LSTS 45. New York: T. & T. Clark, 2004.

Bar-Kochva, Bezalel. "An Ass in the Jerusalem Temple: The Origins and Development of the Slander." In *Josephus' Contra Apionem: Studies in its Character and Context with a Latin Concordance to the Portion Missing in Greek*, edited by Louis H. Feldman and John R. Levison, 310–26. AGJU 34. Leiden: Brill, 1996.

Barrett, C. K. *The Gospel according to St. John.* 2nd ed. Philadelphia: Westminster, 1978.

———. *The Prologue of St. John's Gospel.* London: Athlone Press, 1971.

———. "St. John: Social Historian." *Proceedings of the Irish Biblical Association* 10 (1986) 26–39.

Barth, Fredrik, ed. *Ethnic Groups and Boundaries: The Social Organization of Culture Difference.* Boston: Little, Brown, 1969.

Bauckham, Richard. "For Whom Were Gospels Written?" In *The Gospels for All Christians*, edited by Richard Bauckham, 9–48. Grand Rapids: Eerdmans, 1998.

Baum, Gregory. *Is the New Testament Anti-Semitic? A Re-Examination of the New Testament.* Glen Rock, NJ: Paulist, 1965.

Baumgarten, Albert I. "Marcel Simon's *Verus Israel* as a Contribution to Jewish History." *HTR* 92 (1999) 465–78.

Baur, Ferdinand Christian. *Das Christenthum und die christliche Kirche der drei ersten Jahrhunderte.* 3rd ed. Stuttgart: Friedrich Frommann, 1966.

Beasley-Murray, George Raymond. *John.* 2nd ed. Nashville: Thomas Nelson, 1999.

Bibliography

Beavis, M. A. L. "Anti-Egyptian Polemic in the Letter of Aristeas 130–65 (The High Priest's Discourse)." *JSJ* 18 (1987) 145–51.

Bennema, C. "The Identity and Composition of οἱ Ἰουδαῖοι in the Gospel of John." *TynBul* 60 (2009) 239–63.

Bernier, Jonathan. Aposynagōgos *and the Historical Jesus in John: Rethinking the Historicity of the Johannine Expulsion Passages.* BibInt 122. Leiden: Brill, 2013.

Berry, John W., et al. "Psychological Acculturation of Immigrants." In *Cross-Cultural Adaptation: Current Approaches*, edited by Young Yun Kim and William B. Gudykunst, 62–89. London: Sage, 1987.

Berthelot, Katell. "The Biblical Conquest of the Promised Land and the Hasmonean Wars according to 1 and 2 Maccabees." In *Books of the Maccabees*, edited by Géza G. Xeravits and József Zsengellér, 45–60. Supplements to the Journal for the Study of Judaism 118. Leiden: Brill, 2007.

Bertram, Martin H. "Introduction to 'On the Jews and Their Lies.'" In *Luther's Works* vol. 47, edited and translated by Martin H. Bertram, 137–306. Philadelphia: Fortress, 1971.

Bevans, Stephen B. *Models of Contextual Theology.* New York: Orbis, 1992.

Bickerman, Elias. *The God of the Maccabees: Studies on the Meaning and Origin of the Maccabean Revolt.* Translated by Horst R. Moehring. Leiden: Brill, 1979.

Bieringer, Reimund, Didier Pollefeyt, Frederique Vandecasteele-Vanneuville, eds. *Anti-Judaism and the Fourth Gospel.* Louisville: Westminster John Knox, 2001.

Bilde, Per. *Flavius Josephus between Jerusalem and Rome: His Life, his Works, and Their Importance.* LSTS 2. Sheffield: Sheffield Academic, 1988.

Bilde, Per, ed. *Ethnicity in Hellenistic Egypt.* Aarhus: Aarhus University Press, 1992.

Boer, Martinus C. de. "The Depiction of 'the Jews' in John's Gospel: Matters of Behavior and Identity." In *Anti-Judaism and the Fourth Gospel*, edited by Reimund Bieringer et al., 141–57. Louisville: Westminster John Knox, 2001.

Boismard, M. E. *Moses or Jesus: An Essay in Johannine Christology.* Translated by B.T. Viviano. Leuven: Leuven University Press, 1993.

Borgen, Peder. *Bread from Heaven: An Exegetical Study of the Concept of Manna in the Gospel of John and the Writings of Philo.* NovTSup 10. 2nd ed. Leiden: Brill, 1981.

———. *Early Christianity and Hellenistic Judaism.* Edinburgh: T. & T. Clark, 1996.

———. "God's Agent in the Fourth Gospel." In *The Interpretation of John*, edited by John Ashton, 83–95. Edinburgh: T. & T. Clark, 1997.

Bibliography

———. *The Gospel of John: More Light from Philo, Paul and Archaeology*. NovTSup 154. Leiden: Brill, 2014.

———. "Logos was the True Light." *NovT* 14 (1972) 115–30.

———. "Two Philonic Prayers and their Contexts: An Analysis of *Who is the Heir of Divine Things* (Her.) 24–49 and *Against Flaccus* (Flacc.) 170–75." *NTS* 45 (1999) 291–309.

Bousset, Wilhelm. *Kyrios Christos*. Translated by John E. Steely. New York: Abingdon, 1970.

———. *Die Religion des Judentums im neutestamentlichen Zeitalter*. Berlin: Reuther & Reichard, 1903.

Boyarin, Daniel. "The Ioudaioi in John and the Prehistory of 'Judaism.'" In *Pauline Conversations in Context: Essays in Honor of Calvin J. Roetzel*, edited by J. C. Anderson et al., 216–39. London: Sheffield Academic, 2002.

———. "Semantic Differences; or, 'Judaism/Christianity.'" In *The Ways that Never Parted*, edited by Adam H. Becker and Annette Yoshiko Reed, 68–85. TSAJ 95. Tübingen: Mohr Siebeck, 2003.

Brant, Jo-Ann. *Dialogue and Drama: Elements of Greek Tragedy in the Fourth Gospel*. Peabody, MA: Hendrickson, 2004.

Brawley, Robert L. "An Absent Complement and Intertextuality in John 19:28–29." *JBL* 112 (1993) 427–43.

Brayford, Susan Ann. *Genesis*. Septuagint Commentary Series. Leiden: Brill, 2007.

Brewer, Marilynn B. "In-Group Bias in the Minimal Intergroup Situation: A Cognitive-Motivational Analysis." *Psychological Bulletin* 86 (1979) 307–24.

———. "The Social Self: On Being the Same and Different at the Same Time." *Personality and Social Psychology Bulletin* 17 (1991) 475–82.

Broadhead, Edwin K. *Jewish Ways of Following Jesus*. WUNT 266. Tubingen: Mohr Siebeck, 2010.

Brooke, George J. "The Psalms in Early Jewish Literature in the Light of the Dead Sea Scrolls." In *The Psalms in the New Testament*, edited by Steve Moyise and Maarten J. J. Menken, 5–24. London: T. & T. Clark, 2004.

Brown, Raymond E. *The Community of the Beloved Disciple*. London: G. Chapman, 1979.

———. *The Gospel according to John*. 2 vols. New York: Doubleday, 1970.

Bryan, Steven M. "Consumed by Zeal: John's Use of Psalm 69:9 and the Action in the Temple." *BBR* 21 (2011) 479–94.

———. "Power in the Pool: The Healing of the Man at Bethesda and Jesus' Violation of the Sabbath (Jn. 5:1–18)." *TynBul* 54 (2003) 7–22.

Bibliography

Buckler, W. H., and W. M. Calder. *Monumenta Asiae Minoris Antiqua VI: Monuments and Documents from Phrygia and Caria.* Manchester: Manchester University Press, 1939.

Buell, Denise Kimber. *Why this New Race? Ethnic Reasoning in Early Christianity.* New York: Columbia University Press, 2005.

Bultmann, Rudolph. *The Gospel of John.* Translated by G. R. Beasley-Murray et al. Philadelphia: Westminster, 1971.

———. *Theology of the New Testament.* Translated by Kendrick Grobel. 2 vols. New York: Scribner, 1955.

Burge, Gary M. *The Anointed Community: The Holy Spirit in the Johannine Tradition.* Grand Rapids: Eerdmans, 1987.

Carter, Warren. *John and Empire: Initial Explorations.* New York: T. & T. Clark, 2008.

———. *John: Storyteller, Interpreter, Evangelist.* Peabody, MA: Hendrickson, 2006.

Catto, Stephen K. *Reconstructing the First-Century Synagogue: A Critical Analysis of Current Research.* LNTS 363. New York: T. & T. Clark, 2007.

Charlesworth, James H., ed. *The Old Testament Pseudepigrapha.* 2 vols. New York: Doubleday, 1985.

Chilton, Bruce. *The Temple of Jesus: His Sacrificial Program within a Cultural History of Sacrifice.* University Park, PA: Pennsylvania State University Press, 1992.

Clifford, Hywel. "Moses as Philosopher-Sage in Philo." In *Moses in Biblical and Extra-Biblical Traditions*, edited by Axel Graupner and Michael Wolter, 151–67. BZAW 372. Berlin: de Gruyter, 2007.

Cohen, Naomi G. "The Names of the Translators in the Letter of Aristeas: A Study in the Dynamics of Cultural Transition." *JSJ* 15 (1984) 32–64.

Cohen, Shaye J. D. *The Beginnings of Jewishness: Boundaries, Varieties, Uncertainties.* Berkeley: University of California, 1999.

———. "Crossing the Boundary and Becoming a Jew." *HTR* 81 (1989) 13–33.

———. *From the Maccabees to the Mishnah.* Philadelphia: Westminster, 1987.

Collins, Adela Yarbro. *The Combat Myth in the Book of Revelation.* Missoula, MT: Scholars, 1976.

Collins, John J. *Between Athens and Jerusalem: Jewish Identity in the Hellenistic Diaspora.* 2nd ed. Grand Rapids: Eerdmans, 2000.

Collins, Nina L. *The Library in Alexandria and the Bible in Greek.* VTSup 82. Leiden: Brill, 2000.

Collins, Raymond F. "Speaking of the Jews: 'Jews' in the Discourse Material of the Fourth Gospel." In *Anti-Judaism and the Fourth Gospel*, edited by

Reimund Bieringer et al., 158–75. Louisville: Westminster John Knox, 2001.

Coloe, Mary. *God Dwells with Us: Temple Symbolism in the Fourth Gospel*. Collegeville, MN: Liturgical, 2001.

Colpe, Carsten. *Die Religionsgeschichtliche Schule: Darstellung und Kritik ihres Bildes vom Gnostischen Erlösermythus*. Göttingen: Vändenhoeck & Ruprecht, 1961.

Connolly, Joy. "Being Greek/Being Roman: Hellenism and Assimilation in the Roman Empire." *Millennium* 4 (2007) 21–42.

Cook, M. J. "The Gospel of John and the Jews." *RevExp* 84 (1987) 259–71.

Cory, Catherine. "Wisdom's Rescue: A New Reading of the Tabernacles Discourse (John 7:1–8:59)." *JBL* 116 (1997) 95–116.

Court, John M. *New Testament Writers and the Old Testament*. Eugene, OR: Wipf & Stock, 2002.

Cousland, J. R. C. "Reversal, Recidivism and Reward in *3 Maccabees*: Structure and Purpose." *JSJ* 34 (2003) 39–51.

Croy, N. Clayton. *3 Maccabees*. Septuagint Commentary Series. Leiden: Brill, 2006.

Cullmann, Oscar. *The Johannine Circle*. Translated by John Bowden. Philadelphia: Westminster, 1976.

———. "Der Johanneische Gebrauch Doppeldeutiger Ausdrücke als Schlüssel zum Verständnis des Vierten Evangeliums." *TZ* 4 (1948) 360–71.

Culpepper, R. Alan. *Anatomy of the Fourth Gospel: A Study in Literary Design*. Philadelphia: Fortress, 1983.

———. "Anti-Judaism in the Fourth Gospel as a Theological Problem for Christian Interpreters." In *Anti-Judaism and the Fourth Gospel*, edited by Reimund Bieringer et al., 61–82. Louisville: Westminster John Knox, 2001.

———. "The Gospel of John and the Jews." *RevExp* 84 (1987) 273–88.

———. *The Johannine School*. Missoula, MT: Scholars, 1975.

Dahl, Nils. "The Johannine Church and History." In *Current Issues in New Testament Interpretation*, edited by William Klassen and Graydon F. Snyder, 124–42. London: SCM, 1962.

Daly-Denton, Margaret. *David in the Fourth Gospel: The Johannine Reception of the Psalms*. AGJU 47. Leiden: Brill, 2000.

———. "The Psalms in John's Gospel." In *The Psalms in the New Testament*, edited by Steve Moyise and Maarten J. J. Menken, 119–37. London: T. & T. Clark, 2004.

Daniélou, Jean. *The Theology of Jewish Christianity*. Translated by John A. Baker. London: Darton, Longman & Todd, 1964.

Bibliography

Das, A. Andrew. *Paul, the Law, and the Covenant*. Peabody, MA: Hendrickson, 2001.

Davies, Margaret. *Rhetoric and Reference in the Fourth Gospel*. JSNTSup 69. Sheffield: JSOT, 1992.

Day, Abby. *Believing in Belonging: Belief and Social Identity in the Modern World*. Oxford: Oxford University Press, 2011.

De La Potterie, Ignace. "The Truth in Saint John." In *The Interpretation of John*, edited by John Ashton, 67–82. 2nd ed. Studies in New Testament Interpretation. Edinburgh: T. & T. Clark, 1997.

Dennis, John A. *Jesus' Death and the Gathering of True Israel: The Johannine Appropriation of Restoration Theology in the Light of John 11.47–52*. WUNT 2.217. Tübingen: Mohr Siebeck, 2006.

Diefenbach, Manfred. *Der Konflikt Jesu mit den „Juden."* Münster: Aschendorf, 2002.

Dodd, C. H. *The Interpretation of the Fourth Gospel*. Cambridge: Cambridge University Press, 1953.

Doering, Lutz. "Sabbath Laws in the New Testament Gospels." In *New Testament and Rabbinic Literature*, edited by Reimund Bieringer et al., 207–53. Supplements to the Journal for the Study of Judaism 136. Leiden: Brill, 2010.

Donaldson, Terence L. *Jews and Anti-Judaism in the New Testament*. London: SPCK, 2010.

Doran, Robert. "Independence or Co-existence: The Responses of 1 and 2 Maccabees to Seleucid Hegemony." In *Society of Biblical Literature 1999 Seminar Papers*, 94–103. SBLSP 38. Atlanta: SBL, 1999.

———. *Temple Propaganda: The Purpose and Character of 2 Maccabees*. CBQMS 12. Washington, DC: Catholic Biblical Association of America, 1981.

———. *2 Maccabees*. Minneapolis: Fortress, 2012.

Duke, Paul M. *Irony in the Fourth Gospel*. Atlanta: John Knox, 1985.

Dumbrell, William J. "Grace and Truth: The Progress of the Argument of the Prologue of John's Gospel." In *Doing Theology for the People of God: Studies in Honour of J. I. Packer*, edited by Donald Lewis and Alister McGrath, 105–21. Downers Grove, IL: InterVarsity, 1996.

Dunn, James D. G. *Christology in the Making: A New Testament Inquiry into the Origins of the Doctrine of the Incarnation*. 2nd ed. Grand Rapids: Eerdmans, 1996.

———. "The Embarrassment of History: Reflections on the Problem of 'Anti-Judaism' in the Fourth Gospel." In *Anti-Judaism and the Fourth Gospel*, edited by Reimund Bieringer et al., 41–60. Louisville: Westminster John Knox, 2001.

Bibliography

———. *Jews and Christians: The Parting of the Ways, A.D. 70 to 135*. Grand Rapids: Eerdmans, 1999.

———. "The Justice of God: A Renewed Perspective on Justification by Faith." *JTS* 43 (1992) 1–21.

———. "Let John Be John: A Gospel for its Time." In *The Gospel and the Gospels*, edited by Peter Stuhlmacher, 293–322. Grand Rapids: Eerdmans, 1991.

———. *The New Perspective on Paul: Collected Essays*. Grand Rapids: Eerdmans, 2007.

———. "The Question of Anti-Semitism in the New Testament." In *Jews and Christians: The Parting of the Ways*, edited by James D. G. Dunn, 177–211. Grand Rapids: Eerdmans, 1989.

———. *The Theology of Paul the Apostle*. Grand Rapids: Eerdmans, 1998.

Eckhardt, Benedikt. "Yet another Book on Jewish Identity in Antiquity." In *Jewish Identity and Politics between the Maccabees and Bar Kochba*, edited by Benedikt Eckhardt, 1–10. Supplements to the Journal for the Study of Judaism 155. Leiden: Brill, 2012.

Eddy, Samuel K. *The King is Dead: Studies in the Near Eastern Resistance to Hellenism 334–31 B.C.* Lincoln: University of Nebraska Press, 1961.

Edwards, Ruth B. "ΧΑΡΙΝ ΑΝΤΙ ΧΑΡΙΤΟΣ (John 1.16): Grace and the Law in the Johannine Prologue." *JSNT* 32 (1988) 3–15.

Ego, Beate. "Abraham als Urbild der Toratreue Israels: Traditionsgeschichtliche Überlegungen zu einem Aspekt des biblischen Abrahamsbildes." In *Bund und Tora*, edited by Friedrich Avemarie and Hermann Lichtenberger, 25–40. WUNT 92. Tübingen: Mohr Siebeck, 1996.

Eriksen, Thomas Hylland. *Ethnicity and Nationalism: Anthropological Perspectives*. 3rd ed. London: Pluto, 2010.

Erll, Astrid. *Memory in Culture*. New York: Palgrave Macmillan, 2011.

Esler, Philip Francis. *Conflict and Identity in Romans: The Social Setting of Paul's Letter*. Minneapolis: Fortress, 2003.

———. "Social-Scientific Approaches." In *Dictionary of Biblical Criticism and Interpretation*, edited by Stanley E. Porter, 337–40. London: Routledge, 2007.

Esler, Philip F., and Ronald Piper. *Lazarus, Mary and Martha: Social-Scientific Approaches to the Gospel of John*. Minneapolis: Fortress, 2006.

Evans, Craig A. "Praise and Prophecy in the Psalter and in the New Testament." In *The Book of Psalms: Composition and Reception*, edited by Peter W. Flint et al., 551–79. VTSup 99. Leiden: Brill, 2005.

———. *Word and Glory: On the Exegetical and Theological Background of John's Prologue*. JSNTSup 89. Sheffield: JSOT, 1993.

Bibliography

Farmer, William Reuben. *Maccabees, Zealots, and Josephus: An Inquiry into Jewish Nationalism in the Greco-Roman Period*. New York: Columbia University Press, 1956.

Fearghail, Fearghus O. "The Jews in the Hellenistic Cities of Acts." In *Jews in the Hellenistic and Roman Cities*, edited by John R. Bartlett, 39–54. New York: Routledge, 2012.

Feldman, Louis H. *Jew and Gentile in the Ancient World: Attitudes and Interactions from Alexander to Trajan*. Princeton: Princeton University Press, 1993.

———. "Origen's Contra Celsum and Josephus' Contra Apionem: The Issue of Jewish Origins." *VC* 44 (1990) 105–35.

———. "Philo's View of Moses' Birth and Upbringing." *CBQ* 64 (2002) 258–81.

———. "Pro-Jewish Intimations in Anti-Jewish Remarks Cited in Josephus' Against Apion." *JQR* 78 (1988) 187–251.

Felsch, Dorit. *Die Feste im Johannesevangelium*. WUNT 2.308. Tübingen: Mohr Siebeck, 2011.

Fitzpatrick-McKinley, Anne. "Synagogue Communities in the Graeco-Roman Cities." In *Jews in the Hellenistic and Roman Cities*, edited by John R. Bartlett, 55–87. New York: Routledge, 2012.

Fletcher-Louis, Crispin. "Wisdom Christology and the Parting of the Ways between Judaism and Christianity." In *Christian-Jewish Relations through the Centuries*, edited by Stanley E. Porter and B. W. R. Pearson, 52–68. JSNTSup 192. Roehampton Papers 6. Sheffield: Sheffield Academic, 2000.

Förster, Hans. "Die syntaktische Funktion von ὅτι in Joh 8.47." *NTS* 62 (2016) 157–66.

Fraser, Peter M. *Ptolemaic Alexandria*. 3 vols. Oxford: Clarendon, 1972.

Frayer-Griggs, Daniel. "Spittle, Clay, and Creation in John 9:6 and Some Dead Sea Scrolls." *JBL* 132 (2013) 659–70.

Freed, Edwin D. "Who or What was before Abraham in John 8:58?" *JSNT* 17 (1983) 52–59.

Fretheim, Terence E. *The Deuteronomic History*. Nashville: Abingdon, 1983.

Frey, Jörg. "Auf der Suche nach dem Kontext des vierten Evangeliums: Eine Forschungsgeschichtliche Einführung." In *Kontexte des Johannesevangeliums: Das Vierte Evangelium in religions- und traditionsgeschichtlicher Perspektive*, edited by Jörg Frey and Udo Schnelle, 3–45. WUNT 175. Tübingen: Mohr Siebeck, 2004.

———. "'Die Juden' im Johannesevangelium und die Frage nach der ‚Trennung der Wege' zwischen der johanneischen Gemeinde und der Synagogue." In *Die Herrlichkeit des Gekreuzigten: Studien zu den*

Johanneischen Schriften I, edited by Jörg Frey and Juliana Schlegel, 339–77. WUNT 307. Tübingen: Mohr Siebeck, 2013.

Fuglseth, Kåre Sigvald. *Johannine Sectarianism in Perspective*. NovTSup 119. Leiden: Brill, 2005.

Gager, John C. *The Origins of Anti-Semitism: Attitudes toward Judaism in Pagan and Christian Antiquity*. Oxford: Oxford University Press, 1983.

Gambetti, Sandra. *The Alexandrian Riots of 38 C.E. and the Persecution of the Jews: A Historical Reconstruction*. Supplements to the Journal for the Study of Judaism 135. Leiden: Brill, 2009.

Galinsky, Karl. "The Cult of the Roman Emperor: Uniter or Divider?" In *Rome and Religion: A Cross-Disciplinary Dialogue on the Imperial Cult*, edited by Jeffrey Brod and Jonathan L. Reed, 1–21. WGRWSup 5. Atlanta, GA: SBL, 2011.

———. "In the Shadow (or Not) of the Imperial Cult: A Cooperative Agenda." In *Rome and Religion: A Cross-Disciplinary Dialogue on the Imperial Cult*, edited by Jeffrey Brod and Jonathan L. Reed, 215–25. WGRWSup 5. Atlanta, GA: SBL, 2011.

Gardner, Percy. *The Ephesian Gospel*. London: Williams and Norgate, 1916.

Gaston, Lloyd. *Paul and the Torah*. Vancouver: University of British Columbia Press, 1987.

Gellner, Ernest. *Nations and Nationalism*. Oxford: Basil Blackwell, 1983.

Gerdmar, Anders. *Roots of Theological Anti-Semitism*. Studies in Jewish History and Culture 20. Leiden: Brill, 2009.

Giddens, Anthony. *Modernity and Self-Identity: Self and Society in the Late Modern Age*. Stanford, CA: Stanford University Press, 1991.

Gillingham, Susan. *The Poems and Psalms of the Hebrew Bible*. Oxford: Oxford University Press, 1994.

Glasson, T. F. *Moses in the Fourth Gospel*. London: SCM, 1963.

Goldstein, Jonathan A. "How the Authors of 1 and 2 Maccabees Treated the 'Messianic' Promises." In *Judaisms and their Messiahs at the Turn of the Christian Era*, edited by Jacob Neusner et al., 69–96. Cambridge: Cambridge University Press, 1987.

———. *1 Maccabees*. AB 41. Garden City, NY: Doubleday, 1976.

———. *2 Maccabees*. AB 41A. Garden City, NY: Doubleday, 1983.

Goodblatt, David. *Elements of Ancient Jewish Nationalism*. Cambridge: Cambridge University Press, 2006.

Goodman, Martin. "Diaspora Reactions to the Destruction of the Temple." In *Jews and Christians: The Parting of the Ways A.D. 70 to 135*, edited by James D. G. Dunn, 27–38. WUNT 66 Tübingen: Mohr Siebeck, 1992.

Goudriaan, Koen. "Ethnical Strategies in Graeco-Roman Egypt." In *Ethnicity in Hellenistic Egypt*, edited by Per Bilde, 74–99. Aarhus: Aarhus University Press, 1992.

Bibliography

Granskou, David. "Anti-Judaism in the Passion Accounts of the Fourth Gospel." In *Anti-Judaism in Early Christianity*, edited by Peter Richardson and David Granskou, 201–16. Waterloo, ON: Wilfrid Laurier University Press, 1986.

Gray, W. "Wisdom Christology in the New Testament; its Scope and Relevance." *Theology* 89 (1986) 448–59.

Green, Anna. "Individual Remembering and 'Collective Memory': Theoretical Presuppositions and Contemporary Debates." *Oral History* 32 (2004) 35–44.

Greene, Joseph R. "Integrating Interpretations of John 7:37–39 into the Temple Theme: The Spirit as Efflux from the New Temple." *Neot* 47 (2013) 333–53.

Grodzynski, Denise. "Superstitio." *Revue des Etudes Anciennes* 76 (1974) 36–60.

Gruen, Erich S. *Diaspora: Jews amidst Greeks and Romans*. Cambridge, MA: Harvard University Press, 2002.

Guilding, Aileen. *The Fourth Gospel and Jewish Worship*. Oxford: Clarendon, 1960.

Guite, Harold. "Cicero's Attitude to the Greeks." *Greece and Rome* 9 (1962) 142–59.

Hadas, Moses. *Aristeas to Philocrates*. Eugene, OR: Wipf & Stock, 2007.

Haenchen, Ernst. *John*. 2 vols. Translated by Robert W. Funk. Philadelphia: Fortress, 1984.

Hakola, Raimo. "The Burden of Ambiguity: Nicodemus and the Social Identity of the Johannine Christians." *NTS* 55 (2009) 438–55.

———. "The Counsel of Caiaphas and the Social Identity of the Johannine Community (John 11:47–53)." In *Lux humana, Lux Aeterna*, edited by Antti Mustakallio, 140–63. Helsinki: Finnish Exegetical Society, 2005.

———. *Identity Matters: John, the Jews, and Jewishness*. NovTSup 118. Leiden: Brill, 2005.

———. *Reconsidering Johannine Christianity: A Social Identity Approach*. New York: Routledge, 2015.

———. "Social Identities and Group Phenomena in Second Temple Judaism." In *Explaining Christian Origins and Early Judaism: Contributions from Cognitive and Social Science*, edited by Petri Luomanen, 259–276. BibInt 89. Leiden: Brill, 2007.

Hale, Henry E. "Explaining Ethnicity." *Comparative Political Studies* 37 (2004) 458–85.

Hanson, Anthony T. "John's Citation of Psalm LXXXII." *NTS* 11 (1965) 158–62.

———. "John's Citation of Psalm LXXXII Reconsidered." *NTS* 13 (1967) 363–67.

Bibliography

Hanson, Paul D. *The Dawn of Apocalyptic*. Philadelphia: Fortress, 1975.

Hare, Douglas R. A. "The Rejection of the Jews in the Synoptic Gospels and Acts." In *Antisemitism and the Foundations of Christianity*, edited by Alan Davies, 27–47. New York: Paulist, 1979.

Harnack, Adolf. "Uber das Verhältniß des Prologs des vierten Evangeliums zum ganzen Werke." *ZTK* 2 (1892) 189–231.

Harner, Philip B. *The "I Am" of the Fourth Gospel*. Philadelphia: Fortress, 1970.

Harris, Elizabeth. *Prologue and Gospel: The Theology of the Fourth Evangelist*. JSNTSup 107. Sheffield: Sheffield Academic, 1994.

Harris, Rendel. *The Origin of the Prologue to St. John's Gospel*. Cambridge: Cambridge University Press, 1917.

Harrisville, Roy A., III. *The Figure of Abraham in the Epistles of Saint Paul*. San Francisco: Mellen Research University Press, 1992.

Harstine, Stan. *Moses as a Character in the Fourth Gospel: A Study of Ancient Reading Techniques*. JSNTSup 229. London: Sheffield Academic, 2002.

Haslam, S. Alexander. *Psychology in Organizations: The Social Identity Approach*. London: SAGE, 2002.

Haslam, S. Alexander, et al. "When do Stereotypes Really Become Consensual? Investigating the Group-Based Dynamics of the Consensualization Process." *European Journal of Social Psychology* 28 (1998) 755–76.

Haslam, S. Alexander et al. "Contextual Changes in the Prototypicality of Extreme and Moderate Outgroup Members." *European Journal of Social Psychology* 25 (1995) 509–30.

Hengel, Martin. *The Zealots*. Translated by David Smith. Edinburgh: T. & T. Clark, 1989.

Henten, Jan-Willem, and Ra'Anan Abusch. "The Jews as Typhonians and Josephus' Strategy of Refutation in *Contra Apionem*." In *Josephus' Contra Apionem*, edited by Louis H. Feldman and John R. Levison, 271–308. AGJU 34. Leiden: Brill, 1996.

Hieke, Thomas. "The Role of 'Scripture' in the Last Words of Mattathias (1 Macc 2:49–70)." In *The Books of the Maccabees: History, Theology, Ideology*, edited by Géza G. Xeravits and József Zsengellér, 61–74. Supplements to the Journal for the Study of Judaism 118. Leiden: Brill, 2007.

Hiers, Richard H., and David Larrimore Holland. "Introduction." In *Jesus' Proclamation of the Kingdom of God*, by Johannes Weiss, 1–54. London: SCM, 1971.

Hogg, Michael A., and Kipling D. Williams. "From *I* to *We*: Social Identity and the Collective Self." *Group Dynamics: Theory, Research, and Practice* (2000) 81–97.

Homcy, S. L. "'You Are Gods'? Spirituality and a Difficult Text." *JETS* 32 (1989) 485–91.

Honigman, Sylvie. "'Jews as the Best of All Greeks': Cultural Competition in the Literary Works of Alexandrian Judaeans of the Hellenistic Period." In *Shifting Social Imaginaries in the Hellenistic Period*, edited by Eftychia Stavrianopoulou, 207–232. Mnemosyne Supplements 363. Leiden: Brill, 2013.

———. "Jewish Communities of Hellenistic Egypt: Different Responses to Different Environments." In *Jewish Identities in Antiquity*, edited by Lee I. Levine and Daniel R. Schwartz, 117–35. TSAJ 130. Tübingen: Mohr Siebeck, 2009.

———. *The Septuagint and Homeric Scholarship in Alexandria*. London: Routledge, 2003.

Horbury, William. "Jewish and Christian Monotheism in the Herodian Age." In *Early Jewish and Christian Monotheism*, edited by Loren T. Stuckenbruck and Wendy E. S. North, 16–44. JSNTSupp 263. London: T. & T. Clark, 2004.

Horbury, William, and David Noy, eds. *Jewish Inscriptions of Graeco-Roman Egypt*. Cambridge: Cambridge University Press, 1992.

Hornsey, Matthew J. "Social Identity Theory and Self-Categorization Theory: A Historical Review." *Social and Personality Psychology Compass* 2/1 (2008) 204–22.

Horst, Pieter W. Van der. "Jews and Christians in Aphrodisias in the Light of their Relations in Other Cities of Asia Minor." *NedTTs* 43 (1989) 106–21.

———. *Philo's Flaccus: The First Pogrom*. PACS 2. Leiden: Brill, 2003.

Hoskins, Paul M. "Freedom from Slavery to Sin and the Devil: John 8:31–47 and the Passover Theme of the Gospel of John." *TJ* 31 (2010) 47–63.

———. *Jesus as the Fulfillment of the Temple in the Gospel of John*. Milton Keynes: Paternoster, 2006.

Hossfeld, Frank-Lothar, and Erich Zenger. *A Commentary on Psalms 51–100*. Translated by Linda M. Maloney. Hermeneia. Minneapolis: Fortress, 2005.

Howard, George. "'The Letter of Aristeas' and Diaspora Judaism." *JTS* 22 (1971) 337–48.

Howard, Wilbert Francis. *The Fourth Gospel in Recent Criticism and Interpretation*. London: Epworth, 1931.

Huie-Jolly, Mary R. "Like Father, like Son, Absolute Case, Mythic Authority: Constructing Ideology in John 5:17–23." In *Society of Biblical Literature 1997 Seminar Papers*, 567–95. SBLSP 36. Atlanta: SBL, 1997.

Hunt, Steven A. "And the Word became Flesh—Again? Jesus and Abraham in John 8:31–59." In *Perspectives on our Father Abraham*, edited by Steven A. Hunt, 81–109. Grand Rapids: Eerdmans, 2010.

Bibliography

Hutchinson, John. *The Dynamics of Cultural Nationalism*. Boston, MA: Allen & Unwin, 1987.

Hutchinson, John, and Anthony D. Smith, eds. *Nationalism*. New York: Oxford University Press, 1994.

Hylen, Susan. *Allusion and Meaning in John 6*. BZAW 137. Berlin: de Gruyter, 2005.

Isaac, Jules. *Jesus and Israel*. Translated by Sally Gran. New York: Holt, Rinehart & Winston, 1971.

Ito, Hisayasu. "Johannine Irony Demonstrated in John 9. Part II." *Neot* 34 (2000) 373–87.

Jackson-McCabe, Matt A. "What's in a Name? The Problem of 'Jewish Christianity.'" In *Jewish Christianity Reconsidered*, edited by Matt A. Jackson-McCabe, 7–38. Minneapolis: Fortress, 2007.

Jacoby, F. *Die Fragmente der griechischen Historiker*. 4 vols. Leiden: Brill, 1923.

Janowitz, Naomi. "The Rhetoric of Translation: Three Early Perspectives on Translating Torah." *HTR* 84 (1991) 129–40.

Jenkins, Richard. *Social Identity*. New York: Routledge, 1996.

Jobes, Karen H., and Moisés Silva. *Invitation to the Septuagint*. Grand Rapids: Baker, 2000.

Johnson, Sara Raup. *Historical Fictions and Hellenistic Jewish Identity: Third Maccabees in its Cultural Context*. Los Angeles: University of California Press, 2004.

Jones, Sian, and Sarah Pearce, eds. *Jewish Local Patriotism and Self-Identification in the Graeco-Roman Period*. LSTS 31. Sheffield: Sheffield Academic, 1998.

Jonge, H. J. de. "'The Jews' in the Gospel of John." In *Anti-Judaism and the Fourth Gospel*, edited by Reimund Bieringer et al., 121–40. Louisville: Westminster John Knox, 2001.

Jossa, Giorgio. *Jews or Christians? The Followers of Jesus in Search of their own Identity*. WUNT 202. Tübingen: Mohr Siebeck, 2006.

Judge, E. A. *Social Distinctives of the Christians in the First Century*, edited by David M. Scholer. Peabody, MA: Hendrickson, 2008.

Käsemann, Ernst. *New Testament Questions of Today*. London: SCM, 1969.

———. *The Testament of Jesus: A Study of the Gospel of John in the Light of Chapter 17*. Translated by Gerhard Krodel. Philadelphia: Fortress, 1968.

Kasher, Aryeh. "First Jewish Military Units in Ptolemaic Egypt." *JSJ* 9 (1978) 57–67.

———. *The Jews in Hellenistic and Roman Egypt: The Struggle for Equal Rights*. TSAJ 7. Tübingen: Mohr Siebeck, 1985.

Katz, Steven. "Issues in the Separation of Judaism and Christianity after 70 C.E.: A Reconsideration." *JBL* 103 (1984) 42–76.

Bibliography

Kee, Howard Clark. *Knowing the Truth: A Sociological Approach to New Testament Interpretation*. Philadelphia: Fortress, 1989.

Keener, Craig. *The Gospel of John*. 2 vols. Peabody, MA: Hendrickson, 2003.

Keith, Graham. *Hated without a Cause? A Survey of Anti-Semitism*. Milton Keynes: Paternoster, 1997.

Kelley, Shawn. *Racializing Jesus: Race, Ideology and the Formation of Modern Biblical Scholarship*. New York: Routledge, 2002.

Kerr, Alan R. *The Temple of Jesus' Body*. JSNTSup 220. Sheffield: Sheffield Academic, 2002.

Kierspel, Lars. *The Jews and the World in the Fourth Gospel: Parallelism, Function and Context*. WUNT 2.220. Tübingen: Mohr Siebeck, 2006.

Kim, Stephen S. "The Significance of Jesus' Healing the Blind Man in John 9." *BSac* 167 (2010) 307–18.

Kirschner, Robert. "Apocalyptic and Rabbinic Responses to the Destruction of 70." *HTR* 78 (1985) 27–46.

Klawans, Jonathan. *Purity, Sacrifice, and the Temple: Symbolism and Supersessionism in the Study of Ancient Judaism*. Oxford: Oxford University Press, 2006.

Klink, Edward W. *The Sheep of the Fold: The Audience and Origin of the Gospel of John*. Cambridge: Cambridge University Press, 2007.

Knight, Douglas A. *Rediscovering the Traditions of Israel*. 3rd ed. Atlanta: SBL, 2006.

Kok, Kobus. "The Healing of the Blind Man in John." *Journal of Early Christian History* 2 (2012) 36–62.

Köstenberger, Andreas J. "The Destruction of the Second Temple and the Composition of the Fourth Gospel." *TJ* 26 (2005) 205–42.

Koyama, Kosuke. *No Handle on the Cross*. London: SCM, 1976.

Kraeling, Carl H. *Anthropos and Son of Man: A Study in the Religious Syncretism of the Hellenistic Orient*. New York: Columbia University Press, 1927.

Kraft, Robert A. "In Search of 'Jewish Christianity' and its 'Theology': Problems of Definition and Methodology." In *Judéo-christianisme: Recherches historiques et théologiques offertes en hommage au cardinal Jean Daniélou*, 81–92. Paris: Recherches de science religieuse, 1972.

Lacerenza, Giancarlo. "Jewish Magicians and Christian Clients in Late Antiquity: The Testimony of Amulets and Inscriptions." In *What Athens has to do with Jerusalem: Essays on Classical, Jewish, and Early Christian Art and Archaeology in Honor of Gideon Foerster*, edited by Leonard V. Rutgers, 393–419. Leuven: Peeters, 2002.

LaMarche, Paul. "The Prologue of John." In *The Interpretation of John*, edited by John Ashton, 47–65. 2nd ed. Studies in New Testament Interpretation. Edinburgh: T. & T. Clark, 1997.

Bibliography

Lamb, David A. *Text, Context and the Johannine Community: A Sociolinguistic Analysis of the Johannine Writings.* LNTS 477. New York: T. & T. Clark, 2014.

Lampe, Peter. *From Paul to Valentinus: Christians at Rome in the First Two Centuries.* Translated by Michael Steinhauser. London: Continuum, 2006.

Leon, Harry. *The Jews of Ancient Rome: Updated Edition.* Edited by Carolyn A. Osiek. Peabody, MA: Hendrickson, 1995.

Levine, Lee I., and Daniel R Schwartz, eds. *Jewish Identities in Antiquity: Studies in Memory of Menahem Stern.* TSAJ 130. Tübingen: Mohr Siebeck, 2009.

Levinskaya, Irina. *The Book of Acts in its Diaspora Setting.* Grand Rapids: Eerdmans, 1996.

Lichtenberger, Hermann. "History-writing and History-telling in First and Second Maccabees." In *Memory in the Bible and Antiquity: The Fifth Durham-Tübingen Research Symposium (Durham, September 2004)*, edited by Stephen C. Barton et al., 95–110. WUNT 212. Tübingen: Mohr Siebeck, 2007.

Lidzbarski, Mark. *Das Johannesbuch der Mandäer.* Giessen: Alfred Töppelmann, 1915.

Lieu, Judith. "Anti-Judaism in the Fourth Gospel: Explanation and Hermeneutics." In *Anti-Judaism and the Fourth Gospel*, edited by Reimund Bieringer et al., 101–17. Louisville: Westminster John Knox, 2001.

———. "Anti-Judaism, the Jews, and the Worlds of the Fourth Gospel." In *The Gospel of John and Christian Theology*, edited by Richard Bauckham and Carl Mosser, 168–82. Grand Rapids: Eerdmans, 2008.

———. "Blindness in the Johannine Tradition." *NTS* 34 (1988) 83–95.

———. "The Parting of the Ways: Theological Construct or Historical Reality?" *JSNT* 56 (1994) 101–19.

Lifshitz, B. *Donateurs et Fondateurs dans les Synagogues Juives.* Paris: Gabalda, 1967.

Lincoln, Andrew T. *Truth on Trial: The Lawsuit Motif in the Fourth Gospel.* Peabody, MA: Hendrickson, 2000.

Loader, William. "Jesus and the Law in John." In *Theology and Christology in the Fourth Gospel*, edited by G. Van Belle et al., 135–54. Leuven: Leuven University Press, 2005.

Lohse, Bernard. *Martin Luther's Theology: Its Historical and Systematic Development.* Translated and edited by Roy A. Harrisville. Minneapolis: Fortress, 1999.

Longenecker, Bruce W. *The Triumph of Abraham's God.* Nashville: Abingdon, 1998.

Bibliography

Lowe, Malcolm F. "Who were the Ἰουδαῖοι." *NovT* 18 (1976) 101–30.

Lüderitz, Gert. "What is the Politeuma?" In *Studies in Early Jewish Epigraphy*, edited by Jan Willem Henten and Pieter Willem van der Horst, 183–225. AGJU 21. Leiden: Brill, 1994.

Luthardt, Christoph Ernst. *St. John's Gospel Explained*. Translated by Caspar René Gregory. Edinburgh: T. & T. Clark, 1876.

Luther, Martin. "On the Jews and Their Lies." In *Luther's Works* vol. 47, 137–306. Translated by Martin H. Bertram. Philadelphia: Fortress, 1971.

———. "That Jesus was Born a Jew." In *Luther's Works* vol. 45, 195–229. Translated by Walther I. Brandt. Philadelphia, PA: Fortress, 1962.

Manstead, Antony S.R., Russell Spears, Bertjan Doosje, and Nyla R. Branscombe. "Guilty by Association: When One's Group has a Negative History." *Journal of Personality and Social Psychology* 75 (1998) 872–86.

Maronde, Christopher Allan. "Moses in the Gospel of John." *CTQ* 77 (2013) 23–44.

Martyn, J. L. *History and Theology in the Fourth Gospel*. 3rd ed. Louisville: Westminster John Knox, 2003.

Mason, Steve. "The *Contra Apionem* in Social and Literary Context: An Invitation to Judean Philosophy." In *Religious Rivalries in the Early Roman Empire and the Rise of Christianity*, edited by Leif E. Vaage, 139–73. Waterloo, ON: Wilfrid Laurier University Press, 2006.

McCready, Wayne O. "Johannine Self-Understanding and the Synagogue Episode of John 9." In *Self-Definition and Self-Discovery in Early Christianity*, edited by David J. Hawkin and Tom Robinson, 147–66. Lewiston, NY: Edwin Mellen, 1990.

McGrath, Alister E. *Luther's Theology of the Cross: Martin Luther's Breakthrough*. Oxford: Basil Blackwell, 1985.

Meeks, Wayne A. "'Am I a Jew?' Johannine Christianity and Judaism." In *Christianity, Judaism and other Greco-Roman Cults*, edited by Jacob Neusner, 1:163–86. 4 vols. Leiden: Brill, 1975.

———. *The First Urban Christians: The Social World of the Apostle Paul*. 2nd ed. New Haven: Yale University Press, 2003.

———. "The Man from Heaven in Johannine Sectarianism." *JBL* 91 (1972) 44–72.

———. *The Prophet-King: Moses Traditions and the Johannine Christology*. Leiden: Brill, 1967.

Mendels, Doron. "Memory and Memories: The Attitude of 1–2 Maccabees toward Hellenization and Hellenism." In *Jewish Identities in Antiquity*, edited by Lee I. Levine and Daniel R. Schwartz, 41–54. TSAJ 130. Tübingen: Mohr Siebeck, 2009.

Menken, Martinus J. J. "The Provenance and Meaning of the Old Testament Quotation in John 6:31." *NovT* 30 (1988) 39–56.

Millar, J. G. "Deuteronomy." In *Dictionary of Biblical Theology*, edited by T. Desmond Alexander et al., 159–65. Downers Grove, IL: IVP, 2000.

Miller, David M. "Ethnicity Comes of Age: An Overview of Twentieth-Century Terms for Ioudaios." *CurBR* 10 (2012) 293–311.

———. "Ethnicity, Religion and the Meaning of Ioudaios in Ancient 'Judaism.'" *CurBR* 12 (2014) 216–65.

———. "The Meaning of Ioudaios and its Relationship to other Group Labels in Ancient 'Judaism.'" *CurBR* 9 (2010) 98–126.

Miller, Ed L. "The Johannine Origin of the Johannine Logos." *JBL* 112 (1993) 445–57.

Miller, Paul. "'They Saw His Glory and Spoke of Him': The Gospel of John and the Old Testament." In *Hearing the Old Testament in the New Testament*, edited by Stanley E. Porter, 127–51. Grand Rapids: Eerdmans, 2006.

Misztal, Barbara A. *Theories of Social Remembering*. Philadelphia: Open University Press, 2003.

Modrzejewski, Joseph Mélèze. "How to be a Jew in Hellenistic Egypt?" In *Diasporas in Antiquity*, edited by Shaye J. D. Cohen and Ernest S. Frerichs, 65–92. BJS 288. Atlanta: Scholars, 1993.

———. *The Jews of Egypt: From Ramses II to Emperor Hadrian*. Princeton: Princeton University Press, 1995.

Moehring, Horst R. "The *Acta pro Judaeis* in the *Antiquities* of Flavius Josephus: A Study in Hellenistic and Modern Apologetic Historiography." In *Christianity, Judaism and Other Greco-Roman Cults*, edited by Jacob Neusner, 124–58. Leiden: Brill, 1975.

Moloney, Francis J. *Belief in the Word: Reading the Fourth Gospel, John 1–4*. Minneapolis: Augsburg Fortress, 1993.

———. *Glory not Dishonor: Reading John 13–21*. Minneapolis: Augsburg Fortress, 1998.

———. *Signs and Shadows: Reading John 5–12*. Minneapolis: Augsburg Fortress, 1996.

Morris, Leon. *Jesus is the Christ: Studies in the Theology of John*. Grand Rapids: Eerdmans, 1989.

Motyer, Stephen. "Bridging the Gap: How Might the Fourth Gospel Help Us Cope with the Legacy of Christianity's Exclusive Claim over against Judaism?" In *The Gospel of John and Christian Theology*, edited by Richard Bauckham and Carl Mosser, 143–67. Grand Rapids: Eerdmans, 2008.

———. *Your Father the Devil? A New Approach to John and "the Jews."* Carlisle: Paternoster, 1997.

Moxnes, Halvor. "Honor and Shame." *BTB* 23 (1993) 167–76.

Mueller, James R. "Anti-Judaism in the New Testament Apocrypha." In *Anti-Semitism and Early Christianity: Issues of Polemic and Faith*, edited by

Craig A. Evans and Donald A. Hagner, 253–68. Minneapolis: Fortress, 1993.

Müller, Paul-Gerhard. "Altes Testament, Israel und das Judentums in der Theologie Rudolph Bultmanns." In *Kontinuität und Einheit: Für Franz Mußner*, edited by Paul Gerhard Müller and Werner Stenger, 439–72. Freiburg: Herder, 1981.

Musurillo, Herbert A. *The Acts of the Pagan Martyrs*. Oxford: Oxford University Press, 1954.

Nagel, Joane. "Constructing Ethnicity: Creating and Recreating Ethnic Identity and Culture." *Social Problems* 41 (1994) 152–76.

Neyrey, Jerome H. "Despising the Shame of the Cross: Honor and Shame in the Johannine Passion Narrative. *Semeia* 68 (1994) 113–37.

———. "'I Said You Are Gods': Psalm 82:6 and John 10." *JBL* 108 (1989) 647–63.

———. "John III—A Debate over Johannine Epistemology and Christology." *NovT* 23 (1981) 115–27.

———. "The Trials (Forensic) and Tribulations (Honor Challenges) of Jesus: John 7 in Social Science Perspective." *BTB* 26 (1996) 107–24.

Ngien, Dennis. *The Suffering of God According to Martin Luther's 'Theologia Crucis.'* New York: Peter Lang, 1995.

Nicholson, Godfrey C. *Death and Departure: The Johannine Descent-Ascent Schema*. Chico, CA: Scholars, 1983.

Niehoff, Maren. *Philo on Jewish Identity and Culture*. TSAJ 86. Tübingen: Mohr Siebeck, 2001.

Nicklas, Tobias. *Ablösung und Verstrickung: 'Juden' und Jüngergestalten als Charaktere der erzählten Welt des Johannesevangeliums und ihre Wirkung auf den impliziten Leser*. Frankfurt: Peter Lang, 2001.

Nkomo, S. M., and T. Cox Jr. "Diverse Identities in Organizations." In *Handbook of Organization Studies*, edited by S. R. Clegg et al., 338–56. London: SAGE, 1996.

Nodet, Etienne. "Josephus' Attempt to Reorganize Judaism from Rome." In *Making History: Josephus and Historical Method*, edited by Zuleika Rodgers, 103–22. Supplements to the Journal for the Study of Judaism 110. Leiden: Brill, 2007.

Noth, Martin. *The Deuteronomic History*. Sheffield: JSOT, 1981.

Numada, Jonathan. "Aristeas and Social Identity: Creating Similarity from Continued Difference." *JGRChJ* 11 (2015) 82–103.

———. "The Christological Appropriation of Zeal in John's Use of Psalm 69." In *Johannine Christology*, edited by Stanley E. Porter and Andrew Pitts, 90–110. Johannine Studies 3. Leiden: Brill, 2020.

———. "The Repetition of History? A Select Survey of Scholarly Understandings of Johannine Anti-Judaism from Baur until the End of the Weimar Republic." In *The Origins of John's Gospel*, edited by Stanley E. Porter and Hughson T. Ong, 261–84. Johannine Studies 2. Leiden: Brill, 2016.

O'Day, Gail R. *Revelation in the Fourth Gospel: Narrative Mode and Theological Claim*. Philadelphia: Fortress, 1986.

Odeberg, Hugo. *The Fourth Gospel: Interpreted in its Relation to Contemporaneous Religious Currents in Palestine and the Hellenistic-Oriental World*. Amsterdam: B. R. Grüner, 1968.

Oeming, Manfred. "Der Glaube Abrahams: Zur Rezeptionsgeschichte von Gen 15,6 in der Zeit des zweiten Tempels." *ZAW* 110 (1998) 16–33.

Ong, Hughson T. *The Multilingual Jesus and the Sociological World of the New Testament*. LBS 12. Leiden: Brill, 2015.

Onuki, Takashi. *Gemeinde und Welt im Johannesevangelium: Ein Beitrag zur Frage nach der theologischen und pragmatischen Funktion des johanneische „Dualismus."* Neukirchen-Vluyn: Neukirchener Verlag, 1984.

Orlinsky, Harry Meyer. "Septuagint as Holy Writ and the Philosophy of the Translators." *HUCA* 46 (1975) 89–114.

Ortlund, Dane. "Phinehan Zeal: A Consideration of James Dunn's Proposal." *JSP* 20 (2011) 299–315.

———. "'Zeal without Knowledge': For What Did Paul Criticize his Fellow Jews in Romans 10:2–3?" *WTJ* 73 (2011) 23–37.

Osmer, Richard R. *Practical Theology: An Introduction*. Grand Rapids: Eerdmans, 2008.

Painter, John. "Monotheism and Dualism: John and Qumran." In *Theology and Christology in the Fourth Gospel*, edited by G. van Belle et al., 225–43. Leuven: Leuven, 2005.

Pancaro, Severino. *The Law in the Fourth Gospel*. NovTSup 42. Leiden: Brill, 1975.

Papaioannou, Kim. "John 5:18: Jesus and Sabbath Law—A Fresh Look at a Challenging Text." *Journal of the Adventist Theological Society* 20 (2009) 250–68.

Parker, Barry F. "Works of the Law and Jewish Settlement in Asia Minor." *JGRChJ* 9 (2013) 42–96.

Parkes, James. *The Conflict of the Church and the Synagogue: A Study in the Origins of Antisemitism*. New York: Meridian, 1961.

Parsenios, George L. *Departure and Consolation: The Farewell Discourses in the Light of Greco-Roman Literature*. NovTSup 117. Leiden: Brill, 2005.

Pearce, Sarah. "Belonging and not Belonging: Local Perspectives in Philo of Alexandria." In *Jewish Local Patriotism and Self-Identification in the Graeco-Roman Period*, edited by Siân Jones and Sarah Pearce, 79–105. Sheffield: Sheffield Academic, 1998.

Bibliography

———. "Jerusalem as 'Mother City' in the Writings of Philo of Alexandria." In *Negotiating Diaspora: Jewish Strategies in the Roman Empire*, edited by John M.G. Barclay, 19–36. LSTS 45. New York: T. & T. Clark, 2004.
Pears, Angie. *Doing Contextual Theology*. New York: Routledge, 2010.
Phillips, Peter M. *The Prologue of the Fourth Gospel: A Sequential Reading*. LNTS 294. London: T. & T. Clark, 2006.
Pietersma, Albert. "Beyond Literalism: Interlinearity Revisited." In *'Translation is Required': The Septuagint in Retrospect and Prospect*, edited by Robert J. V. Hiebert, 3–21. SCS 56. Atlanta, GA: SBL, 2010.
———. "Septuagintal Exegesis and the Superscriptions of the Greek Psalter." *The Book of Psalms: Composition and Reception*, edited by Peter Flint et al., 443–75. VTSup 99. Leiden: Brill, 2005.
Plöger, Otto. *Theocracy and Eschatology*. Richmond, VA: John Knox Press, 1968.
Porter, Stanley E. "Can Traditional Exegesis Enlighten Literary Analysis of the Fourth Gospel? An Examination of the Old Testament Fulfillment Motif and the Passover Theme." In *The Gospels and the Scriptures of Israel*, edited by Craig A. Evans and W. Richard Stegner, 396–428. JSNTSup 104. SSEJC 3. Sheffield: Sheffield Academic, 1994.
———. "Further Comments on the Use of the Old Testament in the New Testament." In *The Intertextuality of the Epistles*, edited by Thomas L. Brodie et al., 98–110. Sheffield: Sheffield Phoenix, 2006.
———. "How Do We Define Pauline Social Relations?" In *Paul and His Social Relations*, edited by Stanley E. Porter and Christopher D. Land, 7–33. PAST 8. Leiden: Brill, 2013.
———. *John, His Gospel, and Jesus*. Grand Rapids: Eerdmans, 2015.
Porter, Stanley E., and Andrew K. Gabriel, eds. *Johannine Writings and Apocalyptic: An Annotated Bibliography*. Johannine Studies 1. Leiden: Brill, 2013.
Porter, Stanley E., and Brook W.R. Pearson. "Why the Split? Christians and Jews by the Fourth Century." *JGRChJ* 1 (2000) 82–119.
Rabbie, Jacob M., and Murray Horwitz. "Categories versus Groups as Explanatory Concepts in Intergroup Relations." *European Journal of Social Psychology* 18 (1988) 117–23.
Rajak, Tessa. "The Against Apion and the Continuities in Josephus's Political Thought." In *Understanding Josephus*, edited by Steve Mason, 222–46. LSTS 32. Sheffield: Sheffield Academic, 1998.
———. "Synagogue and Community in the Graeco-Roman Diaspora." In *Jews in the Hellenistic and Roman Cities*, edited by John R. Bartlett, 22–38. New York: Routledge, 2012.
———. "Was there a Roman Charter for the Jews?" *Journal of Roman Studies* 74 (1984) 107–23.

Bibliography

Ramsay, William Mitchell. *The Cities and Bishoprics of Phrygia*. Oxford: Clarendon, 1897.

Rappaport, Uriel. "The Connection between Hasmonean Judaea and the Diaspora." In *Jewish Identities in Antiquity*, edited by Lee I. Levine and Daniel R. Schwartz, 90–100. TSAJ 130. Tübingen: Mohr Siebeck, 2009.

———. "Josephus' Personality and the Credibility of his Narrative." In *Making History: Josephus and Historical Method*, edited by Zuleika Rodgers, 68–81. Supplements to the Journal for the Study of Judaism 110. Leiden: Brill, 2007.

Redlich, E. Basil. *An Introduction to the Fourth Gospel*. London: Longmans, Green, 1939.

Reed, Annette Yoshiko. "The Construction and Subversion of Patriarchal Perfection: Abraham and Exemplarity in Philo, Josephus, and the *Testament of Abraham*." *JSJ* 40 (2009) 185–212.

Reinhartz, Adele. *Befriending the Beloved Disciple: A Jewish Reading of the Gospel of John*. New York: Continuum, 2003.

———. "'Jews' and Jews in the Fourth Gospel." In *Anti-Judaism and the Fourth Gospel*, edited by Reimund Bieringer et al., 213–27. Louisville: Westminster John Knox, 2001.

———. "The New Testament and Anti-Judaism: A Literary-Critical Approach." *JES* 25 (1988) 524–37.

———. *Word in the World: The Cosmological Tale in the Fourth Gospel*. SBLMS 45. Atlanta: Scholars, 1992.

Reitzenstein, Richard. *Poimandres: Studien zur Griechisch-Ägyptischen und frühchristlichen Literatur*. Leipzig: B. G. Teubner, 1904.

Rensberger, David. *Johannine Faith and Liberating Community*. Philadelphia: Westminster, 1988.

Richardson, Peter. "Augustan-Era Synagogues in Rome." In *Judaism and Christianity in First-Century Rome*, edited by Karl P. Donfried and Peter Richardson, 17–29. Grand Rapids: Eerdmans, 1998.

Richey, Lance Byron. *Roman Imperial Ideology and the Gospel of John*. CBQMS 43. Washington, DC: Catholic Biblical Association of America, 2007.

Riffaterre, Michael. *Semiotics of Poetry*. Bloomington, IN: Indiana University Press, 1978.

Ringe, Sharon. *Wisdom's Friends: Community and Christology in the Fourth Gospel*. Louisville: Westminster John Knox, 1999.

Ripley, Jason J. "Killing as Piety? Exploring Ideological Contexts Shaping the Gospel of John." *JBL* 134 (2015) 605–35.

Robert, J., and L. Robert. *Bulletin Épigraphique* (1939).

Robinson, John A. T. *Redating the New Testament*. London: SCM, 1977.

———. *The Priority of John*, edited by J. F. Coakley. Oak Park, IL: Meyerstone Books, 1985.

Rochette, Bruno. "Juifs et Romains: Y a-t-il eu un Antijudaïsme Romain?" *Revue des Études Juives* 160 (2001) 1–31.

Rodriguez, Jeanette, and Ted Fortier. *Cultural Memory: Resistance, Faith, and Identity*. Austin: University of Texas Press, 2007.

Rudolph, Kurt. *Die Mandäer*. 2 volumes. Göttingen: Vändenhoeck & Ruprecht, 1960.

Ruether, Rosemary Radford. *Faith and Fratricide: The Theological Roots of Anti-Semitism*. New York: Seabury, 1974.

Rutgers, L.V. *The Hidden Heritage of Diaspora Judaism*. Leuven: Peeters, 1998.

———. "Roman Policy towards the Jews: Expulsions from the City of Rome during the First Century, C.E." In *Judaism and Christianity in First-Century Rome*, edited by Karl P. Donfried and Peter Richardson, 93–116. Grand Rapids: Eerdmans, 1998.

Rutgers, L. V., et al. "Radiocarbon Dates from the Jewish Catacombs of Rome." *Radiocarbon* 44 (2002) 541–47.

———. "Radiocarbon Dating: Jewish Inspiration of Christian Catacombs." *Nature* 436 (2005) 339.

Sahdra, Baljinder, and Michael Ross. "Group Identification and Historical Memory." *PSPB* 33 (2007) 384–395.

Salvesen, Alison. "A Convergence of the Ways? The Judaizing of Christian Scripture by Origen and Jerome." In *The Ways that Never Parted: Jews and Christians in Late Antiquity and the Early Middle Ages*, edited by Adam H. Becker and Annette Yoshiko Reed, 233–58. TSAJ 95. Tübingen: Mohr Siebeck, 2003.

Sanders, E. P. *Jesus and Judaism*. Philadelphia: Fortress, 1985.

———. *Paul and Palestinian Judaism*. Minneapolis: Fortress, 1977.

Sanders, Jack T. "The Jewish People in Luke-Acts." In *Society of Biblical Literature 1986 Seminar Papers*, 110–29. SBLSP 25. Atlanta: Scholars, 1986.

———. *Schismatics, Sectarians, Dissidents, Deviants: The First One Hundred Years of Jewish-Christian Relations*. Valley Forge, PA: Trinity Press, 1993.

Sandmel, Samuel. "Philo's Place in Judaism: A Study of Conceptions of Abraham in Jewish Literature." *HUCA* 26 (1955) 151–332.

Schäfer, Peter. *Judeophobia: Attitudes towards the Jews in the Ancient World*. Cambridge, MA: Harvard University Press, 1997.

Schapdick, Stefan. "Religious Authority Re-Evaluated: The Character of Moses in the Fourth Gospel." In *Moses in Biblical and Extra-Biblical Traditions*, edited by Axel Graupner and Michael Wolter, 181–209. BZAW 372. Berlin: de Gruyter, 2007.

Schliesser, Benjamin. *Abraham's Faith in Romans 4*. WUNT 224. Tübingen: Mohr Siebeck, 2007.

Schnabel, Eckhard J. *Early Christian Mission*. 2 vols. Downers Grove, IL: Intervarsity, 2004.

———. "Jewish Opposition to Christians in Asia Minor in the First Century." *BBR* 18 (2008) 233–270.

Schnackenburg, Rudolf. *The Gospel according to St. John*. 3 vols. New York, NY: Seabury, 1982.

Schoon, Simon. "Escape Routes as Dead Ends: On Hatred towards Jews and the New Testament, especially in the Gospel of John." In *Anti-Judaism and the Fourth Gospel: Papers of the Leuven Colloquium, 2000*, edited by Reimund Bieringer et al., 144–158. Assen: Royal van Gorcum, 2001.

Schuchard, Bruce G. *Scripture within Scripture: The Interrelationship of Form and Function in the Explicit Old Testament Citations in the Gospel of John*. SBLDS 133. Atlanta: Scholars, 1992.

Schudson, M. "Dynamics of Distortion in Collective Memory." In *Memory Distortion: How Minds, Brains, and Societies Reconstruct the Past*, edited by D. L. Schacter et al., 346–64. Cambridge, MA: Harvard University Press, 1995.

———. "The Present in the Past versus the Past in the Present." *Communication* 11 (1989) 105–13.

Schulz, Siegfried. *Untersuchungen zur Menschensohn-Christologie im Johannesevangelium*. Göttingen: Vändenhoeck & Ruprecht, 1957.

Schürer, Emil. *The History of the Jewish People in the Age of Jesus Christ (175 B.C.–135 A.D.)*, edited by Geza Vermes et al. 3 vols. New York: T. & T. Clark, 1987.

Schwartz, Daniel R. "Doing Like Jews or Becoming a Jew? Josephus on Women Converts to Judaism." In *Jewish Identity in the Greco-Roman World = Jüdische identität in der griechisch-römischen welt*, edited by Jörg Frey et al., 93–110. Ancient Judaism and Early Christianity 71. Leiden: Brill, 2007.

———. "How at Home Were the Jews of the Hellenistic Diaspora?" *Classical Philology* 92 (2000) 349–57.

———. "'Judean' or 'Jew'? How Should we Translate Ioudaios in Josephus?" In *Jewish Identity in the Greco-Roman World = Jüdische identität in der griechisch-römischen welt*, edited by Jörg Frey et al, 3–28. Ancient Judaism and Early Christianity 71. Leiden: Brill, 2007.

———. "The Priests in Ep. Arist. 310." *JBL* 97 (1978) 567–71.

———. *2 Maccabees*. CEJL. Berlin: de Gruyter, 2008.

Scott, E. F. *The Fourth Gospel: Its Purpose and Theology*. Edinburgh: T. & T. Clark, 1920.

Scott, Ian W. "Epistemology and Social Conflict in Jubilees and Aristeas." In *Common Judaism: Explorations in Second Temple Judaism*, edited by Wayne O. McCready and Adele Reinhartz, 195–213. Minneapolis: Fortress, 2008.

———. "Revelation and Human Artefact: The Inspiration of the Pentateuch in the Book of Aristeas." *JSJ* 41 (2010) 1–28.

Scott, Martin. *Sophia and the Johannine Jesus*. JSNTSup 71. Sheffield: Sheffield Academic, 1992.

Seeley, David. *The Noble Death: Graeco-Roman Martyrology and Paul's Concept of Salvation*. JSNTSup 28. Sheffield: JSOT, 1990.

Sevenster, Jan N. *The Roots of Pagan Anti-Semitism in the Ancient World*. NovTSup 41. Leiden: Brill, 1975.

Sheridan, Ruth. "Johannine Sectarianism: A Category Now Defunct?" In *The Origins of John's Gospel*, edited by Stanley E. Porter and Hughson T. Ong, 142–66. Johannine Studies 2. Leiden: Brill, 2015.

———. *Retelling Scripture: "The Jews" and the Scriptural Citations in John 1:19—12:50*. BibInt 110. Leiden: Brill, 2012.

Siegel, J. P. "The Alexandrians in Jerusalem and their Torah Scrolls with Gold Tetragrammata." *IEJ* 22 (1972) 39–43.

Smallwood, E. Mary. *The Jews under Roman Rule: From Pompey to Diocletian: A Study in Political Relations*. Leiden: Brill, 1981.

———. *Legatio ad Gaium*. Leiden: Brill, 1961.

Smiga, George M. *Pain and Polemic: Anti-Judaism in the Gospels*. New York: Paulist, 1992.

Smiles, Vincent M. "The Concept of 'Zeal' in Second-Temple Judaism and Paul's Critique of it in Romans 10:2." *CBQ* 64 (2002) 282–99.

Smith, Anthony D. *The Antiquity of Nations*. Cambridge: Polity, 2004.

———. *Chosen Peoples: Sacred Sources of National Identity*. Oxford: OUP, 2004.

———. *The Ethnic Origin of Nations*. Oxford: Basil Blackwell, 1986.

———. *Ethno-Symbolism and Nationalism*. New York: Routledge, 2009.

Smith, D. Moody. "Postscript for the Third Edition of Martyn." In *History and Theology in the Fourth Gospel*, by J. Louis Martyn, 1–23. 3rd ed. NTL. Louisville: Westminster John Knox, 2003.

Snyder, Graydon F. "The Interaction of Jews with Non-Jews in Rome." In *Judaism and Christianity in First-Century Rome*, edited by Karl P. Donfried and Peter Richardson, 69–90. Grand Rapids: Eerdmans, 1998.

Spaulding, Mary B. *Commemorative Identities: Jewish Social Memory and the Johannine Feast of Booths*. LNTS 396. London: T. & T. Clark, 2009.

Spilsbury, Paul. "Contra Apionem and Antiquitates Judaicae: Points of Contact." In *Josephus' Contra Apionem: Studies in its Character and Context with a Latin Concordance to the Portion Missing in Greek*, edited by Louis H. Feldman and John R. Levison, 348–68. AGJU 34. Leiden: Brill, 1996.

———. *The Image of the Jew in Flavius Josephus' Paraphrase of the Bible*. TSAJ 69. Tübingen: Mohr Siebeck, 1998.

Stark, Rodney, and William Sims Bainbridge. *The Future of Religion: Secularization, Revival and Cult Formation*. Los Angeles: University of California Press, 1985.

Steck, Odil Hannes. *Israel und das Gewaltsame Geschick der Propheten: Untersuchungen zur Überlieferung des deuteronomistischen Geschichtsbildes im Alten Testament, Spätjudentum und Urchristentum*. Neukirchen-Vluyn: Neukirchener Verlag, 1967.

Stegemann, Wolfgang. "Das Verhaltnis Rudolf Bultmanns zum Judentum." *Kirche und Israel* 5 (1990) 26–44.

Stern, Karen B. "Vandals or Pilgrims? Jews, Travel Culture, and Devotional Practice in the Pan Temple of Egyptian El-Kanais." In *"The One Who Sows Bountifully": Essays in Honor of Stanley K. Stowers*, edited by Caroline Johnson Hodge et al., 177–88. BJS 356. Atlanta: SBL, 2013.

Stevick, Daniel B. *Jesus and His Own: A Commentary on John 13–17*. Grand Rapids: Eerdmans, 2011.

Stovell, Beth M. *Mapping Metaphorical Discourse in the Fourth Gospel*. LBS 5. Leiden: Brill, 2012.

Strauss, David Friedrich. *A New Life of Jesus*. Translator anonymous. London: Williams and Norgate, 1865.

Strubbe, Johan H. M. "Curses against Violation of the Grave in Jewish Epitaphs from Asia Minor." In *Studies in Early Jewish Epigraphy*, edited by Jan Willem van Henten and Pieter Willem van der Horst, 70–128. AGJU 21. Leiden: Brill, 1994.

Tal, Oren. "Hellenism in Transition from Empire to Kingdom: Changes in the Material Culture of Hellenistic Palestine." In *Jewish Identities in Antiquity*, edited by Lee I. Levine and Daniel R. Schwartz, 55–73. TSAJ 130. Tübingen: Mohr Siebeck, 2009.

Tannehill, Robert C. "Israel in Luke-Acts: A Tragic Story." *JBL* 104 (1985) 69–85.

Taylor, Miriam S. *Anti-Judaism and Early Christian Identity: A Critique of the Scholarly Consensus*. StPB 46. Leiden: Brill, 1995.

Tcherikover, Victor A. *Corpus Papyrorum Judaicarum*. 3 vols. Cambridge, MA: Harvard University Press, 1964.

———. "The Decline of the Jewish Diaspora in Egypt in the Roman Period." *JJS* 14 (1963) 1–33.

———. *Hellenistic Civilization and the Jews*. Philadelphia: Jewish Publication Society of America, 1959.

———. "The Ideology of the Letter of Aristeas." *HTR* 51 (1958) 59–85.

Bibliography

Thatcher, Tom. *Greater than Caesar: Christology and Empire in the Fourth Gospel*. Minneapolis: Fortress, 2009.

———. "The Sabbath Trick: Unstable Irony in the Fourth Gospel." *JSNT* 76 (1999) 53–77.

Thompson, Marianne Meye. *The God of the Gospel of John*. Grand Rapids: Eerdmans, 2001.

———. "Thinking about God: Wisdom and Theology in John 6." In *Critical Readings of John 6*, edited by R. Alan Culpepper, 221–46. BibInt 22. Leiden: Brill, 1997.

Tilborg, van Sjef. *Reading John in Ephesus*. NovTSup 83. Leiden: Brill, 1996.

Tillich, Paul. *Systematic Theology*. Vol. 1. London: SCM, 1951.

Tomson, Peter J. "'Jews' in the Gospel of John as Compared with the Palestinian Talmud, the Synoptics, and some New Testament Apocrypha." In *Anti-Judaism and the Fourth Gospel*, edited by Reimund Bieringer et al., 176–212. Louisville, KY: Westminster John Knox, 2001.

Trebilco, Paul R. *Jewish Communities in Asia Minor*. Cambridge: Cambridge University Press, 1991.

Trost, Travis. *Who Should Be King in Israel? A Study on Roman Imperial Politics, the Dead Sea Scrolls, and the Fourth Gospel*. New York: Peter Lang, 2010.

Turner, John C. *Rediscovering the Social Group: A Self-Categorization Theory*. Oxford: Basil Blackwell, 1987.

Um, Stephen T. *The Theme of Temple Christology in John's Gospel*. LNTS 312. New York: T. & T. Clark, 2006.

VanderKam, J. C. "Biblical Interpretation in 1 Enoch and Jubilees." In *The Pseudepigrapha and Early Biblical Interpretation*, edited by James H. Charlesworth and Craig A. Evans, 96–125. LSTS 14. Sheffield: Sheffield Academic, 1993.

Visscher, Gerhard H. *Romans 4 and the New Perspective on Paul: Faith Embraces the Promise*. New York: Peter Lang, 2009.

Wahlde, Urban C. von. *The Gospel and Letters of John*. 3 vols. Grand Rapids: Eerdmans, 2010.

———. "'The Jews' in the Gospel of John: Fifteen Years of Research (1983–1998)." *ETL* (2000) 30–55.

———. "The Johannine 'Jews': A Critical Survey." *NTS* 28 (1982) 33–60.

———. "'You are of Your Father the Devil' in its Context: Stereotyped Apocalyptic Polemic in John 8:38–47." In *Anti-Judaism and the Fourth Gospel: Papers of the Leuven Colloquium, 2000*, edited by Reimund Bieringer et al., 418–44. Assen: Royal van Gorcum, 2001.

Ward, W. Peter. *White Canada Forever: Popular Attitudes and Public Policy Toward Orientals in British Columbia*. Montreal: McGill-Queen's University Press, 1978.

Bibliography

Wardy, Bilhah. "Jewish Religion in Pagan Literature." *Principat* 19 (1979) 592–644.
Wasserstein, Abraham, and David J. Wasserstein. *The Legend of the Septuagint*. Cambridge: Cambridge University Press, 2006.
Watson, Francis. *Paul, Judaism, and the Gentiles: Beyond the New Perspective*. Grand Rapids: Eerdmans, 2007.
Wedeck, Harry E. "The Roman Attitude Toward Foreign Influence, Particularly Toward the Greek Influence during the Republic." *The Classical Weekly* 22 (1929) 195–98.
Weiss, Herold. "The Sabbath in the Fourth Gospel." *JBL* 110 (1991) 311–321.
Weiss, Johannes. *Jesus' Proclamation of the Kingdom of God*. Translated by Richard Hyde Hiers and David Larrimore Holland. London: SCM, 1971.
———. *Die Predigt Jesu vom Reichte Gottes*. Göttingen: Vändenhoeck & Ruprecht, 1892.
Weren, W. "The Riot of the Ephesian Silversmiths (Acts 19,23–40): Luke's Advice to his Readers." In *Luke and His Readers*, edited by R. Bieringer et al., 441–56. Leuven: Leuven University Press, 2005.
Westcott, B. F. *The Gospel according to John*. London: John Murray, 1896.
Whitacre, Rodney A. *Johannine Polemic: The Role of Tradition and Theology*. SBLDS 67. Chico, CA: Scholars, 1982.
White, L. Michael. "Synagogue and Society in Imperial Ostia: Archaeological and Epigraphic Evidence." In *Judaism and Christianity in First-Century Rome*, edited by Karl P. Donfried and Peter Richardson, 30–68. Grand Rapids: Eerdmans, 1998.
Williams, Catrin H. *I am He: The Interpretation of 'Anî Hû' in Jewish and Early Christian Literature*. WUNT 2.113. Tübingen: Mohr Siebeck, 2000.
Williams, D. S. "2 Maccabees in Recent Research." *CurBR* 2 (2003) 69–83.
———. "3 Maccabees: A Defense of Diaspora Judaism?" *JSP* 13 (1995) 14–29.
Williams, Jarvis J. *Maccabean Martyr Traditions in Paul's Theology of Atonement*. Eugene, OR: Wipf & Stock, 2010.
Williams, Margaret H. *The Jews among the Greeks and Romans: A Diasporan Sourcebook*. Baltimore: Johns Hopkins University Press, 1998.
———. *Jews in a Graeco-Roman Environment*. WUNT 312. Tübingen: Mohr Siebeck, 2013.
Wilson, Bryan R. *Magic and the Millenium*. New York, NY: Harper & Row, 1973.
———. *Religion in Sociological Perspective*. Oxford: Oxford University Press, 1982.
Wolff, Christian. *Jeremia im Frühjudentum und Urchristentum*. Berlin: Akademie Verlag, 1976.

Wrede, D. W. *Charakter und Tendenz des Johannesevangeliums*. Tübingen: Mohr Siebeck, 1933.
Wright, Benjamin G. *Praise Israel for Wisdom and Instruction: Essays on Ben Sira and Wisdom, the Letter of Aristeas and the Septuagint*. Supplements to the Journal for the Study of Judaism 131. Leiden: Brill, 2008.
Yee, Gale A. *Jewish Feasts and the Gospel of John*. Wilmington, DE: Michael Glazier, 1989.
Zeev, Miriam Pucci ben. *Jewish Rights in the Roman World: The Greek and Roman Documents Quoted by Josephus Flavius*. TSAJ 74. Tübingen: Mohr Siebeck, 1998.
———. "New Perspectives on the Jewish-Greek Hostilities in Alexandria during the Reign of Emperor Caligula." *JSJ* 21 (1990) 227–35.
Zsengellér, József. "Maccabees and Temple Propaganda." In *The Books of the Maccabees: History, Theology, Ideology*, edited by Géza G. Xeravits and József Zsengellér, 181–95. Supplements to the Journal for the Study of Judaism 118. Leiden: Brill, 2007.
Zumstein, Jean. "Crise du Savoir et Conflit des Interprétations selon Jean 9: Un Exemple du Travail de l'École Johannique." In *Early Christian Voices: In Texts, Traditions, and Symbols*, edited by David H. Warren et al., 167–78. Leiden: Brill, 2003.
Zuntz, G. "Aristeas Studies I: 'The Seven Banquets.'" *JSS* 4 (1959) 21–36.

Index of Modern Authors

Abusch, R., 102
Ager, S., 61
Ameling, W., 79-82
Armstrong, J. A., 28
Ashton, J., 14, 17-18, 140, 216
Assmann, J., 31, 102
Augenstein, J., 196
Aune, D. E., 110

Bacon, B. W., 7, 226
Baehrens, A., 106
Bainbridge, W. S., 224-25
Ball, D. M., 145-46, 175-76, 221
Barclay, J. M. G., 26, 43-44, 49, 51, 60, 64, 78-79, 84, 89-90, 99, 110, 117-19, 121-24, 206
Bar-Kochva, B., 102
Barrett, C. K., 17-18, 134, 174, 194
Barth, F., 28
Bauckham, R., 224
Baum, G., 5-6
Baumgarten, A. I., 5, 12
Baur, F. C., 24, 27, 226
Beasley-Murray, G. R., 140-41, 151, 153, 161, 163, 179, 193, 194, 200, 222
Beavis, M. A. L., 57, 124
Bennema, C., 21
Bernier, J., 223
Berry, J. W., 48
Berthelot, K., 54
Bertram, M. H., 232
Bevans, S. B., 219
Bickerman, E., 29, 59
Bieringer, R., 14

Bilde, P., 26, 84, 118
Boer, M. C., 14-15
Boismard, M. E., 146-47, 191, 195, 213
Borgen, P., 112, 143, 144, 150, 151, 188, 195, 196
Bousset, W., 24, 27
Boyarin, D., 14, 15, 16, 26
Branscombe, N. R., 39
Brant, J. A., 134, 162
Brayford, S. A., 169
Brewer, M. B., 35, 36
Broadhead, E. K., 222
Brown, R. E., 7-9, 13, 15, 41, 48, 137, 138, 140, 141, 153, 178, 179, 183, 193, 194, 223
Bryan, S. M., 159
Bultmann, R., 4, 5, 17, 137, 153, 187, 188, 213, 214, 216

Carter, W., 7, 14, 77, 179, 223
Catto, S. K., 80, 99
Charlesworth, J. H., 171
Chilton, B., 157
Clifford, H., 186
Cohen, N. G., 52
Cohen, S. J. D., 26, 30, 52, 60, 82
Collins, A. Y., 110
Collins, J. J., 26, 29, 43, 49, 51, 56, 61, 78, 101
Collins, R. F., 15
Connolly, J., 70
Cook, M. J., 17, 23
Cory, C., 191
Court, J. M., 149

Index of Modern Authors

Cousland, J. R. C., 54
Cox, T., 34
Croy, N. C., 49, 53, 54
Cullmann, O., 16, 134, 223
Culpepper, R. A., 2, 16, 17, 21, 162, 222

Dahl, N., 163
Daly-Denton, M., 147
Daniélou, J., 221–22
Das, A. A., 211
Davies, M., 216, 217
Day, A., 217
Dennis, J. A., 10, 11, 41, 185, 200, 201, 219, 220, 221
Diefenbach, M., 14, 19
Dodd, C. H., 136, 137, 157, 174, 176, 190
Doering, L., 140
Donaldson, T. L., 4, 11
Doosje, B., 39
Doran, R., 49, 53, 55, 58
Duke, P. M., 134, 136
Dumbrell, W. J., 134, 187
Dunn, J. D. G., 2, 6, 8, 9, 11, 27, 133, 157, 211, 223

Eckhardt, B., 26
Eddy, S. K., 59
Edwards, R. B., 187
Eriksen, T. H., 38, 39
Erll, A., 31, 32, 33
Esler, P. F., 40, 41
Evans, C. A., 134, 187, 188, 191, 219

Farmer, W. R., 30
Fearghail, F. O., 92, 93, 96
Feldman, L. H., 66, 67, 102, 117
Fischer, D., 17
Fitzpatrick-McKinley, A., 76, 128
Fletcher-Louis, C., 141, 142, 191
Förster, H., 177
Fortier, T., 33
Frayer-Griggs, D., 154, 195
Freed, E. D., 178
Fretheim, T. E., 168
Frey, J., 13, 22, 81, 217, 218
Fuglseth, K. S., 221, 224, 225

Gager, J. C., 4, 6, 12
Galinsky, K., 48, 146
Gambetti, S., 65
Gardner, P., 226
Gellner, E., 28
Gerdmar, A., 4, 24, 27
Giddens, A., 36
Glasson, T. F., 147, 191, 192
Goldstein, J. A., 49, 55, 58
Goodman, M., 91
Granskou, D., 174
Grodzynski, D., 107
Gruen, E. S., 26, 61, 63, 64, 84, 85, 90, 91, 126
Guite, H., 128

Hadas, M., 49, 52
Haenchen, E., 137, 138, 140, 141, 161, 194
Hakola, R., 8, 9, 10, 16, 39, 41–43, 157, 161, 193, 216, 223
Hanson, P. D., 215
Hare, D. R. A., 12
Harner, P. B., 134
Harris, E., 134, 174, 187
Harrisville, R. A., 169
Harstine, S., 146, 147, 191, 195, 213
Haslam, S. A., 34–39, 113
Hengel, M., 27, 30
Henten, J. W., 102
Hieke, T., 169
Hogg, M. A., 36, 38, 117
Honigman, S., 48, 52, 57, 62, 132, 146, 205, 206
Horbury, W., 60–62, 207
Hornsey, M. J., 34, 36
Horst, P. W., 49, 63, 64, 68–72, 77, 84, 102, 180
Horwitz, M., 35
Hoskins, P. M., 26, 157, 183, 184, 207, 213, 223
Howard, W. F., 23
Huie-Jolly, M. R., 140, 159
Hunt, S. A., 181, 182, 212
Hutchinson, J., 28–30
Hylen, S., 145, 147, 148, 151, 156, 213, 219, 220

Index of Modern Authors

Isaac, J., 5, 6, 226

Jackson-McCabe, M. A., 222
Jacoby, F., 101
Jenkins, R., 28
Johnson, S. R., 49, 54, 57
Jones, S., 26
Jonge, H. J., 21
Judge, E. A., 42

Käsemann, E., 134, 217
Kasher, A., 61, 63, 64, 71
Katz, S., 8
Kee, H. C., 42
Keener, C., 48, 137, 138, 140–44, 148, 151, 154, 163, 178, 179, 181, 183, 193, 194, 200
Keith, G., 12
Kelley, S., 4
Kerr, A. R., 26, 157, 223
Kierspel, L., 20, 188, 216, 234
Kim, S. S., 153, 154
Kirschner, R., 8
Klawans, J., 157
Klink, E. W., 21, 222, 223
Knight, D. A., 93
Kok, K., 154
Köstenberger, A. J., 8, 26, 157, 223
Koyama, K., 235
Kraft, R. A., 221, 222

Lacerenza, G., 64
Lamb, D. A., 224
Lampe, P., 100
Leon, H., 99, 125–28
Levine, L. I., 26
Levinskaya, I., 84, 85, 126
Lieu, J., 3, 6, 7, 17–19, 196
Lifshitz, B., 79
Lincoln, A. T., 140
Loader, W., 188, 189, 194
Lohse, B., 235
Longenecker, B. W., 169
Lowe, M. F., 14, 17
Lüderitz, G., 63, 71
Luthardt, C. E., 17
Luther, M., 232, 233, 235, 236

Manstead, A. S. R., 39
Maronde, C. A., 147, 150, 151, 156, 188, 195, 213
Martyn, J. L., 7–9, 13, 15, 41, 153, 194, 223
Mason, S., 65
McCready, W. O., 217
McGrath, A. E., 235
Meeks, W. A., 134, 150, 151, 163, 188, 195, 216, 222, 231
Mendels, D., 29, 59
Menken, M. J. J., 148
Millar, J. G., 168
Miller, D. M., 205
Miller, P., 181, 183
Misztal, B. A., 31, 32, 204
Modrzejewski, J. M., 54, 205, 226
Moehring, H. R., 84
Moloney, F. J., 137, 138, 141, 142, 158, 187, 188
Morris, L., 146
Motyer, S., 8, 9, 11, 15, 26, 157, 179, 222, 223
Moxnes, H., 213
Müller, P. G., 4

Neyrey, J. H., 136, 137, 140, 213
Ngien, D., 236
Nicholson, G. C., 134, 173
Nicklas, T., 19, 20, 216
Niehoff, M., 64–66, 68, 70, 71, 118, 124
Nkomo, S. M., 34
Nodet, E., 84
Noth, M., 168
Noy, D., 60–62, 99, 128
Numada, J., 13, 17, 158

O'Day, G. R., 134, 136
Odeberg, H., 143
Oeming, M., 168, 169, 170
Ong, H. T., 205
Onuki, T., 225
Ortlund, D., 93

Painter, J., 207
Pancaro, S., 142, 190
Papaioannou, K., 160, 189, 194

Index of Modern Authors

Parker, B. F., 80
Parkes, J., 4, 5, 226
Parsenios, G. L., 134
Pearce, S., 26, 32, 69, 70
Pearson, B. W. R., 23, 132, 133, 226
Phillips, P. M., 134
Piper, R., 40, 41
Plöger, O., 215
Porter, S. E., ix, 14, 22, 23, 42, 132–34, 136, 145–47, 157, 175, 176, 178, 211, 213, 222, 226

Rabbie, J. M., 35
Rajak, T., 84, 120, 205
Ramsay, W. M., 79
Rappaport, U., 29, 84
Reed, A. Y., 66
Reinhartz, A., 2, 16
Rensberger, D., 211, 223
Richardson, P., 126–28
Richey, L. B., 8, 223
Ringe, S., 191
Ripley, J. J., 158
Robert, J., 80
Robert, L., 80
Robinson, J. A. T., 49
Rochette, B., 114, 126
Rodriguez, J., 33
Ross, M., 39
Ruether, R. R., 2, 12
Rutgers, L. V., 26, 43, 44, 99, 125, 126

Sahdra, B., 39
Salvesen, A., 7
Sanders, E. P., 157, 211
Sanders, J. T., 42, 92
Sandmel, S., 66, 67, 182, 205
Schäfer, P., 5, 99, 102, 109, 115–17, 122
Schapdick, S., 146, 149, 151, 156, 192, 195
Schnabel, E. J., 93
Schnackenburg, R., 137, 138, 140–43, 147, 148, 151, 153, 163, 193, 222
Schoon, S., 13
Schuchard, B. G., 157
Schudson, M., 32, 204
Schulz, S., 33

Schürer, E., 65
Schwartz, D. R., 26, 44, 49, 53–55, 59, 60
Scott, E. F., 7, 226
Scott, I. W., 208
Scott, M., 141, 191
Sevenster, J. N., 99, 110
Sheridan, R., 20, 21, 225
Smallwood, E. M., 63, 64, 69
Smiga, G. M., 12
Smith, A. D., 27–29, 31, 34, 167, 191, 214
Smith, D. M., 15, 153
Snyder, G. F., 128
Spaulding, M. B., 219
Spears, R., 39
Spilsbury, P., 50, 117
Stark, R., 224, 225
Steck, O. H., 93
Stegemann, W., 5
Stern, K. B., 60
Stern, M., 101, 104, 108, 109, 115, 116
Stovell, B. M., 219
Strubbe, J. H. M., 77

Tannehill, R. C., 92
Taylor, M. S., 5, 12
Tcherikover, V. A., 26, 49, 52, 90
Thatcher, T., 7, 141, 223
Thompson, M. M., 136, 137, 150, 156, 188, 191, 192, 195, 220
Tilborg, S., 77
Tomson, P. J., 2, 16
Trebilco, P. R., 26, 77–80, 88, 91, 93, 95, 97, 130, 205
Trost, T., 163
Turner, J. C., 33, 34, 36, 37

Um, S. T., 157

VanderKam, J. C., 171

Wahlde, U. C., 14–17, 21, 22, 177, 179, 197, 198, 208
Ward, P. W., 1
Wardy, B., 102, 111, 115
Wasserstein, A., 49, 51, 56
Wasserstein, D. J., 49, 51, 56

Index of Modern Authors

Watson, F., 211
Wedeck, H. E., 128
Weiss, H., 160
Weren, W., 91
Westcott, B. F., 179, 181
Whitacre, R. A., 41, 42, 217
White, L. M., 127
Williams, C. H., 176
Williams, D. S., 59
Williams, K. D., 36, 38, 117

Williams, M. H., 26, 80–83, 99, 105, 107, 114, 125, 126, 128, 129
Wilson, B. R., 219, 222–25
Wintermute, O. S., 171
Wrede, D. W., 7
Wright, B. G., 49, 50, 51

Yee, G. A., 147, 151

Zeev, M. P., 65, 78, 83–87, 90
Zuntz, G., 56

Index of Ancient Sources

OLD TESTAMENT

Genesis

12:11–20	66
15:3–5	171
15:6	168, 169
15:18	173
17:4–19	173
18	182, 183
22	169, 172
22:8	66
26:5	67
26:7–11	66
26:24	171

Exodus

6:25	60
7:1	150
12	192
12:46	189
16	151, 192
16:2	151
16:7–9	151
16:12	151
16:15	149
17:3–4	151
20:4	72
20:13	193
22:28	91
32:19	67

Numbers

9:12	189
20:11–12	67
25:7–13	59

Deuteronomy

1:27–32	151
4:32–35	148
10:16	164
13:1–5	148
18	154
18:15–18	147
18:19	196
30:15–20	142

Joshua

14:1	60

1 Samuel

7:1	60

Nehemiah

9:7–8 LXX	169, 170
9:13–15	149
9:26	93, 147

Psalms

22:18	189
30:19	194
34:20	189

Psalms *(continued)*

41:9	189
43:3	189
56:13	190
68:5–6	144
69 (68 LXX)	157
69:4	189
69:9 (68:10 LXX)	157, 189
69:21 (68:22 LXX)	189
78:24 (77:24 LXX)	149
82:6	161, 189
89:15	190
89:26–27	144
103:13	144
104:6 LXX	171
110:4	189
119:105	189
119:130	189

Proverbs

3:12	144
6:23	189
8:15	143
8:25–31	142
8:35–36	142
9:5	148

Isaiah

2:5	190
6:10	190
9:1–2	175
9:7	189
41:8	171
48:17	143
53:1	190
54:13	143
63:16	144
64:8	144
66:13	144

Jeremiah

4:4	164
31:7–9	144

Ezekiel

28:18	157
37:25	189

Daniel

7:14	189

APOCRYPHA

Judith

5:20	151
12:2	151

Wisdom

14:11	151
18:4	190

Sirach

15:3	148
23:8	151
24	142
24:8–17	142
24:19–23	148
24:19–22	148
24:19–21	170
24:23	142
24:27	189
24:32	189
27:31	151
32:15	151
44:19–21	170
44:19	170

Baruch

4:2	190

1 Maccabees

1:14–15	159
1:60–61	159
2	170, 172
2:34–38	144
2:50	168

Index of Ancient Sources

2:52	168, 169
2:53	168
2:54	168
2:55	168
2:56	168
2:57	168
2:58	168
2:59	169
2:60	169
4	158
8	91
8:17	101
12	91

2 Maccabees

1:1	49
1:2–8	55
1:2–6	59
1:2	51
1:8	55
1:10	49
1:19	139
1:23–36	55
1:27–28	59
1:33–36	59
2:5–10	51
2:12	51
2:21	53
2:30	90
3	56
3:1	139
3:15–20	55
3:16–17	58
3:21	51
3:23	51
3:24–29	55
3:31	55
3:33	55
4:5–6	58
4:11	101
4:35–37	58
5:2–3	55
6:1	55
6:10	159
6:18–31	54
7:1–42	55
7:2	55
7:9	55
7:24	55
7:30	52
7:37	55
8:5	55
10:16	55
10:25	55
10:29	55
11:6	55
11:8	55
11:34–38	91
12:6–7	55
12:45	139
13:10	55
13:14	55
14:15	55
15:12	60
15:13–16	56, 60
15:21–27	55

PSEUDEPIGRAPHA

Apocalypse of Abraham

9:6–7	183

2 Baruch

4:4	183

1 Enoch

62:5–16	189

4 Ezra

1:32	93
2:1	93
3:14	183
7:130	93

Jubilees

17:15–18	170

Letter of Aristeas

2	139
3	52
9	52

Index of Ancient Sources

Letter of Aristeas (continued)

13	57
14	57
15–18	57
15–16	54, 56, 57, 207
15	52, 56, 57
23–24	57
23	50
24	139
26	57
27	52
33	52
36–37	56, 57
36	51, 52
37	139
40–42	52
42	139
44	51, 52
52–82	52
89–116	52
92–99	58
122	52
129–171	58
131–132	50, 56
131	139
134	57
135	139
137–138	139
139	50, 56
144	50, 56
148	50
158	54
177–178	56
177	139
182–300	51, 58
210	139
215	139
233	139
240	50, 56
255	139
261	139
294	52
310–312	52
312–313	50
312	56
317	52, 56, 139
319	52

3 Maccabees

1:3	51, 53, 172
1:5–8	58
1:16	55
1:23	51, 58
1:24	55
2:1–20	55, 58
2:6	51
2:10	51, 55
2:12	51
2:21	145
2:30	51, 90
2:31–33	54
2:31–32	139
2:31	53, 172
3:3	58
3:4–10	53
3:4	51
3:6–7	53
3:7	139
3:8	51
3:18–19	53
3:21–24	53
3:21–23	51, 90
3:21	51, 58
3:23	51
3:27–29	53
4:12	53
4:20	54
5:7–9	55
5:7	51, 145
5:13	53
5:31	58
5:50–51	55
6:1–17	55
6:1–15	58
6:3	51, 145, 172
6:4	51
6:8	51, 145
6:9	51, 53
6:11	53
6:13	51, 53
6:15	53
6:23	51
6:25–26	58
7:1–15	54
7:6	51
7:10	51

Index of Ancient Sources

7:11	58
7:12	51, 172
7:16	51
7:23	51

Psalms of Solomon

4:23	151
9:9	171
18:3	171

Testament of Abraham

1:1–2	182

NEW TESTAMENT

Matthew

5:20	152
11:6	151
13:57	151, 162
15:12	151
17:24–27	151
21:5	31
21:19–20	157
24:10	152
26:31–33	152
27	30

Mark

2:27–28	160
6:3	151
6:4	162
11:4–10	31
11:13–14	157
11:20–21	157
14:27–29	152
15:7	30

Luke

4:24	162
6:15	30
7:5	26, 80
7:23	151
19:30–44	31
23:18–19	30

John

1:4	173
1:9	173
1:11–12	181
1:11	161, 174, 207
1:12–13	198
1:12	173
1:13	198
1:16–18	187
1:17	149
1:18–19	174
1:18	174
1:19—12:50	20
1:21–23	162
1:29–36	145
1:33	136
1:38	151
1:45	149, 150, 189
2–12	208
2:13–25	145, 157
2:14–16	157
2:17	157
2:18	148
2:22	189
2:23	148, 173
2:25	173
3–9	164
3–4	135–39
3:2	148, 151
3:3–8	210
3:4	174
3:11	161
3:13	150, 188
3:15	174
3:16	174, 199, 234
3:18	174
3:19	137, 173, 174, 234
3:20	174
3:21	174
3:22–36	136
3:25	136
3:27	136, 173
3:31–36	136
3:31	174
3:34	136
3:36	174
4	137, 145
4:20–24	139

277

John (continued)

Reference	Pages
4:22–24	10
4:22	137, 138, 207, 208
4:23–24	136, 213
4:26	138
4:44	162
4:46–54	141
4:48	148
5	140, 144, 145, 147, 152, 159, 160, 195
5:1–9a	140
5:8	140
5:9–30	140
5:10	140
5:13	140, 160
5:15	140
5:16–18	160
5:16	140, 160
5:17–23	140
5:17–18	141
5:17	143
5:18	3, 141, 143, 162
5:19–30	142
5:19	143
5:22–27	142
5:22–24	143
5:23	174
5:24	137, 174
5:30–47	191
5:30	142
5:39	188, 191
5:41	173
5:42	173
5:45–47	142
5:45–46	149, 150, 191–92
5:45	191
5:46–47	150
5:46	142
6	145–47, 152
6:1–14	145
6:1–13	147
6:4	145
6:14	147, 148, 162
6:15	30, 147, 162, 151, 206
6:16–21	147
6:22–71	145, 147
6:22–59	146
6:22–58	149
6:24–25	192
6:27	192
6:28	148, 149, 192
6:29	148, 192
6:30–32	192–93
6:30–31	148, 192
6:30	148
6:31	148–50
6:32–40	148
6:32	149
6:35	145, 174
6:37	210
6:40	174
6:41–42	147
6:41	149, 151, 213
6:45–46	142
6:47	174
6:48–51	146
6:48	145
6:49	213
6:51	145, 174
6:54	174
6:56	174
6:57	174
6:58	174, 213
6:60–71	151
6:60–61	151
6:61	151, 152
6:63	136, 152
6:65	152
6:66	151
7–9	3, 21
7:1	3, 162
7:16	151
7:19–25	3
7:19–24	159
7:19–23	193
7:19–20	162
7:19	150, 188, 189, 213
7:22–24	150
7:22	150
7:23	188, 189, 193
7:24	161
7:25	162
7:37–39	153
7:38–39	136
7:38	174, 189
7:40	162
7:41–43	160

Index of Ancient Sources

7:42	188	8:44–45	233
7:49	161, 189	8:44	2, 18, 177, 179, 181, 207
7:51	188, 189	8:45–59	177
7:52–53	161	8:45	183
7:52	160, 175	8:47	174, 177, 183
7:53—8:11	175	8:54b–55a	182, 183
8	18, 173, 183, 185, 206	8:56	182
8:5	188	8:57–59	162
8:12–59	153	8:58	178
8:12–30	184	8:59	162
8:12–20	175, 176	9	152, 160
8:12	153, 174, 175, 178	9:1–7	194, 195
8:14	177	9:1–2	153
8:15–16	174, 177	9:3–5	153
8:15	161	9:5	175, 190
8:17	150, 189, 196	9:6–7	153
8:18–19	177	9:6	154, 195
8:18	175, 178	9:8–13	153
8:19	175	9:8	194
8:21–59	175	9:13	194
8:21–29	175, 176	9:14–16	153, 160
8:23–24	177	9:14	153
8:23	176–78, 207, 210	9:15	154
8:24–25	176	9:16	154
8:24	177, 178	9:17	154, 162, 194
8:25	177	9:19–23	153
8:26–59	177	9:22	153, 194
8:28	151, 178, 184	9:24–41	153
8:30–31	178	9:28–29	150, 154, 194
8:30	162, 176	9:30–33	195
8:31–47	145	9:31	138, 154
8:31	176	9:33	154
8:32–37	177	9:35–41	194
8:32	178	9:35–38	195
8:33–34	179	9:35	154
8:33	173, 178, 180, 181, 183, 206	9:38	154
8:34–36	181	9:39–41	153, 154, 195
8:34–35	181	9:39	174, 195, 196
8:34	174	9:41	196
8:36	173	10:2	174
8:37–41	181	10:12	199
8:37–40	3, 162	10:22	30
8:37	173, 181	10:34–35	188, 189
8:39–40	184	10:34	150, 196
8:39	173, 181–83	10:38	148
8:41	144, 182	10:41	161
8:42–44	182	11	199
8:43	183	11:25	174

Index of Ancient Sources

John (continued)

11:26	174
11:28	151
11:31–36	3
11:38—12:15	200
11:45	3
11:47—12:8	145
11:47–53	162, 210
11:47–52	11, 162, 199, 206
11:47–48	10
11:47	199
11:48	161, 199, 200
11:49	200
11:50	162, 199, 200
11:51–52	200
11:52	173, 200
12:14–16	31
12:25	174
12:31–33	190
12:31–32	137, 174
12:34	189
12:35–36	190
12:35	174
12:36	162
12:42	153
12:44	174
12:45	174
12:46	174
12:47–48	174
12:48	137, 174
13:1—17:26	145
13:13–14	151
13:18	189
13:20	174
13:33	213
14:11	148
14:12	174
14:16–17	139
14:21	174
14:24	174
15:5	174
15:23	174
15:25	189
16:2	153
16:11	174
17:6	173, 210
17:12	189
18:37	174
18:39	136
18:40	30
19:7	188, 189
19:12	163, 199, 200
19:13–42	145
19:15	163, 210
19:24	189
19:28	189
19:36–37	189
19:36	189
19:40	136
20:9	189
20:16	151
20:31	148
21:18–19	48

Acts

1:13	30
13:13–52	93
13:16–41	93
13:21–22	93
13:26	93
13:32	93
13:33–37	93
13:38–39	93
13:40–41	93
13:42–44	93
13:43	93
13:45	27, 93
13:50	93
14	94
14:3	94
14:5	94
17:5	27
19:8–10	95
19:8	92
19:10	92
19:21—20:1	95
19:33–34	93
19:34	95
19:35–40	91
22:3	27

Romans

9–11	200
9:1–8	18
10:1–3	18

Galatians

1:14	27
3:29	18
4:21–31	181
5:12	160

Philippians

3:2	18, 160
3:6	27

1 John

3:23–24	177
4:6–8	177
4:12	177
4:20	177

PHILO OF ALEXANDRIA

Abraham

24	139
52	186
60–61	139
65	139
69–74	67
94	66
98	139
114	182
116	182
129	139
171	139
174–178	66
177	139
190	139
198–199	139
209	66
226–232	66
261	66
275–276	67

Confusion

39	194
62	194

Prelim. Studies

177	194

Flaccus

1	65
3	180
9–29	65
25–31	180
33	180
36–38	118
43	70
44–45	70
45	70
46	70
47	71
48–50	69, 71
48–49	69
48	68, 69, 139
74	70
80	71
98	139
103	139
135	118

Alleg. Interp.

1.18	144

Embassy

4–6	68
4	143
8–13	70
8	69
22	70
111	72
115–117	72
116–117	69
116	139
118	69
119	70
141–149	70
147	69
153–154	69
156	68
157	69, 71
159–160	65
159	69

Index of Ancient Sources

Embassy (continued)

160	72
161	68
172	72
178	72
188	65
191–192	70
192	69
200–203	65
205	72
210	69
212	69
213	139
214	70
215	72
216	139
242	139
245	70, 139
265	71
277	69
279–280	139
281–282	70
297	139
306	68
316	139
319	139
330	70
335	139
347	139
357	69

Migration

89–91	144

Moses

1.4–9	67
1.19	67
1.45–46	67
1.46	139
1.155–156	150
1.158	150
1.163	67
1.183	139
1.187	139
1.189	139
1.193–196	151
1.198	139
1.220	67
1.254	139
1.303	139
1.307	139
1.317	139
2.8	67
2.12	67
2.23	139
2.26	67
2.27–44	67
2.36	67
2.40	139
2.66	139
2.108	139
2.136	139
2.142	139
2.159	139
2.161–162	32
2.165	139
2.170	139
2.192	139
2.216	139
2.260	139
2.270	139
2.284	139

Creation

1.170–171	186

Planting

169	66

Good Person

1.43	186

Sacrifices

10	150

Spec. Laws

1.345	194
2.88	194

Virtues

66	194
102	112
103	112
181–182	112

JOSEPHUS

Ant.

1.122–235	171
1.154–155	120
1.156–157	120
12.416	83
14.99	61
14.116	86
14.127–136	130
14.188	121
14.190–195	85, 86
14.191	83
14.192–195	85
14.192	85
14.194	86
14.196–198	85, 86
14.211–212	86
14.212	85
14.213–216	85, 86
14.213–214	87
14.214	86
14.215	88
14.216	86
14.219–221	83
14.225–227	86
14.226–227	88
14.228–230	86
14.228	87
14.231–232	86
14.232	87
14.235	86, 88
14.241–243	85, 86
14.242–246	88
14.244–246	86
14.245	86
14.256–258	85–87
14.258–264	88
14.259–261	86, 88
14.260	86
14.262–264	86
14.263	86
14.267	83, 86
14.391	83
16.27–28	65
16.31–57	88
16.35–36	88
16.41–42	89
16.42–44	89
16.48	83
16.162–173	88
16.163–172	88
16.163	88
16.167–168	86
16.169–170	65
16.171	86, 88
16.172–173	86
16.173	86
16.175–178	78
16.176–178	86
16.177	87
16.277–283	127
16.332	127
16.344	127
16.354	127
17.324–338	128
18.65–84	126
18.79	114
19.278–279	65
19.280–285	86, 90
19.281–284	90
19.281	90
19.285	90
19.286	90
19.287–291	85, 86, 90
19.288–289	90
19.290	86, 91
20.34–48	26
20.173–177	65

Ag. Ap.

1.1	119
1.2	117
1.7–10	119
1.28–29	119
1.42–43	122
1.42	119
1.54	120

Ag. Ap. (continued)

1.60	139
1.67	123
1.71	120
1.92	120
1.162–165	122
1.162	139
1.164–166	122
1.175	121
1.176–181	121
1.191–192	122
1.200–204	122
1.212	139
1.224	139
1.227–287	118
1.227—2.144	119
1.239	139
1.250–253	120
1.261	139
1.265	120
1.279	120
1.290	120
1.309	120
2.1–144	118
2.27	122
2.28	118
2.38–42	121
2.44	123
2.47	121
2.49–52	123
2.49	123
2.56–61	123
2.61–67	121
2.63	123
2.75–76	123
2.79	89
2.80	89
2.125	139
2.130–131	139
2.134	123
2.144	139
2.146	120, 139
2.148	89
2.156–160	120
2.159	139
2.160	121
2.162–165	122
2.164	123
2.168–169	122
2.168	121
2.170–171	139
2.173	120
2.176–178	121
2.181	120, 139
2.182–183	122
2.184–186	124
2.184	139
2.188	139
2.204	121
2.218–219	122
2.223–224	121
2.255	121, 150
2.257	121, 150, 186
2.258	89
2.278	123
2.281	121, 122
2.282	139
2.291	121, 139
2.293	121, 139

GRECO-ROMAN WRITINGS

Aulus Gellius

Noct. att.

5.14.1–4	118

Cicero

Att.

2.9.1	111

Div.

1.7	107
1.36	108
1.124–126	108
2.19	107

Flac.

66–69	111
66–67	111
67	89, 91, 108, 111
69	89, 115

Index of Ancient Sources

Nat. d.

1.55	108
2.70	107
3.90–92	107

De provinciis consularibus

5.10	110

Dio Cassius

Rom. hist.

57.18.5a	126

Diodorus

Bib. hist.

1.28.1–3	101
1.55.5	101
1.94.1–2	103
2.48.7	113
19.99.3	113
35.1.1–5	102
35.1.3	102, 103
35.1.5	112
40.2	115
40.3.8	102

Horace

Sat.

1.4.139–143	108
1.5.100–101	108
1.9.60–78	117
1.9.65–73	103
1.9.69–71	108
1.9.70–73	111

Juvenal

Sat.

3.290–96	103
6.542–47	110
14.96–106	109, 112

Lydus

De Mensibus

4.53	113

Ovid

Am.

217–220	106

Ars.

1.75–80	106
1.413–416	106

Persius

Sat.

5.176–184	109
5.179–180	106
5.180–181	106

Petronius

Poems

97	106, 109

Satyricon

68.4–8	106
68.5	113

Plato

Leg.

4.718c	89
4.723a	89
7.793b–d	86
10.810e–811e	121
10.888d	89
12.949e–950a	86
12.949e–953e	121

Prot.

326c	121

Index of Ancient Sources

Pliny the Elder

Nat.

pref.25	118
5.15.73	103, 110
12.54.112–113	112, 115
30.2.11	110
31.18.24	106
31.44.95	103, 109

Quintilian

Inst.

3.7.21	108

Seneca

Ep.

95.47	109
95.47.1–3	106

Sextus Empiricus

Pyr.

3.222–223	113

Silius Italicus

Punica

3.605–606	112

Suetonius

Aug.

76.2	107

Cal.

22.2–4	65

Claud.

25.4	108, 113

Dom.

12.2	114

Jul.

84	106
84.5	113
85	107

Nero

40.2	110

Tib.

32.2	105, 114
36	109, 114, 126

Vesp.

4.5	109
5.6	109

Tacitus

Ann.

12.54	116
15.44	105

Hist.

2.78	104
5.2	102
5.3	102
5.3–5	112
5.3–4	102
5.4	104, 111, 112
5.5	105, 111, 112
5.8	115
5.9	105

EARLY CHRISTIAN WRITINGS

1 Clement

35:8	151

Index of Ancient Sources

Augustine

Civ.

4.31	104
6.11	104, 106, 115

Cons.

1.22.30	104
1.23.31	104
1.27.42	104

Eusebius of Caesarea

Hist. eccl.

3.31.3	77
5.24.2	77

Praep. ev.

9.6	26
9.17	101
9.19	101
9.26–27	26
9.26	101
9.27.4	60, 150

John Chrysostom

Adv. Jud.

8	7, 218
8.8.4–5	23

Polycarp

Phil.

6:3	151

www.ingramcontent.com/pod-product-compliance
Lightning Source LLC
Chambersburg PA
CBHW071236230426
43668CB00011B/1467